WHAT'S WRONG
WITH
POSTMODERNISM

Parallax: Re-visions of Culture and Society
Stephen G. Nichols, Gerald Prince, and Wendy Steiner, Series Editors

Christopher Norris

WHAT'S WRONG WITH POSTMODERNISM

Critical theory and the ends of philosophy

THE JOHNS HOPKINS UNIVERSITY PRESS
BALTIMORE

First published in the United States of America in 1990 by
The Johns Hopkins University Press
701 West 40th Street
Baltimore, Maryland 21211-2180

Second printing, paperback, 1992.

Library of Congress Cataloging-in-Publication Data
Norris, Christopher.
  What's wrong with postmodernism: critical theory and
the ends of philosophy/Christopher Norris.
    p.   cm. – (Parallax)
  Includes bibliographical references and index.
  ISBN 0-8018-4136-4 (cloth). – ISBN 0-8018-4137-2 (pbk.)
  1. Postmodernism. 2. Literature – Philosophy.
  3. Methodology. I. Title. II. Series: Parallax
  (Baltimore, Md.)
  B831.2.N67 1990
  909.82'8 – dc20   90-38438
                                                        CIP

In memory of my father,
CHARLES FREDERICK NORRIS

Contents

Acknowledgements

Parts of this book have appeared in various journals during the past four years. I am grateful to the editors and publishers concerned for permission to reprint this material. Sources are as follows:

Chapter 1: *Praxis International* (Basil Blackwell).

Chapter 2: *Comparative Literature* (University of Oregon Press). Some paragraphs from Chapter 2 have also appeared in my book *Spinoza and the Origins of Modern Critical Theory* (Basil Blackwell). My thanks to the publisher for consenting to the incorporation of these passages in slightly modified form.

Chapter 4: *Textual Practice* (Routledge).

Chapter 5: *Criticism* (Wayne State University Press).

Chapter 6: *Ideas and Production* (Cambridge College of Advanced Technology).

Introduction:
Criticism, history
and the politics of theory

I

It is a curious fact – one noted by Perry Anderson in his book *Considerations on Western Marxism* – that the level and quality of theoretical work on the left often seems to vary inversely with the fortunes of left-wing politics at large.[1] Then again, one could argue (and Anderson does) that this should not be any great cause for surprise, since a recourse to theory is typically the response of any marginalised fraction of dissident intellectuals, excluded from the mainstream of political life and left little choice but to cultivate a range of more or less hopeful alternative visions. Still one might think it a curious turn of events when this response takes the form of a deep investment in issues of aesthetics, philosophy of art, and literary theory as the chief areas of concern among a sizeable number of committed left-wing cultural activists. For it is, to say the least, far from self-evident that specialised work in these areas could eventually feed back to exert any influence on the way people live, think, feel, vote, and comport themselves in the public sphere of politically responsible action and choice. The suspicion must be – or so it would seem from a commonsense-realist standpoint – that these theorists are just whistling in the dark, discovering all manner of pseudo-radical rhetorics and postures by which to disguise their own deep sense of political failure or defeat.

Anderson, we should recall, was writing in 1977, at a time when the left scarcely occupied the high ground of British political affairs, but when at least there still existed some measure of right–left consensus on the post-war settlement as regards matters of welfare provision, educational policy, workers' rights, protection of minority cultures and viewpoints, freedom of speech, liberty of the unions to organise effective strike action, and so forth. Twelve years on that situation has changed in a way – or to an extent – that Anderson could scarcely have predicted. The Thatcher years have witnessed what amounts to a full-scale assault on those values, to the point where conservatives can plausibly claim to have carried through a veritable counter-revolution in the social, political and ideological spheres. It is no coincidence that one main target of left literary theory is the appeal to 'commonsense' perception as embodied in the codes and conventions of the so-called 'classic bourgeois realist text'.[2] For it is a sure sign of this conservative hegemony over popular modes of awareness that 'realism' in political matters is nowadays equated with a sensible acknowledgement that the old (progressive or socialist) ideals were just a kind of utopian pie in the sky, that they ignored the plain facts of economic life – competition, market forces, structural unemployment, etc. – and that this lack of 'commonsense' values was itself the chief cause of all our recent (pre-'79) social and economic woes, from inflation to the balance of payments deficit, the 'permissive society' (with AIDS in its wake), single-parent families, social-welfare scroungers, union militancy, and anything else you care to mention as a cause of self-inflicted national decline. And so there has emerged a middle-ground consensus – including many thinkers nominally on the left – that there is simply no point in contesting this swing of opinion, that it articulates a 'genuine' widespread change of popular sentiment, and that therefore the best we can hope for 'realistically' is a compromise settlement on slightly more favourable terms.

That this process of ideological retrenchment has been pushed through with remarkable success is nowhere more evident than in papers like the *Sun*, the *Mail* and the *Express*, where Thatcherite values achieve their most effective (because unthinkingly 'commonsense') form. But it is evident also across a whole range of cultural and socio-political institutions, from television news-broadcasts (with certain striking and honourable exceptions) to adjustments in the balance of university funding and the climb-down on crucial policy issues by the current Labour Party leadership. In each case the measure of right-wing hegemonic power is the extent to which resistance is effectively demobilised through a widespread consensus-view that these are currently the rules of the game, like it or not, and must therefore dictate what shall henceforth count as a genuine (i.e. politically effective or vote-winning) style of approach. What hope, one might ask, for socialist values or left-oppositional thought when a journal like *Marxism Today* can devote most of its monthly space – along with a much-heralded 'New Times' manifesto – to arguments which dump just about every item of socialist principle in an effort to accommodate free-market ideology, consumer politics, 'postmodern' life-styles, the 'end of ideology', the collapse of the real into various forms of mass-media-induced simulation, and so forth?[3] All this, be it noted, in the name of theory, or certain forms of 'advanced' theoretical reflection taking rise from French post-structuralism and its latterly more fashionable offshoots. It does begin to look very much like a gloomy confirmation of the warning note that Perry Anderson sounded way back at a time when left cultural theory still had a certain radical edge, despite its all too obvious lack of purchase on the current realities of power.

For if there is one thing that also needs noting about this last decade it is the fact that theory has maintained its hold and indeed gone from strength to strength, at least if one measures that strength by the sheer range of books, journals, conferences, postgraduate courses, etc. with a mainly 'theoretical' orientation. For a historical parallel one would have to go back to the years of Pitt's government after the French Revolution, when the country witnessed mounting anti-Jacobin hysteria, repressive legislation and a full-scale campaign of ideological warfare, but at the same time produced unprecedented levels of dissenting or left-wing intellectual activity. This parallel is yet more suggestive if one considers the later career of thinkers like Wordsworth and Coleridge, those who renounced their erstwhile revolutionary sympathies and became regular pillars of the Church-and-State establishment. For what is striking about Coleridge's 'mature' reflections is the way that they take up any number of themes from his earlier writing – especially in the way of aesthetics and literary theory – and convert them from a radical or contestatory to a highly conformist cast.[4] This applies especially to Coleridge's ideas (much influenced by Kant) about the powers of creative imagination, a form of 'aesthetic ideology' – in Paul de Man's phrase – that lent itself to both these uses, although the latter has exerted by far the more potent and lasting influence on subsequent literary studies. Elsewhere I have taken up this argument from de Man and suggested that deconstruction is a powerful means of understanding what is at stake in the post-romantic treatment of literature as a source of mystified social and political values.[5] For the moment, however, I just want to remark that there is a similar ambivalence about 'theory' as practised by post-structuralists, post-modernists and other fashionable figures on the current intellectual scene. That is to say, their 'radicalism' has now passed over into a species of disguised apologetics for the socio-political status quo, a persuasion that 'reality' is constituted through and through by the meanings, values or discourses that presently compose it, so that nothing could count as effective counter-argument, much less a critique of existing institutions on valid theoretical grounds.

In short, we have reached a point where theory has effectively turned against itself, generating a form of extreme epistemological scepticism which reduces everything – philosophy, politics, criticism and 'theory' alike – to a dead level of suasive or rhetorical effect where consensus-values are the last (indeed the only) court of appeal. It is a sign of the times that *Marxism Today* has been a main point of entry for postmodernist gurus like Baudrillard, thinkers for whom the whole kit and caboodle of Marxist thought – class conflict, ideology, forces and relations of production, surplus value, alienation and the rest – are just so much useless 'metaphysical' baggage, left over from the old enlightenment meta-narrative of progress, reason and truth.[6] What these thinkers have effected at the level of theory (or anti-theory) is equivalent to the wholesale junking of principles by Labour Party politicians and advisers over the past few years. And they look dead set to continue on this course despite the current signs (November 1989) that the Thatcherite consensus is falling apart, that its ideological project now lacks all credibility, and that developments in Eastern Europe have completely undermined the cold-war rhetoric on which that project has always been based.

The Labour Party decision to abandon its unilateralist stance was to my mind a piece of egregious folly not only on principled or moral grounds but even in terms of the bottom-line pragmatist appeal to 'public opinion', voter perceptions or the electoral main chance. For the case against possession of nuclear weapons was always *unanswerable* as a matter of logic or straightforward demonstrative argument, at least on those (albeit fairly rare) public occasions when debate was allowed to get that far. Nor could their possession be defended on strategic grounds, given all the well-known paradoxes of 'deterrence' (a rhetorical pseudo-concept if ever there was one) and the unthinkability of a real-life situation in which their use – or threatened use – could serve any imaginable purpose.[7] The only result of Labour's about-turn on this issue was to land them with all these impossible questions to answer, plus the problem of needing to argue their case (since socialists are quite properly expected to argue things out, where conservatives can always fall back on their customary stance of ox-like indifference to reasoned objections). Worst of all, this policy change came at precisely the time when radical reforms in the Eastern Bloc countries were creating a situation where continued talk of 'deterrence' by Bush, Thatcher and their like was even more plainly a species of nonsensical (though none the less dangerous) cold-war doublethink. The whole sad episode strikes me as a lesson in the basic fallacy of current neo-pragmatist arguments, raised – as they have been by thinkers like Richard Rorty and Stanley Fish– to a high point of sophistical ingenuity masquerading as straightforward commonsense wisdom.[8] For the appeal to consensus values as a matter of *de facto* self-authorising truth is one that not only fails philosophically (as I argue here in my essay on Fish), but can also go badly wrong as a matter of strategic self-interest. In other words, it may not even pay off in pragmatic (or vote-winning) terms to adopt a thoroughgoing pragmatist line and treat truth as what is presently and contingently 'good in the way of belief'.

This is not to suggest – far from it – that theory will always and inevitably end up by 'deconstructing' the grounds of enlightened critique and thus providing intellectuals with a welcome excuse for acquiescence in the way things are. In fact these essays divide more or less equally between diagnostic treatments of the postmodern-pragmatist malaise (Baudrillard, Fish, Rorty, some aspects of Lyotard) and accounts of what I take to be the continuing critical impulse – the enlightened or emancipatory interest – in thinkers like Derrida, de Man, Roy Bhaskar and Jürgen Habermas. Other essays have to do with the politics of deconstruction, Habermas's quarrel with Derrida, narrative theory as a hermeneutic paradigm, musical aesthetics in relation to literary theory, and various aspects of the postmodernism debate. The long chapter on Stanley Fish brings several of these topics together and could, I suppose, be read as a generalised statement on 'the function of criticism now'. Elsewhere the approach is on occasion more specialised (e.g. in treating de Man's late essays on the topic of aesthetic ideology). But I do want the reader to come away convinced – contrary to Fish's line of argument – that theory has 'consequences' beyond the professional or academic sphere, and that the question whether or not to 'do theory' is always within reach of the larger question whether *anything* we do or think is likely to affect the course of social and political events. As Terry Eagleton has recently put it:

> Children make the best theorists, since they have not yet been educated into accepting our routine social practices as 'natural' . . . 'Where does capitalism come from, mummy?' is therefore the prototypical theoretical question, one which usually receives what one might term a Wittgensteinian reply: 'This is just the way we do things, dear.' It is those children who remain discontent with this shabby parental response who tend to grow up to be emancipatory theorists, unable to conquer their amazement at what everyone else seems to take for granted.[9]

Eagleton goes on to remark that theory can easily be put to other, more conservative uses, as for instance by supplying us with 'new rationales for what we do, ordering and formalizing our experience'. And indeed, there is plenty of evidence for that in some of the fashionable trends surveyed in these essays. One response – the most complex and ambivalent – is de Man's idea of the 'resistance to theory', a resistance that not only comes from outside, so to speak, in the form of institutional hostility and prejudice, but which develops *within and against* the theoretical project as a result of problems that project encounters in the reading of particular texts.[10] (I discuss this argument at length in the chapter here on Fish.) Another is the strong defence of scientific realism offered by Roy Bhaskar, a case with implications for literary theory in so far as it challenges the postmodern-pragmatist view that textual meaning (like the truth-claims of science) can only be a product of the codes and conventions that happen to prevail within this or that historically-contingent interpretative community.[11] In each case theory proves capable of coming up with arguments that resist the currently widespread drift towards forms of ultra-relativist or consensus-based thinking. And it is all the more important to sustain these arguments at a time when 'public opinion' in the West is subject to a vast range of manipulative pressures – always in the name of freedom, democracy, rational self-interest, etc. – whose effect is precisely to reinforce such uncritical consensus values.

II

It is impossible to write about the 'politics of theory' without taking stock of the current dramatic changes in various Eastern European countries. Of course there is no way of predicting how things will turn out, even by the time these words appear in print. After all, it is just a few months since hopes were aroused by the spectacle of mass student protests in Peking, only to be dashed by massive state intervention and reprisals on a scale which can as yet scarcely be guessed at. Already the Nato propaganda machine is moving into gear: don't get too excited, it may not be for real, we've seen it all before (Khrushchev, Dubček), just a short-term distraction from Soviet expansionist designs, no reason yet for making arms cuts, 'lowering our front-line defences', etc. etc. And if there is one thing that is calculated to set back the process of Soviet and Eastern Bloc reform it is precisely this business-as-usual response, since of course it gives comfort to like-minded elements in the Kremlin who wish for nothing more than a continued show of belligerence from the Nato countries. Cynicism is the very rationale of cold-war politics, since without taking the worst possible view of all motives, events and outcomes the rhetoric of nukespeak (or 'Natopolitan' discourse) would collapse into manifest nonsense. There are critical theorists – Lyotard among them – who provide something like a justification for this rock-bottom cynical outlook.

> The 'philosophies of history' that inspired the nineteenth and twentieth centuries claim to assure passages over the abyss of heterogeneity or the event. The names which are those of 'our history' oppose counterexamples to their claim. – Everything real is rational, everything rational is real: 'Auschwitz' refutes speculative doctrine. This crime at least, which is real, is not rational. – Everything proletarian is communist, everything communist is proletarian: 'Berlin 1953, Budapest 1956, Czechoslovakia 1968, Poland 1980' (I could mention others) refute the doctrine of historical materialism: the workers rose up against the Party. – Everything democratic is by and for the people, and vice versa: 'May 1968' refutes the doctrine of parliamentary liberalism. The social in its everydayness puts representative institutions in check. – Everything that is the free play of supply and demand is favorable for the general enrichment, and vice versa: the 'crises of 1911 and 1929' refute the doctrine of economic liberalism. And 'the crisis of 1974–79' refutes the post-Keynesian revision of that doctrine. The passages promised by the great doctrinal syntheses end in bloody impasses. Whence the sorrow of the spectators in this bloody end of the twentieth century.[12]

This passage is the centre-piece of Lyotard's argument that we have now lived on into a postmodern epoch when it is no longer possible to attach any credence to those old 'meta-narrative' schemas (truth, enlightenment, progress and so forth) which once lent support to such grandiose ideas. Henceforth it can only be a matter of 'phrases in dispute', piecemeal items of evidential witness which claim no privileged epistemic status (much less any access to the master-code of history), and which thus submit themselves to the nominalist tribunal of isolated facts, dates, or events. Any theory that attempts to do more – to situate those facts within some larger, more ambitious explanatory paradigm – is ignoring the weight of *de facto* evidence that composes the sad chronicle of history to date.

All of which leads Lyotard to conclude that 'enlightenment' values are totally obsolete; that they have produced nothing more than a lamentable series of failed or miscarried political projects; and therefore that the only viable course is to heed these melancholy lessons and acknowledge the stubborn facticity of events, or the 'abyss of heterogeneity' that opens up beneath every such attempt to comprehend history in rational, purposive, or humanly intelligible terms. This is not to say that Lyotard comes out 'against theory' in the sense of regarding it – like Fish or Rorty– as a wholly inconsequential enterprise, one that cannot possibly make any difference to our first-order (pre-theoretical) habits of conduct and belief. In fact his arguments in this recent book (*Le Différend*) are based on a heterodox reading of Kant that distinguishes the various 'phrase-regimes' of cognitive, practical and speculative reason in order to maintain some margin of hope for the exercise of political thought. Thus he takes Kant's late writings – the essays on freedom, democracy, progress and 'perpetual peace' – as composing what amounts to a nascent *Fourth Critique*, a reflection on the essential forms and modalities of political judgement.[13] What is most important to grasp about these writings, Lyotard argues, is the fact that they appeal to Ideas of Reason – speculative reason – and not to any form of determinate theoretical judgement which could ever be confirmed (or disconfirmed) by recourse to the realm of empirical self-evidence. That is to say, there is no question of consulting past or present events as if to find grounds – probative grounds – for the continued belief in progress, democracy and other such enlightened or emancipatory interests. The relevant analogy here is *not* with theoretical understanding (where intuitions are brought under adequate concepts, as argued in the *First Critique*) but with *aesthetic judgement*, and especially the category of the Sublime, that mode of non-cognitive or 'supra-sensible' judgement where apprehension somehow surpasses all the bounds of phenomenal experience, thus linking the aesthetic – at this point of maximal intensity – with the realm of ethics (or 'practical reason' in the Kantian sense). In Lyotard's words,

> what is discovered is not only the infinite import of Ideas, its incommensurability to presentation, but also the destination of the subject, 'our' destination, which is to supply a presentation for the unpresentable, and therefore, in regard to Ideas, to exceed everything that can be presented. (Lyotard, p. 166)

To imagine otherwise – as by looking to history for *evidence* of progress in this or that determinate respect – is to confuse the two 'phrase-regimes' of cognitive and speculative reason. This deprives thought of its critical power (its capacity to envisage alternative, better worlds) and also risks the more dangerous, potentially totalitarian confusion that seeks to pass straight from political 'enthusiasm' to its implementation in the realm of real-world practical affairs. If 'the sublime is best determined by the indeterminate' (i.e. by ideas that cannot be 'presented' through an act of adequate, self-validating cognitive grasp) then the same ought to apply to revolutions and other such 'great historical events'. For it is the peculiar character of events like these to elude any form of conceptual understanding – or any adequate representation in thought – that would treat them as so many object-lessons for this or that theory of historical development. On the contrary, Lyotard writes: 'they are similar to those spectacles of (physical) nature on whose occasion the viewer experiences the sublime . . . they are formless and without figure in historical human nature' (Lyotard, p. 167). From which it follows that the impulse to treat such episodes as determinate stages in a world-historical progress toward meaning, reason or truth is the worst of all errors, a legacy of that old (Hegelian-Marxist) misreading of Kant which ignored the difference between *Ideas of Reason* on the one hand and *contingent historical events* on the other, and which thus pinned its hope to various forms of delusive meta-narrative (or 'totalising') theory.

Not that these errors can be overcome simply by consulting the historical record to date and noting – as in Walter Benjamin's pregnant image – the manifold catastrophes that have piled up in the wake of such 'enlightened' historicist ideals. For the kinds of aberration that Lyotard has in mind 'result from a confusion (which is *the* political illusion) between the direct presentation of the phenomenon of the *gemeine Wesen* [communal existence] and the analogical presentation of the Idea of a republican social contract' (p. 167). That is to say, they are something like a condition of possibility for political belief in general, and especially those forms of political belief that find an image or a focus in 'great historical events'. Nevertheless, we are mistaken (so Lyotard argues) if we think to comprehend those events in the way of theoretical understanding, i.e. by bringing them under some adequate concept, dialectical schema, or covering-law principle of historical intelligibility. For it is precisely when such category-mistakes occur – when 'enthusiasm' reads the signs of the times as both an index of present realities and a token of future promise – it is at moments like these that revolution passes over into the familiar cycle of excess, terror and counter-revolutionary violence. 'The *Schwärmerei* is accompanied by an illusion: "seeing something beyond all bounds of sensibility", that is, believing that there is a direct presentation when in fact there isn't any' (p. 166). And again, with reference to Kant's critique of the aporias or antinomies of pure speculative reason: 'it [i.e. 'enthusiasm'] proceeds to a noncritical passage, comparable to transcendental illusion, cognizing something beyond the limits of all cognition' (p. 166). In short, the sublime figures for Lyotard as a means of conveying by analogy what cannot be 'presented' to the intellect through any form of direct phenomenal cognition or adequate conceptual grasp.

In this respect it differs from the beautiful, a mode of apprehension – as Kant describes it – where the faculties achieve a feeling of harmonious balance between aesthetic experience and ideas of the *sensus communis*, or realm of shared human values and judgements. Here again, it is a question of passing analogically from one realm to another, although in this case the passage is a good deal more tranquil and involves nothing like the shock to our receptive apparatus involved in confronting the sublime. What occurs when we appreciate a beautiful object – whether an artefact or, more importantly for Kant, a landscape or product of nature – is that the mind effects an imaginative leap whereby our pleasure in the prospect thus afforded comes to strike us as an ideal image or analogy for the *sensus communis* of human understanding raised to its highest power of inter-subjective harmonious grasp. In Lyotard's words,

> in the phrase of the beautiful, the community of addressors and addressees is called forth immediately, without the mediation of any concept, by feeling alone, inasmuch as this feeling can be shared *a priori* . . . The community is already there as taste, but it is not yet there as rational consensus. (p. 169)

Thus the beautiful ministers to a generalised sense that judgements of taste should *in principle* be decided according to the interests of an informed public sphere (or a participatory democracy of values) whose membership would extend to all properly qualified observers, and would hence provide a critical court of appeal for any disputed cases. But these judgements can only have to do with *taste* (i.e. the articulation of agreed-upon subjective standards of response) since they involve what amounts to an idealised version of exactly that existing consensus-model. Kant may disagree with Hume in holding that such standards cannot be reduced to mere expres-sions of individual preference ('de gustibus non est disputandum'), or again, in rejecting the relativist idea that aesthetic values are ultimately a product of socialised habits and conventions. But in treating the beautiful as that which results from a free and harmonious interplay of the faculties – or from the strictly *analogical* linkage between sensuous perceptions and concepts of understanding, achieved through the exercise of aesthetic judgement – Kant in effect makes such values dependent on prevailing (consensus-based) notions of the communal good. And it is here precisely that the sublime differs from the beautiful, pointing as it does toward regions of 'supra-sensible' experience that cannot be brought under the 'phrase-regime' of enlightened consensus values.

'With the sublime', Lyotard writes, 'Kant advances far into heterogeneity, so much so that the solution to the aesthetic antinomy [i.e. the problem of claiming validity for judgements that lack any ultimate conceptual warrant] appears more difficult in the case of the sublime than it does in the case of the beautiful' (p. 169). For the sublime is that which necessarily eludes any form of adequate representation through the concepts and categories of analytic thought. Indeed, it produces a powerful and deep-laid disorder, a perturbation of those categories to the point where understanding is driven to acknowledge its own inadequacy in face of such overwhelming experiences, and must therefore have recourse to the realm of supra-sensible (ethical) Ideas which cannot find a cause – or an adequate object – in the realm of sensuous presentations. The sublime therefore stands as a privileged trope for everything that teases philosophy out of thought, that resists the application of determinant concepts, or compels us to recognise those Ideas of Reason (like Kant's 'republican contract') which may never be borne out by the course of actual historical events. And so it comes about – in Lyotard's reading of Kant – that

> enthusiastic pathos conserves an aesthetic validity, it is an energetic *sign*, a tensor of *Wunsch* . . . The infinity of the Idea draws to itself all the other capacities, that is, all the other faculties, and produces an *Affekt* 'of the vigorous kind', characteristic of the sublime. (p. 169)

Revolutions – the French Revolution in particular – are best thought of as sublime spectacles in exactly this sense, since they exceed all the powers of rational comprehension, or the various dialectical schemas deployed by Hegelians, Marxists and other such believers in history as a progress from stage to stage in some grand providentialist narrative. And the result of such delusory 'totalising' moves is to produce a whole series of untoward consequences, from the arousal of unfulfilled utopian hopes to the mood of disenchanted post-revolutionary despair and, beyond that, the repeated cycle of violence, oppression and suffering.

Of course Lyotard is not suggesting – absurdly – that if we all became better readers of Kant, or learned to distinguish more clearly between the various 'phrase-regimes' of cognitive, ethical and aesthetic judgement, then we might somehow avoid these forms of self-defeating political illusion. On the contrary, his argument tends to imply that there is such a thin line between legitimate aspirations (i.e. regulative 'Ideas of Reason' in the Kantian sense) and erroneous, misplaced or premature forms of political hope that in fact there is little chance of our ever achieving this salutary knowledge of the powers and limits of historical understanding. This is why 'enthusiasm' so easily passes over into *Schwärmerei*, or why the commitment to genuine enlightened ideals of democracy, progress and freedom so often becomes yet another sad episode in the narrative of failed revolutionary movements. All the same he clearly thinks that a better understanding of these issues in the Kantian philosophy of mind would leave us better defended against the various forms of transcendental illusion (or conflation of disparate phrase-regimes) which have so far produced such a melancholy record. At least this knowledge would prevent our imagining that historical events could ever furnish a proof – or a straightforward ground of evidential reasoning – for the validity of this or that socio-political creed. For it is precisely when we fall into the seductive error of equating cognitive with speculative interests (or knowledge-of-events with Ideas of Reason) that we cease to make allowance for the radical contingency that characterises all such 'great historical episodes'.

One further passage from Lyotard may help to define what is at stake in this politicised reading of the Kantian sublime. When appealing to the 'evidence' of such episodes, he writes,

> you are phrasing . . . not according to the rule of direct presentation proper to cognitives but according to the free, analogical presentation to which dialectical phrases in general are held. You can then call upon certain phenomena given through intuition, but they cannot, however, have the value of exempla or of schemata in your argument . . . A single referent – say a phenomenon grasped in the field of human history – can be used *qua* example, to present the object of discourse of despair, but also . . . to present analogically the object of the discourse of emancipation. And along with this guiding thread, one can undertake an analogically republican politics, and be a moral politician. (Lyotard, p. 163)

His essential point here is that nothing could justify our claiming to derive one or the other attitude (belief in progress or a despairing conviction that progress will never come about) from anything pertaining to the record of events as experienced or witnessed hitherto. To assume that we can, in some sense, 'learn from history' is either a species of category-mistake or – as Lyotard would have it – a negative lesson in the sheer contingency of all such events. If there is one thing we should have learned by now (he thinks) it is the message spelled out by Lyotard's catalogue of failed revolutions, twisted ideals, workers' states turning against the workers, communist regimes becoming a vicious parody of communist principles and so forth. On the other hand we should be wrong, he argues, to take these episodes as empirical data that somehow *proved* the bankruptcy of communist or socialist ideas, their historical obsolescence or manifest failure to come up with the promised goods. Such thinking ignores the crucial difference between arguments belonging to the phrase–regime of speculative reason – that is to say, judgements of an ethical, political or social-evaluative character – and those that claim a grounding in past or present historical realities. (These last few months have seen some choice examples as 'free-world' politicians line up to declare that events in Eastern Europe mark the definitive end of socialism as a credible ideology or programme for political change.) What this amounts to – in Lyotard's view – is a premature verdict arrived at by equating truths of experience (or matters of empirical knowledge) with Ideas of Reason in the Kantian sense, i.e. regulative notions that cannot be either proved or disconfirmed by appealing to the documented facts of the case.

But of course there is another side to this argument, one that would rule against anyone who wanted to treat those events as 'proof' that Eastern Bloc communism was working its way through the errors and distortions characteristic of its early development, and was now – at last – within sight of achieving a genuine form of socialist participatory democracy. For in Lyotard's view this could only be another species of 'transcendental illusion', a desire to take the will for the deed, or to treat the current 'spectacle' as something other than a strictly *sublime* event, one that by its nature cannot give rise to truth-claims or probative arguments of any kind. All that we are given to read in such episodes is a 'sign' of progress, justice, liberty, socialist values or whatever. A sign, that is to say, which remains necessarily ambivalent, which may indeed point toward a better, more enlightened state of affairs, but which can always turn out to bear no relation to the longer-term march of historical events. So what Lyotard gives with one hand he promptly snatches away with the other. If political ideals have validity only for reason in its speculative aspect, then there is nothing that could count as an adequate ground for treating this or that 'great historical episode' as an indicator of progress or human emancipation.

Such is precisely Lyotard's understanding of the sublime when transposed into a political or socio-historical key. It is best conveyed in the following passage of commentary on Kant.

The imagination tries to supply a direct, sensible presentation for an Idea of Reason (for the whole is an object of an Idea, as for example, in the whole of practical, reasonable beings). It does not succeed and it thereby feels its impotence, but at the same time, it discovers its destination, which is to bring itself into harmony with the Ideas of Reason through an appropriate presentation. The result of this obstructed relation is that instead of experiencing a feeling for the object, we experience, on the occasion of that object, a feeling for 'the Idea of humanity in our subject' . . . [and hence] the substitution of a reconciliation between the faculties within a subject for the reconciliation between an object and a subject. (Lyotard, p. 170)

In short, the sublime – whether in nature, art or politics – is a figure of radical heterogeneity, of the failure that imagination suffers when it strives to make the passage from one 'phrase-regime' (that of speculative reason) to another (that of our cognitive interest in finding an object adequate to express such ideas). At this point we encounter the limits of phenomenal cognition – along with those of theory, conceptual knowledge, historical understanding and so forth – and are thus enabled, through a kind of redemptive interiorising movement of thought, to conceive ourselves as subjects of an ideal 'suprasensible' community of knowledge and interests whose validity is neither strengthened nor impugned by evidence from that other (cognitive) regime of objects, events, or historical truth-claims. Quite simply, there is a cleavage – an 'abyss', as Lyotard terms it – between judgements brought to bear on the record of events and judgements that derive from the speculative interest in conceiving a better, more just or enlightened social order.

On the one hand this offers a refuge (some would say, a convenient bolt-hole) for thinkers who maintain their belief in socialist ideals against the kind of hard-nosed cynical wisdom that looks to current events in Eastern Europe as proof positive that socialism has failed wherever it has been put into practice, and that therefore we should all accept the 'verdict of history' in favour of capitalism, free-market forces, private enterprise, and so forth. For Lyotard, such arguments would beg the whole question as to whether past or presently-existing social regimes could in any sense be judged according to the standard of genuine (and as yet unrealised) socialist ideals. But on the other hand this means that one must be equally deluded in pointing to those same extraordinary events – the collapse of hardline communist regimes and the emergence of highly effective popular protest movements – as proof that there exists an alternative way forward, a politics of genuine socialist democracy that rejects both existing models, i.e. communism as a form of state monopoly capitalism and the 'free-world' ideology of unrestrained market forces and possessive individualism. From Lyotard's standpoint this could only be another unfortunate example of the confusion between 'cognitive' and 'speculative' language-games, or the specific form of 'transcendental illusion' that impels us to read the 'signs' of history as if they belonged on the side of actual events, rather than on the side of the enthusiast-spectator whose response – as with the sublime – can never find an adequate or commensurable object in the procession of real-world historical developments. So at the end of all Lyotard's immensely subtle and ingenious argumentation we are left with the message – to put it very simply – that political theory is one thing and practical politics quite another, since any passage between these strictly disparate phrase-regimes will give rise either to vain utopian hopes or to a mood of cynical post-revolutionary despair.

This is why the sublime occupies such a central role in Lyotard's thinking. For 'it is not just any aesthetic phrase, but that of the extreme sublime, which is able to supply the proof that humanity is constantly progressing toward the better' (p. 170). The phrase-regime of taste – or of judgements having to do with the beautiful – is unable to afford any such 'proof' since it involves only a *symbol* of the human good as figured analogically in the free play of the faculties, i.e. the harmonious co-operative working of imagination and understanding. With the sublime, on the other hand, one encounters both a limit (or blockage) to this sense of aesthetic gratification, and a consequent impulse to pass beyond it in quest of 'suprasensible' (ethical and political) Ideas of Reason.

> Because the feeling of the sublime is an affective paradox, the paradox of feeling publicly and as a group that something which is 'formless' alludes to a beyond of experience, that feeling constitutes an 'as-if presentation' of the Idea of civil society and even of cosmopolitical society, and thus an as-if presentation of the Idea of morality, right where that Idea nevertheless cannot be presented, within experience. (Lyotard, p. 170)

So it can never be a question of justifying one's political hopes, convictions, or beliefs by appealing to the witness of historical events as if by way of demonstrative proof. This would be an error of judgement similar to that which deludedly seeks a commensurate object (or phenomenal presentation) for feelings of the sublime. That is to say, it gives sovereign powers to the tribunal of cognitive understanding (where intuitions are 'brought under' adequate concepts), and thus leaves no room for the exercise of speculative thought, or Ideas of Reason.

III

Lyotard is by no means alone among present-day thinkers in promoting this turn toward aesthetic models and analogues – especially that of the sublime – in order to raise questions in the realm of socio-political theory. One could take his whole project as a striking (even extravagant) example of the phenomenon noted by Perry Anderson: namely, the fact that theoretical activity on the left tends to assume ever more rarified, abstract or sophisticated forms as the real-world situation offers fewer opportunities for direct political engagement. The recourse to aesthetics would then appear little more than a desperate holding operation, a means of continuing to talk, think and theorise about issues of a vaguely political import while serenely ignoring the manifest 'fact' that socialism is everywhere in a state of terminal decline.

This diagnosis might find additional support in Lyotard's treatment of the sublime as figuring an ultimate discrepancy of 'phrase-regimes' between real-world (cognitive) and ideal (speculative) modes of political discourse. After all, the aesthetic is notoriously a realm of mystified notions and values, a domain that has often been colonised by right-wing ideologues, from Edmund Burke to Roger Scruton. The title of a recent essay by Tony Bennett – 'Really useless "Knowledge": a political critique of aesthetics' – typified at least one familiar line of response among theorists on the left.[14] But to others it has seemed that aesthetics is a topic worth engaging seriously, not so much on account of its intrinsic value or interest (which they would mostly deny), but by reason of its having served so often as a surrogate discourse where political interests were obliquely or covertly in play. Since Burke's time at least, attention has focused on the relation between aesthetic judgement in its various modalities – most crucially, that of the sublime – and those other kinds of cognitive or socio-political interest that supposedly (on the classical reading of Kant) should not figure at all in our responses to art or in the domain of aesthetic understanding. This attitude finds its most doctrinaire expression in present-day conservatives like Scruton, those for whom the appeal to aesthetic values becomes a kind of shibboleth, a touchstone of true, disinterested judgement, as opposed to all forms of critical theory, whether Marxist, post-structuralist, sociological or whatever.[15] For it is a prime concern of philosophers in this tradition to dissociate questions of judgement or taste from questions of theoretical warrant, since the former (*ex hypothese*) have nothing to do with cognitive interests, conceptual truth-claims, determinate ideas, etc.

So one can see very well why aesthetics should have earned such a bad name among thinkers of a left persuasion who regard it as a mystified pseudo-discipline, a strictly 'useless kind of knowledge' invented for no other purpose than to insulate art from more unwelcome forms of socio-historical attention. Then again, some have argued (Terry Eagleton among them) that this makes it all the more important to study the history of aesthetic ideas, since they occupy a crucially contested domain where political interests are often involved, albeit in a highly oblique or attenuated form.[16] And of course there has long existed a counter-tradition of what might be called affirmative left-wing aesthetics, a tradition that runs (roughly speaking) from Schiller to Herbert Marcuse, Ernst Bloch, Fredric Jameson and other such proponents of a secularised redemptive hermeneutic. These critics hold out the saving possibility that theory might recapture the speculative high ground and thus transform aesthetic philosophy into a discourse responsive to art's always latent utopian or emancipatory promise. In which case – so Eagleton argues – we would be wrong to dismiss that whole tradition out of hand, since it offers both positive and negative resources, a means of keeping faith with the utopian impulse while also resisting (like Benjamin and Adorno) any premature appeal to such affirmative ideas.

The most problematical instance here is the work of Paul de Man, especially those essays of his middle and late periods which focus on the topic of aesthetic ideology as a potent force in historical and political affairs.[17] I shall have a good deal to say about de Man at various points in the following chapters. Very briefly, he sets out to rectify a prevalent misreading of certain passages in Kant, passages that concern (among other things) the relation between cognitive and non-cognitive judgements, the role of the Kantian 'productive imagination' as a mediating category throughout the three *Critiques*, and the question as to how aesthetics can figure as a distinctive mode of understanding, given its avowedly non-conceptual character and its lack of any determinate relation to the realm of phenomenal intuition. Like Benjamin, de Man is deeply suspicious of the drive to 'aestheticise politics', as happens – so he argues – when philosophers like Schiller ignore Kant's studious demarcation of the border-lines between these various faculties, and make the aesthetic a privileged term in their ethical and political thinking. What this amounts to is a dangerous (because immensely seductive) vision of how society might turn out if it could only achieve the state of ordered perfection envisaged by the poets and philosophers. Such an order would exist on the far side of all those hateful antinomies that plague the discourse of mere prosaic understanding. It would finally attain the kind of hypostatic union supposedly vouchsafed to poetic imagination by the language of metaphor and symbol, a language that not only transcends the distinction between subject and object (or mind and nature), but which also marks the point of intersection between word and world, time and eternity, the creaturely realm of causal necessity and the realm of free-willing autonomous spirit.

De Man finds this version of aesthetic ideology everywhere implicit in the rhetoric of Romanticism, from its starting-point in the poets and philosophers (Goethe, Coleridge, Wordsworth, Schiller) to its late continuation in mainstream scholars of Romanticism like M.H. Abrams and Earl Wasserman.[18] And it exerts an equally powerful hold on critics of an anti-romantic persuasion, those who followed T.S. Eliot's example in rejecting such high-flown visionary claims and recommending a return to the seventeenth-century virtues of poetic objectivity and wit. For here also the assumption ran deep that language had at some point suffered a fall, a 'dissociation of sensibility', in Eliot's well-known phrase, which marked a kind of cultural watershed in the history of English poetry, and which could only be repaired – if at all – by a fresh cultivation of those long-lost 'organic' qualities.[19] Hence what many critics have noted as a paradox in Eliot's early essays: the fact that they continue to advance a whole series of typically romantic values and imperatives (the reunion of poetic 'thought' and 'sensibility', organic form, creative impersonality and so forth) while at the same time launching a wholesale crusade against Romanticism and all its works.[20] But this episode looks a lot less puzzling if one takes account of de Man's diagnosis, especially his argument – advanced in essays like 'The rhetoric of temporality' – that the entire development of post-romantic literary thought has been shaped by that same aesthetic ideology that holds out an image of renewed social grace figured in the mutual co-operative working of the faculties. And this vision achieves its highest, most satisfying form in the idea of poetry as actually bringing that condition about through the ultimate harmonious fusion of form and content, subject and object, and all those other vexing antinomies bequeathed to us moderns (in Eliot's view) by the baneful spirit of secular rationalism.

Thus it takes no very subtle or sagacious reading to perceive Kant as one of the villain-figures behind Eliot's potent myth of epochal decline. For it is in Kantian philosophy that one finds what amounts to a *rigorous and principled insistence* that the faculties should maintain their internal system of differentiated powers and prerogatives, and not be tempted into various forms of illusory premature synthesis. And conversely, it is the prevalent misreading of Kant by subsequent thinkers in the German idealist tradition

– Schiller chief among them – that seeks to relax these strenuous critical standards and which elevates the aesthetic to a sovereign role over all the other faculties. Indeed, there could be no more apt illustration of de Man's argument than the way that Eliot managed to achieve such widespread credence for his pseudo-historical account of that purely imaginary episode, the 'dissociation of sensibility'. For it is an episode whose signific-ance, dating and subsequent effects are entirely a product of aesthetic ideology, of the values that Eliot located in the poetry and drama of early seventeenth-century England. Hence – in brief outline – the need to project a backward-looking model of 'tradition' in order to accommodate Eliot's beliefs about the decline of European civilisation, the existence of a long-lost 'organic community', and the dire consequences of a rationalist world-view which enforced the separation of 'thought' and 'sensibility', ideas on the one hand and sensuous intuitions on the other. So the whole (albeit sketchy) historical ground-plan of an essay like 'Tradition and the individual talent' can be seen as a mythical working-out of that same aesthetic ideology that de Man would trace back to its sources in Schiller's revisionist reading of Kant.

Nor is this a question of interest only to specialist scholars in the poetics of Romanticism or the background of present-day critical ideas. For it is de Man's major claim throughout these essays of his last period that a great deal hinges, historically and politically, on the way that we interpret such prob-lematic episodes in the legacy of Kantian thought. Roughly speaking, that legacy divides into two main lines of intellectual descent, the one leading (via Schiller and Coleridge) to a mystified form of aesthetic ontology that privileges metaphor or symbol as images of an ultimate reconciliation be-tween subject and object, mind and nature, time and eternity, while the other gives rise to a critical hermeneutics that resists this premature confla-tion of realms and maintains (like Kant) a vigilant awareness of the dangers attendant upon any such failure to respect the powers and limits of the various faculties. For, according to de Man, it is precisely at the point where aesthetics holds out its highest promise that we also find the sources of another, more insidious claim upon our freedoms, one that takes rise within the same complex of thought and emotion but dispenses altogether with the liberal rhetoric adopted by Schiller and his latter-day progeny. De Man makes this point most forcefully in an essay on Kleist's strange parable *Über das Marionettentheater*, a text that he reads deconstructively as figuring the effects of aesthetic ideology when carried to the limit of a formal perfection beyond all the complicating factors of human knowledge, self-consciousness and desire.[21] The central image in this tale is that of a mechanised dance-routine which has the puppets moving in patterns of a preternatural complexity and elegance that far surpasses the powers of any mortal dancer or choreographer. Like Schiller, in a passage cited by de Man from the *Letters on Aesthetic Education*, this suggests that the end-point of such thinking is a kind of austere, self-denying ordinance that equates artistic perfection with the drive to abolish all merely human obstacles to its own attainment. This would be the point at which, in Schiller's words, 'everything fits so skilfully, yet so spontaneously, that everyone seems to be following his own lead, without ever getting in anyone's way'.[22] But Schiller is still thinking of human dancers, whatever the degree of self-discipline required to regulate their movements in keeping with the formal demands of this singular choreography. What emerges more clearly from the Kleist essay is the fact that such perfection only comes about through the forcible (even violent) suppression of attributes that belong on the side of the willing, self-conscious human subject. For here, in the ideal puppet-theatre of Kleist's imagining, we glimpse what de Man calls 'a wisdom that lies somehow beyond cognition and self-knowledge, yet can only be reached by ways of the process it is said to overcome'.[23]

In other words, this tale can be seen as the upshot – the complex, ambivalent, even sinister upshot – of a tradition that includes all the major forms and variants of aesthetic ideology, from Schiller down to the present. Most importantly, it rehearses that crucial stage where self-consciousness (or romantic irony in its specular, reflexive guise) gives way to the quest for an ultimate fusion of content and form, a poetry that would finally achieve the status of Hegel's 'concrete universal', or attain to what Eliot more vaguely envisaged with his talk of an 'objective correlative'. This idea has found numerous echoes and analogues in the language of post-romantic and symbolist aesthetics. It receives perhaps its most powerful expression in the later poetry of Yeats, where one finds a constant series of thematic oppositions between, on the one hand, mortal intimations of time, decay, human fallibility, 'those dying generations', 'the young in one another's arms', and on the other elaborately stylised metaphors of artifice, eternity, 'unaging monuments of human intellect' and other such high-symbolist images and motifs. It is no coincidence that de Man's *Allegories of Reading* begins with a full-scale deconstructive treatment of Yeats's 'Among School Children', a poem that asserts this version of aesthetic ideology in its most doctrinaire and intensely cultivated form.[24] Here again, his point is that these images derive from a notional ideal of poetic objectivity and truth that would have no truck with the messy imprecisions of desire, self-consciousness and will, and would at last bring us out on the far side of such all-too-human concerns. And if we are seeking a source for this complex of ideas then we need look no further than Schiller's seminal misreading of Kant. 'The point', de Man says, 'is not that the dance fails and that Schiller's idyllic description of a graceful but confined freedom is aberrant. Aesthetic education by no means fails; it succeeds all too well, to the point of hiding the violence that makes it possible.'[25]

Nor is this 'violence' just a piece of self-dramatising rhetoric on de Man's part, an exaggerated claim put in to lend his argument a semblance of political point. For it is indeed the case – as anyone will know who has studied the history of German aesthetic philosophy after Kant – that these ideas exerted considerable influence in realms far beyond the more specialised preserve of literary and art-historical scholarship. Thus there developed a powerful irrationalist mystique whose governing metaphor was precisely that of the state as a principle of *organic* growth and development, a quasi-natural entity whose evolutionary character could best be grasped by analogy with the work of art.[26] And from here it is no great distance to the idea of politics as a manifestation of authentic *national* genius, a progress through stages of world-historical spirit or *Geist* where the emergent destiny of cultures and nations obeyed the same laws of profoundly organic development as were exemplified in the sphere of aesthetic production. It hardly needs recalling how such notions entered the mainstream of European (especially German) philosophy after Kant, and what role they played in cultural politics during the period – roughly, from Hegel to Heidegger – when reflections on art and aesthetic experience became central to that whole tradition. And of course there is the evidence of de Man's early writings, published in a wartime Belgian paper under the German occupation, and showing all too clearly how these notions had shaped his own youthful thinking.[27] Small wonder – as I have argued at length elsewhere[28] – that de Man should have devoted his best intellectual efforts over the next three decades and more to deconstructing this strain of aesthetic ideology and pointing out its baneful consequences. For 'the state that is here being advocated [as he puts it in the essay on Schiller and Kleist] is not just a state of mind or of soul, but a principle of political value and authority that has its own claims on the shape and limits of our freedom'.[29]

Hence the specific form that deconstruction takes in the writings of de Man's last period: a relentless critique of monadic or 'totalising' figures, especially metaphor and symbol, allied to a constant reference back to Kant as the thinker who in some sense spawned this whole tradition of mystified aesthetic values, but whose texts can none the less – if we read them aright –provide the best remedy against such errors. Above all, Kant maintains a vigilant suspicion of any attempt to short-circuit the complex order of relationship between theoretical understanding, practical reason and aesthetic judgement as the three chief faculties whose scope it is the task of critical philosophy to determine from an enlightened, unprejudiced standpoint. And one major source of confusion here is the drive – amply witnessed in Schiller and his disciples – to extend the aesthetic far beyond its proper domain by linking it directly to phenomenal perceptions on the one hand and ethical categories on the other. For it is precisely in so far as it collapses this critical distinction – this difference, so crucial to Kant, between our *feelings* of the beautiful or the sublime and the *objects* which occasion that response – it is in this measure that aesthetic ideology can work its untoward effects. Thus 'whenever the aesthetic is invoked as an appeal to clarity and control, whenever, in other words, a symptom is made into a remedy for the disorder that it signals, a great deal of caution is in order'.[30] And again, more explicitly: '[w]hen this same principle [i.e. the project of aesthetic formalisation] is then made to link up with the more objective properties of language revealed by linguistic analysis, the suspicion arises that aesthetic judgement has trespassed beyond its legitimate epistemological reach.'[31] Such trespass would be no great cause for concern – just a species of technical category-mistake – were it not for the extreme seductiveness and power exerted by the model of aesthetic education as developed by poets and philosophers from Schiller to Yeats. For it is by way of this uncritical passage from art to the other dimensions of human experience (ethical, historical, political) that aesthetic ideology has left its disastrous imprint on the past hundred years of European life and thought.

IV

We are now better placed to answer Perry Anderson's question as to why critical theory (and aesthetic philosophy, of all things) should enjoy such a widespread revival of interest at the current low ebb of left political fortunes. One reason may be that nothing concentrates the critical mind like the prospect of a wholesale reactionary drive to mystify social relations and political values through an appeal to notions of commonsense, tradition, 'Victorian values' and so forth, launched in the name of a know-nothing anti-intellectual creed that is currently bent upon destroying the universities as centres of independent thought and – by this and other means –

reducing Britain to one of the most backward pseudo–democracies in the 'free world'. This would go some way toward explaining the interest (the critical-diagnostic interest) in aesthetics as a discourse that has often served in exactly such a mystificatory role.

But there is another side to the story which involves not so much a critique of those mystified values as a wholesale espousal of aesthetic ideology in the name of 'postmodernism' and its claim to have moved way beyond the old dispensation of truth, critique, and suchlike enlightenment values. Perhaps the most depressing aspect of this current intellectual scene is the extent to which fashionable 'left' alternatives (like the ideas canvassed in *Marxism Today*) have set about incorporating large chunks of the Thatcherite cultural and socio-political agenda while talking portentously of 'New Times' and claiming support from postmodernist gurus like Baudrillard. For we have now lived on – so these thinkers urge – into an epoch of pervasive 'hyperreality', an age of mass-media simulation, opinion-poll feedback, total publicity and so forth, with the result that it is no longer possible (if indeed it ever was) to distinguish truth from falsehood, or to cling to those old 'enlightenment' values of reason, critique, and adequate ideas.[32] Reality just *is* what we are currently given to make of it by these various forms of seductive illusion. In fact we might as well give up using such terms, since they tend to suggest that there is still some genuine distinction to be drawn between truth and untruth, 'science' and 'ideology', knowledge and what is presently 'good in the way of belief'. On the contrary, says Baudrillard: if there is one thing we should have learned by now it is the total obsolescence of all such ideas, along with the enlightenment meta-narrative myths – whether Kantian-liberal, Hegelian, Marxist or whatever – that once underwrote their delusive claims. What confronts us now is an order of pure 'simulacra' which no longer needs to disguise or dissimulate the absence of any final truth-behind-appearances.

Baudrillard is perhaps the most extreme instance of this 'postmodern' drive to extend the aesthetic (i.e. the realm of imaginary representations) to the point of collapsing every last form of ontological distinction or critical truth-claim. His main target here is the Marxist discourse of use-value, labour-power, forces and relations of production, etc., since these terms strike him as just one more lingering symptom of the nostalgic desire to separate 'real' human purposes and interests from the delusive shadow-realm of 'ideological' misrecognition.[33] Quite simply, those terms are incapable of sustaining any such normative analysis, since it is nowadays impossible to distinguish genuine needs, values, material forces or whatever from the values and needs that are brought into being through advertising, consumer culture, or the 'artificial' stimulation of demand by these and similar agencies. To pretend otherwise – as by clinging to outmoded Marxist concepts of *Ideologiekritik* or economic determination 'in the last instance' – is merely to betray one's failure to catch up with these new rules of the game. And the same applies to any version of critical philosophy that attempts to distinguish the orders of illusion and reality, *doxa* and *episteme*, or specious from valid forms of argument. For there is simply no point in maintaining such distinctions – so Baudrillard would have us believe – in a world where 'false' appearances go all the way down, and where the only available measure of 'truth' is the capacity to put one's ideas across to maximum suasive effect.

In Chapter 4 I offer a full-length critique of Baudrillard's numerous non-sequiturs, his philosophical muddles and his manifest failure to engage this so-called 'postmodern condition' at any but the most superficial level. For now, his arguments will serve as a signpost of one direction that theorists (or anti-theorists) have taken in response to the widespread sense of crisis affecting the present-day human sciences. It amounts to a wholesale version of aesthetic ideology, a project of annulling all the terms and distinctions that Kant so strenuously sought to hold in place, and a consequent refusal to acknowledge any limits to the realm of imaginary representation. Lyotard is a rather more complex case, since in *Le Différend* he makes a point of insisting – unlike Baudrillard – that we should not mix up the various 'phrase-regimes' (cognitive, speculative, aesthetic etc.) which have to do with different orders of judgement. But his work exhibits a similar aestheticising drift in its tendency to downplay the interests of theory (i.e. phrases belonging to the cognitive regime) and to emphasise those that appeal either to speculative Ideas of Reason or to the sublime as the most extreme case of intuitions that cannot be brought under the rule of any adequate concept. Thus:

> Marx built the International Association of Working Men. He interprets the sign that is the enthusiasm aroused by the Commune as if it signalled the political project of the real class and as if it outlined the organization of a real party. This is a second illusory 'passage'; the first passes from the sign that is solidary enthusiasm to the ideal of a revolutionary subject, the proletariat; the second passes from this ideal to the real political organization of the real working class. (Lyotard, p. 172)

So the end of all Lyotard's subtle argumentation is to enforce the message that political theory had better stick to the realm of speculative reason and not make the all-too-frequent mistake of translating its ideas into this-worldly, practical terms. For the result of such confusions – as Lyotard reads them – is a dreary catalogue of historical events ('Berlin 1953, Budapest 1956, Czechoslovakia 1968', etc.) that can only give the lie to any hopes built up through the exercise of speculative reason.

It seems to me that this trick of playing Kant off against Marx has a lot more to do with events near home – that is to say, 'Paris '68' and the disillusioned mood of French left intellectuals during the subsequent decade – than with anything on the broader European front. It also raises the obvious question: how are we to interpret those other, more hopeful 'signs' that have emerged from Eastern Europe over the past few months of extraordinary political developments? From Lyotard's standpoint these developments might inspire 'enthusiasm' (i.e. a response of excited fellow-feeling in sympathy with the hopes and aspirations manifest in such 'great historical events'). But we should be wrong to interpret them as in any sense providing *evidence* (i.e. material grounds) for believing that Eastern Bloc communism was working its way toward a better, more enlightened or democratic form of socialist practice. For this would be to fall into the trap that opened up for Marx when he misread the 'sign' of the Paris Commune and attempted to discover an objective correlative for it in the domain of actually-existing socialist movements or working-class political activity. In other words, these events would belong to the order of sublime experience, happenings on a scale that solicited the utmost of sympathetic human involvement, but which for that very reason could never be brought under a form of determinate historico-political judgement. For this is the upshot of Lyotard's argument: that we will always go wrong – and in potentially catastrophic ways – if we think to extrapolate from one phrase-regime to another, as by looking to history for *evidence* that 'things are getting better', or (conversely) allowing events to disconfirm our belief in such desirable Ideas of Reason. For 'it can then be proven [as Lyotard phrases it, summarising Kant] that humanity's natural predisposition to make use of speculative reason can indeed be realized, and that a constant progress toward the better can be anticipated in history, without fear of error' (p. 165). But the price of this immunity turns out to be nothing less than a willingness to sever all links between political theory (as the exercise of speculative reason) and political events (where one might – naïvely – hope to find some evidence that such ideas were capable of being carried into practice).

This would all tend to bear out Anderson's thesis about the retreat into theory among left intellectuals at times of widespread political disenchantment. There is an interesting parallel in some essays of de Man's middle period where he reads passages from Wordsworth's *Prelude* as symptomatic of the poet's withdrawal from politics – or his mood of chastened post-revolutionary consciousness – and links this feeling to the sense of the sublime as an experience that always exceeds and baffles the powers of cognitive judgement. 'For the interpreter of history', de Man writes, 'it is never a simple and uniform movement like the ascent of a peak or the installation of a definitive social order.' On the contrary: what we learn through Wordsworth's highly complex and self-occupied narration of events is the lesson that history must always appear

> much more in that twilight in which . . . the crossing of the Alps was bathed, in which the coming-to-consciousness is in arrears *vis-à-vis* the actual act, and consequently is to be understood not as a conquest but rather as a rectification or even a reproach.[34]

It is not hard to see how this reading might be motivated, at least in part, by de Man's own need to disavow his involvement in a history – that of Belgium under the wartime German occupation – which he now had every reason to conjure away through such appeals to the movement of reflective 'interiorisation' and its privileged trope, the Wordsworthian sublime.[35] But my purpose here is to make the more general point: that this recourse to the aesthetic as a means of handling complex *political* questions is one that can take a variety of forms, some of them profoundly conservative in character, others more progressive or radical. For the aesthetic has been installed within Western philosophy since Kant as the problematic ground where various faculties or truth-claims have established a provisional court of appeal whereby to adjudicate their often conflicting interests. As such, it exerts what de Man came to recognise as a decisive 'claim upon our freedoms', a claim that may lead on the one hand to forms of subtly coercive aesthetic ideology, and on the other – at Lyotard's opposite extreme – to a politics of pure speculative reason devoid of all probative or empirical warrant.

For it is precisely on this contested terrain that theory comes up against the crucial question: how far, and at what analogical remove, can the interests of reason assert their claim to deliver significant truths about the meaning and nature of political events? To this question Lyotard returns what amounts to a confidently negative response. For him, there is no possible 'passage' between language-games belonging to the genre of speculative reason and language-games that assert some cognitive or truth-telling relation to the way that history has turned out so far. Any such passage will always prove to involve a fundamental category-mistake, a desire to leap over the properly unbridgeable gulf between judgements aimed toward an ideal *sensus communis* of emancipated human interests and judgements that bear upon the question of what *actually happened* in this or that set of historical circumstances. Hence his appeal to the Kantian sublime – generalised far beyond its role in the original context of argument – as a principle of ultimate 'heterogeneity', a means of driving this doctrinal wedge between the two supposedly disparate phrase-regimes of knowledge and speculative reason. In which case Marxism can only retain its viability as a discourse of political justice in so far as it appeals to Ideas of Reason (e.g. the Idea of a 'republican social contract'), and renounces any form of the cognitive appeal to determinate class interests, revolutionary movements etc. In Lyotard's words:

> Marxism has not come to an end, but how does it continue? . . . The wrong is expressed through the silence of suffering, through feeling. The wrong results from the fact that all phrase universes and all their linkages are or can be subordinated to the sole finality of capital (but is capital a genre?) and judged accordingly. Because this finality seizes upon or can seize upon all phrases, it makes a claim to universality. The wrong done to phrases by capital would then be a universal one. Even if the wrong is not universal (but how can you prove it? it's an Idea), the silent feeling that signals a differend remains to be listened to. Responsibility to thought requires it. This is the way in which Marxism has not come to an end, as the feeling of the differend. (Lyotard, p. 171)

In short, there is no future for Marxist thinking in so far as it persists in the illusory belief that events past or present might actually have some bearing on the validity of its larger (theoretical or speculative) claims, or indeed that those claims might actually be borne out by future historical developments. For this is to ignore what Lyotard considers the decisive refutations of Marxist doctrine that arise as soon as one contemplates the record of failed revolutionary movements to date. It was here that Marx himself went wrong – or misconstrued the nature of his own project – by seeking to validate one type of 'phrase' by standards that pertained to quite another. 'In suffering and in class struggle, which is a referent for cognitive phrases (the phrases of the historian, the socialist, and the economist), he thinks he hears the demands of the proletariat, which is the object of an Idea, an ideal of reason, namely an emancipated working humanity' (p. 171). And if Marxism continues to elide these categories – thus laying itself open to empirical disproof with each new set-back or predictive failure – then it is condemned to obsolescence, along with all the other 'grand narratives' of enlightenment, progress and truth.

It is not at all hard to find reasons for Lyotard's extreme non-cognitivist stance with regard to these questions in the province of historical and socio-political theory. One obvious reason is 'May '68', a phrase that he regards as spelling an end to many of the confident assumptions that once underwrote the truth-claims of both liberal and Marxist salvation-histories. Like Foucault, he sees such claims as amounting to nothing more than a species of grandiose delusion, a trick whereby the self-appointed revolutionary vanguard (or the class of 'universal intellectuals') sets itself up as the possessor of some ultimate truth, some omniscient or God's-eye perspective from which to theorise the logic and meaning of historical events.[36] This lesson was brought home with particular force – so the story runs – when Marxist luminaries (Althusser among them) proved utterly incapable of grasping what had happened or advising the best course of action, and when history itself, in the wake of *les évènements*, turned into a sad mockery of everything that might have been predicted according to the grand dialectical narrative schema. Hence the whole range of disenchanted stances – post-Marxist, postmodern, post-historical, post-enlightenment, post-just-about-everything – that have since come to characterise 'advanced' French thought during the past two decades. What these movements have in common is a deep suspicion of any theory that claims a vantage-point of knowledge or truth, a self-assured position of 'scientific' method from which to criticise the various forms of 'ideological' false-seeming or commonsense perception. If these notions once possessed a certain delusive appeal – as undoubtedly they did for the proponents of Althusserian 'theoretical practice' during the early-to-mid 1960s – they can no longer be taken seriously by anyone who has witnessed the collapse of such high-flown intellectual ambitions on the left or the break-up of socialist programmes and principles in face of subsequent historical events.[37] In short, the only option for critical theorists – in so far as that phrase still applies – is to accept this predicament as best they can and carry on working as 'specific intellectuals' in this or that localised field of activity, without any claim to have privileged access to some truth behind the ideological façade or some ultimate ('meta-narrative') theory that *explains* why history should have taken this untoward turn. Least of all can they afford to indulge nostalgic ideas of criticism as class struggle carried over into the realm of 'theoretical practice', a notion whose authority once invested such figures as Sartre and Althusser (whatever their deep intellectual differences), but which now shows up – in light of subsequent events – as a form of overweening intellectual presumption. For it should now be self-evident (according to thinkers like Foucault, Lyotard and Baudrillard) that the time is long past when anyone could claim to speak or write in the name of some vanguard party of truth whose authority transcended the limiting conditions of its own, historically-specific time and place.

Where these issues converge is on the question of *representation*, understood in the twofold sense of that term as used by critical theorists and philosophers in the post-Kantian tradition. On the one hand it signifies the capacity of reason to grasp and interpret truths of experience that present themselves before the critical tribunal of adequate or answerable knowledge. To Lyotard's way of thinking – as also for neo-pragmatists like Rorty and Fish – this whole set of notions must now be given up since it appeals to standards of validity and truth that amount to nothing more than one 'final vocabulary' among others, or one phrase-regime (that of cognitive judgements) which possesses no ultimate or binding authority. Other versions of this anti-foundationalist drive can be seen in the various critiques of representation that characterise post-structuralist thinking (with its attack on that much-maligned mythical entity, the 'classic realist text') and postmodernism, with its attitude of thoroughgoing sceptical doubt in regard to questions of truth, meaning and historical interpretation. On the other hand these movements reject the idea that intellectuals (i.e. critical thinkers) could ever claim the right to *represent* human interests, needs or political aspirations that go beyond their own, necessarily partial and self-interested view of events. For this is to ignore precisely those lessons that postmodernism draws from its reading of the way that history – especially recent history– has failed to live up to these grandiose 'totalising' plans and projections. That is to say, they adopt an enlightenment rhetoric of critique, reason, progress and truth at the very moment when those values are most under siege from the pressure of unlooked-for political developments (e.g. what has happened in Eastern Europe) and the sheer contingency of historical events. So 'representation' becomes a doubly problematical notion and maybe – as some of these thinkers would have it – a henceforth discredited category. For it carries an appeal to standards of truth whose ultimate locus is the transcendental subject of Kantian philosophy, a subject whose powers of discriminating judgement (between truth and illusion, science and ideology, concepts of understanding and ideas of reason) are in fact nothing more than a transient product of the will-to-power that masks behind a rhetoric of pure, disinterested knowledge. And if this is the case then we had better abandon any idea of representation that trades on either the epistemological or the politico-juridical sense of that term.

These are some of the factors that have evidently conspired to produce the current postmodernist turn in French intellectual debate. With Lyotard, this turn is somewhat qualified by the desire to conserve at least some elements of Kantian or 'enlightened' thought, namely, the principle that reason has its role in phrases bearing upon issues of political justice, freedom and responsibility, though only in so far as such phrases are treated as belonging to the genre of speculative truth-claims ('Ideas of Reason'), and not as possessing any cognitive value for our knowledge of historical events. For others – Baudrillard among them – there is simply no point in hanging on to these and kindred philosophical notions. Enlightenment is now a thing of the past, a closed chapter in the history of European thought, and the only way forward is to junk such ideas and revel in the prospect of a postmodern epoch devoid of all truth-claims, all standards of valid argumentation or efforts to separate a notional 'real' from the various forms of superinduced fantasy or mass-media simulation. Least of all can we hope to redeem the high promise of enlightened emancipatory thought at a time when that project has run up against such a range of historical counter-examples, anti-foundationalist arguments and so forth. What these thinkers have in common – despite Lyotard's much greater powers of cogent exposition – is this sense of an unprecedented crisis affecting all the concepts and categories of adequate representation.

V

However, it should be obvious to anyone who has read Marx's *Eighteenth Brumaire of Louis Bonaparte* that such crises have a much longer prehistory than might be guessed from these current modish variations on the 'end-of-ideology' theme.[38] In fact Marx anticipates just about everything that Lyotard and Baudrillard will have to say about the collapse of enlightened meta-narratives, the breakdown of theory – 'classic' Marxist theory – in the face of contingent historical events, and the way that such absurd happenings as the Bonapartist coup confront dialectical reason with a challenge that apparently exceeds its furthest powers of explanatory grasp. The best-known passage of the *Eighteenth Brumaire* is the sentence from its opening paragraph: 'Hegel remarks somewhere that all facts and personages of great importance in world history occur, as it were twice. He forgot to add: the first time as tragedy, the second as farce' (Marx, p. 103).

And the text goes on to develop this argument to a point where – as recent commentators have noted – all the axioms of Marxist 'scientific' method are subject to a kind of self-deconstructive parody, a series of wildly exuberant set-piece descriptions which seem to stand historical progress on its head and to leave no room for any form of dialectical reprise.[39] Thus the nephew (Louis Bonaparte) sets out to re-enact the previous triumphs of the uncle, but succeeds only in producing a species of out-and-out involuntary farce, a mockery of everything that had gone before. And this effect proves contagious when Marx gets around to describing and explaining the course of events that somehow led up to this farcically regressive chapter in the history of French political institutions. For everything about the *Eighteenth Brumaire* – its metaphors, parentheses, narrative strategies, offhand observations, stylistic devices, ironic reversals, relentless piling up of detail, etc. – seems to carry the same message: that reason (dialectical reason) is here completely out of its depth, since there exists no possible paradigm or theory by which to make sense of such a thoroughly absurd episode.

Least of all can this evidence be marshalled to support a Marxist reading along classic (economic-determinist) lines, i.e. a reading that invokes such concepts as class interest, forces and relations of production, or any variant of the base/superstructure model. For if there is one lesson that this text drives home with relentless force it is the failure of theory to establish any link – any kind of causal or structural relation – between the categories of Marxist analysis and the morass of anarchic detail thrown up in the effort to portray this whirligig sequence of events. The problems are most evident in another much-quoted passage where Marx seemingly goes out of his way to insist that this episode makes no kind of sense from the standpoint of a 'classic' Marxist analysis based on ideas of determinate class interest, 'representative' state or civil institutions and so forth. Hence his description of the motley entourage that supported Louis Bonaparte:

> Alongside aging *roués* with dubious means of subsistence and of dubious origin, alongside ruined and adventurous offshoots of the bourgeoisie, were vagabonds, discharged soldiers, discharged jailbirds, escaped galley-slaves, rogues, mountebanks, pickpockets, tricksters, gamblers, brothel-keepers, porters, *literati*, organ-grinders, rag-pickers, knife-grinders, tinkers, beggars – in short, the whole indefinite, disintegrated mass, thrown hither and thither, which the French term *la bohème*; from this kindred element Bonaparte formed the core of the Society of December 10 . . . This Bonaparte, who constitutes himself *chief of the Lumpenproletariat*, who here alone discovers in mass form the interests which he personally pursues, who

recognises in this scum, offal, refuse of all classes the only class upon which he can base himself unconditionally, is the real Bonaparte, the Bonaparte *sans phrase*. (Marx, p. 149)

It is not hard to see why this passage has been cited by commentators of a postmodernist or deconstructive bent who read in it the ultimate *mise-en-abîme* of Marxist theory and all such 'totalising' schemes of historical explanation. For the rhetorical effect – so these critics argue – is to play dialectics right off the field by creating such a mass of random, unassimilated detail that no kind of theory (or historical meta–narrative) can possibly reduce it to order. Marx's language can only give 'adequate' expression to this sense of a scandalous breakdown in the categories of representation by allowing its descriptive energies to run wild, thus creating a grotesquely surreal proliferation of metonymic class-substitutes, of parasitic stand-ins for what ought to be the bearers of 'authentic' class interest and consciousness according to the classic Marxist paradigm. In the end there is no accounting for this thoroughly exorbitant episode except by abandoning the protocols of Marxist 'science' and allowing language to play all manner of mischievous deconstructive games with the notions of historical representation and socio-economic determinism (whether or not, as the saving formula would have it, 'in the last instance').

So the upshot of Marx's precocious experiment in postmodern narrative techniques is to show that this whole way of thinking collapses when it tries to understand how history repeats itself, the second time around as farce. In short, there is no appealing to the 'real foundations' of socio-economic life when history is always liable to take such a ridiculous and wholly unpredictable turn toward forms of regressive imaginary investment, episodes that only make sense according to a weird pseudo-logic of uncanny repetition. Thus the *Eighteenth Brumaire* becomes a kind of test-case for the methods and procedures of Marxist criticism, much as Balzac's *Sarrasine* serves Barthes as an instance of the 'bourgeois realist text' pushed up against the limits of its own commitment to a classic economy of meaning, value and truth.[40] From which it is a short step to the conclusion that Marxism no longer possesses any interest except as a period-specific episode of thought which at least had the virtue – the diagnostic virtue – of self-deconstructing when it reached the limits of its own explanatory grasp.

This is why a text like the *Eighteenth Brumaire* has become such a focus of interest at precisely the time when Marxist ideas are under attack from various political and intellectual quarters. For here more than anywhere

Introduction

Marx comes close to conceding that certain historical turns of event may baffle or frustrate the best efforts of dialectical-materialist thought. And moreover, this realisation comes about through a text that exhibits all the characteristic features of postmodernism *avant la lettre*. That is to say, Marx encounters such obstacles to the straightforward narration of these events – to the process of bringing them under adequate concepts, or fitting them into some self-assured dialectical schema – that his writing becomes a kind of object-lesson in the breakdown of Marxist representational categories. The better Marx appreciates the absurdity of this whole episode, the more he seems drawn into a farcical scene of instruction where he – the aspiring omniscient narrator – becomes tied up in *Tristram Shandy*-like knots of his own fictive contriving.

> Only when he [*Napoléon le petit*] has eliminated his solemn opponent, when he himself now takes his imperial role seriously and under the Napoleonic mask imagines he is the real Napoleon, does he become the victim of his own conception of the world, the serious buffoon who no longer takes world history for a comedy but his comedy for world history. (Marx, pp. 149–50)

And in passages like this – so the postmodern reading goes – we can see how the 'serious' discourse of Marxist criticism falls prey to a species of monstrous self-parody that threatens to disrupt all its concepts and categories and leave them devoid of explanatory power. For such is the confusion of identities, class-roles, narrative sequence, historical epochs and so forth that this welter of profligate representations exceeds all the bounds of intelligible form.[41]

Of course there is more at stake in this reading of the *Eighteenth Brumaire* than an attempt to claim at least one text of Marx for the purposes of postmodernist literary criticism. Looming behind this whole debate is the shadow of Althusserian Marxism, that high-theoreticist project of an earlier decade which sought above all to give scientific status to the axioms and truth-claims of Marxist theoretical discourse. With the collapse of that project – more or less taken for granted by the current postmodernist consensus – Marxism itself underwent a deep crisis which left scarcely one of those conceptual foundations in place.[42] In particular, it brought out the sheer impossibility of Marxism's supposed 'meta-narrative' stance, i.e. its assumption that theory could occupy a vantage-point of reason and truth beyond all the vagaries of first-hand ('ideological') experience or awareness. In the *Eighteenth Brumaire* such theories receive what looks very much like their final come-uppance, a demonstration that there is simply no available ground – no bed-rock certainties of method or theory – from which to conduct the kind of high-level abstract critique of 'commonsense' representations envisaged by Althusserian Marxists. For readers willing to heed its message this text spells out the following lessons: (1) that the narration of historical events cannot be subject to higher ('metanarrative') forms of explanatory comment or control; (2) that this distinction (like the formalist categories of *récit* and *discours*, or 'story' and 'plot') is at best just a handy heuristic device, subject to all manner of complicating tensions as soon as one actually begins to read; and (3) that we should therefore give up thinking in these typecast theoreticist terms and accept the plain fact that all our sense-making strategies are provisional constructions out of the chaos of history, and hence liable to summary disconfirmation at each new turn of the story so far. What the *Eighteenth Brumaire* would then represent – in so far as it managed to 'represent' anything at all – is the total obsolescence of Marxist (especially Althusserian-Marxist) theory, and the advent of a so-called 'postmodern condition' that finally dispenses with all such delusive transcendental guarantees.

But this is, to say the least, a very partial reading and one that focuses on isolated passages (like those cited above) which dovetail neatly with the present-day fashion for discovering self-deconstructive narratives at work in just about every kind of text. For one could just as well argue to opposite effect: that the *Eighteenth Brumaire* is a triumphant vindication of Marxist historiography applied to the most intractable sequence of chaotic images, memories and events.[43] For what is really most impressive about Marx's text – taken as a whole and not read piecemeal by critics looking sharp for proto-deconstructionist moves – is the way that it deploys such an extraordinary range of stylistic and narrative devices in the course of making good its opening statements on the complex, overdetermined, repetitive nature of all such revolutionary (or pseudo-revolutionary) episodes. These sentences are worth recalling since they tend to drop out of sight when critics get around to the more exciting business of catching Marx out in fictive games of his own unwitting invention.

> Men make their own history, but they do not make it just as they please; they do not make it under circumstances chosen by themselves, but under circumstances directly encountered, given and transmitted from the past . . . And just when they seem engaged in revolutionizing themselves and things, in creating something that has never yet existed, precisely in such periods of revolutionary crisis they anxiously conjure up the spirits of the past to their

service and borrow from them names, battle-cries and costumes in order to present the new scene of world history in this time-honoured disguise and this borrowed language. (Marx, pp. 103-4)

And the *Eighteenth Brumaire* goes on to substantiate this argument through a series of detailed comparisons between earlier revolutionary movements and leaders – from the Roman Republic to Luther, Cromwell, Robespierre, Danton, Napoleon – and those events in France from 1848 to '51 that brought the Nephew (Louis Bonaparte) to power and reduced this whole process to the level of out-and-out farce. What is more, it marshalls an impressive (at times overwhelming) range of documentary sources, first-hand descriptions, statistics, day-to-day chronological records, etc. in order to support this reading of the episode and make better sense of it in world-historical terms. So there is no good reason to suppose – like the current postmodernising critics – that the *Eighteenth Brumaire* signals a breakdown or prefigures some kind of latter-day terminal crisis in the project of Marxist-dialectical thought. What it does bring out with particular vividness and force is the extent to which Marxism is capable of adopting more resourceful (even proto-deconstructionist) narrative strategies in handling events that cannot be described – much less explained – on the classic determinist model.

Now of course it is always *possible* to read this text as a lesson in the ultimate futility of historical explanations, a narrative that explodes all the basic Marxist categories of meaning, logic, temporal progression, representative class interests, ideological formations and so forth. This reading gains force from the currently widespread mood of disenchantment with 'enlightened' thinking in all its forms, in particular that version of enlightenment reason – whether Kantian, Marxist or whatever – which claims to distinguish truth from illusion, or the interests of rational critique from those of dominant consensus-belief or imaginary misrecognition. We have seen already how this doctrine has taken hold among 'postmodern' thinkers like Lyotard and Baudrillard, producing what amounts to a vote of no confidence in the political relevance of theory, or (as Lyotard would have it) the non-correspondence between judgements belonging to the 'phrase-regime' of speculative reason and judgements pertaining to matters of cognitive or real-world socio-political import. From this point of view the *Eighteenth Brumaire* is a text uncannily prescient of all the problems, set-backs and unthinkable paradoxes in the nature of historical representation suffered by Marxist theory over the past few decades. What Marx observes of events in France between 1848 and 1851 would then

apply point for point to the predicament of Marxist or left-wing intellectuals at the present time, confronted with the spectacle of history going
into reverse, so to speak, and throwing up all manner of absurdly regressive
values and political programs.

> An entire people, which had imagined that by means of a revolution it had
> imparted to itself an accelerated power of motion, suddenly finds itself set
> back into a defunct epoch and, in order that no doubt as to the relapse may
> be possible, the old dates rise again, the old chronology, the old edicts,
> which had long become a subject of antiquarian erudition, and the old
> myrmidons of the law, who had seemed long decayed . . . They have not
> only a caricature of the old Napoleon, they have the old Napoleon himself,
> caricatured as he must appear in the middle of the nineteenth century.
> (Marx, p. 105)

The present-day parallels are obvious enough, with politicians like
Thatcher promoting a return to so-called 'Victorian values', busily undoing all the social advances of the past quarter-century and more, and
reducing the currency of political debate to the level of knockabout farcical
exchange that Marx so brilliantly captures in the *Eighteenth Brumaire*. In
fact one could envisage an updated version of the text that substituted
'Thatcher' for 'Louis Bonaparte' and discovered all manner of living rep-
resentatives – self-made Tory grandees, ex-politicians-turned-best-selling-
novelists, advertising agents dictating party policy, City whiz-kids, yup-
pies, insider-dealers, kowtowing civil servants 'economical with the truth',
etc. – to match Marx's catalogue of the *déclassé* rabble that accompanied
the Nephew in his rise to power. And this exercise would probably do
more to explain the Thatcherite phenomenon than any amount of patient
analysis along standard (class-based or economic-determinist) Marxian
lines. For there is, undeniably, a sense in which history – or the history of
the Western 'free-world' democracies – has entered a phase of absurd self-
parody which can ony be captured by some such wildly exorbitant means
of representation.

An example (one of many, but peculiarly apt) would be Thatcher's
invocation of a high-toned Churchillian rhetoric in order to dignify her
shameless use of the Malvinas/Falklands campaign as a means of whipping
up nationalist fervour in time for the 1983 election. Like the Nephew
sedulously aping the Uncle – and producing nothing more than a species
of squalid and brutal farce – this episode perfectly illustrates Marx's point
about the patterns of compulsive repetition that characterise such periods
of widespread regressive fantasy. Indeed, the past ten years of British

politics would provide plentiful material for a 'postmodern' narrative treatment and analysis after the style of the *Eighteenth Brumaire*. To some extent this explains why so many erstwhile left thinkers have gone over to an attitude of cynical acquiescence in versions of the 'end of ideology' thesis, the idea that enlightened or progressive values have nowadays fallen upon such hard times that it is no longer possible – 'realistically' possible – to espouse any version of Marxist or liberal-progressive thinking. Such attitudes follow from the commonplace error of equating our present, depressed conditions of political life with the limits of what is thinkable in terms of a better, more just, enlightened or truly *representative* sociopolitical order. For Lyotard, the principal source of confusion consists in mistaking speculative for cognitive judgements, thus producing forms of 'transcendental illusion' that seek some substantive historical evidence for the claims of political freedom, justice, progress, etc. But it is just as mistaken, I would argue, to swing right over and embrace the opposite tendency, i.e. by rejecting any form of enlightened critique that involves some appeal to the *manifest disparity* between things-as-they-are and things as they might be according to the standards of enlightened critical reason. In Lyotard's writing this tension disappears, since the two 'phrase-regimes' are treated as realms apart, orders of judgement that must not be confused lest reason (speculative reason) surrender its purely *ethical* authority and become entangled with the crass contingencies of history, politics and real-world events.

The postmodern reading of the *Eighteenth Brumaire* can be seen to make the same point in a yet more negative or quasi-deconstructionist style. That is to say, it offers a set-piece demonstration of the way that all those fine old Marxist values – reason, truth, freedom, progress, the emancipating power of enlightened critique – are dragged down, as the story goes along, into a morass of random, chaotic, unintelligible detail, a sense of irretrievable collapse affecting all the codes and conventions of Marxist 'meta-narrative' theory. But this is not at all what happens in the *Eighteenth Brumaire*, any more than it happens (necessarily) when thinking confronts the grotesque absurdities of Thatcher's 'revolution' over the past decade, or the ongoing farce of North American politics under the Reagan–Bush dispensation. Postmodernism chooses to read such events as spectacular examples of the 'textualisation' of reality, the way in which representation breaks down in face of the so-called 'hyperreal', a procession of endless simulated images and media illusions which cut the ground from under any attempt to revive the outmoded concepts and categories of Marxist *Ideologiekritik*. But this conclusion is both historically premature and – more important – philosophically misguided. For it should be clear to any reader of Marx's text not wholly in the grip of this last-ditch irrationalist persuasion that the narrative succeeds quite brilliantly in making sense of that apparently senseless episode and moreover in conserving and appreciably refining the categories of Marxist historical analysis. What is truly remarkable about this text is not so much the breakdown of narrative representation as the fact that it provides such a marvellously detailed and convincing *explanatory* account of events that would otherwise beggar description.

In short, the postmodernist reading gets things completely upsidedown. Far from exemplifying the ultra-textualist thesis – i.e. that narrative is here pushed beyond the limits of adequate historical representation to the point of grotesque self-parody and surreal fabrication – the *Eighteenth Brumaire* makes deliberate use of exactly those stylistic resources in order to convey *with the maximum degree of verisimilitude* just how fantastic were the events that took place during this absurd interlude of history. And it is perhaps worth noting that this argument is perfectly compatible with what Derrida says in his notorious (and widely misinterpreted) remark that 'there is no "outside" to the text' ('il n'y a pas de hors-texte').[44] For his point here is not to endorse the postmodernist line, i.e. the notion that truth and reality are simulated values, products of an infinitised textual 'freeplay', so that nothing could count as an effective critique of past or present ideologies and systems of representation. On the contrary, as I have argued at length in this volume and elsewhere, Derrida's writings are always aimed at locating the stress-points or moments of self-contestation where texts come up against the ineluctable limits of their own ideological project.[45] If the *Eighteenth Brumaire* can indeed be described as a protodeconstructionist narrative, then it is in this sense precisely that the term applies, and not by virtue of its somehow slipping all the bonds of historical verisimilitude or explanatory grasp. And this means in turn that deconstruction – unlike its postmodernist offshoots and derivatives – belongs much more to the tradition of enlightened *Ideologiekritik* than many of its proponents are currently willing to acknowledge.

VI

I set down these reflections (you will have to take my word for it) on the last day of 1989, at a time when political developments, at home and abroad, seem to justify the claim that we are living through a period of momentous – indeed world-historical – change. A half-century ago W.H. Auden looked back on the 1930s as a 'low, dishonest decade', a description that almost inevitably comes to mind when reflecting on the social panorama of hypocrisy, greed and sheer human waste that have marked Margaret Thatcher's ten years in office.[46] As I have suggested, one way to interpret this episode is to reread the *Eighteenth Brumaire* and follow Marx's hard-put effort to comprehend how history can sometimes assume such a retrograde, anomalous and thoroughly exorbitant guise. That the effort succeeds to a remarkable degree – and through a style of narration that deploys many tricks in the current postmodernist book – should at least give pause to those thinkers who have written Marxism off as a relic of the old enlightenment ethos, a clanking machinery of ironcast concepts and categories quite unable to cope with these present 'New Times' of all-pervasive hyperreality.

Take the following passage, where Marx's description of the Nephew suggests any number of comparisons with the Thatcher style of government and its twists and turns during the past ten years:

> As the executive authority which has made itself an independent power, Bonaparte feels it to be his mission to safeguard 'bourgeois order'. But the strength of this bourgeois order lies in the middle class. He looks on himself, therefore, as the representative of this middle class and issues decrees in this sense. Nevertheless, he is somebody solely due to the fact that he has broken the political power of the middle class and daily breaks it anew. Consequently, he looks on himself as the adversary of the political and literary power of the middle class. But by protecting its material power, he generates its political power anew. The cause must according be kept alive; but the effect, where it manifests itself, must be done away with. But this cannot pass off without slight confusions of cause and effect, since in their interaction both lose their distinguishing features. New decrees that obliterate the border line . . . This contradictory task of the man explains the contradictions of his government, the confused, blind to-ing and fro-ing which seeks now to win, now to humiliate first one class and then another and arrays them all of them uniformly against him, whose practical uncertainty forms a highly comical contrast to the imperious, categorical style of the government decrees, a style which is faithfully copied from the uncle. (Marx, p. 194)

Again, this passage appears to lend itself ideally to a reading in the standard deconstructionist vein, one that brings out the 'uncanny' substitution of causes for effects and vice versa, the absence of any governing 'meta-narrative' logic and the breakdown of all those categories – class interest, forces and relations of production, economic determinism 'in the last instance' and so forth – which are taken as constitutive of Marxist discourse in general. In short, these symptoms could be seen to prefigure what numerous commentators are now hailing as the terminal 'crisis' of Marxism in our time, a crisis whose effects may also be read in the collapse of all those old 'grand narrative' schemas that once promised to explain history on the basis of adequate concepts, paradigms or models of representation. It is no coincidence that such ideas should enjoy a wide currency among literary critics, cultural commentators and other purveyors of intellectual fashion at a time when events in Eastern Europe are likewise greeted as signalling the end of 'socialism' in whatever form or guise. For the whole political thrust of postmodernist thinking is to legitimise the kind of inert consensus-ideology that refuses all notions of enlightened critique (or reform of existing social institutions) and identifies the meaning of historical events with the way they are represented according to this or that dominant propaganda-line or rhetorical strategy. It is a short step from the claims of postmodern sceptical historiography – as exemplified in the work of Hayden White – to the arguments of proselytising right-wing historians who more or less openly advocate a return to the teaching of history as a vehicle for Thatcherite values and principles.[47]

One thing that the *Eighteenth Brumaire* makes clear is the difference between real historical events and 'farcical' occurrences (like those in France after 1848) that adopt the rhetoric of previous such episodes in order to dissimulate their own unreality or lack of political substance. Thus:

> at another stage of development, a century earlier, Cromwell and the English people had borrowed speech, passions and illusions from the Old Testament for their bourgeois revolution. When the real aim had been achieved, when the bourgeois transformation of English society had been accomplished, Locke replaced Habbakuk . . . Thus the resurrection of the dead in those revolutions served the purpose of glorifying the new struggles, not of parodying the old; of magnifying the given task in imagination, not of fleeing from its solution in reality; of finding once more the spirit of revolution, not of making its ghost walk about again. (Marx, p. 105)

These words have a singular and direct relevance to the current state of world political affairs. They help to explain what is so laughable about Thatcher's welcoming the collapse of Eastern Bloc communist dictatorships as a sign that all the world is now discovering the virtues of unrestrained capitalist enterprise, free-market doctrine and 'democracy' in her own (decidedly idiosyncratic) understanding of the word. What has happened in the Soviet Union, Czechoslovakia, East Germany, Poland and Romania during the past few months is a series of events without pattern or precedent, events that would have struck the best qualified observers as strictly unthinkable until they actually occurred. These are indeed 'real' revolutions in Marx's sense of that term, popular risings that find what inspiration they can in the history of previous struggles, but which do so with the purpose of actively transforming the way things are, rather than 'fleeing from solutions in reality' or 'making their ghost walk about again'. The impulse behind these events is one that takes heart from the massive and blatant contradiction between communist ideals and communist practice, or socialism as envisaged by its best proponents and 'actually-existing socialism' as it has turned out under the multiple pressures of global militarisation, capitalist encirclement and internal repression brought about largely by these and allied causes. (This, incidentally, is by far the most plausible reading of Orwell's allegorical intentions in *Animal Farm*, contrary to the standard gloss placed upon it during the last fifty years of cold-war educational propaganda.)[48]

It is therefore something more than an expression of pious hope – an utterance belonging to the 'phrase-regime' of pure speculative reason, as Lyotard might say – that these events in Eastern Europe may presage the emergence of a new form of genuine, working socialist democracy. Of course we can expect the propaganda-battle to continue apace, with Western politicians routinely ignoring the difference betwen 'socialism' and communist dictatorship, with right-wing ideologues once again announcing the 'end of ideology' or the 'end of history', and with the capitalist think-tanks busily drawing up plans for the 'rescue' of those under-developed economies by application of the usual incentives (i.e. massive loans with a crippling burden of interest repayment and all kinds of strings attached, among them the need for political 'reconstruction' along lines laid down by multinational corporate interests). The newspapers are currently full of confident expert opinions to exactly this effect, many of them written by old hands in the 'end-of-ideology' game who were saying just the same in the late 1950s and now find history indeed repeating itself, the second time around pretty much unchanged except for the wider geopolitical stage. But these prognoses ignore one significant point: the failure of capitalism to produce anything like those promised benefits (equal opportunity, respect for human rights, genuine representative government, freedom of the press, extension of welfare provision, etc.) that once underwrote its claim to represent the best interests of humanity at large. And this failure is of a quite different order from the failure of 'actually existing socialism' as witnessed by the collapse of communist dictatorships. For in this latter case it is the *manifest contradiction* between theory and practice – a contradiction perceived and lived out in every aspect of social and political life – that in the end mobilises popular feeling to the point of spontaneous revolution. In the 'free-world' democracies, conversely, such is the power of mass-media misrepresentation and simulated ideological consensus that there appears no longer to exist any gap between what people 'want' (as reflected in opinion polls, electoral surveys, personality-ratings, etc.) and what their leaders promise (as likewise manufactured through this highly elaborated feedback mechanism).

And so there comes a point (prefigured in the *Eighteenth Brumaire*) where all distinctions between reality and illusion begin to fall away, where genuine interests are replaced by a range of imaginary pseudo-fulfilments, and where politicians can carry on talking about 'principles' – no matter how absurd or mendacious – in the confident knowledge that their words will not be subject to even the most elementary forms of critical appraisal. Or indeed a stage beyond that when questions of truth and falsehood scarcely arise since the simulated rhetoric and image-mongering become second nature and it is impossible to say – as with Thatcher's more ludicrously high-toned pronouncements – that the words are 'insincere' or hypocritical. With a few minor shifts of pronominal reference one could rewrite Marx's description of the Nephew to provide a most appropriate commentary on Thatcher's style of heroic self-presentation during the Falklands/Malvinas conflict. Thus: 'Only when she has eliminated her solemn opponent, when she herself now takes her imperial role seriously and under the Churchillian mask imagines she is the real Churchill, does she become the victim of her own conception of the world, the serious buffoon who no longer takes world history for a comedy but her comedy for world history' (adapted from Marx, pp. 149–50). To this extent thinkers like Baudrillard are right when they diagnose the postmodern condition as a generalised crisis in the order of signs and representations that works to efface all sense of the difference between truth and falsehood, reality and illusion, serious and non-serious discourse. But their argument goes wrong when it moves from describing the symptoms of this present malaise to asserting that in fact things were ever thus; that 'truth' was always a chimerical notion that could just as well be paraphrased 'good in the way of belief'; and that now, finally, we have learned to make terms with the failure of all those grand enlightenment concepts (reason, critique, reality *versus* appearances, etc.) that once managed to exert such a potent appeal. This fashionable line amounts to nothing more than a latter-day *trahison des clercs*, a willing abrogation of their critical role on the part of jaded Western intellectuals ready to adopt whatever self-image they can rescue in these present hard times.

Meanwhile, altogether elsewhere, history is being made on a scale and under conditions that Marx himself – let alone the current post-Marxists – could scarcely have imagined. But this is not to say (as the Western propagandists and think-tank pundits would have it) that events in Eastern Europe have finally signalled the bankruptcy of socialist ideas and – more specifically – the demise of Marxism as a thoroughly discredited episode in the history of thought. For those events can only be understood as the working-out of chronic contradictions between the true principles of socialist justice and the brutal distortion to which those principles were subject during the period of 'actually existing' communist rule. And the chief causal factors here were the pressures of unceasing Western hostility, the ever-present threat of war on various fronts and the consequent massive deflection of economic resources into the armaments programme. Of course there is no hint of all this in the standard Thatcherite line on Eastern Europe, namely, that socialism is inherently destined to produce such forms of oppressive dictatorial rule since it involves centralised planning or some version of command economy, as opposed to the 'liberal' or 'democratic' virtues of free-market capitalist enterprise. But this argument falls down on three main counts. Firstly, it ignores the degree of selective coercion exercised by governments (Thatcher's chief among them) that have striven to *enforce* free-market doctrine through the curtailment of union activities, the extension of police powers to intervene in industrial disputes, the manipulative use of legal machinery to protect the 'public interest' in these and related areas, the withdrawal of numerous welfare provisions from those most acutely in need of them, and the redistribution of wealth and taxation benefits in order to create an ever-widening gap between the highest and lowest income groups.[49] Secondly, it fails to understand that socialism represents the only principled and consistent philosophy that envisages a way beyond these forms of blatant social injustice, and which does so, moreover, *despite and against* the abuses that have so often been practised in its name by dictatorships of various colour. And thirdly – most relevant in the British context – it takes no account of the massive contradictions that are opening up between the rhetoric of freedom, prosperity, unlimited opportunity and so forth and the stark realities of unemployment, social deprivation, economic failure (as witnessed by the trade figures from month to month, no matter how expertly 'adjusted' or fiddled for public consumption), and above all the mounting evidence of conflicts at the heart of the Thatcherite ideological project. In light of all this, there is indeed something comical – not to say patently absurd – about the claim that current events in Eastern Europe are at last setting those countries on the high road to free-market capitalism, private enterprise and the outright rejection of socialist ideals. (They forgot to add: the next time around as another episode of increasingly brutal farce.)

VII

We can now return once more to Perry Anderson's nagging question – what price theory in an age of widespread disillusionment on the left? – with a sharpened sense of the issues it raises for Western intellectuals at the present time. One response is the retreat to a 'postmodern' stance of all-out sceptical indifference, a stance that involves (as in Baudrillard's case) the willingness to jettison every last notion of truth, justice, or critical understanding. Another – exemplified by Lyotard – is the more refined version of postmodernist thinking that preserves those ideas but only on condition of driving a wedge between judgements of a speculative (ethical) order and cognitive truth-claims of whatever kind. Then again, there is the turn toward that thoroughly depoliticised version of deconstructionist thought that reduces all concepts to metaphors, all philosophy to an undifferentiated 'kind of writing', and hence all history to a play of ungrounded figural representations. In each case – so I have argued – theory has served as an escape-route from pressing political questions and a pretext for avoiding any serious engagement with real-world historical events. Worst of all, these ideas deprive critical thought of the one resource most needful at present, i.e. the competence to judge between good and bad arguments, reason and rhetoric, truth-seeking discourse and the 'postmodern' discourse of mass-induced media simulation.

Let me cite some recent comments by Derrida – in his second-round response to John Searle – lest anyone object that this argument goes clean against the whole drift of 'deconstructionist' precept and practice.

> A few moments ago, I insisted on writing, at least in quotation marks, the strange and trivial formula, 'real-history-of-the-world', in order to mark clearly that the concept of text or of context which guides me embraces and does not exclude the world, reality, history. Once again . . . as I understand it (and I have explained why), the text is not a book, it is not confined in a volume itself confined to the library. It does not suspend reference – to history, to reality, to being, and especially not to the other since to say of

history, of the world, of reality, that they always appear in an experience, hence in a movement of interpretation which contextualizes them according to a network of differences and hence of referral to the other, is surely to recall that alterity (difference) is irreducible. *Différance* is a reference and vice versa.[50]

Among other things, this passage should serve to remind us of the complex relationship between ethical and epistemological questions that has characterised the tradition of modern (post-Kantian) philosophy over the past two centuries. In a thinker like Lyotard these issues are still very much on the agenda, though deflected – as I have argued – toward a form of modish aesthetic ideology that elevates the Kantian sublime into a *de jure* principle of non-correspondence between cognitive and speculative judgements. For Derrida, on the contrary, 'the value of truth . . . is never contested or destroyed in my writings, but only reinscribed in more powerful, larger, more stratified contexts'. In which case, as he says, it must always be possible – indeed, a matter of absolute and principled necessity– 'to invoke rules of competence, criteria of discussion and of consensus, good faith, lucidity, rigour, criticism, and pedagogy'.[51] For without these strictly *indispensable* protocols – however complex their articulation in the reading of specific texts – deconstruction will lack all critical force and become just another sophisticated bag of rhetorical tricks, a strategy designed to place the maximum distance between 'theory' and the ethico-political demands that such thinking should properly entail. And this is, to say the least, a period of world history when we can ill afford to indulge such forms of collusive mystification.

Notes

1. Perry Anderson, *Considerations on Western Marxism* (London: New Left Books, 1977).
2. See for instance Roland Barthes, *S/Z*, trans. Richard Miller (London: Jonathan Cape, 1975); Colin MacCabe, *James Joyce and the 'Revolution of the Word'* (London: Macmillan, 1978); Catherine Belsey, *Critical Practice* (London: Methuen, 1980).
3. For a representative collection of essays, see Stuart Hall and Martin Jacques (eds.), *New Times: the changing face of politics in the 1990s* (London: Lawrence & Wishart, 1990).
4. On this topic see Paul Hamilton, *Coleridge's Poetics* (Oxford: Basil Blackwell, 1983).
5. Christopher Norris, *Paul de Man: deconstruction and the critique of aesthetic ideology* (New York and London: Routledge, 1988).

6. See for instance Mark Poster (ed.), *Jean Baudrillard: selected writings* (Cambridge: Polity Press, 1988).

7. On this topic see especially Jacques Derrida, 'No apocalypse, not now (full speed ahead, seven missiles, seven missives)', *Diacritics*, vol. 20 (1984), pp. 20–31; also Christopher Norris, 'Against postmodernism: Derrida, Kant and nuclear politics', *Paragraph*, vol. 9 (March, 1987), pp. 1–30.

8. See Richard Rorty, *Consequences of Pragmatism* (Minneapolis: University of Minnesota Press, 1982) and Stanley Fish, *Doing What Comes Naturally: change, rhetoric and the practice of theory in literary and legal studies* (Oxford: Clarendon Press, 1989).

9. Terry Eagleton, *The Significance of Theory* (Oxford: Basil Blackwell, 1989), p. 34.

10. See especially Paul de Man, *The Resistance to Theory* (Minneapolis: University of Minnesota Press, 1986).

11. Roy Bhaskar, *Scientific Realism and Human Emancipation* (London: Verso, 1986).

12. Jean-François Lyotard, *The Differend: phrases in dispute*, trans. Georges van den Abbeele (Minneapolis: University of Minnesota Press, 1988). All further references given by 'Lyotard' and page-number in the text.

13. See Hans Reiss (ed.), *Kant's Political Writings* (Cambridge: CUP, 1966).

14. Tony Bennett, 'Really useless "Knowledge": a political critique of aesthetics', *Literature and History*, vol. 13, no. 1 (1987), pp. 38–57.

15. See for instance Roger Scruton, *The Aesthetic Understanding* (London: Methuen, 1983); also Christopher Norris, 'Aesthetics and politics: reading Roger Scruton', in *The Contest of Faculties* (London: Methuen, 1985), pp.123–38.

16. See especially Terry Eagleton, *The Ideology of the Aesthetic* (Oxford: Basil Blackwell, 1989).

17. Most relevant here are the essays collected in de Man's posthumously-published volumes: *The Rhetoric of Romanticism* (New York: Columbia University Press, 1984) and *The Resistance to Theory* (*op. cit.*).

18. See especially de Man, 'The rhetoric of temporality', in *Blindness And Insight: essays in the rhetoric of contemporary criticism* (London: Methuen, 1983), pp. 187–228.

19. T.S. Eliot, 'Tradition and the individual talent' and 'The Metaphysical poets', in *Selected Essays* (London: Faber, 1964).

20. See for instance Frank Kermode, *Romantic Image* (London: Routledge & Kegan Paul, 1957).

21. Paul de Man 'Aesthetic formalization: Kleist's *Über das Marionettentheater*', in *The Rhetoric of Romanticism* (*op. cit.*), pp. 263–90.

22. Friedrich Schiller, *On the Aesthetic Education of Man, in a series of letters*, trans. E.M. Wilkinson and E.A. Willoughby (Oxford: Clarendon Press, 1967), p. 300. Cited by de Man in *The Rhetoric of Romanticism* (*op. cit.*), p. 263.

23. De Man, 'Aesthetic formalization', p. 265.

24. De Man, *Allegories of Reading: figural language in Rousseau, Nietzsche, Rilke, and Proust* (New Haven: Yale University Press, 1979), pp. 11–12.

25. De Man, 'Aesthetic formalization', p. 289.
26. On this topic see for instance G.S. Rousseau, *Organic Form: the life of an idea* (London: Routledge & Kegan Paul, 1966).
27. See de Man, *Wartime Writings*, eds. Werner Hamacher, Neil Hertz and Thomas Keenan (Lincoln, Nebraska and London: University of Nebraska Press, 1988); also *Responses: on Paul de Man's wartime journalism* (same editors and publisher, 1989).
28. See Norris, *Paul de Man* (*op. cit.*), especially pp. 177–98.
29. De Man, 'Aesthetic formalization', p. 264.
30. De Man, 'Reading and History', in *The Resistance to Theory* (*op. cit*), pp. 54–72; p. 64.
31. *ibid.*, p. 64.
32. See Poster (ed.), *Jean Baudrillard: selected writings* (*op. cit.*).
33. See especially Baudrillard, *The Mirror of Production*, trans. Mark Poster (St Louis: Telos Press, 1975) and *For a Critique of the Political Economy of the Sign*, trans. Charles Levin (St Louis: Telos Press, 1981).
34. Paul de Man, 'Wordsworth and Hölderlin', in *The Rhetoric of Romanticism* (op. cit.), pp. 47–65; p. 58.
35. See Norris, *Paul de Man* (*op. cit.*), especially pp. 5–11.
36. See for instance Michel Foucault, *Power/Knowledge: selected interviews and other writings* (Hemel Hempstead: Harvester Wheatsheaf, 1980).
37. See Gregory Elliott, *Althusser: the detour of theory* (London: Verso, 1987) for an admirably lucid and detailed account of this chapter in French intellectual history.
38. Karl Marx, *The Eighteenth Brumaire of Louis Napoleon*, in *Karl Marx and Friedrich Engels: Collected Works* Vol. 2 (London: Lawrence & Wishart, 1979), pp. 103–97. All further references given by 'Marx' and page-number in the text.
39. See especially Jeffrey Mehlman, *Revolution and Repetition* (Berkeley and Los Angeles: University of California Press, 1979).
40. Roland Barthes, *S/Z* (*op. cit.*).
41. This paragraph is largely a summary account of Mehlman's argument in *Revolution and Repetition* (*op. cit.*).
42. See Elliot, *Althusser: the detour of theory* (*op. cit.*); also Ted Benton, *The Rise and Fall of Structural Marxism* (London: Routledge, 1984).
43. For a powerfully-argued critique of Mehlman's reading, see Terry Eagleton, *Walter Benjamin, or towards a revolutionary criticism* (London: New Left Books, 1981), pp. 162–70.
44. Jacques Derrida, *Of Grammatology*, trans. Gayatri C. Spivak (Baltimore: Johns Hopkins University Press, 1976), p. 158.
45. Christopher Norris, *Derrida* (London: Fontana and Cambridge, Mass.: Harvard University Press, 1987).
46. W.H. Auden, 'September 1, 1939', in *Selected Poems*, ed. Edward Mendelson (London: Faber, 1979), pp. 86–9.
47. On this topic see Norris, 'Postmodernizing history: right-wing revisionism and the uses of theory', *Southern Review*, vol. 21, no. 2 (July, 1988), pp. 123–40.

48. As argued by Stephen Sedley, 'An immodest proposal: *Animal Farm*', in Christopher Norris (ed.), *Inside The Myth: Orwell – views from the left* (London: Lawrence & Wishart, 1984), pp. 155–62.
49. See especially Ruth Levitas (ed.), *The Ideology of the New Right* (Cambridge: Polity Press, 1986).
50. Jacques Derrida, 'Afterword: toward an ethic of discussion', in *Limited Inc*, 2nd edn. (Evanston, Ill.: Northwestern University Press, 1989), p. 137.
51. *ibid.*, p. 146.

rather as the upshot of a widespread failure to think through the problems bequeathed by that tradition. Where Habermas goes wrong, I shall argue, is in failing to acknowledge the crucial respects in which Derrida has distanced his own thinking from a generalised 'postmodern' or post-structuralist discourse.

More specifically, Habermas misreads Derrida in much the same way that literary critics (and apostles of American neo-pragmatism) have so far received his work: that is to say, as a handy pretext for dispensing with the effort of conceptual critique and declaring an end to the 'modernist' epoch of enlightened secular reason. I have no quarrel with Habermas's claim that the 'post-' in postmodernism is a delusive prefix, disguising the fact that theorists like Foucault, Lyotard and Baudrillard are still caught up in problems that have plagued the discourse of philosophy at least since the parting of ways after Kant. He is right to point out how their work re-capitulates the quarrels that emerged between those various thinkers (left- and right-wing Hegelians, objective and subjective idealists) who at-tempted – and failed – to overcome the antinomies of Kantian critical reason. One need only look to Lyotard's recent writings on philosophy, politics and the 'idea of history' to remark this resurgence of Kantian themes (albeit deployed to very un-Kantian ends) in the discourse of postmodern thought.[1] And the same applies to Foucault's genealogy of power/knowledge, as Habermas brings out very clearly when he traces its various intellectual antecedents in the line of counter-enlightenment philosophies running from Nietzsche to Bataille. In each case, he argues, thought has suffered the disabling effects of an irrationalist doctrine that can only take hold through a form of self-willed amnesia, a compulsive repetition of similar episodes in the previous (post-Kantian) history of ideas. *PDM* is in this sense an exercise of large-scale rational reconstruc-tion, an essentially therapeutic exercise whose aim is to provide a more adequate understanding of those episodes, and thus to recall the present-day human sciences to a knowledge of their own formative prehistory.

All this will of course be familiar enough to any reader moderately versed in Habermas's work over the past two decades. Where these lec-tures break new ground is in specifying more exactly the terms of his quarrel with French post-structuralism, deconstruction and other such forms of – as Habermas would have it – militant latter-day unreason. To some extent the ground had already been prepared by debates on and around his work in journals like *Praxis* and *New German Critique*. One could summarise the issues very briefly as follows. To his opponents it has seemed that Habermas's thinking belongs squarely within the enlightenment tradition of oppressive, monological reason. That is to say, he has sought a means of reinstating the Kantian foundationalist project – the belief in transcendental arguments, truth-claims, critique of consensual values and so forth – at a time when that project has at last been shown up as a mere historical dead-end, a discourse premised on false ideas of theoretical mastery and power. In support of this argument they point to such instances as the reading of Freud that Habermas offers in *Knowledge and Human Interests*, a reading that interprets psychoanalysis as a therapy designed to overcome the blocks and distortions of repressed desire by bringing them out into the light of a conscious, rational self-understanding.[2] To this they respond by drawing on Lacan's very different account of the 'talking cure', namely his insistence that language is *always and everywhere* marked by the symptoms of unconscious desire, so that any attempt to ecape or transcend this condition is deluded at best, and at worst a technique of manipulative reason in the service of a harsh and repressive social order.[3]

These opposing viewponts can each claim a warrant in Freud's notoriously cryptic statement: 'where id was, there shall ego be.' For Habermas, on the one hand, this sentence should be read as signalling an alignment of interests between psychoanalysis and the wider project of enlightened or emancipatory thought. For the Lacanians, conversely, it enforces the message that the ego is always a plaything of unconscious desire, and that therefore any version of ego-psychology (to which doctrine, in their view, Habermas subscribes) is necessarily a hopeless and misguided endeavour. On their reading the sentence should be paraphrased: 'Wherever reason thinks to explain the unconscious and its effects, there most surely those effects will resurface to disrupt such a project from the outset.' In this case there would seem little to choose between Habermas's talk of 'transcendental pragmatics', 'ideal speech-situations', etc., and those previous modes of foundationalist thought (the Cartesian *cogito*, the Kantian transcendental subject or Husserl's phenomenological reduction) whose claims – or so it is argued – have now been totally discredited. The fact that he has been at some pains to distance himself from that tradition apparently counts for nothing in terms of the current polemical exchange. So these thinkers bring two main charges against Habermas: firstly that he attempts the impossible (since reason is in no position to legislate over effects that exceed its powers of comprehension), and secondly that his project is politically retrograde (since it clings to a form of enlightenment thinking whose covert aim is to repress or to marginalise everything that falls outside its privileged domain). And their criticisms will no doubt find ample confirmation now that Habermas has offered his response in the form of these recent lectures. He will still be treated as a last-ditch defender of the strong foundationalist argument, despite the very clear signals that he – no less than his opponents – wants to find a basis for the conduct of rational enquiry that will not have recourse to anything resembling a Kantian epistemological paradigm.

It seems to me that Habermas goes wrong about Derrida mainly because he takes it for granted that deconstruction is one offshoot – a 'philosophical' offshoot – of this wider postmodernist or counter-enlightenment drift. In what follows I shall point to some crucial respects in which Derrida's work not only fails to fit this description but also mounts a resistance to it on terms that Habermas ought to acknowledge, given his own intellectual commitments. In fact I shall argue that deconstruction, properly understood, belongs within that same 'philosophical discourse of modernity' that Habermas sets out to defend against its present-day detractors. But it may be useful to preface that discussion with a brief account of the very different readings of Derrida's work that have now gained currency among literary theorists and philosophers. This will help to explain some of the blind spots in Habermas's critique, based as it is on a partial reading which tends to privilege just one of these rival accounts.

II

Commentators on deconstruction are divided very roughly into two main camps: those (like Rodolphe Gasché) who read Derrida's work as a radical continuation of certain Kantian themes,[4] and those (like Richard Rorty) who praise Derrida for having put such deluded 'enlightenment' notions behind him and arrived at a postmodern-pragmatist stance relieved of all surplus metaphysical baggage.[5] Nevertheless they are agreed in thinking that we can't make sense of Derrida without some knowledge of the relevant intellectual prehistory. Where they differ is on the question of whether those debates are still of real interest – 'philosophical' interest – or whether (as Rorty would have it) they have failed to come up with any workable answers, and should therefore be regarded as failed candidates for Philosophy Honours and awarded nothing more than a Pass Degree in English, Liberal Studies or Comp. Lit.

On Rorty's view we can still put together an instructive *story* about the way that thinkers from Descartes and Kant on down have so misconceived their own enterprise as to think they were offering genuine solutions to a range of distinctively 'philosophical' problems. But we will be wrong – simply repeating their mistake – if we try to give this story an upbeat conclusion or a Whiggish meta-narrative drift suggesting that we have *now*, after so many errors, started to get things right. The story is just that, a handy little pragmatist narrative, and the most it can do is stop us from believing in all those grandiose philosophical ideas. For Gasché, on the contrary, Derrida is still very much a philosopher, if by this we understand one whose work is both committed to an ongoing critical dialogue with previous thinkers (notably, in this case, Kant, Hegel and Husserl), and centrally concerned with issues in the realm of truth, knowledge and representation. This dialogue may take an unfamiliar or disconcerting form, as when Derrida questions the categorical bases of Kantian argument and sets out to demonstrate what Gasché calls the 'conditions of impossibility' that mark the limits of all philosophical enquiry. But even so his work remains squarely within that tradition of epistemological critique which alone makes it possible to raise such questions against the more accommodating pragmatist line espoused by thinkers like Rorty. These different readings of Derrida are also, inseparably, different readings of the whole philosophical history that has led up to where we are now. And in Hegel's case likewise there is a conflict of interpretations between those (again including Rorty) who would accept a kind of 'naturalised' Hegelianism, a story of philosophy that includes all the major episodes but dispenses with the vantage-point of reason or truth, and those who reject this compromise solution and regard the dialectic as something more than a species of edifying narrative.

One could make the same point about all those philosophers whose work has come in for revisionist readings as a consequence of the currently widespread scepticism as regards truth-claims and foundationalist arguments of whatever kind. On the one hand it has led to a new intellectual division of labour, a situation where thinkers like Rorty feel more at home in humanities or literature departments, while the 'real' (analytical) philosophers tend to close ranks and leave the teaching of Hegel, Nietzsche, Heidegger, Derrida, etc. to their colleagues with less exacting standards of argument. On the other, it has persuaded literary theorists that philosophy has no good claim to monopolise the texts of its own tradition, since the current guardians seem overly zealous to protect their canon from any form of unauthorised reading (which is to say, any reading that treats it on rhetorical, hermeneutic or 'literary' terms). And so it has come about that 'theory' now denominates an area (not so much a 'discipline') which straddles the activities of philosophy and literary criticism, taking charge of those figures (the Hegel-Nietzsche-Derrida line) who lend themselves to just such a non-canonical approach. But even within this camp one finds disagreements (as between Rorty and Gasché) concerning the extent to which philosophy may yet be conserved as a discipline with its own distinct mode of conceptual or analytic rigour. Thus 'theory' is construed as post-philosophical *either* in the sense that it dissolves philosophy into a textual, rhetorical or narrative genre with no distinctive truth-claims whatsoever (the Rorty argument), *or* in the sense (following Gasché) that it presses certain Kantian antinomies to the point where they demand a form of analysis undreamt of in the mainstream tradition. Both sides have an interest in claiming Kant since he stands at precisely the cardinal point where their histories will henceforth diverge. On the one hand there is the line that leads from Kant, via Hegel to the various speculative systems and projects that make up the 'continental' heritage. On the other it is clear that Kant provides the basis for most of those debates about language, logic and truth that have occupied the analytic schools.

One reason why *PDM* seems blind to certain aspects of Derrida's work is that it more or less identifies deconstruction with the Rortyan-postmodern-pragmatist reading, and thus tends to perpetuate the view of it as a species of literary-critical activity, an attempt to colonise philosophy by levelling the genre-distinction between these disciplines. Now of course this corresponds to one major premise of Derrida's thought: namely, his insistence that philosophy is indeed a certain 'kind of writing', a discourse which none the less strives to cover its own rhetorical tracks by aspiring to an order of pure, unmediated, self-present truth. Thus a deconstructive reading will typically fasten upon those moments in the philosophic text where some cardinal concept turns out to rest on a latent or sublimated metaphor, or where the logic of an argument is subtly undone by its reliance on covert rhetorical devices. Or again, it will show how some seemingly marginal detail of the text – some aspect ignored (not without reason) by the mainstream exponents – in fact plays a crucial but problematic role in the entire structure of argument.[6] One result of such readings is undoubtedly to challenge the commonplace assumption that philosophy has to do with concepts, truth-claims, logical arguments, 'clear and distinct ideas', etc., while literary criticism deals with language only in its rhetorical, poetic or non-truth-functional aspects. What Derrida has achieved – on this view at least – is a striking reversal of the age-old prejudice that elevates philosophy over rhetoric, or right reason over the dissimulating arts of language.

This is the reading of Derrida's work that Habermas offers in his

'Excursus: on levelling the genre-distinction between philosophy and literature' (*PDM*, pp. 185–210). That is to say, he takes it as read that Derrida is out to reduce all texts to an undifferentiated 'freeplay' of signification where the old disciplinary border-lines will at last break down, and where philosophy will thus take its place as just one 'kind of writing' among others, with no special claim to validity or truth. More specifically, Derrida makes a full-scale program of ignoring those different kinds of language-use that have separated out in the modern (post-Kantian) discourse of enlightened reason. He has privileged just one of these uses (language in its poetic, rhetorical or 'world-disclosive' aspect) and failed to see how the others demand a quite different mode of understanding. Thus, according to Habermas,

> [t]he rhetorical element occurs *in its pure form* only in the self-referentiality of the poetic expression, that is, in the language of fiction specialized for world-disclosure. Even the normal language of everyday life is ineradicably rhetorical; but within the matrix of different linguistic functions, the rhetorical elements recede here . . . The same holds true of the specialized languages of science and technology, law and morality, economics, political science, etc. They, too, live off the illuminating power of metaphorical tropes; but the rhetorical elements, which are by no means expunged, are tamed, as it were, and enlisted for special purposes of problem-solving. (*PDM*, p. 209)

It is the main fault of Derrida's work, as Habermas reads it, that he has failed to observe these essential distinctions and thus over-generalised the poetic (rhetorical) aspect of language to a point where it commands the whole field of communicative action. The result is to deprive thinking of that critical force which depends on a proper separation of realms, and which has come about historically – so Habermas contends – through the increasing specialisation of language in its threefold social aspect. By extending rhetoric so far beyond its own legitimate domain Derrida has not only collapsed the 'genre-distinction' between philosophy and literature but also annulled the emancipating promise that resides in the poetic (or world-disclosive) function of language. For this promise is likewise dependent on the existence of a 'polar tension', a sense of what specifically differentiates literature from 'everyday' communicative language, on the one hand, and those specialised problem-solving languages on the other. Derrida, says Habermas,

> holistically levels these complicated relationships in order to equate philosophy with literature and criticism. He fails to recognize the special status

that both philosophy and literary criticism, each in its own way, assume as mediators between expert cultures and the everyday world. (*PDM*, p. 207)

Now I think that these criticisms apply not so much to what Derrida has written but to what has been written about him by various (mostly American) commentators. Or more accurately – on the principle 'no smoke without fire' – they find some warrant in certain of his texts, but can then be made to stick only through a very partial reading, one that sets out quite deliberately to level the distinction between philosophy and literature. The favoured texts for this purpose would include Derrida's response to John Searle on the topic of speech-act theory;[7] the closing paragraph of 'Structure, sign and play', with its apocalyptic overtones and Nietzschean end-of-philosophy rhetoric;[8] and, more recently, the 'Envois' section of *La Carte postale*, where Derrida goes about as far as possible toward undermining the truth-claims of logocentric reason by recasting them in fictive or mock-epistolary form.[9] One could then go back to Derrida's earliest published work – his Introduction to Husserl's essay 'The origin of geometry' – and cite the well-known passage where he appears to encounter a moment of choice between 'philosophy' and 'literature', or the quest for some pure, univocal, self-present meaning (Husserl) as opposed to the prospect of a liberating 'freeplay' of the signifier glimpsed in such writings as Joyce's *Finnegans Wake*.[10] In so far as he has confronted this choice – so the argument goes – Derrida has come out firmly on the side of a literary approach to the texts of philosophy, one that pays minimal regard to their truth-claims or structures of logical argument, and which thus frees itself to treat them as purely rhetorical constructs on a level with poems, novels, postcards or any other kind of writing.

So it might seem that Habermas's arguments are fully warranted by the 'levelling' or undifferentiating character of Derrida's generalised rhetoric. What drops out of sight is the complex and highly-evolved relationship between (1) everyday communicative language, (2) the mediating discourses of philosophy and criticism and (3) the various forms of 'expert' or specialised enquiry ('art, literature, science, morality') which would otherwise tend to float free in a conceptual universe of their own creating. Criticism can only perform this essential task so long as it maintains a due sense of its own distinctive role *vis-à-vis* those other disciplines. Where philosophy occupies the middle ground between 'ordinary language' and specialised questions of ethics, epistemology, metaphysics, theory of science, etc., criticism stands in much the same relation to everyday language on the one hand and artistic or literary innovation on the other. And it is also imperative that criticism and philosophy should not become mixed up one with another and thus produce the kind of hybrid discourse that Habermas thinks so damaging in Derrida's work.

The point is best made by quoting him at length, since this is the passage where the charge is pressed home with maximum force.

> Literary criticism and philosophy . . . are both faced with tasks that are paradoxical in similar ways. They are supposed to feed the contents of expert cultures, in which knowledge is accumulated under one aspect of validity at a time, into an everyday practice in which all linguistic functions are inter-meshed. And yet [they] are supposed to accomplish this task of mediation with means of expression taken from languages specialized in questions of taste or of truth. They can only resolve this paradox by rhetorically expand-ing and enriching their special languages . . . [Thus] literary criticism and philosophy have a family resemblance to literature – and to this extent to one another as well – in their rhetorical achievements. But their family relation-ship stops right there, for in each of these enterprises the tools of rhetoric are subordinated to the discipline of a *distinct* form of argumentation. (*PDM*, pp. 209–10)

What is presented here is a qualified version of Kant's doctrine of the faculties. It is qualified mainly by Habermas's wish to avoid any hint of a Kantian foundationalist legacy by reasoning in terms of the different lan-guages – 'everyday', 'expert', 'specialised', etc. – which between them mark out the range of communicative options. He can thus maintain a critical attitude toward Derrida's 'levelling' of genre-distinctions without having to argue that philosophy has access to some privileged realm of a priori concepts or uniquely self-validating truth-claims. We can afford to give up that outworn tradition, he argues, just so long as we grasp that *language* itself is oriented toward a better understanding of those blocks, aporias, misprisions and so forth which get in the way of our (everyday or specialised) communicative acts.[11] But on Derrida's account – so Haber-mas believes – this process could never make a start, let alone achieve the levels of complexity and sophistication required by the various present-day arts and sciences.

This follows from Derrida's extreme form of contextualist doctrine, that is, his argument – enounced in the debate with John Searle – that (1) meaning is entirely a product of the various contexts in which signs play a role; (2) that such contexts can in principle be multiplied beyond any possible enumerative grasp; and (3) that therefore meaning is strictly un-decidable in any given case. But we are simply not obliged to accept this conclusion if – as Habermas suggests – we drop the idea of an open-ended general 'context' and recognise the various *specific* normative dimensions that exist within the range of communicative action. For Derrida, in short,

> linguistically mediated processes within the world are embedded in a *world-constituting* context that prejudices everything; they are fatalistically delivered up to the unmanageable happening of text-production, overwhelmed by the poetic-creative transformation of a background designated by arche-writing, and condemned to be provincial. (*PDM*, p. 204)

'Provincial', one supposes, in the sense that it seeks to reduce all language to a single paradigm, and thereby annexes every form of communicative action to the province of poetic or literary language. Thus Habermas cites Roman Jakobson and the Prague Structuralists by way of insisting that the poetic function be defined more specifically, i.e. in terms of those features (like self-reflexivity or lack of informative content) that set it apart from other uses of language. Where Derrida has gone wrong (he argues) is in failing to perceive the constitutive difference between speech-acts engaged in the normative activities of problem-solving, theorising, giving information, etc., and speech-acts that are not so engaged, and can therefore be construed as fictive, non-serious, parodic or whatever. Otherwise Derrida would not have been misled into extending the poetic function so far beyond its proper reach, or discounting those normative constraints upon language that save it from the infinitised 'freeplay' of an open-ended contextualist account. 'The frailty of the genre distinction between philosophy and literature is evidenced in the practice of deconstruction: in the end, *all* distinctions are submerged in one comprehensive, all-embracing context of texts – Derrida talks in a hypnotizing manner about a "universal text" ' (*PDM*, p. 190). The result of this confusion is to give language up to the effects of an infinite regress (or 'unlimited semiosis') which excludes all possibility of rational understanding.

III

The first point to note about Habermas's critique of Derrida is that it more or less restates John Searle's position with regard to the supposedly self-evident distinction between 'serious' and other (deviant) kinds of speech-act.[12] That is, it assumes that Searle has both commonsense and reason on his side of the argument, while Derrida is content to make 'literary' play with certain marginal or merely rhetorical aspects of Austin's text. In which case Searle would be the serious, the faithful or properly authorised exponent of Austin's ideas, while Derrida would stand to Austin in much the same relation as the sophists to Socrates: a gadfly rhetorician merely anxious to display his own ingenuity and wit, and lacking any regard for wisdom or truth. But this ignores several important points about the three-sided debate between Austin, Derrida and Searle. It fails to register the extent to which Austin invites and solicits a deconstructive reading by himself putting up all manner of resistance to the project of a generalised speech-act theory. I have written at length on this topic elsewhere – as have a number of other commentators, including Jonathan Culler and Shoshana Felman – so there is no need to rehearse the details over again here.[13] Sufficient to say that Austin, like Derrida, shows a fondness for marginal or problematic cases, speech-acts which cannot be securely assigned to this or that typecast category. Thus he often comes up with supposedly deviant instances which then turn out to be typical of the kind, or to indicate features that necessarily pertain to all possible varieties of speech-act. Or again, he will pause to illustrate a point with some odd piece of anecdotal evidence, only to find that it creates real problems for his classificatory system.

What is distinctive about Austin's approach – aligning it with Derrida as against Searle – is this readiness to let language have its way with him and not give in to the systematising drive for method and clear-cut theory. Partly it is a matter of the 'Oxford' ethos, the attitude of quizzical detachment mixed with a passion for off-beat linguistic detail that Derrida encountered on his trip to Oxford (narrated in *La Carte postale*). But we would be wrong to see this as a downright rejection of philosophical 'seriousness', an opting out in favour of stylistic 'freeplay' or the possible worlds of his own fictive devising. Certainly Derrida goes a long way toward deconstructing the terms of this old opposition. Thus *La Carte postale* takes up a great variety of philosophic themes, among them the relationship of Plato and Socrates, the Heideggerian questioning of Western metaphysics, the status of truth-claims in the discourse of Freudian psychoanalysis and the way that all these topics return to haunt the seemingly detached, almost clinical idiom of Oxford linguistic philosophy. But it does so by way of a fictional *mise-en-scène*, a correspondence carried on by postcard, and specifically through a series of fragmentary love-letters inscribed on numerous copies of a card that Derrida discovered in the Bodleian Library. This card reproduces an apocryphal scene which apparently has Plato dictating his thoughts to Socrates and Socrates obediently writing them down at Plato's behest. It thus stages a comic reversal of the age-old scholarly assumption: namely, that Socrates was the thinker who *wrote nothing* – whose wisdom prevented him from entrusting his thoughts to the perilous medium of writing – while Plato, his disciple, gave in to this bad necessity in order to preserve Socrates' teaching for the benefit of later generations. So one can see why this postcard so fascinated Derrida. What it offered was a kind of zany confirmation of his own thesis (in *Of Grammatology* and elsewhere) that writing is the 'exile', the 'wandering outcast' of Western logocentric tradition, the repressed term whose disruptive effects are none the less everywhere manifest in the texts of that same tradition.[15]

So *La Carte postale* is undoubtedly a work of 'literature' in so far as it exploits the full range of fictive possibilities opened up by this scandalous reversal of roles between Socrates and Plato. From here it goes on to develop various other counter-factual, extravagant or apocryphal themes, along with a running debate among the scholars as to the authenticity or otherwise of Plato's letters, a 'correspondence' (by postcard, what else?) between Heidegger and Freud, a quizzical commentary on Ryle, Austin and the Oxford tradition of linguistic philosophy and a whole series of anachronistic swerves and redoublings which enable Derrida to play havoc with accredited notions of history and truth. His point in all this is to show how philosophy has excluded certain kinds of writing – letters, apocrypha, 'unauthorised' genres of whatever sort – while allowing them a place on the margins of discourse from which they continue to exert a fascination and a power to complicate received ideas. And there is something of this even in the Oxford tradition – for all its analytical 'seriousness' – when thinkers like Austin cite (or invent) their various speech-act examples, and then find their argument beginning to get out of hand. 'I adore these theorizations, so very "Oxford" in character, their extraordinary and necessary subtlety as well as their imperturbable naivety, "psychoanalytically speaking"; they will always be confident in the law of quotation marks.'[16] Derrida's reference here is to the problem of naming, and more specifically the difference between *using* and *mentioning* a name, as theorised by Russell and Ryle among others. But where this distinction serves analytical philosophers as a technique for avoiding trouble – for resolving the kinds of paradox that emerge when the two linguistic functions are confused – its appeal for Derrida has more to do with the undecidability of names in general, their tendency to migrate across the border-lines of authorised genre, history, etc., and thus to create all manner of intriguing fictive scenarios.[17] 'Psychoanalytically speaking', it is by no means certain that philosophy can control these potential aberrations of language, or lay down rules for the proper conduct of logical debate.

Thus Derrida cites a 'very good book' by one such analytical thinker, a book which advises us not to be misled by the seeming identity of names-as-used and names as merely cited, mentioned or placed between quotation marks. To which Derrida responds by asking: what kind of *de jure* regulation can back up this confident policing operation, designed to cure language of its bad propensity for conjuring up phantom nominal presences? The 'law of quotation marks' could achieve this purpose only on condition that language be treated as *already having attained* what Habermas describes as an 'ideal speech-situation', that is, a transparency of meaning and intent that would admit no impediment to the wished-for meeting of minds. But this condition is impossible – so Derrida implies – for reasons that return us to Freud, Lacan and the arguments of French (post-structuralist) psychoanalysis. That is to say, it ignores the effects of a 'structural unconscious' that forever divides the speaking self ('subject of enunciation') from the self spoken about ('subject of the enounced'). Thus:

[t]he author of the book of which I am speaking, himself, not his name (therefore he would pardon me for not naming him) is himself reserved as concerns the very interesting 'position of Quine' ('a word-between-quotation-marks is the proper name of the word which figures between the quotation marks, simultaneously an occurrence of the word which is between the quotation marks and an occurrence of the word-between-the-quotation-marks, the latter including the former as a part' – and it is true that this logic of inclusion perhaps is not very satisfying in order to account for the 'simultaneously', but small matter here), and making an allusion to a 'forgetting', his word, a forgetting 'evidently facilitated by the resemblance that there is between a word and the name of this word formed by its being placed between quotation marks', he concludes, I quote, 'But one must not let oneself be abused by this resemblance, and confuse the two names . . .'. Okay, promised, we won't any more. Not on purpose anyway. Unless we forget, but we will not forget on purpose, it's just that they resemble each other so much . . .[18]

This passage is typical of *La Carte postale* in the way that it picks up numerous themes, cross-references, cryptic allusions and so forth, among them the 'correspondence' between philosophy and psychoanalysis (or Socrates and Freud), staged as a kind of running encounter where reason confronts its own 'structural unconscious' in the form of a promiscuously generalised writing that circulates without origin or proper addressee. Hence the link that Derrida perceives between philosophy as a 'serious', responsible discourse and the postal service (in its 'grand epoch') as a smoothly-functioning system of exchange which ensures that letters arrive on time and at the right destination. But there is always the residue of mail that has not been correctly addressed, that bounces back and forth between various recipients and ends up in the dead-letter office. Or again, those items that arrive out of the blue with some intimate yet wholly undecipherable message, and thus give rise to all manner of pleasing conjecture. So it comes about that

> the guardians of tradition, the professors, academics, and librarians, the doctors and authors of theses are terribly curious about correspondences . . . about private or public correspondences (a distinction without pertinence in this case, whence the post card, half private half public, neither the one nor the other, and which does not await the post card *stricto sensu* in order to define the law of the genre, of all genres. . .).[19]

It is on this level that the 'Envois' can be read as relating to the essays on Freud and Lacan that make up the remainder of *La Carte postale*. For here also Derrida is concerned with the status of a certain theoretical enterprise (psychoanalysis) which attempts to secure itself on the basis of an authorised truth passed down from founder to disciple, but which runs into all manner of speculative detours and swerves from origin. In each case there is a strong *proprietory* interest at work, a tendency to anathematise those various distortions, misreadings or perversions of the Freudian text that would compromise its original (authentic) meaning. In Freud himself, this takes the form of an obsessive desire to keep psychoanalysis 'in the family', to save it from the egregious falsehoods put about by his erstwhile colleagues and disciples.[20] With Lacan, it produces an allegorical reading of Poe's story 'The purloined letter', treated as a virtual *mise-en-scène* of the dialogue between analyst and patient, a dialogue whose meaning can never be fully brought to light, caught up as it is in the shuttling exchange of transference and counter-transference, but which none the less points to an ultimate truth identified with the 'letter' of the Freudian text.[21] In both instances, so Derrida argues, this desire takes the form of a putative master-discourse that attempts to put a frame around the various episodes, case-histories, speculative ventures, correspondences and so forth that make up the proper, self-authorised legacy of Freud's life and work. But these projects cannot reckon with the undecidability of all such narrative frames, or the way that events from 'outside' the frame – whether textual events, as in Poe's short story, or episodes from the life, as in Freud's troubled correspondence with Fliess – may always return to complicate the record beyond all hope of a straightforward, truth-telling account. Here

```
           PRINCETON
           UNIVERSITY
              STORE
                      01/21/94
   TYPE                   2  #
  MCLERK                500  #
    SKU 1

           280088097138  #
  N.J ROAD PC         3.25  I
    SKU 1

           280014043010  #
  EMMA                4.50  I
    SKU 1

           280063118718  #
  TRUTH ABOU         19.95  I
    SKU 1

           280080184137  #
  WHATS WRON         14.95  I
  SUBTOTAL           42.65
  NJ TAX              2.56
  CHECK-TD TL        45.21


        THANK  YOU
  #194487 C123 R11 T13:48
```

again, it proves impossible for thinking to master the effects of a generalised writing (or 'structural unconscious'), some of whose canniest adepts
– like Freud and Lacan – may yet be caught out by its uncanny power to
disrupt their projects at source.

Now it might well seem – from what I have written so far – that
Habermas is absolutely right about Derrida, since *La Carte postale* is a
'literary' text which exploits various philosophical themes merely as a
springboard for its own extravagant purposes. This is certainly the reading
that most appeals to a postmodern pragmatist like Rorty, one for whom
philosophy is in any case a dead or dying enterprise, best treated (as
Derrida apparently treats it here) with a fine disregard for the protocols of
truth and an eye to its fictive potential or entertainment value. Thus if
Rorty has problems with the 'early' Derrida – too serious by half, too
argumentative, too much inclined to take a term like *différance* and give it
the status of a privileged anti-concept – these problems disappear with *La
Carte postale*, where philosophy receives its final come-uppance at the
hands of literature. But Rorty's reading is open to challenge, as indeed is
Habermas's assumption (in *PDM*) that Rorty has read Derrida aright, and
therefore that the two of them must be saying much the same kind of
thing. What this ignores is the extent to which a text like *La Carte postale*
continues to engage with philosophical problems which do not simply
disappear when approached from a fictive, apocryphal or 'literary' standpoint. After all, philosophers in the mainstream tradition – from Plato to
Austin – have often had recourse to invented case-histories, parables,
counter-factual scenarios and so forth, in order to make some critical point
about our language or commonplace habits of thought. Hence one of the
problems that Derrida remarks in connection with Austin's procedure:
namely, his exclusion of 'deviant' or 'parasitical' speech-acts (e.g. those
merely cited, placed between quotation marks, uttered in jest, on the
stage, in a novel, etc.) as not meriting serious philosophical attention. For
it is surely the case (1) that *all* speech-acts must perform, cite or rehearse
some existing formulaic convention (since otherwise they would carry no
recognised force); (2), that this creates a real problem for Austin's distinction between 'serious' and 'non-serious' cases; and (3) that the majority of
Austin's own examples are speech-acts contrived specifically for the purpose of illustrating speech-act theory. Once again, the 'law of quotation
marks' turns out to have effects far beyond those allowed for on the
standard, unproblematical account.

My point is that Habermas mistakes the character of deconstruction
when he treats it as having simply *given up* the kinds of argument specific

to philosophy, and opted instead for the pleasures of a free-wheeling 'literary' style. It is true that Derrida's writings can be roughly divided – as Rorty suggests – into two main categories. On the one hand there are texts (like the essays collected in *Margins of Philosophy*) that argue their way through a rigorous and consequential treatment of the various blind-spots, aporias or antinomies that characterise the discourse of philosophic reason. On the other there are pieces (like the 'Envois' section of *La Carte postale* or Derrida's prolix and riddling response to John Searle) where undoubtedly he is making maximum use of 'literary' devices in order to provoke or to disconcert the more self-assured guardians of that mainstream tradition. But we would be wrong to suppose – as Rorty does – that Derrida has gone over from the one kind of writing to the other, renouncing 'philosophy' and its self-deluded claims for the sake of a henceforth uninhibited devotion to 'literature'. This ignores the extent to which 'Envois' and 'Limited Inc' (the rejoinder to Searle) continue to work within the same problematics of writing, language and representation that Derrida addresses more explicitly elsewhere. And it also fails to recognise the distinct kinship between deconstruction and those passages of off-beat, speculative musing in Austin's text ('so very "Oxford" in character, their extraordinary and necessary subtlety, as well as their imperturbable naivety, "psychoanalytically speaking" ') which Derrida singles out for attention in *La Carte postale*.

IV

There are, I think, several reasons for Habermas's inability to grasp the philosophical pertinence of Derrida's work. One is the fact that he (Habermas) clearly does not have much concern for the finer points of style, writing as he does in a manner that surpasses even Hegel in its heavyweight abstractions, its relentless piling up of clause upon clause, and the sense it conveys that strenuous thinking is somehow incompatible with 'literary' arts and graces. One can therefore understand why he (like Searle) might regard Derrida's stylistic innovations with a somewhat jaundiced eye. But the antipathy goes much deeper than that, as can be seen from those passages in *PDM* where Habermas sets out his reasons for opposing any attempt to level the genre-distinction between philosophy and literature. Again, I shall need to quote at some length since – at risk of labouring the point – Habermas's style does not exactly lend itself to concise summary statement.

Derrida and Rorty are mistaken about the unique status of discourses differentiated from ordinary communication and tailored to a single validity dimension (truth or normative rightness), or to a single complex of problems (questions of truth or justice). In modern societies, the spheres of science, morality, and law have crystallized around these forms of argumentation. The corresponding cultural systems of action administer *problem-solving capacities* in a way similar to that in which the enterprises of art and literature administer *capacities for world-disclosure*. Because Derrida overgeneralizes this one linguistic function – namely, the poetic – he can no longer see the complex relationship of the ordinary practice of normal speech to the two extraordinary spheres, differentiated, as it were, in opposite directions. The polar tension between world-disclosure and problem-solving is held together within the functional matrix of ordinary language; but art and literature on the one side, and science, morality, and law on the other, are specialized for experiences and modes of knowledge that can be shaped and worked out within the compass of *one* linguistic function and *one* dimension of validity at a time. (*PDM*, p. 207)

It is clear from this passage that Habermas is still working within a broadly Kantian architectonic, a doctrine of the faculties that insists on maintaining the distinction between pure reason, practical reason and aesthetic judgement. In this respect his arguments in *PDM* are continuous with the project set forth in an early work like *Knowledge and Human Interests*, despite what is presented as a crucial shift of emphasis, from an overtly Kantian ('epistemological' or 'foundationalist') approach to one that takes its bearings from speech-act theory, pragmatics and the study of communicative action. The continuity can be seen clearly enough in Habermas's way of separating out those uses of language 'specialised' for the purposes of problem-solving, argument or rational critique. It is likewise evident in the distinction that Habermas maintains between 'ordinary' and 'extraordinary' language-games, or those that have their place in 'normal speech' and those that belong more properly to art, literature and the 'world-disclosive' function of aesthetic understanding. Here we have the nub of Habermas's case against Derrida: the charge that he has effectively *disenfranchised* critical reason by allowing this promiscuous confusion of realms within and between the various linguistic orientations.

What this argument cannot countenance is any suggestion that *one and the same text* might possess both literary value (on account of its fictive, metaphorical or stylistic attributes) and philosophic cogency (by virtue of its power to criticise normative truth-claims). Thus Habermas would need to reject as non-philosophical not only a text like *La Carte postale*, but also those numerous border-line cases – among them Plato, Augustine, Hegel,

Kierkegaard, Austin, Borges, Calvino – where fiction and philosophy are closely intertwined. And if the list were then extended to philosophers who had once in a while made use of fictive devices or analogies, then it would also include Aristotle, Kant, Husserl, Frege, Quine, Searle and just about every thinker in the Western tradition. So Habermas is pretty much out on a limb when he seeks to demarcate the types and conditions of language according to their various specialised roles. And this applies even more to his argument that literary criticism – at least as that discipline has developed since the eighteenth century – should also be regarded as a language apart from those texts that constitute its subject-domain. Thus:

> it [criticism] has responded to the increasing autonomy of linguistic works of art by means of a discourse specialized for questions of taste. In it, the claims with which literary texts appear are submitted to examination – claims to 'artistic truth', aesthetic harmony, exemplary validity, innovative force, and authenticity. In this respect, aesthetic criticism is similar to argumentative forms specialized for propositional truth and the rightness of norms, that is, to theoretical and practical discourse. It is, however, not merely an esoteric component of expert culture but, beyond this, has the job of mediating between expert culture and everyday world. (*PDM*, p. 207)

This last sentence might appear to qualify Habermas's rigid demarcation of realms by allowing that criticism (like philosophy) must have contact with 'ordinary language', at least to the extent of being understood by persons outside the 'expert culture' specifically devoted to such questions. But the passage makes it clear that Habermas conceives this alignment of interest as basically a two-term relationship, holding between 'ordinary language' on the one hand and aesthetics, art-criticism and literary theory on the other. That is to say, he excludes the possibility that this semi-specialised or mediating discourse might also respond to stylistic innovations in literary language, of the kind most strikingly exemplified in Derrida's texts. For Habermas, such developments have exactly the opposite effect. As literature becomes more 'autonomous' – more preoccupied with matters of style, form and technique – so criticism has to insist more firmly on the distance that separates its own language ('specialized for questions of taste') from the language of poetry or fiction. For otherwise – so Habermas implies – criticism will be in no position to claim a knowledge of the text that the text itself has not already made explicit. Only in so far as it maintains this stance can criticism adjudicate in those questions of 'aesthetic harmony, exemplary validity, innovative force, and authenticity' which constitute its own proper sphere of understanding. And in order to do so it will need to be aligned not so much with 'literature' as with 'philosophy', since it is here that such normative validity-claims are most thoroughly tried and tested.

I have already perhaps said enough to indicate just how remote these arguments are from Derrida's practice of a 'philosophical criticism' (for want of any better term) that deliberately mixes the genres of literature and theory. But we should not be misled into thinking that he has thereby renounced philosophy and given himself up to a mode of 'extraordinary' language that severs all links between itself and critical reason on the one hand, or itself and the interests of communal understanding on the other. What Habermas fails to recognise is the extent to which so-called 'ordinary' language is in fact shot through with metaphors, nonce-usages, chance collocations, Freudian parapraxes and other such 'accidental' features that cannot be reduced to any normative account. Henry Staten makes the point well when he describes how Wittgenstein, like Derrida, develops a style that is 'radically errant', one which effectively 'unlids all the accidence concealed by "normal" uses of words in order to show how many different routes it would be possible to take from any given point in the discourse'.[22] Staten is here arguing specifically against those mainstream readings of Wittgenstein which fasten on his talk of 'language-games' and 'forms of life', and use it as a warrant for confining authentic, serious or meaningful discourse to the range of usages sanctioned within some existing cultural community. On the contrary, says, Staten: Wittgenstein is just as much concerned as Derrida with the radical 'accidence' of language, the way that it can open up unlooked-for possibilities of meaning precisely through the absence of such binding communal constraints. And the same applies to Derrida and Austin if their texts are read with sufficient regard to these innovative byways of language, routes which 'we had simply not thought of because we were bemused by normality'.[23]

Staten argues a convincing case for Derrida as one who has pushed the project of post-Kantian critical reason to the point of acknowledging its covert involvement in a general problematics of language, writing and representation. This is why his book pays careful attention to Derrida's reading of Husserl, and more specifically those passages where the claims of transcendental phenomenology are subject to a certain dislocating pressure brought about by the effects of linguistic *différance*. It is here, Staten writes, that Derrida most decisively 'wrests the concept of meaning away from the moment of intuition in order to attach it *essentially* to the moment of signification'. Thus language (or writing, in Derrida's extended sense of the term) cannot be confined to its traditional role as a mere vehicle for thoughts and intuitions that would otherwise exist in a state of ideal self-presence or intelligibility. Rather, it is the signifying structure of language – that system of differential marks and traces 'without positive terms' – that constitutes the very possibility of meaning, and thus creates all manner of problems for Husserl's philosophical enterprise.[24] But again we should be wrong to see in this encounter a straightforward instance of philosophy's undoing at the hands of literature, writing or rhetoric. As Staten says,

> [w]hat is both original and problematic about Derrida's own project is that it does *not* pursue Joyce's path, but remains faithful to the problematic of that 'univocity' that Derrida sees as underlying Joyce's equivocity, while yet opening out the univocal language in which he works, the language of philosophy, to that spread of meaning Joyce explored.[25]

It is precisely this possibility that Habermas excludes when he takes it that Derrida's levelling of the genre-distinction between philosophy and literature deprives thinking of its critical force and thus betrays the very project of enlightened thought.

One could offer many instances from Derrida's work that would count strongly against this reading. Thus his essay on Foucault ('Cogito and the history of madness')[26] makes exactly the point that Habermas is making when he asks what kind of *argumentative* force could possibly attach to Foucault's critical genealogies. More specifically: what is the status of a discourse that reduces all truths to the level of an undifferentiated power-knowledge; that denounces reason as merely an agency of ever-increasing surveillance and control; and that claims not only to speak on behalf of that madness which reason has constructed as its outcast other, but moreover to speak the very language of madness from a standpoint beyond any rational accountability.[27] For Habermas, this serves to demonstrate the sheer dead-end that thought runs into when it follows the line of reactive counter-enlightenment rhetoric that leads from Nietzsche to Bataille, Foucault and other such present-day apostles of unreason. It also goes to show how much they have in common with that one-sided view of modernity and its discontents adopted by an earlier generation of Frankfurt theorists (notably Adorno and Horkheimer in their book *Dialectic of Enlightenment*). For them, as for Foucault, 'modernity' is more or less synonymous with the advance of an instrumental reason that subjugates everything – nature, social existence, art, philosophy, language – to its own homogenising drive. Thus 'Foucault so levels down the complexity of societal modernization that the disturbing paradoxes of this process cannot even become apparent to him' (*PDM*, p. 291). And he can do so only by ignoring the crucial distinction between instrumental reason – as developed in the service of scientific mastery and power – and those other forms of reason (communicative, critical or emancipatory) which point a way beyond this deadlocked condition.

Derrida is arguing to similar effect when he remarks on the strictly *impossible* nature of Foucault's undertaking and the fact that any such discourse on madness will necessarily have resort to a different order of language, logic and validity-claims. Thus:

> if discourse and philosophical communication (that is, language itself) are to have an intelligible meaning, that is to say, if they are to conform to their essence and vocation as discourse, they must simultaneously in fact and in principle escape madness. They must carry normality within themselves . . . By its essence, the sentence is normal . . . whatever the health or madness of him who propounds it, or whom it passes through, on whom, in whom it is articulated. In its most impoverished syntax, logos is reason and, indeed, a historical reason.[28]

Where this differs from Habermas's reading is in its argument that Foucault has *not* in fact achieved what he thinks to achieve, i.e. a decisive break with the protocols of reason and truth. Since no such break is possible – since every sentence of Foucault's writing betrays an opposite compulsion – Derrida can acknowledge the critical force of that writing *despite and against* its avowed purpose. 'Crisis of reason, finally, access to reason and attack of reason. For what Michel Foucault teaches us to think is that there are crises of reason in strange complicity with what the world calls crises of madness.'[29] For Habermas, conversely, Foucault exemplifies that levelling of the difference between reason and unreason which heralds the 'postmodern condition' and the ultimate betrayal of enlightenment values. In short, Habermas takes Foucault at his word as having left behind all the rational criteria, normative truth-claims, standards of validity, etc. which constitute the 'philosophical discourse of modernity'. And this despite his clear recognition elsewhere that 'Foucault only gains this basis [that is, the explanatory matrix of power-knowledge] by not thinking genealogically when it comes to his *own* genealogical historiography and by rendering unrecognizable the derivation of this transcendental-historicist concept of power' (*PDM*, p. 269). For ultimately Habermas cannot conceive that Foucault's project, deriving as it does from the Nietzschean counter-enlightenment lineage, might yet possess a power of demystifying insight that works against its own professed aims and interests.

Derrida can allow for this ambivalence in Foucault's work because (unlike Habermas) he does not draw a firm, juridical line between reason and rhetoric, philosophy and literature, the discourse of enlightened critique and the capacity of language (even 'extraordinary' language) to reflect on the inbuilt limits and aporias of that same discourse. But it is simply not the case, as Habermas asserts, that Derrida has thereby abandoned the ground of post-Kantian critical thought or gone along with that 'drastic levelling of [the] architectonic of reason that results from the Nietzsche-inspired reading of Kant' (*PDM*, p. 305). On the contrary: several of his recent essays are concerned with questions in precisely this sphere. They include Derrida's writings on the modern university and its division of intellectual labour, especially as this relates to Kant's doctrine of the faculties and their role *vis-à-vis* the cardinal distinction between 'pure' and 'applied' forms of knowledge.[30] Here as in Habermas, philosophy is assigned to its proper place as the discipline that legislates in questions of validity and truth, while the other, more practical or research-oriented disciplines have their separate domains marked out according to their own specific ends and interests. Certainly Derrida calls this system into question, remarking on the various conflicts, aporias or boundary-disputes that arise within and between the faculties. Moreover, he does so by way of a rhetorical reading that suspends the privileged truth-claims of philosophy and asks more specifically what *interests* are served by this policing of the various faculty limits. But there is no question of simply revoking the Kantian paradigm and declaring a break with that entire heritage of enlightened critical thought. In fact Derrida repeatedly insists on the need to keep faith with this 'vigil' of enlightenment, a vigil whose term is not ended (as 'postmodern' thinkers would have it) on account of these constitutive blind spots in its own project. Those who profess to deconstruct Kant's doctrine of the faculties 'need not set themselves up in opposition to the principle of reason, nor need they give way to "irrationalism" '.[31] While questioning the modern university system and its forms of self-authorised knowledge, they can nevertheless assume, 'along with its memory and tradition, the imperatives of professional rigor and competence'.

V

Perhaps the most interesting text in this regard is Derrida's essay 'Of an

apocalyptic tone recently adopted in philosophy'.[32] The title is borrowed
almost verbatim from Kant, who used it for a piece of philosophical polemics
against those who saw fit to reject the dictates of enlightened reason, and
who relied instead on their own unaided intuition as to questions of truth
and falsehood or right and wrong. Kant has nothing but scorn for these
enthusiasts, these adepts of the 'inner light', imagining as they do that one
can bypass the critical tribunal of the faculties and arrive at truth without
benefit of reasoned debate. And of course their presumption has religious
and political overtones, laying claim to a freedom of individual conscience
that goes far beyond Kant's prescription for the exercise of citizenly virtues
in a liberal-democratic state. In short, this text bears a close resemblance to
Habermas's critique of Derrida, especially those passages where he locates
the origins of deconstruction in a 'subject-centred' pre-enlightenment discourse which in turn goes back to the 'mysticism of being', and which thus
provides a starting-point for Heidegger and Derrida alike. 'If this suspicion
is not utterly false, Derrida returns to the historical locale where mysticism
once turned into enlightenment' (*PDM*, p. 184). On this reading, deconstruction is the upshot of a fateful error in the history of thought, a path
wrongly chosen at precisely the point where philosophy might have set out
on the high road of rational self-understanding.

Thus Habermas takes Derrida to task – just as Kant once chastised the
fake illuminati and apostles of unreason – for rejecting that alternative, far
preferable course that led *through and beyond* Kant and Hegel to the
theory of communicative action. In short, Derrida's deconstructive reading of Heidegger 'does not escape the aporetic structure of a truth-
occurrence eviscerated of all truth-as-validity' (*PDM*, p. 167). And again:

> unabashedly, and in the style of *Ursprungsphilosophie*, Derrida falls back on
> this *Urschrift* [viz., *Arche-écriture*] which leaves its traces anonymously,
> without any subject . . . As Schelling once did in speculating about the
> timeless temporalizing inter-nesting of the past, present and future ages of
> the world, so Derrida clings to the dizzying thought of a past that has never
> been present . . . He too [like Heidegger] degrades politics and contempor-
> ary history to the status of the ontic and the foreground, so as to romp all the
> more freely . . . in the sphere of the ontological and arche-writing. (*PDM*,
> pp. 179–81)

This passage tends to confirm the impression that Habermas has based his
critique on a very partial knowledge of Derrida's work. It is a reading that
conspicuously fails to take account of his more recent texts on the 'principle of reason', the politics of representation and the role of the modern

university system as a site where Kant's doctrine of the faculties is both reproduced and subjected to forms of destabilising pressure and critique. But the point can be made more specifically with reference to Derrida's essay 'Of an apocalyptic tone', and the way that it rehearses not only Kant's quarrel with the mystagogues but also – at least by implication – the issue between Habermas and Derrida.

For it is simply not the case (or *not simply* the case) that Derrida here 'deconstructs' the pretensions of enlightenment discourse in order to gain a hearing for those sophists, rhetoricians or purveyors of an occult wisdom whose extravagant teachings Kant holds up to ridicule in the parliament of plain-prose reason. Thus when Derrida offers his own free paraphrase of Kant's case against the mystagogues it could easily be taken for a passage from one of Habermas's chapters on Derrida in *PDM*. 'This cryptopolitics is also a cryptopoetics, a poetic perversion of philosophy' (AT, p. 14). And again: 'this leap toward the imminence of a vision without concept, this impatience turned toward the most crypted secret sets free a poetico-metaphorical overabundance' (p. 12). For Kant, 'all philosophy is indeed prosaic', since it is only by submitting to the democratic rule of reason – to the various 'faculties' duly assembled in parliament, along with all their delegated powers and provisions – that thinking can avoid the manifest dangers of a direct appeal to individual conscience or naked, self-advocating will. Hobbes is a warning presence in the background here, as he is in those passages where Habermas reproaches Foucault for abandoning the ground of enlightened critique, as evolved through the various forms and procedures of civil-administrative reason. What is most to be feared is a wholesale levelling of the faculties which would deprive reason of its moderating role and thereby reduce history, philosophy and politics to a mere force-field of contending interests or rhetorical strategies. And according to Habermas deconstruction is complicit in this process, since it over-extends the province of rhetoric to the point of annulling reason itself, along with all those crucial distinctions that emerged in the sphere of socio-political debate.

Again, these are arguments that Derrida rehearses – and the term seems just right in this context – when he speaks up for Kant and the values of enlightenment, as against the purveyors of a false knowledge vouchsafed by mere intuition. Thus the mystagogues 'scoff at work, the concept, schooling . . . To what is given they believe they have access effortlessly, gracefully, intuitively or through genius, outside of school' (AT, p. 9). Where these characters offend most gravely is in 'playing the overlord', in 'raising the tone' of philosophy (or pseudo-philosophy) to such a pitch that it rejects all rational obligations, all the rules of civilised exchange among equals that make up an emergent and developing public sphere. In so doing they seek 'to hoist themselves above their colleagues or fellows and wrong them in their inalienable right to freedom and equality regarding everything touching on reason alone' (AT, p.11). And the signs of this attitude are there to be read in the various forms of *rhetorical* overreaching – hyperbole, multiplied metaphor, prosopopeia, apostrophe and other such tropes – whose effect is to disrupt the parliament of faculties by giving voice to a language that respects none of its agreed-upon rules and protocols. As Derrida writes, again paraphrasing Kant: '. . . they do not distinguish between pure speculative reason and pure practical reason; they believe they *know* what is solely *thinkable* and reach through feeling alone the universal laws of practical reason' (p.12). Hence their resort to an 'apocalyptic tone' that takes effect through its sheerly *performative* power, its use of an oracular, 'inspired' or prophetic style of speech where the truth-claims of reason (or of language in its constative aspect) have no part to play.

Now it is clear that Derrida is not unambiguously taking Kant's side in this attack on the pretensions of any philosophy that thinks to place itself above or outside the jurisidiction of plain-prose reason. For one thing, his essay is itself shot through with apocalyptic figures and devices, among them various mystical injunctions from Jewish and Christian source-texts. To this extent Derrida is asking us to see that the ethos of Kantian civilised reason has sharp juridical limits; that it has only been able to impose its rule through a constant policing of the border-lines between reason and rhetoric, concept and metaphor, 'genuine' philosophy and a discourse that lays false claim to that title. But we should be wrong to conclude that the essay comes out squarely *against* Kant, or that Derrida's use of an apocalyptic tone signals yet another 'postmodern' break with the discourse of enlightened reason. What sustains this project, he writes, is the 'desire for vigilance, for the lucid vigil, for elucidation, for critique and truth' (AT, p. 22). Of course it may be said that Derrida is here not speaking 'in his own voice'; that this essay is a kind of ventriloquist performance, mixing all manner of citations, intertextual allusions, contrapuntal ironies and so forth, so that anyone who instances this or that passage as evidence for their own preferred reading is surely missing the point. But this objection is itself wide of the mark in so far as it ignores the distinctly Kantian form of Derrida's argument, namely, his questioning of enlightenment values and truth-claims through a debate whose terms are inescapably set by that same Kantian tribunal. That is to say, Derrida is asking what might be the *conditions of possibility* for the exercise of a critical reason that thinks to keep itself pure by excluding or denouncing all other forms of discourse.

To regard this essay as a mere assemblage of 'literary' tricks and devices is to make the same error that Habermas makes when he criticises Derrida for supposedly levelling the genre-distinction between philosophy and literature. It involves the kind of typecast binary thinking that refuses to see how a 'literary' text – or one which exploits a wide range of stylistic resources – might yet possess sufficient *argumentative* force to unsettle such deep-laid asumptions. Derrida belongs very much with those philosophers (Wittgenstein and Austin among them) who resist this habit of compartmentalised thinking. He wants to keep open the two-way flow between so-called 'ordinary' language and the various extra-ordinary styles, idioms, metaphorical usages, 'expert' registers and so forth which help to defamiliarise our commonplace beliefs. But he also sees – unlike Habermas or Searle – that 'ordinary language' is a gross misnomer, since there is no possibility of laying down rules (or extracting a generalised speech-act theory) that would separate normal from deviant instances. It is the idea that such rules *ought* to be available – and that philosophy is the discipline specialised (as Habermas would say) for the purpose of producing them – that actually prevents philosphy from perceiving how manifold, inventive and remarkable are the varieties of 'ordinary' language. The result of such thinking is to isolate philosophy in a realm of meta-linguistic theory and principle where it can have no contact with those energising sources.

Derrida's point– to put it very simply – is that philosophy is indeed a 'kind of writing', but a kind which (contrary to Rorty's understanding) cannot be collapsed into a generalised notion of rhetoric or intertextuality. It is unfortunate that Habermas takes his bearings in *PDM* from a wide-spread but none the less fallacious idea of how deconstruction relates to other symptoms of the so-called 'postmodern condition'. What Derrida gives us to read is *not* philosophy's undoing at the hands of literature but a literature that meets the challenge of philosophy in every aspect of its argument, form and style.

Notes

1. See for instance Jean-François Lyotard, 'The sign of history', in Derek Attridge, Geoff Bennington and Robert Young (eds.), *Post-Structuralism and the Question of History* (Cambridge: CUP, 1987), pp. 162–80.

2. Habermas, *Knowledge and Human Interests*, trans. Jeremy J. Shapiro (London: Heinemann, 1972).
3. For a useful account of these differences, see Rainer Nägele, 'Freud, Habermas and the dialectic of Enlightenment: on real and ideal discourses', *New German Critique*, vol. 22 (1981), pp. 41–62.
4. See Rodolphe Gasché, *The Tain of the Mirror: Derrida and the philosophy of reflection* (Cambridge, Mass.: Harvard University Press, 1986).
5. Richard Rorty, 'Philosophy as a kind of writing', in *Consequences of Pragmatism* (Minneapolis: University of Minnesota Press, 1982), pp. 89–109. See also Rorty, 'Deconstruction and circumvention', *Critical Inquiry*, vol. 11 (1984), pp. 1–23.
6. See especially Jacques Derrida, *Margins of Philosophy*, trans. Alan Bass (Chicago: University of Chicago Press, 1982).
7. Derrida, 'Limited Inc. abc', *Glyph*, vol. 2 (1977), pp. 162–254.
8. Derrida, 'Structure, sign and play in the discourse of the human sciences', in *Writing and Difference*, trans. Alan Bass (London: Routledge & Kegan Paul, 1978), pp. 278–93.
9. Derrida, *The Post Card: from Socrates to Freud and beyond*, trans. Alan Bass (Chicago: University of Chicago Press, 1987). I have slightly modified Bass's translation in some of the passages cited.
10. Derrida, *Edmund Husserl's 'Origin of Geometry': an introduction*, trans. John P. Leavey (Pittsburgh: Duquesne University Press, 1978).
11. In this connection see especially Habermas, *Communication and the Evolution of Society*, trans. Thomas McCarthy (London: Heinemann, 1979).
12. John Searle, 'Reiterating the differences', *Glyph*, vol. 1 (1977), pp. 198–208.
13. See Norris, *Derrida* (Cambridge, Mass.: Harvard University Press, 1987), pp. 172–93; also Jonathan Culler, 'Convention and meaning: Derrida and Austin', *New Literary History*, vol. 13 (1981), pp. 15–30 and Shoshana Felman, *The Literary Speech-Act: Don Juan with J.L. Austin, or seduction in two languages*, trans. Catherine Porter (Ithaca, NY: Cornell University Press, 1983).
14. See J.L. Austin, *How To Do Things With Words* (London: OUP, 1962) and *Philosophical Papers* (London: OUP, 1961), especially the essay, 'A plea for excuses', pp. 123–52.
15. Derrida, *Of Grammatology*, trans. Gayatri C. Spivak (Baltimore: Johns Hopkins University Press, 1976).
16. Derrida, *The Post Card* (*op. cit.*), p. 98.
17. On this topic see also Derrida, *Signsponge*, trans. Richard Rand (New York: Columbia University Press, 1984).
18. Derrida, *The Post Card*, (*op. cit.*), p. 99.
19. *ibid.*, p. 62.
20. Derrida, 'To speculate – on "Freud" ', in *The Post Card* (*op. cit.*), pp. 257–409.
21. Jacques Lacan, 'Seminar on "The purloined letter" ', trans. Jeffrey Mehlman, *Yale French Studies*, no. 48 (1972), pp. 38–72. Derrida's essay, 'Le facteur de la vérité', appears in *The Post Card* (*op.cit.*), pp. 411–96.
22. Henry Staten, *Wittgenstein and Derrida* (Lincoln and London: University of Nebraska Press, 1984), p. 75.
23. *ibid.*, p. 75.

24. See Derrida, '*Speech and Phenomena*' *and other essays on Husserl's theory of signs*, trans. David B. Allison (Evanston, Ill.: Northwestern University Press, 1973).

25. Staten (*op. cit.*), p. 48.

26. Derrida, 'Cogito and the history of madness', in *Writing and Difference* (*op. cit.*), pp. 31–63.

27. Michel Foucault, *Madness and Civilization: a history of insanity in the age of reason*, trans. Richard Howard (New York: Pantheon, 1965). Foucault responded to Derrida's essay in his appendix to the second edition of *Folie et Déraison* (Paris: Gallimard, 1972), pp. 583–603.

28. Derrida, 'Cogito and the history of madness' (*op.cit.*), pp. 53–4.

29. *ibid.*, p. 63.

30. See for instance Derrida, 'The principle of reason: the university in the eyes of its pupils', *Diacritics*, vol. 19 (1983), pp. 3–20.

31. *ibid.*, p. 17.

32. Derrida, 'Of an apocalyptic tone recently adopted in philosophy', trans. John P. Leavey, *The Oxford Literary Review*, vol. 6, no. 2 (1984), pp. 3–37. Hereafter cited in the text as AT.

Chapter 2

Right you are (if you think so): Stanley Fish and the rhetoric of assent

I

Stanley Fish's imposing volume *Doing What Comes Naturally** brings together most of the essays that the author has published during his ten years of high productivity since *Is There A Text In This Class?*[1] It is a wide-ranging collection in the sense that Fish writes about issues in literary theory, linguistics, jurisprudence, philosophy, economics, psychoanalysis, professional ethics, historiography and several other disciplines. Or again one could say – and Fish says it himself in the Preface – that in fact it is a thoroughly predictable and repetitive work, one which goes through the same argumentative moves over and again with wearisome regularity. But if this is the case, Fish argues, then it signals something of interest about the current state of play in those various disciplines. For in his view they have all fallen prey to a certain kind of deep-laid philosophical error – what Fish calls 'theory-hope', positive or negative – which crops up repeatedly and therefore needs debunking wherever it appears.

So he is happy enough to acknowledge the charge that 'every essay in this book is the same: no matter what its putative topic each chapter finally reduces to an argument in which the troubles and benefits of interpretive theory are made to disappear in the solvent of an enriched notion of practice' (Fish, p. ix). But we would be wrong (Fish implies) to put this down to some tedious obsession on his part or some perverse delight in showing how all such arguments self-deconstruct in the end. For it is

* Stanley Fish, *Doing What Comes Naturally: Change, Rhetoric and the Practice of Theory in Literary and Legal Studies*, Oxford: Clarendon Press, 1989. All references to this work are given by page number in the text.

precisely his point that deconstruction and other kinds of 'negative' theory – Marxist, post-structuralist, Freudian or whatever – cannot have the least effect in changing our beliefs or bringing us to abandon habits of thought already in place. Or rather, any effect they may have can only come about by persuading us *rhetorically* to substitute one such item of belief for another, quite apart from their claim to 'theoretical' cogency or truth. In which case we might as well drop all the theory-talk and acknowledge that belief goes all the way down, since on the one hand truth just *is* what we believe (or what we take as sufficiently proof against counter-argument), while on the other – as a matter of plain psychological self-evidence – it is impossible both to believe something and to entertain a negative theory that would show up that belief as erroneous, misguided, or a product of ideological conditioning. If we are convinced by any such argument then this must mean, according to Fish, that the theory falls square with certain pre-existent notions as to what properly counts as a valid, persuasive, or good-faith manner of reasoning. On this point he finds himself happily in agreement with a range of anti-foundationalist thinkers – among them Wittgenstein, Quine, Rorty, Davidson, Derrida and Foucault – whose combined efforts have at last succeeded in demolishing that old 'epistemological' paradigm.

This applies just as much to negative as to positive theories, since in neither case can there be any question of our breaking altogether with previous habits of thought on account of some utterly new and unlooked-for intellectual discovery. Quite simply, there is no external viewpoint – no independent ground or neutral observation-language – from which one could survey the whole range of our present beliefs (or indeed any item among them) and apply determinate standards of truth and falsehood. For anyone who adopted, or who thought to adopt, such a stance would be ignoring three main points: (1) that all truth-claims take rise from some particular set of values, priorities, conventions, procedures of verification, etc.; (2) that any challenge to existing claims – whatever its supposed 'theoretical' grounding – will necessarily involve some alternative (but no less conventional) background of belief; and (3) that this need not be a cause for anxiety since it *makes no difference* to the way we normally argue things out at the level of straightforward, honest disagreement on this or that topic of concern. If theory thus has no 'consequences', positive or negative, then neither does the decision to stop doing theory, or the willingness to acknowledge what Fish regards as the knock-down persuasive force of his arguments to that effect. If we were all won over to Fish's way of thinking then the only result would be to leave more time for the discussion of genuine, substantive differences of view. And this would be a wholly desirable result, though one quite devoid of theoretical significance.

Fish offers several arguments in support of this case. One is the point – pushed home relentlessly in each of these essays – that theory can never do more than offer a *post hoc* rationalisation of beliefs that must always already be in place if its rhetoric is to carry conviction with us or other members of our own 'interpretive community'. On its broadest definition this latter may extend to the whole socio-cultural context or framework of values within which we live, work and think as late-twentieth-century citizens of one or another Western bourgeois democracy. More narrowly, it signifies our membership of various more specialised interest groups – political parties, academic disciplines, professional bodies and so forth – which also set the terms for what shall count as an effective, worthwhile or acceptable contribution to debate. On the one hand, any truly radical theory – any argument that broke altogether with existing interpretative constraints – would *ipso facto* be wholly unintelligible to people within the relevant community, and would thus be either ignored, misconstrued or consigned to the limbo of 'incompetent' or 'eccentric' thought. On the other, any theory that *claimed* to be 'radical' but in fact enjoyed widespread acceptance – or even a modest degree of success among like-minded colleagues – would for this very reason have to be seen as part of an existing consensus, no matter how small or how marginal its membership. In short, critical theorists cannot have it both ways, assuming an imaginary standpoint of knowledge outside and above their interpretative community, while expecting their ideas to be received, taken up or merely understood by members of that same community. They are caught (so Fish would argue) in a classic double-bind predicament, since their claims to speak genuinely on behalf of an alternative, dispossessed or minority culture must become less plausible with each new step toward gaining a wider currency for their views.

This leads on to Fish's second point: that theory cannot have 'consequences' in the strong sense of effecting some change in the social, political or intellectual sphere that could not have been effected by other (i.e. non-theoretical) means. Of course, as he concedes, it may have *results* in persuading us or others that the beliefs we hold are more than just beliefs; that they possess some ultimate validity or truth that can only be arrived at through theory. But if so then this remains an empirical fact about the psychology of assent or the workings of persuasive argument. That is to say, it offers no grounds whatsoever for the strong thesis that theory makes a difference *in and of itself*, that by learning to criticise received ideas from a higher, theoretical standpoint we can change those ideas and thus bring about a more adequate, enlightened or progressive state of knowledge. 'In what follows', he writes,

> I will contend (1) that in whatever form it appears the argument for theory fails, (2) that theory is not and could not be used . . . to generate and/or guide practice, (3) that when 'theory' is in fact used it is . . . in order to justify a decision reached on other grounds, (4) that theory is essentially a rhetorical and political phenomenon whose effects are purely contingent, and (5) that these truths are the occasion neither of cynicism nor of despair. (Fish, p. 380)

His last item here is intended as a simple recognition of the fact that, just as 'doing theory' has absolutely no consequences, for better or worse, so giving up theory will have no real effect on the quality, range or intellectual level of debate. As for his own arguments – and the obvious question as to what would be the 'consequence' if people found them wholly convincing – Fish can afford to take a relaxed line. The ideal outcome, he suggests, would be a couple of letters saying 'You're right!' and then a complete silence on the topic of theory (for or against) and a switch of attention to other, more important matters. But really nothing much will have changed since the theorists were always debating those matters – starting out from various kinds of value-judgement, political conviction, disciplinary interest or whatever – and producing theoretical arguments or truth-claims only to achieve an extra degree of persuasive force. So the real benefit of ceasing to talk about theory is that it would remove these obstacles in the way of straightforward discussion and thus leave us free to continue the argument exactly where we last left off.

Fish's third point has to do with the distinction between 'positive' and 'negative' versions of theory. The positive theorists are those who think we need reasons, principles, or justifying grounds for the conduct of debate on interpretative questions. They would include, for instance, a thinker like E.D. Hirsch, whose early book *Validity in Interpretation* came up with a range of theoretical arguments for the case that an author's intentions are constitutive for the meaning of his or her text, and that critics should therefore make every effort to recover the 'original' sense before going on to raise questions of present-day 'significance' or meaning-for-us.[2] But to Fish this whole enterprise seems nothing more than a massive example of misapplied scholarly ingenuity. For it is simply a fact about the way we understand language – whether everyday speech-acts or literary texts – that we *do* try to figure out the utterer's intentions and thus make sense of their meaning to the best of our ability. And when this effort does not pay off for some reason (maybe on account of confused expression, changes of linguistic usage or wilful obscurity) then no kind of theory can possibly help us to determine what the speaker or the author might have had in mind. And the same goes for theorists in other disciplines – notably exponents of liberal jurisprudence like Ronald Dworkin – who argue for the existence of 'grounds' or 'principles' by way of backing up their interpretative claims.[3] Here again Fish finds their thinking inconsequent in the sense that it simply cannot make any difference whether or not one's beliefs come equipped with some notional back-up apparatus of theory. Of course there are reasons – strategic or rhetorical reasons – for taking an avowedly principled stand on this or that question, and thus claiming to occupy the moral high ground. But in the end such talk comes down to a species of self-induced mystification. What it has to ignore is the straight-forward fact that we believe what we believe on various issues of politics, justice, social values, etc., and that nothing follows – in theory or in principle – from the effort to justify these suasive techniques. Thus 'if "law as integrity" [Dworkin's paradigm] is anything, it is either the name of what we already do (without any special prompting) or a rhetorical/political strategy by means of which we give a certain necessary colouring to what we've already done' (Fish, p. 388).

The 'negative theorists' (i.e. the deconstructors) are in even worse trouble, according to Fish. For it is their main argument – at the opposite extreme from a hardline intentionalist like Hirsch – that texts very often *do not and cannot* mean what they say; that there is simply no access to authorial intentions (or original meaning) since language complicates the process of reading to the point of an ultimate 'undecidability'; and therefore that we had best discount all these delusory surrogates for the author's self-present voice and instead pay attention to the conflicts that develop between logic, grammar and rhetoric, or language in its literal and figural modes.[4] Then again, there is the Marxist version of 'negative theory' which holds that texts may be seen to conceal their true (class-specific or historically determinate) meaning in the interests of some dominant ideology whose workings can best be exposed to view through an immanent critique of their blind spots, contradictions or moments of unwitting self-revelation. Much the same applies to the Freudian distinction between 'manifest' and 'latent' sense, or indeed to any form of diagnostic reading that claims this prerogative of somehow knowing more than the author can plausibly be held to have known about his or her meanings, motives or intent. In each case the critic effectively disowns any belief in the maxim that language, for the most part, means what it says and says what it means.

Fish's response to all this – as might be expected – is a downright denial that it could ever apply to our experience as members of an interpretative community engaged in making sense of literary or other kinds of text. For it is a precondition of belonging to any such community that one's readings will only be acceptable in so far as they are addressed to the common understanding of like-minded scholars, critics, informed laypersons, competent judges and so forth. And beyond these relatively specialised subgroups there is also the larger – maybe universal – set of assumptions about meaning, intention, or speech-act implicature which simply define what it is to 'make sense' in any given context of utterance. So the negative theorists cannot be taken seriously, Fish argues, when they put forward their case for a modern 'hermeneutics of suspicion' that would somehow revoke one or all of these basic conventions, and thus produce readings that purport to go against every notion of a commonsense interpretative grasp. Once again, it is something like a performative version of the Cretan Liar predicament: *either* these readings are intelligible to the wider community (in which case they cannot be as radical as they claim), *or* they really do subvert all established ideas of readerly competence (in which case nobody could begin to understand them). And since the theorists concerned are mostly prominent figures on the academic scene it is the first option that clearly provides the best means of resolving this pseudo-paradox.

There is no denying the elegance and persuasiveness of Fish's arguments when applied to some of the more wayward examples of modish all-purpose scepticism. But his real target – among 'positive' and 'negative' thinkers alike – is the claim that theory can indeed make a difference, and not the idea (which in fact he would very willingly endorse) that it amounts to just one more species of persuasive rhetoric. One can best view Fish as the latest in a line of debunking anti-philosophers which goes back at least to Protagoras and his quarrel with the truth-claims of Socratic reason. This is why he is able to beat the modern sceptics (or some of them at least) at their own game. It also gives a handle for other players, like Walter Benn Michaels and Steven Knapp, who go along with the whole neo-pragmatist case (against theory) but then proceed to catch Fish out in some covert theoretical move or failure to stick with his own principles.[5] To which Fish responds – quite predictably – by showing that these critics have misconstrued his argument, and done so moreover since they

/assent*

themselves are in the grip of some residual theoreticist illusion. Clearly there can be no end to this game so long as one carries on playing by the same rules. For it is always possible for Fish to trump any opposing (pro-theory) argument by offering the standard neo-pragmatist response: that what presently counts as a worthwhile, serious or valid contribution to debate will appear so only in light of our existing professionalised habits of judgement.

To suppose otherwise – as by arguing for standards of validity or truth independent of prevailing consensus norms – is to fall straight back into the same old self-deluding trap that has always characterised the academic disciplines, philosophy chief among them. This is the idea that one could somehow get *outside* those prevailing norms by an effort of self-critical reflection (or 'consciousness-raising') which enabled one to see where the beliefs in question proved somehow inadequate, revealed their own 'ideo-logical' blind spots, or – as argued by canny dialecticians from Socrates to Derrida – gave rise to antinomies which rendered them suspect by their own philosophical lights. On the contrary, says Fish:

> [s]uch a realization could only have this effect if it enabled the individual who was constituted by historical and cultural forces to 'see through' those forces and thus stand to the side of his own convictions and beliefs. But that is the one thing a historically conditioned consciousness cannot do – scrutinize its own beliefs, conduct a rational examination of its own convictions; for in order to begin such a scrutiny, it would first have to escape the grounds of its own possibility, and it could only do that if it were not historically conditioned and were instead an acontextual or unsituated entity of the kind that is rendered unavailable by the first principle of the interpret-ivist or conventionalist view. (Fish, p. 245)

From which it follows – among other things – that literary critics are exhibiting a peculiar blindness to the enabling conditions of their own activity when they espouse the kind of high-toned ethical stance which rejects such arguments as merely a pretext for Fish's style of geared-up professionalist approach. In fact the widespread pejorative use of terms like 'professionalism' as a stick to beat careerist academics is one that strikes Fish as nicely symptomatic of the deep confusion that currently attends such debates. For it clearly implies that there *are* certain absolute standards of judgement – scholarly integrity, objectivity, interpretative insight, crit-ical acumen or whatever – which transcend the currently existing consen-sus, and which thus hold good for any qualified observer who can take a decently disinterested view. But this argument collapses into manifest

83*

nonsense, Fish thinks, if one asks *from what possible vantage-point of principle or theory* a critic could claim both the competence to judge in such matters (i.e. the requisite degree of inside knowledge) and also the capacity to stand right back, diagnose the workings of professional bias, and thus come up with a judgement untainted by those same consensus values. For this is just another (ethical) variant of the familiar theoreticist mistake, that of claiming to occupy some high ground of principle where all contingent factors – or self-interested motives - would at last drop away, leaving the interpreter free to exercise his or her powers of unaided, self-authenticating judgement. But there is not and cannot be any such standpoint if, as Fish argues, 'it is only with reference to the articulation and hierarchies of a professional bureaucracy that a sense of the self and its worth – its merit – emerges and becomes measurable' (p. 244).

That is to say, we are all professionals, like it or not, including those staunch defenders of the anti-professionalist ethos who are able to gain a platform for their views precisely on account of the deep-laid bias against 'mere' professionalism which to a large extent defines the profession's accustomed self-image. Hence the upshot to Fish's argument, seemingly a species of wilful paradox but, as he would have it, nothing more than a clear-eyed acceptance of the way things are.

> The professional who is 'spoken' in his every thought and action by the institution and yet 'speaks' in the name of essences that transcend the institution and provide a vantage-point for its critique is not acting out a contradiction, but only acting in the only way human beings can. (p. 246)

And the same applies to those theorists of various persuasion, positive or negative, who *cannot do other* than espouse their (deluded) theoretical claims, since those claims are constitutive of a certain – currently prestigious – mode of academic discourse which not only sets the relevant terms for debate but provides them (the theorists) with a sense of intellectual, which is just to say professional, identity. So it would not make sense to be 'against theory' if this meant asking everyone to stop taking an interest in such matters and henceforth adopt a wholly different line of approach. All that is needed is a scaling-down of the claims, a decision to substitute 'theory-talk' for 'theory', or to jettison all that old philosophical baggage and just accept that what is true (or theoretically valid) is just what happens to work for present suasive or rhetorical purposes. This is why, in Fish's words, the distinction between theory and theory-talk is a distinction between a discourse that stands apart from all practices (and no such discourse exists) and a discourse that is itself a practice and is therefore consequential to the extent that it is influential or respected or widespread. (p. 14)

Fish has no real objection to theory-talk among literary critics, just as he has no objection to talk about 'principles' and 'integrity' among proponents of liberal jurisprudence like Dworkin, or to anti-professionalism as a mode of legitimising rhetoric whereby professionals standardly mark off their distance from other trades and occupations. Where he does find fault is with the further, strong-consequentialist belief that one can actually *do theory* in a sense of that phrase that would involve something more than a preferential idiom, that is to say, a set of principles, truth-claims, validating grounds, etc. which could bring about a decisive shift in the way we habitually do things with words. For this is mere delusion, he thinks, and moreover has the harmful consequence of promoting contempt for professional values (or consensus beliefs) to which we all of us subscribe even when conducting such arguments, since otherwise – quite simply – they would not *count* as arguments for us or anyone else. To this extent theorists and anti-theorists, professionals and anti-professionals, are all in the same boat. Some of them hope to steer according to fixed coordinates of method and principle, while others (the deconstructionists and partisans of various radical persuasion) prefer to rock the boat by showing that no such coordinates can possibly exist. Fish sees both kinds of enterprise as perfectly valid on their own given terms, so long as they accept the on-board condition of sailing in the same broad cultural enterprise, and do not pretend to have some ultimate anchor-point in truth, reality or reason.

II

These issues are by no means confined to the more specialised reaches of literary theory and philosophy. If Fish is right – whatever that could mean – then his argument has large implications in every area of social, political and intellectual life. Take for instance his case against 'blind submission', the practice of reviewing scholarly articles without knowledge of the author's name, rank, or standing in the academic world. To those who recommend this procedure – most often on principled ethical grounds – it would seem self-evident that blind submission is a worthwhile attempt to screen out the habits of routine deferential judgement that conspire to keep the established big names in print and to marginalise other, less authoritative voices. But they are wrong, Fish argues, for the simple reason that if one ever succeeded (*per impossible*) in discounting all such 'extraneous' grounds of appeal, then there would be nothing left – no operative values or standard of pure, 'disinterested' judgement – by which to assess the merits of incoming articles. In short, 'bias is just another word for seeing from a particular perspective as opposed to seeing from no perspective at all, and since seeing from no perspective at all is not a possibility, bias is a condition of consciousness and therefore of action' (Fish, p. 176). So the argument for blind submission – however well-meant in principle – turns out to be just another version of the same old fallacy, the idea that there exists some realm of absolute standards or values quite apart from the various kinds of prejudice, self-interest or contingent motivation that govern our day-to-day evaluative practice. Fish's title for this essay – 'No bias, no merit' – puts the case in a nutshell.

Elsewhere he offers a number of detailed case-histories, designed to make the point that what counts as a competent reading at any given time is always a product of interpretative conventions, and never established through the straightforward appeal to standards of validity or truth. Fish's favourite example is *Paradise Lost*, no doubt because his own reading of the poem has undergone some drastic changes over the years, changes that can only be accounted for (he thinks) in terms of the wider academic and professional interests that have come into play.[6] In fact it is an ideal case for treatment from his point of view since Milton's reputation has veered so sharply – at least among the arbiters of orthodox fashion – during that period (roughly the past fifty years) that marks the emergence of English Studies as a fully professionalised discipline. Fish's essay starts out by citing a 1972 article where the critic (Raymond Waddington) offers his confident opinion that 'few of us today could risk echoing C.S. Lewis's condemnation of the concluding books of *Paradise Lost* as an "untransmuted lump of futurity" '.[7] What interests Fish is firstly the question just *how* this change occurred – through what efforts of 'constructive' reinterpretation, new alignments of scholarly interest, critical methodology, etc. – and secondly the larger (but related) question of where such authority comes from, or how it could happen that Lewis's self-assured negative judgement came to look so eccentric, or at any rate 'risky', to critics of a later generation. His answer is predictable: the great shift occurred because a number of influential Miltonists set about 'proving' that Books XI and XII were not just chunks of undigested theological material worked up into dubiously poetic form, but in fact possessed all kinds of distinctive literary

merit. Sometimes this project took a modestly revisionist form, as by
arguing that Milton displayed all those qualities (vivid metaphor, intricate
verbal texture, 'sensuous enactment' or whatever) which previous critics –
Eliot and Leavis among them – had found so conspicuously lacking in his
verse. Elsewhere it involved the more contentious idea that those values
were narrowly conceived, or applicable only to poets (like Shakespeare and
Donne) who had enjoyed canonical status among critics of the earlier
persuasion. But in each case the claim to have discovered something
'there' in the text – something passed over (or perversely ignored) by
previous readers – was in fact nothing more than a species of enabling
rhetoric, an appeal to supposedly self-evident values whose existence was
entirely a product of their own creation.

Of course their campaign would never have achieved such striking success if these critics had been fully converted to Fish's way of thinking, i.e. if
they had come to regard their own efforts as 'merely' a suasive or rhetorical exercise, a redescription of the poem in terms more suited to the
project in hand. For in this case their arguments would have carried no
conviction, either with themselves or with other members of the relevant
interpretative community. In short, the new Miltonists *had no choice* but
to believe absolutely in the truth (or justice) of their own interpretative
claims, and to treat the opposition either as labouring in the grip of a
restrictive aesthetic creed or as having been prompted – like Lewis – by
'extraneous' motives of a religious or ideological nature. But this is
nothing more than an empirical fact about the psychology of belief or, as
Fish would have it, the structure of unavoidable self-deception built into
all such interpretative truth-claims. It is the same with those proponents of
'positive theory' who need their talk of principles, grounds, a priori values
and so forth by way of self-legitimising argument, or again with those
negative theorists for whom terms like 'ideology', 'aporia', or 'critique'
function as a source of much-needed psychological assurance. In the
Milton debate this conviction comes across as a belief that the text has
certain intrinsic properties which critics have hitherto been prone to ignore but which should now be apparent, given the nature of criticism as a
progressive, self-improving art. Thus:

in his [Waddington's] sentences Miltonists are always 'recognizing' this or
'becoming aware' of that; the dominant image is one of seeing, either clearly
or through a glass darkly, and seeing is itself never seen as contextually
determined, as an activity that is performed in accordance with the possibilities and options that are inherent in a particular historical moment. (p.
250)

Again, Fish has no quarrel with this notion in so far as it provides Waddington and others with the kind of psychological back-up needed to pursue their scholarly (i.e. professional) interests. Where the error comes in – and it is an error so widespread as to constitute something very like a *de facto* condition of possibility for the human sciences at large – is in mistaking this inveterate habit of belief for some ultimate truth about language, literature, or the grounds of critical evaluation.

This argument is repeated with minor (though ingenious) variations in every chapter of Fish's book. He has clearly spent much of his time over the past ten years looking sharp for such handy illustrative cases of the way that foundationalist thinking tends to reassert itself even in the work of critics and theorists who would claim to have no truck with such ideas. Thus Fish's main objection to exponents of left-wing or radical jurisprudence – especially the Critical Legal Studies movement – is that they cannot have it both ways, on the one hand denouncing all talk of principles, adjudicative grounds, procedural rules, etc. as just another version of the 'formalist' trick that dissimulates the real workings of political power, while on the other proposing to deconstruct the rhetoric of mainstream (liberal) thought by applying their own kind of negative theory.[8] For then they fall into what Fish describes as the 'characteristically left error', the mistake of supposing 'that an insight into the source of our convictions (they come from culture, not from God) will render them less compelling' (p. 395). The Critical Legal Studies people are right – that is to say, in agreement with Fish – when they argue against the received idea that law is (or should be) a neutral adjudicative discourse, one that possesses its own special standards of truth, justice and procedural logic quite aside from all merely 'political' interests or motives. They are also quite entitled to make this point by deconstructing the various binary oppositions that have propped up the legal enterprise to date, for example, those between perspicuous and 'hard' cases, rule-governed procedure and interpretative licence, or verdicts arrived at by an appeal to established (constitutional or case-law) precedent and verdicts based on the supposedly self-evident facts of the case in hand. For these distinctions are manifestly open to challenge, as for instance when the CLS writers show that each and every judgement involves some degree of interpretative latitude; that 'facts' are self-evident only from a certain, highly selective angle of vision; or that any appeal to 'rules' must always involve the logical regress that results when one asks what authority those rules can possess apart from their belonging to a culture-specific set of legalised codes and conventions. In short, the radicals are well placed to criticise the blindspots of prejudice, self-interest, or professional *amour propre* that mask behind the rhetoric of principled argument in defenders of the mainstream tradition. Where their case falls apart – according to Fish – is in thinking to offer an *alternative* theory, a set of adequate (non-circular) grounds or reasons for rejecting what they see in their high-toned liberal opponents as a merely 'rhetorical' stance. There is just no way that they can claim to reoccupy this high ground of theory and principle, having made such a show of deconstructing its truth-claims from a negative (demystifying) standpoint.

Fish sees this as yet another striking instance of the curious double logic (or the self-exempting clause) that allows theorists to remain somehow blind to their own governing interests and motives. What they fail to perceive in adopting this stance is the fact that *all* arguments, truth-claims, or assertions – along with all criticism directed against them – take rise within some given context of belief which inevitably sets the agenda for anyone wishing to participate. It is a point that Fish develops throughout this book against thinkers of otherwise diverse persuasions, among them Noam Chomsky, Stephen Toulmin, Jürgen Habermas, Terry Eagleton, Roberto Unger, E.D. Hirsch and H.L.A. Hart. They are united in adhering to some version (positive or negative) of the strong consequentialist thesis, namely, the idea that changing our beliefs is a matter of attaining an improved, more perspicuous or self-conscious grasp of the motives that led us to adopt those beliefs in the first place. On the contrary, says Fish:

> The fact that change can neither be willed nor stopped means that critical self-consciousness is at once impossible and superfluous. It is impossible because there is no action or motion of the self that exists apart from the 'prevailing realm of purposes' [Unger's phrase], and therefore no way of achieving distance from that realm; and it is superfluous because the prevailing realm of purposes is, in the very act of elaborating itself, turning itself into something other than it was . . . The failure of critical self-consciousness is a failure without consequences since everything it would achieve – change, the undoing of the status quo, the redistribution of power and authority, the emergence of new forms of action – is already achieved by the ordinary and everyday efforts by which, in innumerable situations, large and small, each of us attempts to alter the beliefs of another. (Fish, pp. 463–4)

And this argument extends – as in Chomsky's case – to any theory that claims a generalising power outside or above our ordinary, everyday practice as language-using creatures. In fact Fish's first example in the book is taken from a work of linguistic philosophy (Ruth Kempson's *Presupposition and the Delimitation of Semantics*) which raises precisely this question, i.e. how far one can analyse language in formal or logico-semantic terms without bringing in all manner of implicit assumptions, background knowledge, contextual information, and so forth.[9] The answer, for Kempson as for Fish, would appear to be 'not very far', since formal categories like entailment, synonymy and semantic structure can never get close to encompassing all the items of tacit presupposition that make up the meaning of a given speech-act in a given context of utterance.

But here again the argument reaches a point where the theorist seems unwilling or unable to accept the full implications of her own best insight. Thus Kempson veers around, in the space of a single sentence, from entertaining the idea of a 'speaker-relative concept of presupposition' to declaring flatly that any such theory *must* include a 'finite set of predictive rules', along with a formalised account of semantic entailment and a framework for explaining 'the systematic relation between the meaning of lexical items and the syntactic structure of the sentence' (cited by Fish, p. 2). Now it may well be – Fish concedes – that this working assumption goes so deep into the project of theoretical linguistics that Kempson (like Chomsky) could scarcely give it up without relinquishing that project once and for all. Still he thinks it worthwhile to track the notion down wherever it appears and demonstrate the manifest impossibility of doing what these theorists claim to do. One likely reason for Fish's extreme pertinacity comes out if one considers the self-avowed relation in Chomsky's work between technical questions in the realm of syntactic theory and issues of a wider socio-political import.[10] For of course it was (and is) one of Chomsky's main contentions that theory does indeed have 'consequences'; that any position one adopts with regard to (e.g.) the nature and scope of human linguistic 'competence' will also have a bearing on topics in the philosophy of mind and, beyond that, on the sense one attaches to ideas of moral and political accountability.

Oddly enough, Fish has nothing to say about these further controversial claims on Chomsky's part, restricting his discussion to the same basic point (i.e. the limits of any formalised linguistic theory) that he had previously made in relation to Kempson's argument. But it is clear that his quarrel with the theorists on 'technical' grounds is always within reach of this larger, political dimension where the issue is one of consensus-values versus the stance of dissenting intellectuals, or the claims of oppositional critique. For Fish such arguments simply do not make sense, whether offered in support of positive theories – like Dworkin's language of principles, Chomsky's rationalist linguistics, or Habermas's talk of 'transcendental pragmatics', 'ideal speech-situations', etc. – or couched in the negative, demystifying idiom favoured by the current (mainly left-wing) hermeneutics of suspicion. But for all this appearance of even-handed treatment it is the latter – what Fish calls 'anti-foundationalist theory-hope' – that attracts his most detailed, persistent and vigorous rebuttals. 'If critical self-consciousness is anything, it is the self-description of a persuasive agenda that dare not speak its name; for if it were to do so and acknowledge itself as a design, it could no longer claim the purity that supposedly marks it off from every other form of coercion and constraint' (Fish, p. 464). Or again, with reference to the negative theorists: '. . . the man [*sic*] who says "I am going to change" and means it is really saying "I have already changed": he is simply reporting the conclusion of a process marked by none of the reflective self-consciousness with which he now, and retroactively, endows it' (p. 463). In short, the delegitimisers cannot evade the reflexive application of their own best insight, according to which – as Fish construes it – nothing can alter the simple fact that we believe what we believe (or reject what we do not believe) on the basis of convictions that are always already in place, and which remain wholly unaltered by any such effort of *post hoc* rationalisation.

III

It would, I think, be wrong to dismiss these arguments as merely the product of a subtle but perverse intelligence determined to beat the critical theorists at their own demythologising game. No doubt this is one, fairly sizeable motive for Fish's having written what must seem – on the face of it – a singularly negative sequence of essays whose upshot is always to catch someone out in arguing a case that fails to square with their own rhetorical practice. After all, these essays constantly home in on the point that professionals, academics, or practitioners of this or that discipline are surely deceiving themselves (and others) if they think that one could ever do more than devise ingenious new variations on a handful of current *idées reçues*. The best one can do is work within the existing rules of the game while seizing every opportunity for novel moves and counter-moves, at the same time keeping close watch on one's opponents for any rule-breaking moves on their part. So anyone who thought to criticise Fish for striking such a narrowly professional stance – or for addressing issues that were only of interest to a company of like-minded adepts – would then have to reckon with everything he says against the claims of theory as a 'consequential' enterprise, one that somehow makes it possible to break with the existing range of agreed-upon topics and problems. This position is indefensible, he thinks, since it rests on the long-since discredited idea of knowledge as a free-floating realm of enquiry where minds are able to scrutinise their own false beliefs, where truth awaits discovery through a process of critique quite apart from all given (institutional) constraints, and where intellectual merit is measured in terms of its resistance to mere consensus-values and assumptions. Those who cling to this old, foundationalist paradigm are merely evincing their failure (or unwillingness) to grasp the plain fact of its historical obsolescence.

Thus even in philosophy, the discipline where strong foundationalist arguments have traditionally carried most weight, Fish can summon up a whole series of influential names – Wittgenstein, Quine, Rorty, Putnam and others – whose mention seems enough to support his general case. And on the point about professonalism (that is to say, Fish's claim that professional interests go 'all the way down', that they define not only our working habits of belief but our very sense of intellectual ideentity) he can likewise draw upon a wide range of sources, from psychology to Foucauldian discourse-theory and the applied sociology of knowledge. Thus:

> it is only with reference to the articulation and hierarchies of a professional bureaucracy that a sense of the self and its worth – its merit – emerges . . . which is another way of saying that the self of the professional is constituted and legitimized by the very structures – social and institutional – from which it is supposedly aloof. (Fish, p. 245)

In which case anti-professionalism is just another kind of misplaced theory-hope, one that holds out for the saving power of intellectual and personal integrity, just as thinkers in the Kantian enlightenment tradition had staked their claims on the idea of knowledge as giving access to a realm of transcendent, self-evident, or a priori truth. But again, nothing follows in practical terms from the realisation that this is the way things are, since to acknowledge the force of Fish's arguments is also to see that they can make no difference to our everyday practice as critics, philosophers, moralists or 'concerned' citizens.

Hence the repeated twist-in-the-tail effect that one comes to recognise as a hallmark, of Fish's thinking in its latest phase. Thus his case against theory ends up by conceding that theory-hope cannot be assuaged or subdued – much less 'deconstructed' by some novel turn of argument – since we all of us experience its seductive pull in every aspect of our professional and intellectual lives. And it is the same with those other obsolete ideas (principles, concepts, truth-claims and so forth) which likewise turn out to resist his best efforts of rhetorical demystification. The following passage makes the point with maximum relish and flair, though one could find similar examples on almost every page of Fish's book.

> Professionalism cannot do without anti-professionalism; it is the chief support and maintenance of the professional ideology; its presence is a continual assertion and sign of the purity of the profession's intentions. In short, the ideology of anti-professionalism – of essential and independent values chosen freely by an independent self – is nothing more or less than the ideology of professionalism taking itself seriously. (Fish, p. 245)

Now it is certainly possible to view such arguments as just a kind of routine point-scoring exercise, carried off – one must admit – with great virtuosity but otherwise of small interest outside the peculiar hothouse climate of professional Eng. Lit. debate. However, as I suggested above, there is more to this book than might appear if one reads only with an eye to its stake in the current academic game. For if Fish is right – once again, suspending the question of just what that could mean, given his dismissal of truth-values in every shape and form – then this argument extends far beyond the province of literary critics, and takes on some fairly drastic implications for every other field of enquiry or activity of thought. And of course Fish himself is quick to make the point by addressing these essays not only to specialists in the 'soft' (i.e. hermeneutic or interpretative) disciplines, but also to those – philosophers, economists, political theorists, professors of jurisprudence, transformational grammarians, historians of science and the rest – who standardly claim something more in the way of methodological rigour, explanatory power or truth-conditional warrant. Such arguments would only hold up if they issued from some ideal vantage-point of neutral observation, some wholly external or objective ground whence to adjudicate other, less privileged claims. And since, as Fish contends, this idea is quite simply unintelligible – since every judgement entails a whole range of self-legitimising presuppositions – it is clear that all truths must at last come down to the level of presently warranted belief.

In short, there is no discipline, however 'scientific' its credentials, which does not take rise within a given context of agreed-upon values and beliefs, or against some backdrop of enabling assumptions which provide its only possible ground of appeal. In which case we might as well give up the attempt to distinguish between the various kinds of knowledge (sciences/humanities, *Erklären/Verstehen*, theory/interpretation and their manifold cognates) which have so far exerted such a deep hold on the conduct of academic life. For Fish – as for others in the pragmatist camp like Richard Rorty – such efforts are just a melancholy sign that we (or some of us) have not yet acknowledged the radical contingency of all truth-claims, all attempts to 'cut nature at the joints', to ascend from *doxa* to *episteme*, or to achieve some perfect, self-validating match between concepts and sensuous intuitions. In fact Rorty is one of the very few thinkers – Thomas Kuhn and Jacques Derrida are others – whose work Fish cites without then going on to remark this or that unfortunate lapse into bad old 'theoretical' habits of thought. But we should not be deceived by this combative style into thinking that Fish is an isolated voice, or even that he represents a minority viewpoint in terms of current intellectual debate. For despite all the show of being up against 'theory-hope' resurgent on every side, like Abdiel alone against the forces of night, Fish knows well enough that he is swimming with the tide, or at least that things have been moving his way across a wide range of disciplines during the past decade and more.

Thus in sanguine moments he can muster quite a roll-call of thinkers who would agree pretty much with what he says, at least to the extent of regarding all knowledge as a product of contingent discovery-procedures, or as resting on assumptions taken for granted within this or that 'interpretive community'. Rorty no doubt comes closest to Fish in his willingness to push this argument to the limit and embrace a full-blown pragmatist doctrine of truth as what is (currently and contingently) 'good in the way of belief'.[11] But there is also – as Fish argues – much support to be had from Wittgenstein's anti-foundationalist teaching about 'language-games' and cultural 'forms of life', from Quine's well-known attack on the analytic/synthetic distinction (which effectively relativises both kinds of truth-claim to contingent ideas of where that line should be drawn),[12] from Thomas Kuhn on the shifting contexts (or paradigms) of scientific enquiry, and from latter-day Nietzschean genealogists like Foucault for whom 'truth' is nothing more than a transient product of the epistemic will-to-power that masks behind notions of 'scientific' objectivity or disinterested scholarly method.[13] And to these one could add the tradition of thought, descending from Heidegger to Gadamer and other such exponents of the 'hermeneutic circle', which holds that every act of understanding takes place within a given interpretative 'horizon' which alone makes it possible to decide what shall count as a good-faith, adequate, or answerable mode of response.[14] All of which suggests – despite his fondness for a rhetoric of tough-minded pragmatist dissent – that Fish in fact has plenty of allies in his case against the lingering 'enlightenment' ethos of theory, reason and truth.

This is why his book merits serious attention from thinkers outside Departments of English or Comparative Literature. It is not just that Fish makes a point of annexing adjacent disciplines, as by telling the lawyers and philosophers that they can learn some useful lessons from literary critics who have been through that old theoreticist phase and come out with a healthy commonsense mistrust of everything it once stood for. This is certainly a major motive in his enterprise, as indeed one ought to expect, given Fish's deep conviction that professional self-interest is the only thing that counts when it comes to making a mark on the intellectual scene. But what is really disturbing about this whole line of argument is the fact that it follows *of necessity* from the premises that govern so many current versions of the anti-foundationalist case. That is to say, there is no resisting the cynical upshot of Fish's case if one accepts that all forms of intellectual enquiry come down to a more or less successful attempt to trim one's sails to the prevailing wind of professional or academic fashion. At this point Fish would most certainly protest that I have misconstrued the whole nature of his project, since after all *nothing follows*, in practical, terms, from any choice we might make 'for' or 'against' the truth-claims of theory, positive or negative. So he could bounce straight back with the now familiar line of response: that everything will carry on as normal when we stop talking about theory, principles, truth at the end of enquiry and so forth, except that our debates will then be conducted at the level of honestly-argued belief and conviction, and not hung up on the pointless search for non-existent justifying grounds. In which case – contrary to my statement above – there would be nothing in the least degree 'cynical' or nihilist about Fish's suggestion that we dump those obsolete ideas and just learn to live with the straightforward fact that our beliefs have no possible justification outside the practices, contexts, or language-games that happen to prevail at present.

Still I guess that many readers will share my sense that if Fish's arguments hold then philosophers, lawyers, ethical theorists, literary critics and others might as well close up shop straight away, since nothing would remain of the intellectual values that have so far justified their activity. Of course Fish can argue (once again) that this is the wrong way to pose the question, since (1) those values are strictly contingent, justified by the work they do in given professional or cultural contexts; (2) they will anyway remain firmly in place whatever their perceived lack of theoretical foundations; and (3) any argument against them will itself be launched from a situated standpoint – or against some background of likewise enabling (even if negative) beliefs – which can claim no more in the way of ultimate 'theoretical' warrant. So we need not worry: business as usual except, maybe, for the hardline theorists, philosophers and (mostly left-wing) intellectuals still hooked on the idea of separating truth from the currencies of consensus-belief. Fish cites a passage from Israel Scheffler – arguing against Kuhn and the relativist drift in current philosophy of science – as sadly indicative of the way such thinkers expose their adherence to an outworn paradigm of objective rationality and truth. What Scheffler perceives at the end of this road is a condition of 'epistemological and moral anarchy', a state in which nothing could any longer count as a valid (or indeed a falsifiable) description of the way things stand in reality.

> Independent and public controls are no more, communication has failed, the common universe of things is a delusion, reality itself is made . . . rather than discovered . . . In place of a community of rational men [*sic*] following objective procedures in the pursuit of truth, we have a set of isolated monads, within each of which belief forms without systematic constraints. (cited by Fish, p. 322)

'The centre cannot hold' . . . 'Mere anarchy is loosed upon the world': clearly we are expected to view this apocalyptic scenario as a piece of patently absurd over-reaction, a response engendered by Scheffler's mistaken belief that without absolute standards of validity, reason and truth there is nothing to prevent the relativist slide into chaos and old night. He (Fish) is able to strike this attitude of sturdy commonsense wisdom because he can rely on it that a good many readers will be half-way convinced from the outset, having picked up enough in the way of currently popular anti-foundationalist views to make Scheffler's argument appear just a species of alarmist over-reaction.

Now I think that Fish is wrong in all this, and wrong moreover on grounds susceptible of argued, demonstrative proof, rather than reducing – as he would surely claim – to a difference of opinion (or a clash of incommensurable beliefs) beyond any hope of rational adjudication. Firstly, it is by no means apparent that conventionalist arguments have won the day in those disciplines – theory of science, epistemology, analytical philosophy of language, etc. – where it might be expected that the realist (or strong truth-conditional) case would put up the maximum resistance. For in fact some of the best recent work in these fields has maintained a commitment to exactly such values, and done so with an argumentative force quite unmatched by the neo-pragmatist partisans of truth as a product of consensus ideas, or what is 'good in the way of belief'. The work of Roy Bhaskar – especially his book *Scientific Realism and Human*

Emancipation – is relevant here on several counts.[15] It combines a strong, transcendental-realist account of scientific knowledge with an emphasis on socialised modes of production, on various ideological determinants (e.g. the positivist paradigm as a form of pre-critical, naïve or reified under-standing), and also on the need for some normative standard – as in Habermas – by which to criticise such fallings-short of rational debate. In the course of these arguments Bhaskar succeeds in showing how any form of conventionalism, when applied to the history of science, either collapses into manifest self-contradiction or produces antinomies that land it back in the province of metaphysical realism or idealist mystification.

As against this regressive or dead-end philosophy, Bhaskar puts forward the following alternative:

> Facts are possibilities inherent in the cognitive structures agents reproduce and transform but never create, with voluntarism, committed in conven-tionalism (and, more radically, in super-idealism), and reification in positiv-ism, forming contrasting and complementary mistakes. Facts are indeed paradigmatic social institutions. They are *real*, in as much as but for them certain determinate states of the physical world, for which our intellectual agency is a necessary condition, could not occur. They are *social*, in as much as, though dependent upon human agency, they are irreducible to a purely individual production. But although all facts are social results, not every social result is a fact: facts are the results of specific cognitive, and more especially empirically grounded, processes of social production. (Bhaskar, p. 49)

If such passages lack the persuasive elegance of Fish's formulations, they none the less knock some sizeable holes in his argument for the socially-constituted nature of *all* knowledges and truth-claims. What Bhaskar terms 'transcendental realism' is shown to be the only set of assumptions on which science makes sense as an activity of jointly theoretical and empirical investigation producing determinate (cognitive) effects in our dealing with the world of natural forces and events. Most importantly, it challenges the notion – advanced by thinkers like Foucault, Feyerabend and Rorty – that science (or knowledge in general) is entirely a product of socialised codes and conventions that set the agenda for debate in various disciplines and cannot be dislodged except by the adoption of some alter-native 'discourse', 'paradigm' or 'final vocabulary'. For this would mean that any such change could only occur through some mysterious shift in the prevailing currency of ideas, and could never come about as the result of genuine criticism, whether prompted by recalcitrant experimental data or by perceived contradictions, blindspots, anomalies, etc. in the theoretical discourse of this or that science. In which case science becomes a wholly meaningless enterprise, lurching from one unaccountable paradigm-shift to the next, and carried on by workers whose differences of view – within or across generations – cannot be rationally assessed since they belong to 'incommensurable' paradigms, interpretative communities, or spheres of knowledge-production.

Bhaskar is surely right in regarding this as a thoroughly implausible picture of the way that scientists proceed or that debate is conducted on questions capable of argued (empirical or theoretical) justification. He makes the point as follows in a passage that again needs quoting at length since it pinpoints the basic fallacy in Fish's and Rorty's line of argument. What is required is a clear distinction between

> (a) the principle of *epistemic relativity*, viz that all beliefs are socially pro-
> duced, so that knowledge is transient and neither truth-values nor criteria of
> rationality exist outside historical time and (b) the doctrine of *judgmental
> relativism*, which maintains that all beliefs are equally valid in the sense that
> there are no rational grounds for preferring one to another. I accept (a), so
> disavowing any form of epistemic absolutism, but reject (b), so upholding
> judgmental rationality against irrationalism . . . Relativists have mistakenly
> inferred (b) from (a), while anti-relativists have wrongly taken the unaccept-
> ability of (b) as a reductio of (a). (Bhaskar, p. 54)

This argument amounts to a two-pronged attack on the various currently fashionable versions of extreme relativist doctrine. It enables Bhaskar to defend both the basic rationality of science as an enterprise aimed toward better, more adequate grounds of judgement, and also the need for critique as a process of reflective understanding that questions 'absolutist' truth-claims by revealing their partial, self-interested, or socially-motivated character. Thus his approach does justice to the manifest achievements of science as a constructive, problem-solving activity whose power to produce real-world effects (or knowledge thereof) could only be doubted by theorists wedded to some version of transcendental solipsism. But it also keeps open the possibility of criticising reified (e.g. positivist) notions of scientific method and truth through an immanent critique of their involvement with socialised structures of knowledge and power.

Bhaskar provides the groundwork of a flexible but strictly non-relativist epistemology which respects the claims of scientific realism while also leaving room for a strong form of Marxist *Ideologiekritik*. On the one hand, as he argues, 'it is because we are material beings, with a position in space and a point of view in time, that a material object language forms the only possible meta-language for science conceived as the study of the enduring and trans-factually efficacious mechanisms of nature' (p. 91). But on the other he acknowledges that science may well become the locus of reified (positivist) truth-claims whose social determinants – or whose ideological character – it is the task of criticism to expose and demystify. In short,

> facts are real, but they are historically specific social realities . . . Fetishism, by naturalizing facts, at once collapses and so destratifies their generative or sustaining social context and the mode of their production, reproduction, and transformation in time, *ipso facto* dehistoricizing and eternalizing them. The fact form then acts so as to obscure, from scientists and non-scientists alike, the historically specific (cognitive and non-cognitive) structures and relations governing sense-experience in science. (Bhaskar, p. 283)

The most important point to grasp here is that the theory which challenges such naïve, pre-critical assumptions is no less 'materialist' than the scientific world-view it sets out to criticise. That is to say, it maintains a strongly argued commitment to the following basic propositions: (1) that there exists a real world of objects, processes and events which science attempts to describe or explain; (2) that this enterprise is subject to varying constraints as imposed, for instance, by current technology, research programs, descriptive frameworks, 'commonsense' habits of perception, etc.; (3) that any item of accredited knowledge may conceivably turn out to be unfounded, erroneous or a product of ideological interests; and (4) that, despite this, the realist argument still holds, since the process of criticising scientific truth-claims can always be extended to include such forms of reified consensus thinking.

Thus there is nothing in the least contradictory about Bhaskar's twin commitment to scientific realism on the one hand, and on the other to a socialised theory of science as always a product of given (knowledge-constitutive) interests and values. As he puts it:

> the fact form is an objective mystification, partly analogous to the value form, generated by the very nature of the activities in which we engage. Thus we represent facts as hard, stubborn, brute, recalcitrant. A considerable mystique accrues spontaneously to this concept. This is alright if the source of the mystique . . . is located firmly in the social structure, where it belongs, and not in the natural world, where positivism, following commonsense, places it. (Bhaskar, p. 282).

So it is not so much a question of ingeniously squaring these two philosophical viewpoints (i.e. scientific realism and *Ideologiekritik*) as of showing that in fact they are mutually supportive; that science requires a systematic reflection on its own socio-historical contexts of emergence; and that the failure to sustain this critical awareness is the source of various illusory or mystified knowledge-effects. In short, there is no reason to conclude – along with Fish, Rorty and other neo-pragmatist thinkers – that truth simply drops out of the picture (or becomes just a piece of redundant conceptual baggage) as soon as one concedes the fact of its involvement with changing historical conditions. What this argument ignores is the close *dialectical* relationship between science as a mode of practical, transformative engagement with real-world objects and events and criticism as a form of reflective understanding that questions any premature or naturalised appeal to the positive self-evidence of scientific truth.

'Such a critique,' Bhaskar writes, 'inasmuch as it casts light on unexpected or recondite sources of determination, facilitates the development of emancipatory practices oriented to emancipated (free) actions' (p.133). This passage of course carries echoes of Habermas, especially those early writings (like *Knowledge and Human Interests*) where he offers a detailed historical genealogy of the process that Bhaskar here describes.[16] That is to say, the chief object of Habermas's work is to explain how science – or the positivist ideology of science – has developed in the service of an instrumental reason that maintains itself precisely through the absence of any critical reflection on its own social role. And at the same time philosophy has followed a path of increasingly self-occupied or specialised concern that leaves it ill-equipped to engage with issues in the practical or scientific sphere. Hence the major tasks of present-day critical theory: to remedy this chronic divergence of interests *firstly* by restoring a critical-reflective dimension to the practices of scientific method, and *secondly* by recalling philosophy to a sense of its involvement with science and other such real-world transformative activities. Only thus, Habermas thinks, can science be enlisted on the side of progressive or 'emancipating' reason, and philosophy rescued from its present marginal status as a discipline lacking all relevance or force in matters of urgent socio-political concern.

Bhaskar sees Aristotle and Marx as the two most significant precursors for this idea of knowledge as the joint application of empirical discovery-procedures and critical reflection on the methods, values and grounding assumptions which characterise scientific discourse at any given time. It is therefore his contention – indeed, the central thesis of his book – that

the special, qualitative kind of becoming-free or liberation which is emancipation, and which consists in the transformation . . . from an unwanted
and unneeded to a wanted and needed source of determination, is both
causally presaged and logically entailed by explanatory theory, but that it can
only be effected *in practice* . . . In this special sense an emancipatory politics
or practice is necessarily both grounded in scientific theory and revolutionary
in objective or intent. (Bhaskar, p. 171)

Like Habermas, Bhaskar is committed to redeeming the 'unfinished project' of modernity, conceived as the potential for emancipating science (or
practical-cognitive interests) from the dominance of a reified means-ends
rationality imposed by narrowly positivist conceptions of knowledge,
method and truth. Where he improves on Habermas's somewhat abstract
and generalised argument is in offering a range of specific examples from
the history of scientific thought, and also – most impressively – deducing
the *conditions of possibility* for each of these cases from a strong
transcendental-realist account of how such episodes occur.

In short, there is no reason to suppose – as Rorty or Fish would have it –
that such arguments have been thoroughly discredited by the
postmodern-pragmatist turn 'against theory' across various present-day
disciplines of thought. What this movement comes down to is a widespread failure of intellectual nerve, coupled with a basic refusal to conceive
how those same disciplines – science, criticism, philosophy, sociology of
knowledge – might yet be related in the common effort to think their way
through and beyond the limits of received consensus-belief. For otherwise,
as he argues, there is simply no accounting for science *either* in its genuinely productive aspect (i.e. its capacity to effect real changes in the lifeworld of practical knowledge) *or* in its mystified, positivist form (where the
resort to absolute grounds and truth-claims can only be revealed as a form
of self-legitimising ideological fiction by treating it from a critical standpoint possessed of its own theoretical principles). Thus 'science is, indeed,
a continuous process; but it is a continuous process with a point: deepen-
ing knowledge of the ever deeper transfactually active mechanisms of
nature' (p. 85). And it is precisely this characteristic feature, in Bhaskar's
view, which 'supplies the most significant reference points for the development of any rational criteriology of scientific knowledge or praxiology of
scientific work', since it offers the only adequate means of relating science
to the wider interests of practical-emancipatory reason.

In one sense this amounts to nothing more than an elaborate restate-
ment of the commonplace assumptions that have always – or at least since
the early-modern period – governed the practice of scientific enquiry. That

is to say, it defends the following basic propositions: (1) that there exists a material world of objects, processes and events which science attempts to understand or predict with maximal accuracy; (2) that any advance in this direction will involve the shedding of illusory truth-claims, prejudices, unexamined suppositions, etc.; (3) that such activity demands a constant testing of theories (or hypotheses) against the evidence provided by various kinds of empirical research; and (4) that this enterprise can itself be subject to critical assessment in terms of both its specialised procedures and its wider (socio-political) accountability. If one then asks the obvious question, that is, why these principles currently require such an elaborate defence, then one need look no further than the arguments advanced by thinkers like Rorty and Fish. For it is their major claim that nothing could possibly count as a reason (or an evidential ground) for abandoning some item of received knowledge backed up by the existing consensus of informed professional belief. Or, to put it more plausibly, any such change could only come about in so far as there already existed a paradigm, a language-game or set of descriptive conventions within which the 'new' way of thinking made sense to a broad enough community of qualified opinion. So there is no question of scientists – or anyone else – coming up against evidence that their theories are basically unsound, or that their findings necessitate some large-scale revision of the paradigm currently in place. Where such shifts do occur it can only be a matter of exchanging one vocabulary for another, a process that may indeed transform the whole range of agreed-upon topics for debate, but which cannot then claim to represent 'reality' in a better, more perspicuous or accurate fashion. For this would be to occupy a standpoint of ultimate truth *outside and above* the various discourses, metaphysical assumptions, research programmes and so forth which effectively decide what shall count as knowledge at any given time. And to think in these terms is to fall straight back into the old epistemological fallacy, the notion that there exists some primordial, truth-telling discipline – whether science, philosophy or theory in general – which could somehow 'cut nature at the joints', or achieve a perfect correspondence between objects and concepts, facts and propositions, or the way things stand in reality and the way they are represented in the well-ordered mind. On the contrary, say Rorty and Fish: once remove such delusive notions of privileged epistemic access and we are left with the simple (though belated) recognition that 'reality' just *is* what we currently make of it in accordance with this or that 'final vocabulary', language-game, or cultural form of life.

So Bhaskar is by no means tilting at windmills when he mounts such a

detailed philosophical case in support of scientific realism. Where the pragmatists go wrong is in equating all talk of 'truth' with the reductive
(positivist) treatment of truth-claims as *either* a matter of empirical self-
evidence, verified through observation-sentences, *or* a purely analytical
relation between synonymous terms ('All men are mortal, Socrates was a
man . . .', etc.) that are otherwise devoid of factual or informative content.
That is to say, they conclude from the failure of this project – and from
various attacks on it like Quine's critique of the analytic/synthetic distinction – that 'truth' itself is a redundant term, or just the product of that old
philosophical desire to separate knowledge (authentic knowledge) from
the currencies of mere belief. Thus Rorty can see no grounds for claiming
that Galileo or Copernicus were in any sense *right* (i.e. justified by the facts
of the case) when they argued against the received idea – backed up by the
authority of Church and State – that the Earth was the centre of the visible
universe and the sun one of its fixed planets.[17] It is just that we have
inherited their way of thinking, along with all its associated models and
metaphors, and are therefore in no position to grasp how things might
have gone had the traditionalist picture won out. That Rorty has gained
such widespread credence for this and similar arguments is a sign of the
influence currently exerted by various forms of extreme cultural-relativist
argument. It is also one good reason why Bhaskar should have devoted
much of his work to defending the claims of scientific realism against
exactly these varieties of sceptical argument. For if indeed it is the case that
positivist conceptions of science run up against intractable problems – like
those noted by Quine – it does not follow at all that scientific truth-claims
must henceforth be regarded as operative fictions, accountable only in
terms of their role within this or that present-day context of belief.

IV

Now Fish sees clearly that these issues in the philosophy of science have a
crucial bearing on wider issues of interpretative validity and warrant. It is
for this reason that he is keen to recruit thinkers like Quine, Putnam and
Kuhn to his side of the argument. After all, the natural sciences are one
domain where there is still – as he would regard it – a strong standing
prejudice in favour of realist or objectivist epistemologies,
correspondence-theories of truth and other such supposedly unworkable
ideas. So if these philosophers have come around to a broadly pragmatist
conception of science then Fish should not have much difficulty

convincing others in the 'softer' disciplines (e.g. jurisprudence, literary criticism, linguistics or sociology) that there is nothing to be gained by harking back to outmoded notions of theoretical rigour, consistency and truth.

However, this argument ignores quite a number of complicating factors. One is the fact that the philosophers he cites – Quine in particular – are far from agreeing that scientific truth-claims come down to a matter of consensus-opinion or what is good in the way of belief. Thus Quine's classic essay 'Two dogmas of empiricism' starts out by attacking the analytic–synthetic distinction as a piece of surplus metaphysical baggage, but then goes on to argue for a naturalised, quasi-behaviourist version that would treat some statements as 'stimulus-analytic' in so far as they evoke an identical response across various language- or culture-specific contexts of usage.[18] Certainly Quine would resist the kind of levelling consensus view that regards science (or the truth-claims of scientific method) as just another voice in what Rorty terms the ongoing cultural 'conversation of mankind'. Putnam represents a more ambivalent case, having shifted ground more than once on the question as to whether philosophy can manage without some form of realist metaphysical commitment.[19] And with Kuhn there is still a large measure of disagreement as to just how far his relativism goes; whether, that is to say, he can really be claimed as an ally by post-structuralists, neo-pragmatists, Foucauldians and others who standardly invoke his name. At any rate there is something rather premature – even disingenuous – about Fish's confidently orthodox assumption that the brightest philosophers on the analytic scene have mostly come round to his own point of view as regards the obsolescence of truth-values, transcendental arguments, realist ontologies and so forth.

But Fish could well afford to concede this point with regard to philosophy of science and still maintain that his argument holds for the interpretative or hermeneutic disciplines. For here – with few exceptions – there is a general agreement that different standards apply; that the reading of texts cannot be a matter of rigorous or demonstrative argument, since it always involves some foregone appeal to meanings, conventions, evaluative judgements, cultural 'forms of life' and other such components of a tacit dimension (or a realm of interpretative 'pre-understanding') that eludes the grasp of determinate truth-claims. The exceptions would include those diverse schools of formalist or structuralist theory – from Aristotle to the present – which have sought to place criticism on a 'scientific' basis by eschewing mere interpretation and instead offering to explain how literature *works* in terms of its various stylistic devices, narrative forms, generic constraints and so forth. But again, it can always be argued by sceptics like Fish that this is inherently a hopeless (because circular) endeavour, a quest for first principles – or explanatory grounds – that only looks plausible so long as one forgets that *all* interpretation takes place in some context of pre-existent values and beliefs.

This applies just as much to other varieties of formalist doctrine, as for instance in the field of jurisprudence, where the time-honoured appeal to 'self-evident' distinctions like that between statute-law and case-law (or determinate judgements and 'hard cases') can also be seen as a handy escape-route from the problems thrown up by every such interpretative act. 'To be sure', Fish writes,

> you can always cite a statute or a piece of the Constitution and declare roundly that you stand on it and will not go beyond it; but, in fact, you will *already* have gone beyond it, if by 'it' you understand a meaning that declares itself and repels interpretation. Meanings only become perspicuous against a background of interpretive assumptions in the absence of which reading or understanding would be impossible. A meaning that seems to leap off the page, propelled by its own self-sufficiency, is a meaning that flows from interpretive assumptions so deeply embedded that they have become invisible. (Fish, p. 358)

In which case it follows – once again – that there is simply no escaping the closed circle of interpretative foreknowledge, since any claim to have achieved such a thing (whether by appealing to theory, principle, statutory warrant or evidential grounds) will always involve a whole range of tacitly agreed-upon communal rules and restraints. The most that these arguments can do – and it is no small benefit, according to Fish – is provide a sense of moral uplift (or radical edge) to positions that would otherwise be forced to acknowledge their own unavoidably rhetorical character. So the booby-prizes divide pretty evenly between high-minded liberals like Dworkin, those who entertain a generous vision of 'law as integrity', or who want to ascend 'from the battleground of power politics to the forum of principle', and those – like the Critical Legal Theorists – who think they can demolish the whole rotten enterprise by pointing out its inbuilt contradictions, aporias, or instances of plain bad faith. In both cases the argument fails because it cannot do otherwise than rehearse strategic moves that have always been allowed for in advance by some existing set of interpretative beliefs.

Now it is clearly no use objecting at this point that Fish's message comes down to a counsel of despair, a recommendation that we simply accept whatever meanings, values or standards of judgement happen to be available within our own community at any given time. For then of course he will come straight back with the standard line of response: (1) that this is just the way things are, like it or not; (2) that any counter-arguments we can muster will always have resort to some more or less familiar suasive rhetoric (in the absence of which they would lack all power to convince); (3) that this makes *absolutely no difference* to the conduct of debate across the various disciplines, since we can carry on arguing exactly as before without the appeal to theory, principles, etc.; and (4) that in any case the resultant picture is not so bleak if one acknowledges the range of rhetorics, professional interests, disciplinary frameworks, or belief-systems that characterise the present-day cultural scene. So there is still plenty of room for significant differences of view on this or that topic just so long as we do not then erect these disputes into a matter of truth *versus* falsehood, science versus ideology, or theory as opposed to the various forms of pre-reflective commonsense belief.

But I think we should be wrong to take comfort from this argument, whatever its undoubted suasive appeal. For despite all the current postmodernist talk of multiplying language-games, opening up discourses, decentring subject-positions and so on it still remains the case that some of those language-games (not others) will exert a hegemonic force, and also – on Fish's view of the matter – that nothing could conceivably count as a reason for critiquing or resisting that force. What Fish will not acknowledge (and what puts him markedly at odds with a thinker like Quine) is the standing possibility that beliefs may change in some drastic or far-reaching way as the result of *discoveries* – not mere shifts of preferential viewpoint, vocabulary, or descriptive paradigm – that come about through empirical or theoretical research, and which create such upheavals in the framework of accredited knowledge as to constitute a genuine 'revolution' of thought for the discipline concerned. That episodes of this kind have indeed occurred in the history of the natural sciences is a fact that should not need documenting here. That there are consequences to be drawn for the philosophy of science – and for philosophy in general – is the burden of Bhaskar's argument, as summarised above. (It is also, contrary to Fish's understanding, what Quine has in mind when he argues that even the most entrenched metaphysical categories – like the analytic/synthetic distinction – might conceivably have to be revised in light of some new development affecting the hitherto unshaken 'foundations' of science and philosophy alike.) But the question remains: is there any equivalent case to be made with regard to those disciplines (like literary criticism) where validity-claims are undoubtedly subject to a much wider range of disagreement? Or, to put it in Fish's preferred idiom: do interpretative conventions go all the way down, thus rendering 'theory' just a species of rhetorical/ psychological back-up for beliefs that are always already in place before the theorist gets to work on them?

It is the Marxists, left-wingers and other dissenting intellectuals who mostly come in for this treatment. Thus Fish cites a passage from Terry Eagleton which supposedly exemplifies the recurrent slide into versions of the old theoreticist delusion.

> After having pointed out (quite correctly) that 'becoming certified . . . as proficient in literary studies is a matter of being able to talk and write in certain ways', he [Eagleton] comments indignantly,'it is this which is being taught, examined and certificated, not what you personally think or believe'. (Fish, p. 236)

To which Fish counters, quite predictably, that such complaints miss the mark since the values they invoke – authenticity, selfhood, 'personal' response – are themselves nothing more (if nothing less) than the upshot of a certain academic training in what *counts* as a properly authentic mode of expression. Behind Eagleton's statement he detects the idea 'that true purposes and genuine beliefs exist apart from social and institutional forms which provide artificial or manufactured motives that are subversive of the real self' (p. 236). And of course this provides yet another knock-down example of Fish's favourite paradox, the fact that 'anti-professionalism' is precisely the means by which literary critics assert their distance – their *professional* distance – from any kind of routine, workaday or service activity. But where Fish treats this as an amiable weakness in other (left-liberal or mildly reformist) thinkers, he seizes on its appearance in Eagleton's text as a symptom of blatant bad faith. 'Indeed, Eagleton's real complaint (although he would hardly acknowledge it) is that the validation of professional activities is "merely" social' (p. 237).

It is hard to deny that he does have a point in picking this quarrel with one of Eagleton's less canny pronouncements. What also needs saying, however, is that the passage occurs in a popularising text where Eagleton comes closer to Fish's line of argument than anywhere else in his work.[20] In fact it is a broadly narrative account of episodes in the history of recent literary theory, leading up to a polemical closing chapter which more or less rejects all the various claims and counter-claims, then argues that we should drop this impossible enterprise and instead view criticism as a branch of applied rhetoric, thus acknowledging both its suasive (or performative) character and its prime function as a mode of ideological discourse. In other words Eagleton pretty much endorses the Fish–Rorty line of neo-pragmatist argument, albeit with different political ends in view. So it is odd that Fish should single out this text – as opposed to one of Eagleton's more avowedly theoretical works – in order to make his standard point. On the other hand the passage is, undeniably, a gift for his debunking purposes, and the irony is compounded if one then goes on to consider just why this should be the case. For it is precisely when Eagleton comes out 'against theory' – when he abandons the high ground of method and argument previously occupied in works like *Criticism and Ideology* (1976) – that one finds him falling back on this voluntarist rhetoric of personal values and beliefs. All of which suggests that the pragmatist escape-route is in fact something more like a blind alley or intellectual dead-end. That is to say, it cannot account for the process of change – for the capacity of criticism to *make a difference* to the way we read texts, assess arguments, or conduct our lives – without invoking some bedrock standard of private authenticity and truth-to-experience. Furthermore, as I shall argue, this applies just as much to Fish's highly circumspect statement of the case as to Eagleton's brief and untypical flirtation with the modish 'against theory' line.

Paul de Man's late writings help to explain what is at stake in this current dispute about the powers and limits of rhetoric. Thus he remarks that 'the resistance to theory . . . which is also a resistance to reading, appears in its most rigorous and theoretically elaborated form among the theoreticians of reading who dominate the contemporary theoretical scene'.[21] One way of grasping de Man's point here is to unpack the various meanings contained in this string of seemingly redundant or pleonastic terms. These critics are still theorists (or 'theoreticians') to the extent that they offer, like Fish, a generalised account of the reading process which in turn links up with speech-act philosophy, hermeneutics and rhetoric in its widest, most inclusive sense. More than that: their work can indeed be called 'rigorous' and 'theoretically elaborated' in so far as it provides a persuasive and – on its own terms at least – a simply *irrefutable* case for believing that theory can never do more than reproduce existing consensus-ideas of what counts as a competent, qualified reading. That is to say, the whole drift of such theories is to show that conventions go all the way down; that meaning is a product of interpretative codes (or moves in the game of reader-response) that define the very nature of literary competence; and therefore that it cannot make sense for theory to reject these conventions in favour of some other, more 'radical' line of approach.

But it is precisely de Man's point that this argument involves a 'resistance to theory' which is also and inseparably a 'resistance to reading', or a means of avoiding those obstacles that rhetoric puts in the way of a straightforward consensus-theory of meaning and truth. For Fish's case will only seem convincing – only carry the kind of knock-down force it is clearly intended to exert – if one accepts his implicit confinement of rhetoric to language in its suasive, performative or strictly non-cognitive aspects. It is by means of this concealed premise, this avoidance of what de Man calls the 'epistemology of tropes' (i.e. rhetoric as a form of immanent critique) that Fish can always show, or persuasively 'prove', how pointless and redundant are the truth-claims of theory. And so it turns out, in de Man's words, that 'the resistance to theory is in fact a resistance to reading, a resistance that is perhaps at its most effective . . . in the methodologies that call themselves theories of reading but nonetheless avoid the function they claim as their object' (*RT*, pp.17–18). For what emerges from a properly rhetorical close-reading is the fact that these two dimensions of rhetoric (the suasive and the cognitive, or the performative and the epistemological) are bound up with each other at every point and cannot be neatly separated out in the fashion that Fish requires. In short – as de Man argues most forcefully in an essay on Pascal – one has to take account of those structures of sense 'which are no less rhetorical and no less at work in literary texts, but which are of the order of persuasion by *proof* rather than persuasion by seduction'.[22] For otherwise there is simply no accounting for the way that texts can and do have a power to resist our most stubborn preconceptions, or to change our minds by not falling in with this or that prevailing consensus-ideology or settled habit of response.

Curiously enough, one can find what looks like a strong statement of exactly this position in the works that Fish wrote before arriving at his current neo-pragmatist standpoint. These books (*Surprised By Sin*, his study of Milton, and its sequel *Self-Consuming Artifacts*) were aimed squarely against the formalist presumption that literary meaning was somehow objectively 'there' in the text, embodied in certain distinctive attributes of form, structure or style.[23] The American New Critics had raised this belief into a matter of doctrinal orthodoxy. For them, the poem was a 'verbal icon', a structure of inwrought 'irony', 'paradox' or other such privileged tropes, and hence sealed off in a realm of timeless aesthetic values indifferent to the mere vicissitudes of reader-response[24] Fish set out to counter this high formalist position by proposing what he called an 'affective stylistics', an account of what happened from moment to moment in the process of interpreting texts, negotiating various problems or obstacles, and sometimes coming up with ingenious solutions in the face of some particular interpretative crux. In the Milton book this approach went along with a claim that the reader was thereby placed in the same situation as characters in the poem like Satan, Adam and Eve, confronted with a series of complex and wholly unpredictable choices which they – characters and readers alike – had to make on the instant and without any guidance from rules or conventions already in place. And with *Self-Consuming Artifacts* – as the title suggests – this approach was extended to various poems and prose-texts which (as Fish read them) could be seen to subvert any notion of autonomous, self-possessed 'form' by bringing the interpreter up against a series of blocks or resistances to easy comprehension, and thus giving rise to a constant quest for new and more adaptable strategies of reading. So on the face of it nothing could be further removed from Fish's later line of argument, his insistence that texts can only be construed in accordance with some pre-existing set of interpretative values and protocols. In fact, he would appear to have swung right over from a position that maximises reader-involvement, unpredictability and *resistance* in the text to one that completely rejects these notions in favour of a blanket consensus-theory where nothing could ever come as a surprise since everything is always known in advance.

But this change of tack will appear less drastic if one recalls what de Man has to say about the effect of any theory that equates rhetoric with language in its purely suasive dimension, and which thus avoids taking cognizance of rhetoric in the other, more unsettling or troublesome sense of that term. For it can then be seen that Fish has not so much renounced his earlier convictions as devised a different model of reader-response, one that is still conceived in *psychological* rather than epistemological terms. That is to say, he has simply switched from a theory that focuses on what goes on 'in' the individual reader to one that takes the whole community of readers (or those properly qualified to judge) as its final court of appeal. In neither case does he leave any room for those tensions that arise – as de Man argues – between rhetoric considered as a mode of persuasion and rhetoric as a form of immanent critique (or an 'epistemology of tropes') that inherently tends to question or problematise those same persuasive effects. Thus, although the early Fish thinks always in terms of resistances, obstacles or blocks – textual features that get in the way of some habitual mode of reading – still these effects are treated psychologically, as conflicts that arise from some local interference of attitudes, mind-sets or reader expectations. In short, there is no question for Fish – early or late – that language might harbour a potential for the kind of disruptive self-critical undoing of its own rhetorical devices that de Man finds everywhere at work in the texts of literature, criticism and philosophy. His theories (both of them) are able to achieve such a high degree of persuasiveness and force precisely because they take no account of this complicating factor in the analysis of language. Hence de Man's observation that

> to empty rhetoric of its epistemological impact is possible only because its tropological, figural functions are being bypassed. It is as if . . . rhetoric could be isolated from the generality that grammar and logic have in common and considered as a mere correlative of an illocutionary power. (*RT*, pp. 18–19)

For the upshot of all such arguments – whether advanced under the banner of reader-response criticism or that of 'interpretative communities' – is to render it strictly unthinkable that language should muster an effective resistance to the workings of suasive ideology.

It might be thought that de Man goes a long way around to make a point that most readers (or those unseduced by fashionable lit. crit. opinion) would accept readily enough. That is to say, there is nothing in the least problematic or counter-intuitive about the notion that texts can put up a resistance to received ways of understanding; that sometimes they will not turn out to mean what we expect according to this or that set of in-place linguistic, cultural, or readerly conventions. The same goes for Bhaskar's elaborate defence of the realist position in philosophy of science, an argument that might seem to make heavy weather of some obvious facts about the nature of scientific enquiry, that is, that it has to do with real-world objects, processes and events that exist independently of the various descriptive or explanatory frameworks by which we attempt to comprehend them. But in both cases the point needs making with considerable detail and refinement on account of the currently widespread drift toward extreme forms of relativist or anti-realist doctrine. And for this reason it is important to grasp what unites the otherwise very different projects of de Man and Bhaskar. They are each committed to a strong version of the following interconnected claims: (1) that truth is not just what we make of it in accordance with prevailing consensus-beliefs; (2) that those beliefs may encounter real obstacles, whether in the form of empirical counter-evidence, theoretical inconsistencies, textual aporias or other such blocks to understanding; (3) that when problems of this kind occur it is due to some determinate error of understanding which can then become an object of further critical enquiry; and (4) that such errors typically arise through the presence of ideological motives or interests that remain obscure – necessarily so – to those who identify truth *tout court* with what is currently 'good in the way of belief'. There is no room here for a detailed account of how these claims are made good in de Man's late essays on the topic of 'aesthetic ideology'.[25] Sufficient to say that they show what is wrong with any simplifed notion of rhetoric – like Fish's – that treats it in purely suasive or performative terms, and which thus takes no account of its power to subvert our more placid, taken-for-granted modes of readerly response.

Fish would of course reject this argument as yet another showing of the old theoreticist delusion. He would claim that deconstruction offers further evidence – if any were needed – of the plain *impossibility* of any such occurrence, given that every reading takes place within a certain horizon of pre-understanding, or (to vary the metaphor) against some background of tacit assumptions which decide in advance what shall count as a competent reading of the text in hand. Thus he cites a passage from Derrida's *Positions* where the project is described in the following terms. To deconstruct a text, Derrida writes,

> is to work through the structured genealogy of its concepts in the most scrupulous and immanent fashion, but at the same time to determine from a certain external perspective that it cannot name or describe what this history may have concealed or excluded, constituting itself as history through this repression in which it has a stake. (cited by Fish, p. 492)

Now on the face of it this passage goes clean against the drift of Fish's argument. If deconstruction really does what it claims to do here – or what de Man likewise claims to show by examining the complex field of tensions that exist between the logical, grammatical and rhetorical aspects of a text – then it is hard to see how such readings could result from the kind of purely circular, self-confirming process that Fish finds everywhere at work. But in fact he sails breezily past this objection by interpreting the passage on his own preferred terms:

> The 'external perspective' is the perspective from which the analyst knows in advance (by virtue of his commitment to the rhetorical or anti-foundationalist worldview) that the coherences presented by a text (and an institution or an economy can in this sense be a text) rests [*sic*] on a contradiction it cannot acknowledge, rests on the suppression of the challengeable

rhetoricity of its own standpoint, a standpoint that offers itself as if it came from nowhere in particular and simply delivered things as they really (i.e., nonperspectivally) are. (Fish, pp. 492–3)

And of course this fits in with the widespread view – widespread at least among literary critics and disabused philosophers like Rorty – that deconstruction works best if we ignore its occasional (misguided) claims to validity or truth, and treat it as just another 'kind of writing', on a level with fiction, poetry, criticism, or the cultural 'conversation of mankind'.[26] It would then be Derrida's signal virtue to have cut philosophy down to size by showing that in fact this was always the case, even (or especially) when 'serious' thinkers – from Plato to Searle – strove to hold those distinctions in place. Deconstruction would figure as a kind of belated ironic revenge, a postmodern 'turn' in the history of thought whereby rhetoric won out over reason, metaphor over concept, sophistics over dialectic, or Gorgias and Protagoras – the earliest heroes in Fish's story – over their old opponents, Socrates and (arguably) Plato. In other words, we should then have come around at last to acknowledging what Fish takes as the bottom line of all interpretative enquiry: that 'truth' is nothing more than an honorific term for beliefs that can muster sufficient rhetorical force to pass themselves off as such. If there is one thing that deconstructionists *cannot* afford to do – at least without inviting the charge of manifest inconsistency – it is to grant their own case a privileged exemption from this otherwise ubiquitous rule.

Or so says Fish, basing his assertion on some carefully selected passages from Derrida and de Man. Thus,

> when de Man approvingly quotes Nietzsche's identification of truth with 'a moving army of metaphors, metonymies and anthropomorphisms', a rhetorical construction whose origin has been (and must be) forgotten, he does not exempt Nietzsche's text from its own corrosive effects. If Nietzsche declares . . . that there is 'no such thing as an unrhetorical, "natural" language', for 'tropes are not something that can be added to or subtracted from language at will', the insight must be extended to that very declaration . . . The 'rhetorical mode', the mode of deconstruction, is a mode of 'endless reflection', since it is 'unable ever to escape from the rhetorical deceit it announces'. (Fish, p. 494)

This sentence offers a handy example, in miniature, of the technique that Fish regularly uses to enlist sundry thinkers on his side of the argument. If one works through the thicket of nested quotations one can see how the key term 'rhetoric' is reduced to a kind of polemical place-filler, an all-purpose slogan that serves to head off any question as to just what de Man might have meant by his own (more ambivalent yet precisely delineated) use of that term. As it functions in his chapters on Nietzsche (*Allegories of Reading*) 'rhetoric' signifies *both* the persuasive or performative aspect of language *and* that other complicating function (what de Man calls the 'epistemology of tropes') which generates resistance to readings based on the persuasive dimension alone.[27] It is by virtue of this double-aspect theory that de Man can argue his case for deconstruction as a powerful resource for the uncovering of ideological errors and illusions. More specifically, it reveals those moments of 'blindness' in the received (canonical) reading of texts where the *materiality* of language is ignored in favour of a premature *phenomenalist* reduction that collapses the ontological difference between language and the realm of natural processes and events.[28] Hence those late essays on Kant, Schiller, Hegel and others where de Man addresses the topic of 'aesthetic ideology' and argues that a certain misreading of crucial passages in Kant has given rise to a whole tradition of dangerously mystified pseudo-organicist thinking. Hence also his insistence – as against critics like Fish – that rhetorical close-reading has more work to do than appears on the levelling consensus-view that equates rhetoric with language in its purely suasive aspect.

What disappears entirely in Fish's treatment of the question – what *must* disappear, given his own rhetorical *parti pris* – is any notion that language could constitute an obstacle to meanings and values imposed upon it in accordance with current interpretative beliefs. But his case will only appear to possess this knock-down force if one accepts the basic premise that reading is *always and everywhere* confined to the hermeneutic circle of tacit foreknowledge. Otherwise it will seem a highly questionable argument, one that starts out from the (indeed self-evident) fact that we do approach texts with certain strong-held beliefs about language, relevance, aesthetic value, authorial intentions, etc., in the absence of which interpretation could not get off the ground, but which then goes on to draw the unwarranted conclusion that reading can do nothing other than confirm those beliefs since they constitute the absolute horizon of intelligibility for each and every act of interpretative grasp. Of course this idea finds plenty of support from thinkers in the modern hermeneutic tradition like Heidegger and Gadamer, as well as those philosophers (Wittgenstein included) who see no way beyond the bottom-line appeal to a rhetoric of 'language-games' or cultural 'forms of life'. It is also the dominant assumption among literary critics in the post-romantic line of descent for whom questions of meaning (or interpretative method) have nothing whatsoever to do with cognitive interests, truth-values, or standards of veridical utterance. One can trace this attitude back to its origins in the history of scriptural hermeneutics, where it first became a matter of urgent necessity to argue that scripture could still be meaningful (i.e. lend itself to the subtleties of textual exegesis) even though scholarship had shown up its manifold anachronisms, conflicting claims, narrative inconsistencies and so forth.[29] When this approach was carried over into the practice of secular criticism it produced the characteristic present-day belief – common to a wide range of schools and methods, from I.A. Richards to the 'old' New Critics and at least some varieties of American deconstruction – that literary language is somehow *sui generis*, unbeholden to commonplace notions of argumentative validity or truth, and exhibiting instead those distinctively aesthetic attributes (ambiguity, irony, paradox) which served to mark it off from other, less rewardingly complex kinds of discourse.

It is precisely this assumption that de Man sets out to challenge in his essays on the topic of aesthetic ideology. That is to say, he argues first that criticism should concern itself with those rhetorical structures which alone offer a hold for detailed textual understanding; second, that such structures are inherently resistant to any clear-cut methodical approach that would reduce them to an orderly taxonomy (or 'grammar') of tropes; and third, that the sources of this inbuilt resistance can only be revealed by an analytic reading alert to the various conflicts and tensions that arise between the logical, grammatical and rhetorical orders of sense. For then it will appear – *contra* Fish – that there is nothing absurd about the analogy between bumping up against recalcitrant facts in the realm of empirical knowledge and bumping up against anomalous details in the reading of familiar texts. Wlad Godzich makes the point with reference to Aristotle in his Editor's Foreword to *The Resistance to Theory*:

[t]he term resistance names a property of matter recognized since antiquity: its perceptibility to touch and inertial resistance to muscular exertion. For Aristotle, *ta physika* are characterized by the resistance they oppose to us and they thus become objects of our cognition: it is by virtue of this resistance that we know them to be outside of ourselves and not illusions foisted upon us by our unreliable sensory apparatus . . . To the extent that theory has cognitive pretensions, resistance is very important to it as a precondition for the theory's cognitive reach into the phenomenal. (*RT*, p. xii)

It is a major part of de Man's argument in these essays that this principle can indeed be extended into the fields of criticism, philosophy, hermeneutics, textual exegesis and the 'human sciences' at large. What enables deconstruction to effect this program is its return to the classical trivium (the distinction between logic, grammar and rhetoric) as a means of revealing how the model comes under strain as soon as one perceives the extent to which rhetoric subverts or complicates the workings of logic and grammar. In other words, rhetoric (or the 'epistemology of tropes') always has this power to unsettle any system based on the presumed equivalence between logic (as the rational 'grammar' of thought), grammar (as the 'logic' of linguistic structures that preserve this same isomorphic relation) and reality as that which grounds this order of perspicuous representation in so far as it exhibits factual states of affairs which already possess an intelligible, structured character. According to the standard model, in short, '[g]rammar stands in the service of logic which, in turn, allows for the passage to the knowledge of the world' (*RT*, p. 14). In which case rhetoric would figure in a strictly ancillary role, tolerable only in so far as it respected the *de jure* priority of logic and grammar, and confined its persuasive strategies to the business of serving or enhancing those functions. To this way of thinking it is a scandal (or simply inconceivable) that rhetoric should trespass onto the epistemological domain and assert its power to disrupt or reconfigure the relation between logic, grammar and the world. For de Man, on the contrary,

> this is the point at which literariness, the use of language that foregrounds the rhetorical . . . intervenes as a decisive but unsettling element which, in a variety of modes and aspects, disrupts the inner balance of the model and, consequently, its outward extension to the nonverbal world as well. (*RT*, p. 14)

We can now see more clearly how Fish's use of 'rhetoric' works to foreclose any real understanding of the ways in which textual close-reading can complicate a given interpretative consensus to the point of overturning its deepest, most cherished assumptions. His aim is to render such occurrences wholly unthinkable by narrowing the term to just one of its senses (i.e. 'rhetoric of persuasion'), and then – by an opposite but complementary movement of thought – extending 'rhetoric' thus redefined to cover the entire field of argument. It is as if – to recall de Man's cryptic sentence – rhetoric could be 'isolated' from logic and grammar, deprived (that is to say) of any possible relation to cognitive or truth-seeking interests, and henceforth treated as a repertoire of purely suasive strategies (or as the 'mere correlative of an illocutionary power'). Thus Fish takes over the trivium model but reverses its classical order of priorities so that rhetoric now becomes a catch-all term, a tactic for rubbishing the truth-claims of theory (whether positive or negative), for discounting all ideas of critical (as opposed to consensus) accountability, and for showing – at least to his own satisfaction – that nothing counts save the power to persuade oneself and others that presently existing beliefs are just fine by presently existing standards.

V

It is a neat trick, carried off by Fish with undeniable brilliance and flair. On occasions it does capture something of the unpredictability, the random (or at any rate highly overdetermined) character of changes in the currency of lit. crit. opinion. This is why Fish is at his best in essays (like the piece here on Milton) which take a fairly extended chapter of reception-history and bring out the sheer variety of viewpoints that have achieved orthodox standing – or widespread acceptance – from one period to the next. Another nice example is his essay on irony ('Short people got no reason to live') where Fish takes his cue from a song by Randy Newman which offered a range of arguments in support of this contention ('small voices, beady little eyes, and the inconvenience of having to pick them up in order to say "hello" ' [Fish, p.180]). A lot of short people were very annoyed by this song, so it seems, and organised protests which succeeded in getting it banned from the airwaves by at least one act of state legislature. At this stage Newman intervened, saying that the song was supposed to be ironic, that he had meant it as a satire on all kinds of prejudice, for example, against women, blacks, Jews, or other marginalised groups, and that his critics had simply failed to take the obvious point. To which Fish responds by asking in what sense such a point could ever be obvious, given the well-documented fact that ironies are always liable to be misconstrued, often rebounding on the well-intentioned author with similar unfortunate results. He then offers various examples from Voltaire, Jane Austen, Swift and others to enforce this argument that irony is never demonstrably 'there' in the text, that it cannot be read off from the 'words on the page' by applying some form of reliable test-procedure, and that the only court of appeal in such arguments is the 'interpretive community' which finally decides which reading makes the best sort of sense.

On the way to this conclusion Fish has some fun with tidy-minded theorists like Wayne Booth who evince a clear sense of unease with the topic. Thus Booth's book *A Rhetoric of Irony* attempts to bring order out of chaos by locating the indubitable 'marks' of ironic intent, and also by distinguishing 'stable' instances (i.e. those that respond to such treatment) from cases where the critic finds himself uncomfortably bereft of reliable signs or indices.[30] But according to Fish this attempt is bound to fail, first because there are no such signs to be read, and second because they are simply not required when interpreters proceed – as they always will – on the strength of some existing consensus-view of what counts as an adequate, persuasive reading. 'For someone like Booth', he writes,

> this state of affairs is distressing since it seems to doom us to an infinite regress of unstable interpretation; but one can just as easily say that it graces us with an endless succession of interpretive certainties, a reassuring sequence in which one set of obvious and indisputable facts gives way to another. (Fish, p. 196)

Fish can thus take it as a strong argument in support of his own neopragmatist case that Booth should appear so anxious about irony – so keen to discover interpretative ground-rules, criteria, textual signposts and so forth – whereas he (Fish) can live quite happily with the absence of all such delusory props. That is to say, these anxieties would simply fall away if critics like Booth would just accept the fact that irony is always a product of interpretation, that it is never a question of discovering features objectively 'there' in the text, but also – the by now familiar twist of argument – that this is (or should be) no cause for concern, since the current consensus gives all that is required in the way of legitimising grounds. Of course there is another, equally powerful convention which demands that interpreters ignore this fact in order that their readings should carry more conviction with members of the relevant intepretative community. Thus it is suddenly 'discovered' – by dint of close-reading, what else? – that Swift's problematical 'Verses on the death of Dr. Swift' are *in fact* shot through with all manner of reflexive ironies, so that the poem no longer looks like a piece of embarrassingly overt self-praise, and becomes yet another striking example of Swift's fierce honesty in confronting his own (as well as other people's) delusions of moral grandeur. But such claims are nothing more than a necessary ruse, a self-protecting gambit by which critics avoid facing up to the facts of interpretative contingency, time and change.

Now in one sense clearly Fish must be right: it is impossible to defend the objectivist case about irony when the record offers so many well-known examples of readers failing to take the point, authors denying (as against the critics) that they meant to be 'ironic' in the first place, or works

– like the Fourth Book of *Gulliver's Travels* – which continue to provoke heated debate between partisans of this or that reading. What is by no means so clear is that these problems will vanish, or at any rate become less pressing, if one just accepts the notion of 'interpretive communities' and gives up the quest for objective meaning and truth. Thus Fish cites a passage from Booth which, in his view, reveals both the cause of anxiety and the pointlessness of trying to assuage that anxiety by invoking such non-existent standards.

> If irony is, as Kierkegaard and the German romantics taught the world, 'absolute infinite negativity', and if, as many believe, the world or universe or creation provides at no point a hard and fast resistance to further ironic corrosion, then all meanings dissolve into one supreme meaning: No meaning. (cited by Fish, p. 183)

Fish sees this as, in effect, a piece of needless melodramatics, a conjuring-up of nihilist demons which only exist in Booth's somewhat fevered imagination. For if irony cannot be made 'stable' or determinate – if it is the product of interpretative moves and conventions which lack any objective characterising marks – this need not mean that we are henceforth plunged into an 'absurd multiverse' (Booth again) where 'all propositions about it are ultimately absurd . . . [and] there is no such thing as a "fundamental violation" of the text' (p. 183). Such dire prophecies will only carry weight with critics still hooked on the old opposition between fixed, univocal meanings on the one hand and last-ditch relativism or cognitive anarchy on the other. But this problem disappears – so Fish would persuade us – if one simply relocates the source of interpretative authority *not* in the 'words on the page' (which after all have no meaning whatsoever in and of themselves) but in the whole ensemble of conventions, values, reading practices, professional standards, etc. which make up the current pluralist consensus. Booth is merely choosing to stake his claim on one such set of assumptions, a doctrine with sufficiently widespread support to give it a certain suasive commonsense appeal. And if other critics (e.g. the deconstructionists) prefer to operate with ideas of romantic irony, *mise-en-abime*, textual undecidability and other such exotic notions, then it is equally the case that those notions can only make sense within a recognised alternative language-game, one with its own preferred rhetoric of crisis, its philosophic mentors, elective prehistory, practised modes of argument and so forth. The one thing that neither party can achieve – Booth or the adepts of romantic irony – is an argument on grounds philosphical or textual that would settle the question once and for all.

As I say, Fish's case is at its strongest when he deals with irony as a paradigm instance of the conflict of interpretations. In fact it is Booth who is notably out on a limb in attempting to pin irony down to a determinate (objective) structure of meaning demonstrably there on the page. But Fish still begs any number of questions in arguing that the problem can be laid to rest through the appeal to rhetoric (or interpretative conventions) as a kind of universal solvent. One only has to read de Man's essays on this subject – in particular 'The rhetoric of temporality'[31] – to see that Booth is not alone in supposing that irony is a tricky, subversive topic; that it creates problems far beyond those envisaged on Fish's rather cosy consensus-view; and furthermore, that these problems are not resolved by any straightforward appeal to meanings and conventions presupposed in the very act of reading. For it is de Man's main point that if we approach such texts with anything like the requisite degree of attentiveness and care then we are compelled to recognise tensions or obstacles that cannot be accounted for by a purely 'performative' reading in Fish's preferred mode. In this respect irony is the most extreme case of that textual 'resistance' which eludes the kind of clear-cut methodical approach essayed by critics like Booth, but which also demands a more rigorous treatment than Fish sees fit to provide. That is to say, it requires that rhetoric be conceived *not only* under the aspect of suasive utterance, but also in terms of that figural dimension (de Man's 'epistemology of tropes') where language is subject to complicating tensions beyond the grasp of any simplified performative model. What is most important to grasp about this process – and what sets it at odds with Fish's understanding of irony – is the fact that it opens a space for language to escape the closed circle of interpretative foreknowledge that otherwise delimits the sphere of intelligible meaning.

In short, the 'resistance to theory' as de Man conceives it should be understood *both* in institutional terms (as a deep-laid mistrust of readings aimed toward forms of rhetorical demystification) *and* as a resistance that theory generates within and against its own more methodical claims. Such is the double burden of these late essays where de Man develops the critique of ideology to a high pitch of subtlety and refinement. The following passage is perhaps the best statement of de Man's case (though it makes few concessions to orthodox ideas of interpretative consistency and truth):

Technically correct rhetorical readings may be boring, monotonous, predictable and unpleasant, but they are irrefutable . . . They are, always in theory, the most elastic theoretical and dialectical model to end all models and they can rightly claim to contain within their own defective selves all the other defective models of reading-avoidance, referential, semiological, grammatical, performative, logical or whatever. They are theory and not theory at the same time, the universal theory of the impossibility of theory . . . Nothing can overcome the resistance to theory since theory is itself this resistance. (*RT*, p. 19)

Taken out of context this passage might be read as a version – albeit a tortuous version – of the argument that Fish deploys against theory at every opportunity. Thus de Man, like Fish, rejects the idea that one could ever come up with a systematic method (or covering-law principle) for explaining what happens in the encounter between reader and text. He is likewise sceptical of theory's claim to provide a generalised rhetoric – or exhaustive taxonomy of tropes and figures – which would then serve as a working basis for the project of a formalist or structuralist poetics. The problem with such theories, according to de Man, is that they always achieve this delusive sense of explanatory grasp by ignoring the specific obstacles that arise in the rhetorical close-reading of texts. They are 'defective models of reading-avoidance' to the extent that they substitute theoretical precepts and principles for the detailed activity of textual exegesis. Again like Fish, de Man sees no prospect of success for methods (e.g. *Rezeptionsaesthetik* or reader-response criticism) that do take some account of this activity, but only in the hope of moving beyond it to establish a firm theoretical groundwork.[32] In each case, he argues, there is a tendency – a motivated drive – to bypass the difficulties of a full-scale rhetorical analysis for the sake of securing some ultimate appeal to meaning, history, aesthetic criteria, readerly competence, or other such reassuring substitute values. What these methods cannot account for is the residue of unresolved tensions or discrepancies that will always emerge through a deconstructive reading alert to the signs of textual resistance.

So one might suppose that de Man comes around to something very like Fish's sceptical attitude with regard to the claims of theory. But this ignores his point that 'performative' approaches – that is, those appealing to speech-act theory or a generalised rhetoric of persuasion – are equally liable to turn into pretexts for the avoidance of reading as a genuine encounter with linguistic complications that cannot be allowed for by any such all-purpose model. It is by way of this ubiquitous strategy that Fish can demonstrate over and again that texts simply *must* turn out to mean what we expect in accordance with this or that set of current interpretative beliefs; that theory is powerless to affect this situation in any way; and that the sophists had it right (or as nearly 'right' as one can get in such matters) when they failed to see the point of all that abstract philosophical talk. I have argued, on the contrary, that Fish gets it wrong – for demonstrable reasons – when he essays this wholesale reduction of truth to what is (currently and provisionally) good in the way of belief. The possibility that texts may resist certain kinds of partial, 'common-sense' or ideologically-motivated reading is one that survives all Fish's attempts to prove otherwise. And this despite de Man's seeming suggestion – in the passage cited above – that theory is always a self-defeating exercise, a perpetual lesson in the unreliability of its own more ambitious, methodical or formalised procedures.

So when he speaks of deconstruction (or rhetorical close-reading) as a practice which tends to undo those procedures – or as 'the universal theory of the impossibility of theory' – it is not with a view to demolishing the whole enterprise. Rather, it is by way of making the point that theory's failures are in some sense *exemplary* failures; that one can only gain a knowledge of rhetorical effects that exceed all the powers of systematic thought by repeatedly encountering the limits of theory in the reading of particular texts. Hence de Man's otherwise incomprehensible claim that 'nothing can overcome the resistance to theory since theory is itself this resistance' (*RT*, p.19). Hence also his assertion – in another late essay – that

> mere reading . . . prior to any theory, is able to transform critical discourse in a way that would appear deeply subversive to those who think of the teaching of literature as a substitute for the teaching of theology, ethics, psychology, or intellectual history (*RT*, p. 24)

What de Man here describes as 'mere reading' is that process of rhetorical demystification which language makes possible *despite and against* the various forms of ideological misrecognition.

For de Man, therefore, literary theory is both an impossible project and one that remains absolutely prerequisite to any critical reflection on the powers and limits of textual understanding. 'Close reading accomplishes this [i.e. the deconstruction of premature systematising models] often in spite of itself because it cannot fail to respond to structures of language which it is the more or less secret aim of literary teaching to keep hidden' (*RT*, p. 24). Among those models – and the one most congenial to interpreters in the mainstream romantic tradition – is the idea that language (especially the language of poetry) partakes of an organic continuity with objects and processes in the natural world, thus collapsing the ontological difference between sensuous intuitions on the one hand and concepts (or signifying structures) on the other. This is where de Man locates the origin of that widespread 'aesthetic ideology' which took hold among post-Kantian idealist philosophers like Schiller, and whose effects are still with us in the various schools of latter-day formalist and reader-response criticism. Thus 'the link between literature (as art), epistemology, and ethics is the burden of aesthetic theory at least since Kant . . . It is because we teach literature as an aesthetic function that we can move so easily from literature to its apparent prolongations in the spheres of self-knowledge, of religion, and of politics' (*RT*, p. 25). To resist this premature conflation of realms is *not* to drive a wedge between literature and politics, or to assert that close reading is somehow incompatible with the interests of *Ideologiekritik*. On the contrary: it amounts to the strongest possible claim for deconstruction as a form of negative dialectics aimed toward uncovering those symptomatic blind spots – notably in the reading of Kant – that have worked to promote a mystified conception of language, history and theory itself. Therefore, as de Man provocatively says, '[t]hose who reproach literary theory for being oblivious to social and historical (that is to say ideological) reality are merely stating their fear at having their own ideological mystifications exposed by the tool they are trying to discredit. They are, in short, very poor readers of Marx's *German Ideology*' (*RT*, p.11).

Nothing could be further from Fish's claim that 'theory' is a wholly redundant activity, one that we indulge for various contingent psychological reasons – to bolster an argument, win out in debate, convince other people of the rightness of our beliefs (or the wrongness of their own), etc. – but which cannot have 'consequences' other than those that are just as well secured by abandoning theory and adopting a straightforward rhetoric of persuasion. For if this were the case then it could not make sense for de Man to speak of a 'resistance' that texts put up despite our inclination to read them in accordance with received ideas of what they have to say. Of course it would beg all the relevant questions to urge that Fish *must* be mistaken since his position amounts to a standing disproof of de Man's whole case for the uses of literary theory. But I think we should be wrong to treat this as an ultimate stand-off, a situation where both arguments work on their own preferred terms of debate and there is no possibility of settling the issue between them. What enables us to avoid this depressing conclusion is the sheer cogency of de Man's readings, the fact – as he puts it in the above-cited passage – that rhetorical exegeses in the deconstructive mode 'may be boring, monotonous, predictable and unpleasant, but they are irrefutable' (*RT*, p.19).

The question then arises as to how one can reconcile this talk of routine predictability with the claim that deconstruction makes *discoveries* – often startling, even counter-intuitive discoveries – about the structures of signification at work in various kinds of text. It is a case that I have argued at length elsewhere, but the elements of which may perhaps be grasped through de Man's reading of Kant, as mentioned above.[33] That this reading goes strongly against the consensus of mainstream Kantian scholarship is evident enough from various bewildered (and more or less hostile) responses, tending to evoke the composite figure 'de Mannuel Kant' in order to dismiss what they take to be this strange and perverse misconstrual of the *Third Critique*. Other commentators – Rodolphe Gasché among them – register the strangeness while also acknowledging that de Man's account has a rigour and a quality of sustained argumentative power which make it all the more disconcerting.[34] That is to say, he seizes upon details of the text – rhetorical figures like hypotyposis – which are standardly ignored, or treated as marginal to the interests of 'serious' philosophical enquiry. But the upshot of these essays, as Gasché rather fretfully concedes, is to focus one's attention on those problematic details in the Kantian text which make it simply *impossible* to continue in the self-assured belief that no such problems exist, or that they need not concern anyone except bother-headed literary theorists like de Man.

So 'technically correct rhetorical readings' may indeed be 'predictable' (even 'boringly' so) to the extent that they result from a regular pattern of interference between habits of readerly expectation and structures of language that turn out to resist those same expectations. But this does not mean that such readings are predictable in the sense that one could ever know in advance – or easily guess – what specific complications are bound to arise in the deconstructive reading of individual texts. It is the same point that Godzich makes when he compares de Man's rhetoric of textual 'resistance' with the Aristotelian definition of matter as that which, on occasion, withstands or obstructs our pre-existing habits of thought.[35] This is why de Man can claim to have discovered certain discrepant, anomalous features of the Kantian text that go clean against the consensus reading accepted not only by most philosophers but also by mainstream scholars of literary Romanticism (like M.H. Abrams and Earl Wasserman) who tend to reproduce that same reading.[36] In both cases there is a failure to perceive those deep-laid linguistic tensions — as between the literal and figural, the constative and the performative, or the grammatical and rhetorical structures of sense – that make it strictly impossible to maintain the orthodox interpretative stance. In short, aesthetic theory has not yet succeeded in 'its admirable ambition to unite cognition, desire and morality in one single synthetic judgment' (*RT*, p. 25). Nor can it thus succeed, according to de Man, unless one counts 'success' – in pragmatist terms – as the ability to impose its preconceived values and assumptions through a process of canonical self-authorisation inherently blind to certain crucial details of the Kantian text. 'Whether a reading of the *Critique of Judgment*, as distinct from its simplified version in Schiller and his offspring, would confirm this assertion [i.e. the synthesising power of the aesthetic] certainly stands in need of careful examination' (p. 25). And one effect of such detailed scrutiny, so de Man argues, would be to expose not only the inadequacy of readings that take this power for granted, but also the very real dangers – moral, social and political dangers – that result from the extension of aesthetic values into other realms of thought.

From what we know of his ill-famed writings in Belgium during World War II, as well as from the evidence of these (vastly more sophisticated) late essays, it is clear that de Man was not inclined to underestimate the harmfulness of aesthetic ideology as a source of mystified communal values.[37] Indeed, the 'resistance' that de Man locates in language – or the tensions he discovers between rhetoric in its suasive and its cognitive aspect – offer the only means, as he later came to think, for criticism to shield itself against just those forms of delusive rhetorical appeal. (Of course the word assumes a yet more complex and ironic charge if one considers the context of de Man's wartime writings and the current debate as to whether they suggest any possible, albeit covert alignment with the Belgian resistance movement.)[38] But my purpose here is not to comment further on this already well-publicised chapter in de Man's life-history. What is more to the point is his subsequent determined refusal to allow that language lends itself passively to effects of ideological indoctrination or mystified value-laden rhetoric. And this refusal is nowhere more evident than in de Man's steadfast opposition to readings of Kant that privilege aesthetic judgement as a synthesising power, a faculty that somehow transcends, unites or reconciles the various orders of thought and perception. As he puts it:

> literary theory raises the unavoidable question whether aesthetic values can
> be compatible with the linguistic structures that make up the entities from

which those values are derived . . . What is established is that their compatibility, or lack of it, has to remain an open question and that the manner in which the teaching of literature, since the later nineteenth century, has foreclosed the question is unsound, even if motivated by the best of intentions. (*RT*, p. 25)

Hence the quite extraordinary sense of urgency and tension that inhabits these avowedly 'technical' essays in the applied rhetoric of reading. For it is de Man's argument that only by revealing this resistance to premature totalising creeds – to 'aesthetic ideology' in its manifold forms – can criticism avoid the seductive appeal of organicist models and metaphors.

VI

I have suggested three main grounds of philosophical dissent from Fish's blanket case 'against theory' and all its works. One is the strong scientific-realistic standpoint, as developed by Bhaskar from his starting-point in Kant and the critique of idealist or speculative reason. The second – following directly from this – is the argument for a Marxist account of knowledge-constitutive motives and interests which would examine the specific *ideological* formations (e.g. positivism) that achieve the status of self-evident truth within this or that interpretative community. Clearly these first two positions are interdependent to the extent that any realist ontology presupposes the capacity to discriminate valid from false (or ideological) modes of understanding, while any version of Marxist *Ideologiekritik* will likewise involve the supposition that truth-claims are not just a matter – as Fish would have it – of currently accepted values and interests. At this point he (Fish) will of course turn the argument around and observe that both parties, Marxists and scientific realists alike, have nothing more to fall back on than their own preferred set of rhetorical strategies and in-place consensus-beliefs. But we need not be over-impressed by such arguments if they fail to give any satisfactory account of how change comes about in various disciplines through the process of critical self-examination and the encounter with resistant or problematic cases. Whence, as I have argued, the pertinence of deconstruction – or de Man's counter-canonical 'allegories of reading' – as proof that criticism need not be confined to the hermeneutic circle of tacit foreknowledge, but may sometimes discover textual complications which in turn give rise to unpredictable changes in the sense of what counts as an adequate interpretative grasp.

That Fish sees no great problem here is evident from the following passage, intended to meet precisely such objections by shifting them back on to his own rhetorical ground. An interpretative community, he writes,

> rather than being an object of which one might ask 'how does it change?' is an engine of change. It is an engine of change because its assumptions are not a mechanism for shutting the world out but for organizing it, for seeing phenomena as already related to the interests and goals that make the community what it is. The community, in other words, is always engaged in doing work, the work of transforming the landscape into material for its own project; but that project is then itself transformed by the very work it does. (Fish, p. 150)

But this response merely begs the obvious question: if the agenda for change is already laid down by some pre-existing set of communal 'interests and goals', then the notion becomes strictly tautologous, or devoid of any genuine (descriptive or explanatory) power. For there is another, hidden agenda to be glimpsed behind Fish's non-consequentialist arguments, one that surfaces on occasions like this despite his repeated declarations that it *would not make the least bit of difference* if we all followed his sensible advice and gave up 'doing theory' forthwith. The difference it would make is the crucial difference between taking beliefs on trust and subjecting those beliefs to the kinds of criticism that the various disciplines – 'sciences' and 'humanities' – have evolved for the purpose of distinguishing truth from falsehood, or for separating valid from invalid orders of argument, reasoning, or interpretative method. The idea of hermeneutics (or textual comprehension) as the paradigm case of knowledge in general is one that has lately done a good deal of harm through its suggestion that all truth-claims come down to a level of constitutive pre-understanding, such that no encounter with discrepant details could escape the inherent circularity of knower and known. What we had much better do is reverse this order of assumptions and acknowledge – like de Man – that 'reading is an epistemological event prior to being an ethical or aesthetic value'. Or again, as he puts in the same essay:

> what makes a reading more or less true is simply the predictability, the necessity of its occurrence, regardless of the reader or of the author's wishes . . . It depends, in other words, on the rigor of the reading as argument. Reading is an argument . . . because it has to go against the grain of what one would want to happen in the name of what has to happen. . .[39]

Fish's essays only manage to exert such persuasive force because we – that

is to say, us literary critics, his target 'community' of like-minded readers –
can mostly be relied upon to accept the idea that meaning is a product of
consensus-belief, that truth (or validity) is beside the point in issues of
interpretative judgement, that there is no appeal to standards of right
reading, argumentative rigour, etc. This belief has taken hold very largely
as a result of that potent 'aesthetic ideology' whose origins de Man locates
in the widespread misreading of crucial passages in Kant's *Third Critique*.
It is virtually an item of faith among modern literary critics, with the
exception of those – like William Empson in his sadly neglected book *The
Structure of Complex Words*[40] – who resist the equation of aesthetic value
with a range of privileged rhetorical tropes (irony, paradox, ambiguity)
presumed to raise poetry into a realm apart from the requirements of
logical consistency and truth. The American New Critics were among the
most orthodox in this regard, treating poetry as an utterly distinctive kind
of language, hedged about with various doctrinal sanctions amounting to
a form of wholesale aesthetic ideology.[41] But there was – de Man reminds
us – another aspect to this 'old' New Critical programme, one that
emphasised the virtue or necessity of rhetorical close-reading, even to the
point where such reading subverted its own more doctrinaire claims. In
this way it revealed what de Man takes to be the single most important
truth about literature as a mode of un-self-deceiving reflection on the
powers and limits of aesthetic judgement.

> Attention to the philological or rhetorical devices of language is not the
> same as aesthetic appreciation, although the latter can be a way of access to
> the former. Perhaps the most difficult thing for students and teachers of
> literature to realise is that their appreciation is measured by the analytical
> rigor of their own discourse about literature, a criterion that is not primarily
> or exclusively aesthetic. Yet it separates the sheep from the goats, the con-
> sumers from the *professors* of literature, the chit-chat of evaluation from
> actual perception. (*RT*, p. 24)

One way of reading this passage is to find it pretty much in agreement with
Fish as regards the professionalised character of literary studies and the
appeal to standards of competence which happen to prevail in this or that
'interpretive community'. De Man's favoured talk of 'analytical rigor' and
'actual perception' would then appear just a species of enabling rhetoric, a
useful device for securing assent to propositions which only carry weight in
so far as they invoke some given (in this case deconstructionist) set of
values and beliefs. The question is whether such a reading is borne out by
what occurs – 'actually' occurs, as de Man would have it – in those essays

where his argument is put to the test of detailed rhetorical analysis. For it is here, if anywhere, that literary theory turns out to resist the kind of wholesale neo-pragmatist view of language and truth that Fish has raised to such a high point of sophistical refinement.

It is, one might think, a very curious feature of the current intellectual scene that these questions should receive their most intensive treatment at the hands of literary theorists. One reason emerges clearly enough from Fish's repeated line of argument: that interpretation goes 'all the way down', in which case other disciplines – philosophy, law, ethics, linguistics, historiography, theory of science, etc. – yield up their erstwhile privileged claims and stand revealed as so many equal partners in the ongoing cultural conversation. It is the same idea that gives rise to talk of the 'linguistic turn', the 'hermeneutic circle' and other such forms of anti-foundationalist thinking whose appeal is currently widespread across all those disciplines. To which one might add the 'postmodern' diagnosis essayed by fashionable thinkers like Lyotard and Baudrillard,[42] along with those philosophers (Rorty chief among them) who adopt a broadly similar line. This is the idea that we are witnessing a break with all 'enlightened' meta-narrative schemas, or a collapse of those outmoded binary distinctions (truth/falsehood, science/ideology, real/imaginary, history/fiction) that once made sense – or enjoyed a large measure of credence – among progressive intellectuals, social reformers, left-wing ideologues and the like. What should now be apparent, so these thinkers urge, is the total obsolescence of all such (in any case illusory) values, and the fact that 'reality' is defined through and through by the various belief-systems, cultural codes, media images, opinion polls, advertising slogans and so forth that make up the lifeworld of late twentieth-century culture. And so it comes about that literary theory – hitherto something of a cinderella among the disciplines – now begins to look like the only one capable of coping with this new situation. For if philosophy, history and the others all turn out to be so many fictive or rhetorical constructs, then clearly there is a sense in which literary criticism provides the best, least deluded means of address to the problems thrown up by our present 'postmodern' condition. In which case nothing could be more misguided – or more out of key with the spirit of the times – than de Man's (and my own) uphill attempts to redeem the values of truth and critique from the currency of postmodern-pragmatist thought.

It is against this background of ideas – taken as a matter of informed consensus belief – that Fish can carry off his ingenious series of rhetorical sleights of hand. I have argued that in fact they possess nothing like the kind of knock-down demonstrative force that Fish standardly attributes to them. More specifically, they represent the triumph of rhetoric only in so far as that term is narrowed down and subject to stipulative limits in accordance with Fish's polemical purpose. That is to say, 'rhetoric' is equated *tout court* with what de Man calls 'rhetoric of persuasion', and is thus taken to exclude any further enquiry into the sources of rhetorical mystification, the grounds of valid argument (in literary theory as in other disciplines) and the capacity of criticism to think its way through and beyond the untruths, errors and prejudices that characterise our (always partial) state of present understanding. As Fish sees it, 'another word for anti-foundationalism *is* rhetoric, and one could say without too much exaggeration that modern anti-foundationalism is old sophism writ large' (p. 347). But one could just as well argue that this way of putting things amounts, yet again, to a wilful narrowing of the options and a fixed resolve to exclude any alternative view. Bhaskar's arguments in defence of scientific realism provide evidence enough that philosophy can take full measure of the anti-foundationalist case without giving up its claims to consistency and truth. They also demonstrate, contrary to Fish's way of thinking, that these claims can be upheld alongside the commitment to a version of Marxist *Ideologiekritik* (or applied sociology of knowledge) which questions science – or theory in general – with regard to its knowledge-constitutive interests. And one form that such criticism may take is that of deconstruction, or rhetorical analysis in something other – more consequent and rigorous – than anything allowed for in Fish's understanding of the term.

This is no doubt what de Man has in mind with his comment that 'to empty rhetoric of its epistemological impact is possible only because its tropological, figural functions are being bypassed' (*RT*, pp. 18–19). For he then goes on to elaborate the point precisely in connection with Fish's claim that rhetorical criticism begins and ends with the accounting for language in its purely persuasive aspect. Thus 'the equation of rhetoric with psychology rather than epistemology opens up dreary prospects of pragmatic banality, all the drearier if compared with the brilliance of the performative anlaysis' (p. 19). And indeed it is true that Fish's essays are brilliant set-piece examples of the pragmatist move to assimilate theory (or criticism in general) to a mode of persuasive utterance devoid of epistemological truth-claims. Fish is certainly the cleverest sophist around, or the thinker who has most successfully revived that strain of all-purpose rhetorical professionalism that Socrates considered such a scandalous affair. Nobody could honestly claim that these essays bear out de Man's

Stanley Fish and the rhetoric of assent

description of the 'dreary prospects of pragmatic banality' threatened by readings that assimilate rhetoric to a straightforward persuasive or performative model. But the question remains as to whether such readings are indeed – as Fish would have it – strategically proof against the kinds of counter-argument, 'positive' or 'negative', offered by theorists like Bhaskar and de Man. It seems to me that Fish's essays achieve their rhetorical effect only in so far as they evade this question by treating the 'end-of-theory' thesis as a matter of established consensus belief, and thus as presumptively immune from any further challenge or critique. It is a neat bag of tricks, one has to admit, but hardly a reason to give up on the quest for more adequate, truthful, or intelligent ways of understanding.

'Theory's day is dying; the hour is late; and the only thing left for a theorist to do is say so, which is what I have been saying here, and, I think, not a moment too soon' (Fish, p. 341). If wishing (or urging) could make it so then these pronouncements could scarcely fail of their intended perlocutionary effect. That is to say, Fish's book would mark the end not only of literary theory but of philosophy, ethics, political science, sociology of knowledge, historiography and every other discipline that presumes to offer reasons for not just 'doing what comes naturally', that is, going along with accepted, commonsense, or unreflective habits of thought. Which would of course be no bad thing, according to Fish, since those habits – like it or not – are where we always start out from and always finish up, whatever our convictions to the contrary. But one may, as I have argued, take leave to doubt both the benefits promised and the tactics deployed in pursuit of this foregone conclusion. For theory is united with common-sense on one point at least: that the human mind may have to labour against all sorts of stubborn prejudice or erroneous belief, but that it does – on occasion – make genuine discoveries which (to vary Fish's favourite line of baseball metaphor) knock all its expectations for six. Any argument that does not take account of this fact is sure to be a non-starter, whatever its degree of rhetorical ingenuity.

Notes

1. Stanley Fish, *Is There A Text In This Class? The authority of interpretive communities* (Cambridge, Mass.: Harvard University Press, 1980).
2. E.D. Hirsch, *Validity In Interpretation* (New Haven: Yale University Press, 1967).
3. See for instance Ronald Dworkin, *Law's Empire* (London: Fontana, 1987).

4. See especially the essays collected in Paul de Man, *The Resistance to Theory* (Minneapolis: University of Minnesota Press, 1986).

5. Steven Knapp and Walter Benn Michaels, 'Against theory', in W.J.T. Mitchell (ed.), *Against Theory: literary theory and the new pragmatism* (Chicago: University of Chicago Press, 1985), pp. 11–30.

6. Stanley Fish, *Surprised By Sin* (New York: Macmillan & Co., 1967).

7. Raymond B. Waddington, 'The death of Adam: vision and voice in Books XI and XII of *Paradise Lost*', *Modern Philology*, vol. 70 (1972), pp. 9–21.

8. For further discussion of Fish's case against the Critical Legal Studies movement, see Norris, 'Law, deconstruction, and the resistance to theory', *Journal of Law and Society*, vol. 15, no. 2 (1988), pp. 166–87.

9. Ruth Kempson, *Presupposition and the Delimitation of Semantics* (Cambridge: CUP, 1975).

10. See for instance Noam Chomsky, *Language And Responsibility* (Hemel Hempstead: Harvester Wheatsheaf, 1979).

11. See Richard Rorty, *Philosophy and the Mirror of Nature* (Princeton, NJ: Princeton University Press, 1979); *Consequences Of Pragmatism* (Mineapolis: University of Minnesota Press, 1982); *Irony, Contingency, Solidarity* (Cambridge: CUP, 1989).

12. See especially W.V. Quine, 'Two dogmas of Empiricism', in *From A Logical Point Of View* (Cambridge, Mass.: Harvard University Press, 1953), pp. 20–46.

13. See for instance Michel Foucault, *Language, Counter-Memory, Practice*, trans. and ed. Donald F. Bouchard and Sherry Simon (Ithaca, NY.: Cornell University Press, 1977).

14. Hans-Georg Gadamer, *Truth And Method*, trans. Garrett Barden and John Cumming (London: Sheed & Ward, 1975).

15. Roy Bhaskar, *Scientific Realism and Human Emancipation* (London: Verso, 1986). All further references given by 'Bhaskar' and page-number in the text.

16. Jürgen Habermas, *Knowledge And Human Interests*, trans. Jeremy J. Shapiro (London: Heinemann, 1972).

17. Rorty, *Philosophy and the Mirror of Nature* (*op. cit.*).

18. Quine, 'Two dogmas of Empiricism' (*op. cit.*).

19. See for instance Hilary Putnam, *Reason, Truth And History* (Cambridge: CUP, 1981) and *Realism And Reason* (Cambridge: CUP, 1983).

20. Terry Eagleton, *Literary Theory: an introduction* (Oxford: Basil Blackwell, 1983).

21. Paul de Man, *The Resistance to Theory* (*op. cit.*), pp. 17–18. All further references given by *RT* and page-number in the text.

22. Paul de Man, 'Pascal's allegory of persuasion', in Stephen J. Greenblatt (ed.), *Allegory And Representation* (Baltimore: Johns Hopkins University Press, 1981), pp. 1–25; p. 23.

23. Stanley Fish, *Surprised By Sin* (*op. cit.*) and *Self-Consuming Artifacts* (Berkeley: University of California Press, 1972).

24. See for instance W.K. Wimsatt, *The Verbal Icon: studies in the meaning of poetry* (Lexington, Ky.: University of Kentucky Press, 1954) and Cleanth Brooks, *The Well-Wrought Urn* (New York: Harcourt Brace, 1947).

25. See especially Paul de Man, 'Phenomenality and materiality in Kant', in Gary Shapiro and Alan Sica (eds.), *Hermeneutics: Questions and Prospects* (Amherst: University of Massachusetts Press, 1984), pp. 121–44. See also de Man, 'Sign and symbol in Hegel's *Aesthetics*', *Critical Inquiry*, vol. 8, no. 4 (1982), pp. 761–75.
26. Richard Rorty, 'Philosophy as a kind of writing', in *Consequences Of Pragmatism* (*op. cit.*), pp. 89–109.
27. See de Man, *Allegories Of Reading: figural language in Rousseau, Rilke, Nietzsche, and Proust* (New Haven: Yale University Press, 1979).
28. de Man, 'Phenomenality and materiality in Kant' (*op. cit.*).
29. On this topic, see for instance Frank Kermode, *The Genesis of Secrecy* (Cambridge, Mass.: Harvard University Press, 1979).
30. Wayne Booth, *A Rhetoric of Irony* (Chicago and London: Chicago University Press, 1974).
31. de Man, 'The rhetoric of temporality', in *Blindness And Insight: essays in the rhetoric of contemporary criticism* (London: Methuen, 1983), pp. 187–228.
32. See de Man, 'Reading and history', in *The Resistance to Theory* (*op. cit.*), pp. 54–72.
33. De Man, 'Phenomenality and materiality in Kant' (*op. cit.*).
34. Rodolphe Gasché, 'In-Difference to philosophy: de Man on Kant, Hegel, and Nietzsche', in Lindsey Waters and Wlad Godzich (eds.), *Reading de Man Reading* (Minneapolis: University of Minnesota Press, 1989), pp. 259–94.
35. See Godzich, Introduction to *The Resistance to Theory* (*op. cit.*).
36. See de Man's discussion of these and other scholar-critics of Romanticism in 'The Rhetoric of Temporality' (*op. cit.*).
37. See de Man, *Wartime Writings* (Lincoln, Nebr.: University of Nebraska Press, 1988); also Werner Hamacher, Neil Hertz and Thomas Keenan (eds.), *Responses: on Paul de Man's wartime journalism* (Nebraska, 1989) and Christopher Norris, *Paul de Man: deconstruction and the critique of aesthetic ideology* (New York and London: Routledge, 1988).
38. See Jacques Derrida, 'Like the sound of the sea deep within a shell: Paul de Man's war', *Critical Inquiry*, vol. 14, no. 3 (1988), pp. 590–652.
39. De Man, Foreword to Carol Jacobs, *The Dissimulating Harmony* (Baltimore: Johns Hopkins University Press, 1978), pp. vii–xiii; p. xi.
40. William Empson, *The Structure of Complex Words* (London: Chatto & Windus, 1951).
41. See for instance Wimsatt, *The Verbal Icon* (*op. cit.*).
42. For useful introductory material, see Mark Poster (ed.), *Baudrillard: selected writings* (Cambridge: Polity, 1988) and Andrew Benjamin (ed.), *A Lyotard Reader* (Oxford: Basil Blackwell, 1989).

Chapter 3

Limited Think:
How not to read Derrida

I

I am in sympathy with John Ellis's book *Against Deconstruction** on several counts, not least his insistence that deconstruction – or those who speak in its name – be held accountable to the standards of logical rigour, argumentative consistency and truth. He is also perfectly right to maintain that such ideas need testing through a process of genuine and open intellectual debate; that deconstructionists are failing this test if they resort to a notion of open-ended textual 'freeplay' or all-purpose rhetorical 'undecidability'; and furthermore, that one simply cannot make sense of arguments that claim allegiance to a different, alternative or uniquely 'Derridean' kind of logic whose terms they are then unable to specify with any degree of exactitude. Of course it is absurd – and Ellis has a keen eye for such moments in the secondary literature – for critics to raise obscurity to a high point of principle, so that anyone who writes about deconstruction with a measure of lucidity and intellectual grasp will most likely be attacked for 'taming radical new ideas', or for deploying 'the conceptual tools of conservatism'. It is equally absurd (a palpable hit for Ellis) when one comes across the argument that deconstructionist logic has to be distinguished from the 'old' (binary) logic, a distinction that could only be maintained – as he remarks – by falling back into that same old habit of thought.

Nor would I reject out of hand his complaint about the tendency of *some* deconstructionists, when answering hostile criticism, to protest that

* John M. Ellis, *Against Deconstruction* (Princeton, New Jersey: Princeton University Press, 1989). All references to this work are given by page number only in the text.

their opponents have not read all the texts in question – a fairly massive undertaking in Derrida's case – or that they have read them in a wrong, that is, hostile or anti-deconstructionist spirit, thus forgoing any claim to have really understood what those texts are all about. Ellis makes this point by way of a comparison with Wittgenstein's much-discussed 'private language' argument. As he remarks:

> in the unlikely event that anyone were to insist that only those who were sympathetic to Wittgenstein, or who set their analysis of this one issue in the context of a comprehensive treatment of the entire corpus of his thought, could be regarded as a serious contributor to the debate, the result would be derisive laughter. (pp. viii–ix)

And the reason for this, in Ellis's view, is that any theory, philosophical position or argument worth the name will be capable of accurate statement in a form that can then be judged on its merit by anyone who has taken the trouble to understand it, and not just by those – the born-again converts – who have read absolutely everything and done so, moreover, in a spirit of unquestioning acceptance. For otherwise, he protests, there is simply no room for informed rational debate on matters that should not be confined to a circle of like-minded adepts and initiates.

Least of all should we accept their claim that any critique of deconstruction presuming to summarise Derrida's arguments – to explain what they amount to in words other than his own – is necessarily to this extent 'reductive' and distorting, and therefore (once again) scarcely worth the attention of those already in the know. As Ellis says, '[i]t is one thing to make the *general* point that two different sets of terms cannot always be assumed to be functionally equivalent in a given context; it is quite another thing to face the issue in the *specific* way demanded by a particular situation' (p.145). Most often, he finds, the deconstructionists take refuge in a wholesale appeal to the incommensurability thesis while failing to provide any material evidence that this or that passage has been misconstrued, taken out of context, or subjected to some other form of wilful hermeneutic violence. For this latter charge to stick, 'it would be necessary to argue against the change of terms by showing that in this particular case the substitute terms are functionally quite different, and thus that the *substance* of the argument had been changed by the substitution' (p.145). And in the absence of such cases we should not be too impressed by attempts to shift the burden of proof by denying that texts have any 'substance' (i.e. any content of determinable meanings, truth-claims, propositional entailments and so forth) as apart from the endless 'freeplay' of unanchored signification. In fact, as Ellis notes, there is another fairly obvious logical problem here, since if these critics are right (whatever that could mean) – if texts are indeed open to any number of readings with no possible appeal to standards of validity or truth – then they can hardly complain that opponents have got them wrong, or that attacks on deconstruction amount to nothing more than a species of reductive travesty.

Up to this point I can still muster some sympathy with Ellis's style of brisk no-nonsense riposte. That is to say, I would agree that any worthwhile debate on such issues must involve some appeal to substantive ideas of what counts as an adequate, rational, good-faith, or competent address to the topic in hand. There is absolutely no reason why deconstruction should be exempted from respecting these standards of argumentative validity, even if – as its exponents often remind us – the appeal to such standards can become a pretext for adhering to the straightforward, canonical sense of things and ignoring any textual complications that get in its way. But again, these arguments must lose all their force if applied at a level of blanket generality where *all* texts supposedly self-deconstruct once read with an eye to their rhetorical blind spots, or where *every* such reading leads up to the point of an utterly predictable *mise-en-abîme*. 'In theoretical discourse', Ellis writes, 'argument is met by argument; one careful attempt to analyze and elucidate the basis of a critical concept or position is met by an equally exacting and penetrating scrutiny of its own inner logic' (p. 159). And this applies just as much to literary criticism (where traditionally matters of rhetoric and style have played a prominent role) as to other disciplines, like philosophy and intellectual history, where they have not – up to now – been thought of as deserving such detailed or meticulous attention. What Ellis hopes to show – and it is a point worth making – is that all these efforts will be thrown away if they amount to nothing more than a routine insistence on the infinite 'deferral' of meaning, the arbitrary character of interpretative constraints, or the absence of a 'transcendental signified' that would limit the otherwise boundless 'freeplay' of textual signification. This is where Ellis locates the main weakness of deconstructionist criticism: in its tendency to jump clean over 'from one extreme (meaning is a matter of fixed, immutable concepts) to the other (meaning is a matter of the indeterminate, infinite play of signs)' (p. 66). In the process, he argues, it abandons every last claim to discriminate valid from invalid arguments, or to offer any principled case in support of its own declared position.

So the real question here – the main point at issue between Ellis and the

Derridean camp-followers – has to do with the status of theory itself as a constructive and properly accountable discipline of thought. More specifically, it concerns the extent to which ideas, arguments and truth-claims may be judged as achieving (or as failing to achieve) a degree of conceptual autonomy, such that they would not be subject to the vagaries of 'free-play', 'dissemination', 'iterability' and the various cognate terms of Derridean-textualist thought. Ellis sees no reason to equivocate here: clarity and conceptual rigour are the prime virtues in every field of intellectual endeavour, and if deconstruction turns out to lack those virtues – or makes a point of flouting them at every opportunity – then so much the worse for deconstruction. Theoretical argument must therefore 'proceed with great care . . . it must be above all a careful, patient, analytical process: its strengths must lie in precision of formulation, in well-drawn distinctions, in carefully delineated concepts' (pp. 158–9). Hence Ellis's principled objection to what he takes as the standard deconstructionist response when confronted with any such argument. This is the idea that 'textuality' goes all the way down, that language (including the language of philosophy or theory) is metaphorical through and through, and – following Nietzsche – that 'concept' is merely an honorific usage, a name we attach to those privileged philosophemes whose figural origin has now been forgotten through a process of erasure or selective oblivion.[1] On this account theory would have to yield up all its time-honoured powers and prerogatives. It would henceforth exist (in Richard Rorty's phrase) as just another 'kind of writing', a genre devoid of all truth-claims, validating grounds, or epistemological guarantees, and one moreover whose sole distinguishing mark was its attachment to that old, self-deluding order of 'logocentric' concepts and categories.[2]

Such is at any rate the version of Derrida that has gained wide currency among literary critics, as well as neo-pragmatists like Rorty who see it as a handy tactical resource against foundationalist arguments of whatever kind. This is why Ellis regards deconstruction as a thoroughly perverse and mischievous doctrine, an affront to all decent standards of scholarly and critical debate. Before its advent, he writes, literary theory 'worked against the laissez-faire tendencies of criticism; but now deconstruction, an intensified expression of those tendencies, has attempted to seize the mantle of theory in order to pursue [an] anti-theoretical program' (p.159). That is to say, deconstruction encourages the idea of criticism as a kind of free-for-all hermeneutic romp, an activity where no constraints apply save those brought to bear by some arbitrary set of interpretative codes and conventions. In a previous book (*The Logic of Literary Criticism*, 1974) Ellis had argued a similar case with regard to the various competing schools which jostled for attention in the decades before deconstruction made its mark on the US academic scene.[3] His point, then as now, was that theory should be seen as essentially a normative and clarifying enterprise, one whose only use was to sort out the 'logic' (i.e. the implicit orders of truth-claim, evaluative judgement, ontological presupposition, etc.) which characterised the discourses of literary criticism. All too often interpreters ran into trouble through simply not perceiving the logical entailments of their own practice, or by adopting a language that failed to respect the elementary requirements of consistency and truth. Ellis's approach was clearly much influenced by modern analytical philosophy, in particular those forms of conceptual exegesis (or logico-semantic investigation) espoused by thinkers in the post-war Anglo-American camp. Like them, he took a firmly no-nonsense line as against the more adventurous, 'metaphysical' or speculative schools of literary theory. On this point he agreed with Wittgenstein: that the only result of such misguided endeavours was to cut criticism off from its source in the shared enterprise of human understanding, one that should involve the widest possible community of readers, and not have recourse to all manner of specialised jargon or professional shop-talk.

It is the same line of argument that Ellis takes up in his present crusade against deconstruction. The object of literary theory, as he sees it, is to analyse the logic of critical discourse, as revealed in various representative samples, good and bad; to clarify the beliefs that underlie such discourse, most often at the level of tacit presupposition; and thus to arrive at a better understanding of the errors or the cross-purpose arguments that result from hitherto unperceived conflicts of aim and principle. From which it follows that theory should *not* be concerned with a whole range of other (currently fashionable) activities, among them the invention of ever more subtle and elaborate techniques for discovering occult meanings at work, or levels of significance beyond the grasp of readers unequipped with such specialised hermeneutic skills. In this respect, according to Ellis, there is little to choose between deconstruction and those other forms of pseudo-liberationist rhetoric (like reader-response theory) which reject all notions of determinate meaning in favour of an open-ended 'textualist' approach, a willingness to let the work mean what it will in this or that phase of its reception-history, or from each individual reading to the next. For if one pushes this argument to its logical conclusion – a procedure that Ellis very rightly recommends – then one is led to the point of denying all standards of interpretative consistency, relevance, or truth. In which case these current modes of thought are 'anti-theoretical' in the sense that they promote a kind of easy-going pluralist tolerance which leaves no room for significant disagreement on issues of principle and practice.

It is worth quoting Ellis at some length on this point since it is here that his book most clearly reveals its limitations of scope and intellectual grasp. In fact, as I shall argue, it mounts a strong case against 'literary' deconstruction (i.e. the US-domesticated variant) while failing to engage with Derrida's work beyond the most superficial or second-hand level of acquaintance. 'Typically', he writes,

> theorists, by their very nature, do not grant this kind of licence to people or situations to do or be whatever they wish; theory always moves in the opposite direction. Nor do theorists generally reach such an easy peace with the strong undercurrents of the status quo of a field as deconstruction's accommodation with the prevalent laissez-faire of critical practice. Typically, theorists analyze situations to investigate the relations between aspects of current beliefs and practices and reach conclusions about the relative coherence or incoherence of ideas. That kind of analysis will always exert pressure on particular aspects of the status quo, a pressure that will introduce new restraints more than it will abolish them. By contrast, the kind of thinking that tends towards removing such restraints represents a resistance to making distinctions and so a resistance to any real scope for theoretical analysis. (p. 158)

There are three main points to be made about this passage, as indeed about Ellis's book as a whole. First, it mistakes its target by assuming that 'deconstruction' is synonymous with a handful of overworked catch-words ('textuality', 'freeplay', 'dissemination' and the rest) whose promiscuous usage at the hands of literary critics bears no relation to the role they play in Derrida's work. Second, everything that Ellis says apropos of 'theory' in his strong, approving sense of the term would apply point for point to deconstruction as practised not only by Derrida but also by those others (like Paul de Man) whose writings maintain a principled resistance to the dictates of literary-critical fashion.[4] It is precisely on account of this resistance – this concern with the 'relative coherence or incoherence of ideas', along with its refusal to accommodate 'current beliefs and practices' – that deconstruction differs so markedly from the work of neo-pragmatist adepts like Richard Rorty or Stanley Fish. And third, through a similar effect of ironic reversal, Ellis ends up by undermining his own case when he states (with good reason) that theory is more concerned to criticise erroneous, incoherent, or unwarranted beliefs than to offer new pretexts for self-display on the part of ingenious interpreters. For it requires no very deep or extensive acquaintance with the writings of Derrida and de Man to see that they are not involved *in any way* with the 'laissez-faire' attitude that Ellis condemns among literary critics, or the seeking-out of multiple meanings, verbal nuances, alternative reader-responses and so forth, in order to stake some claim to interpretative novelty or – in Harold Bloom's terms – 'strong revisionist' power. On the contrary: their writings do exactly what all good 'theory' should do, as Ellis conceives it. That is to say, they engage in a close and critical reading of texts, drawing out the various orders of co-implicated sense (logical, grammatical and rhetorical) that organise those texts, and only then – with the strictest regard for such protocols – locating their blind spots of naïve or pre-critical presupposition. For Ellis to equate this procedure *tout court* with the wilder excesses of reader-response criticism is a sure sign that he, like so many others, has set about attacking deconstruction without having read enough of Derrida's work or read it with sufficient attentiveness to detail. Had he done so – and this is by far the most charitable assumption – then Ellis would have been in no position to make such a series of ungrounded charges, mistaken attributions and wholesale misconstruals of the deconstructionist case.

Of course this response falls plump into Ellis's sights as just another instance of the 'textualist' idea: that one cannot engage Derrida on substantive issues of theory without first scanning every word of his voluminous output. But one could just as well turn this argument around and ask how far we should trust any commentator who erects non-reading into a positive virtue, thus allowing himself to ignore not only those texts that do not fit in with his argument but almost the entirety of Derrida's production, aside from some few choice passages which – suitably construed – may appear to support the oppositional case. For it has to be said that Ellis's account of deconstruction falls woefully short of what the subject demands by way of serious intellectual engagement and willingness to treat Derrida's writings at their own high level of sustained argumentative force. Where Ellis goes wrong is in taking it more or less for granted that deconstruction comes down to a species of all-out hermeneutic licence, a pretext for indulging super-subtle games at the expense of some typecast naïve position (like the single-right-reading intentionalist case) which serves to screen out alternative, more sensible or logically sophisticated views. On Ellis's absurdly reductionist account, this tendency is best explained in terms of the well-known French predilection *pour épater les bourgeois*, a desire that is perhaps understandable (he grants) on account of the dominant positivist tradition in Francophone literary studies that runs

all the way from Taine to Lanson, and which treats works of literature as so
much material for factual-documentary research or routine *explication de
texte*. But in North America, according to Ellis, the reverse situation ob-
tains: not a rigid traditionalism imposed from above by some outworn
scholastic paradigm but, on the contrary, a pluralist ethos where everything goes and new ideas are taken up without the least concern for their
genuine intellectual merits. What is required by way of countering this
free-for-all attitude is 'a greater degree of inhibition against the acceptance
into this chaos of yet another ideology . . . more agreement on standards
of argument, coherence, and usefulness so that new movements such as
deconstruction might be given closer scrutiny before they are imported'
(p. 86). And for Ellis this means, roughly speaking, a sizeable injection of
healthy anti-Gallic commonsense rationalism, plus a fortifying dose of
elementary logic and a strict avoidance of exotic stimulants in the textualist
vein.

II

As against all this there are certain basic truths about Derrida's work that
apparently need restating since so many of his critics (Ellis included)
prefer to rest their case on minimal exposure to that work. One can best
begin with the simple point that deconstruction has relatively little to do
with the past or present state of French literary criticism. Ellis's excursion
into the comparative sociology of culture merely shows that he is working on the same false premise that he attacks in the US deconstruction
industry, that is, the idea that philosophical arguments can migrate
across disciplines (in this case from philosophy to literary criticism) without suffering a consequent loss of theoretical cogency and rigour. This
explains quite a number of Ellis's misunderstandings, among them his
persistent (and tactically useful) habit of equating deconstruction with
reader-response theory, subjective criticism and the various forms of
free-wheeling 'textualist' approach that in fact owe nothing to Derrida's
influence beyond the adoption of a vaguely libertarian ethos. On the one
hand Ellis argues that deconstruction is bad philosophy – and a baneful
influence on literary theory – on account of its illogicality, its evasion of
crucial argumentative issues and its habit of collapsing conceptual distinctions in the name of an all-purpose Nietzschean rhetoric that leaves
no room for substantive debate. On the other he endorses that view by
virtually ignoring the entire *philosophical* dimension of Derrida's work

141

and treating it as just another fashionable craze among literary critics, one whose main effect has been to license all manner of wild and wilful interpretative games. But this is to attribute to Derrida a position that Ellis has himself created through a resolutely partial reading of Derrida's texts and a heavy reliance on secondary sources which mistake the force and pertinence of deconstructionist thought. It is only by creating this imaginary scenario – one in which the 'movement' takes rise, for Derrida and his US disciples alike, by way of a revolt against the cramping orthodoxies of academic literary study – that Ellis can give his argument any semblance of historical or diagnostic truth.

In so doing he is obliged to ignore the following essential points: (1) that Derrida's writings are only marginally concerned with the business of interpreting literary texts; (2) that where he does engage in something that resembles this activity (e.g. in the essays on Mallarmé, Blanchot and Sollers)[5] the resultant readings are generically quite distinct from literary criticism or commentary in any of its familiar forms; and (3) that these essays have much more to do with distinctively *philosophical* topoi like the status of mimetic representation, the nature and modalities of aesthetic judgement, the problematic character of speech-act conventions (fictive or otherwise) and the way in which 'literature' itself has been constructed – along with related categories like metaphor, fiction, rhetoric, form and style – in the course of a long and complex prehistory (from Plato to Kant, Husserl and J.L. Austin) whose workings can only be grasped through a process of rigorous genealogical critique.[6] In short, Derrida's texts stand squarely within the tradition of Western philosophical thought, and none the less so for his seeking to contest or 'deconstruct' that tradition at points where its foundational concepts and values are open to a non-canonical reading. This is what makes it so absurd for Ellis to claim that Derrida is just one more arch debunker of typecast 'bourgeois' complacencies, or that his 'method' has only managed to create such a stir by setting up a variety of simplified target-positions and then proceeding to shoot them down in the usual triumphalist fashion.

There is only one instance in Derrida's work where he resorts to anything like the 'typical' procedure that Ellis describes. It is – notoriously – his article 'Limited Inc abc', written in response to the philosopher John Searle, who had taken Derrida roundly to task on the topic of Austinian speech-act theory.[7] This essay has been widely canvassed – by admirers and detractors alike – as setting out to demolish Searle's arguments through a range of ultra-textualist gambits ('brilliant' or 'perverse' according to taste), or as attempting to play 'philosophy' right off the field by showing

how all such debates come down to an endless 'dissemination' of meanings, speech-acts, codes and conventions whose import can never be
determined *either* by appealing to utterer's intentions (since these are
inherently unknowable and subject to various kinds of circumstantial
qualification), *or* as a matter of straightforward contextual grasp (since the
possible 'contexts' of any given utterance can be multiplied beyond the
explanatory powers of a theory – like Searle's – that seeks to maintain the
normative distinctions between authentic and inauthentic, serious and
non-serious, or 'real' and 'fictive' speech-act genres). Now it is certainly
the case that Derrida allows himself considerable fun and games at Searle's
expense. Thus he makes the central point about 'iterability' (i.e. the capacity of speech-acts to function across a vast – potentially infinite – range of
contexts, situations, or discourses) by citing the *entirety* of Searle's original
response, but citing it piecemeal to his own strategic ends, with the object
of activating latent or unlooked-for possibilities of sense which thus become the basis for a scrupulously *literal* reading which none the less goes
clean against the intentional or manifest drift of Searle's argument. There
is also a good deal of knockabout play with signatures, proper names,
copyright conventions, Searle's claim to speak as the 'authorised' exponent of genuine speech-act philosophy, and other such pointers to what
Derrida sees as a strong proprietary drive, a desire that Austin's texts
should not be exposed to any reading that questions their 'obvious', self-
validating import. So one can well understand why 'Limited Inc' has
acquired its reputation as the *ne plus ultra* of Derridean sophistical 'freeplay', as opposed to the plain good sense and sobriety of Searle's corrective
intervention.

Such is at any rate Ellis's view of the Searle/Derrida exchange, serving
as it does – at several points in his book – as a flagrant example of Derrida's
unwillingness to engage in reasoned, responsible debate, and his lack of
regard for the elementary protocols of shared understanding. It is precisely
these failings, in Ellis's view, that should prevent us from taking such
performances seriously as a genuine contribution to philosophy or literary
theory. 'By contrast', he writes,

> the beginning of other attempts to advance thought is normally taken to
> require a focus on the highest and most advanced level of thinking that has
> been achieved on a given question; we start with the latest state of the art
> and go on from there. (p. 137)

For deconstructionists, conversely, criticism beats a defensive retreat 'away from the most sophisticated thought achieved to date, back to unsophisticated, simple notions' (pp. 137–8). But it is hard to conceive how anyone who had studied the exchange between Derrida and Searle could possibly judge Searle to have argued more effectively or mounted a stronger *philosophical* case. For the truth is – and I make no apology for putting it like this – that Derrida not only runs rings around Searle at the level of 'sophisticated' word-play, but also draws attention to antinomies, blind spots, non-sequiturs, aporias and moments of unwitting self-contradiction which are manifestly *there* in Searle's essay and which render his arguments vulnerable to a deconstructive reading.

There is one case-in-point that has particular relevance here since it concerns an objection brought against Derrida by Searle, Ellis and others who adopt a likewise dismissive attitude. Their argument, in short, is that Derrida goes wrong – or succeeds in creating all kinds of unnecessary trouble – through his insistence on a rigidly binary logic, an 'all-or-nothing' stance whereby it is made to appear that dogmatic certainty or out-and-out scepticism are the only available alternatives. Thus Derrida maintains (or so these critics would have us believe) that meaning is *either* fully determinate or subject to a limitless 'undecidability'; that *unless* there exist some clearly specifiable rules for interpreting speech-act conventions, then those conventions are *necessarily* just *ad hoc*, makeshift products of this or that uniquely-occurring situation, and can thus possess no binding or intelligible force from one such context to the next; that if 'logocentrism' (or the Western 'metaphysics of presence') turns out to entail a deeply problematical set of assumptions, then there is *no possibility* of meaning what one says or effectively saying what one means; that if language does not work in quite the way envisaged by naïve referentialist theories – on account of the 'arbitrary' nature of the sign, or complicating factors pointed out (less dramatically) by philosophers in the modern analytical tradition – then we *must* be deluded in the commonsense belief that words can get a good enough grip on the world to serve for most practical purposes. According to Searle and Ellis these are just some of the absurd conclusions to which Derrida is driven by following out the logic of his equally absurd premises. And the best way to avoid such muddles, they argue, is to give up the habit of thinking exclusively in binary, 'either-or' terms, a habit that can only lead to all manner of sterile antinomies and conceptual dead-ends. Once rid of these distracting pseudo-problems philosophy can then get on with its proper business of describing the various speech-act conventions, nuances of meaning, contextual criteria and so forth which help to explain how we do in fact succeed – at least most of the time – in achieving a decent measure of shared linguistic grasp.

Derrida has two main points to make in response to Searle's confidently orthodox rejoinder. One is that he (Searle) is hardly in a strong position to advance such arguments since his whole case rests on the charge that Derrida has ignored certain basic distinctions in speech-act theory (e.g. those between real-life and fictive, genuine and pretended, 'felicitous' and 'infelicitous' examples of the kind), thus wilfully ignoring the plain sense of Austin's text, as well as the obvious practical need to keep these categories in place. So there is an unwitting irony about Searle's attack on Derrida for adopting a rigidly exclusivist logic, an 'all-or-nothing' attitude which holds that (in Searle's words) 'unless a distinction can be made rigorous and precise, it isn't really a distinction at all'.[8] But then Derrida turns this argument around by *not* taking the line – as might be expected – that such categories need deconstructing in order to reveal their 'metaphysical' or 'logocentric' nature, but declaring on the contrary that they remain *indispensable* to any project of thought (his own included) which seeks to achieve philosophical cogency and rigour. What makes Searle a bad, inattentive reader of Austin and Derrida alike is his failure to perceive the rigorous necessity of maintaining these distinctions, even – and especially – at the point where they encounter a deep-laid resistance to straightforward 'commonsense' application. 'In fact', Derrida writes,

> not only do I find this logic strong, and, in conceptual language and analysis, *an absolute must (il la faut)*, it must (this 'it must' translates my love for philosophy) be sustained against all empirical confusion, to the point where the same demand of rigour requires the structure of that logic to be transformed and complicated . . . What philosopher ever since there were philosophers, what logician since there were logicians, what theoretician ever renounced this axiom: in the order of concepts (since we are speaking of concepts and not of the colours of clouds or the taste of certain chewing gums), when a distinction cannot be rigorous or precise, it is not a distinction at all. (*Limited Inc*, p. 123–4)

I have cited this passage at length because it states very firmly what should have been obvious to Searle, Ellis and other commentators who routinely chide Derrida for his well-known aversion to 'serious' argument. Their mistake is to suppose that first-rate philosophy – analytical work of the highest order – cannot be conducted in a style that partakes of certain 'literary' figures and devices, or which makes its point through a skilful interweaving of constative and performative speech-act genres. For if there is one thing that Austin should have taught them – so Derrida implies –it is the need to press these cardinal distinctions as far as they will go, but also to keep an open mind when dealing with instances, anecdotes, off-beat usages, anomalous cases and so forth which might seem to 'play Old Harry' (Austin's own phrase) with all such tidy categorical schemes. There is a nice example at the turning-point in *How To Do Things With Words*, when Austin decides – on account of various problems with the evidence so far – that the straightforward constative/performative distinction just will not hold up, and therefore switches to a three-term descriptive model based on the notions of 'locutionary', 'illocutionary' and 'perlocutionary' force.[9] But in thus shifting ground he is not giving up on the quest for conceptual clarity and rigour, any more than Derrida does when he plays certain (shrewdly Austinian) games with Searle's unquestioning, 'serious' attachment to the canons of orthodox speech-act theory.

So Derrida is perfectly entitled to offer what amounts to a classic *tu quoque* response in countering Searle's arguments. Let me quote further from the above-cited passage by way of returning to Ellis's book and its confused understanding of deconstruction as a species of last-ditch relativist abandon.

> If Searle declares explicitly, seriously, literally that this axiom [i.e. the true/false distinction and its various speech-act correlatives] must be renounced . . . then, short of practising deconstruction with some consistency and of submitting the very rules and regulations of his project to an explicit reworking, his entire philosophical discourse on speech acts will collapse . . . To each word will have to be added 'a little', 'more or less', 'up to a certain point', 'rather', and despite all this, the literal will not cease to be somewhat metaphorical, 'mention' will not stop being tainted by 'use', the 'intentional' no less slightly 'unintentional', and so forth. Searle knows well that he neither can nor should go in this direction. He has never afforded himself the theoretical means of escaping conceptual opposition without empiricist confusion. (*Limited Inc*, p. 124)

One could hardly wish for a clearer affirmation of Derrida's commitment, not only to 'philosophy' in some vague and all-encompassing sense of the word, but precisely to those standards of logical rigour, consistency and truth which deconstruction is reputed to reject out of hand. Of course Searle and Ellis could still maintain that *in fact* Derrida's writings display nothing like this high regard for the commonplace intellectual decencies; that if one goes back to his original essay on Austin – not to mention his 'outrageous', 'nonsensical' riposte to Searle – then one finds him indulging all the usual deconstructionist tricks of the trade and blithely discounting all the 'serious' objections that rise up against him. But then it can only be a matter (*pace* Ellis) of reading all three texts over again – Derrida on Austin, Searle on Derrida, Derrida's book-length commentary on Austin and Searle – and judging those texts strictly on their argumentative merits, in the first place according to generalised criteria of validity and truth (standards which Derrida by no means abandons), and then, more specifically, as read-ings of Austin alive to the peculiar problems, subtleties and potential aberra-tions of speech-act theory. On both counts Derrida wins hands down, not merely as a skilful rhetorician, one who contrives to tie Searle up in philosophical knots of his own creation, but also as by far the more rigorous thinker and perceptive exponent of Austin's ideas.

So it hardly comes as a surprise that the one crucial document missing from the latest edition of *Limited Inc** is Searle's essay 'Reiterating the dif-ferences', written in response to Derrida. Gerald Graff provides a brief but accurate summary, while judiciously advising readers to consult the full text as it appeared in *Glyph*, vol. 2 (1977). For Searle the debate is now closed and the exchange nothing more than a lamentable instance – on Derrida's side – of the muddles that result when literary theorists presume to encroach upon the specialised preserve of 'serious' philosophical thought. Ellis draws the same lesson from this episode, taking it as read – or at least with very little in the way of supporting argument – that Searle's essay was an adequate (indeed definitive) response and Derrida's follow-up just another piece of deconstruc-tionist word-spinning nonsense. Furthermore, he finds evidence of sophistry (not to say blatant double-dealing) in Derrida's claim *on the one hand* that textual meaning is indeterminate, authorial intentions unknowable, etc., and *on the other* that Searle has misstated his position and – whether wilfully or not – offered a reading that fails to respect the requirements of interpretative fidelity and truth. This latter

> is indeed a far cry from the claim that Derrida's position cannot be stated as others can (or that a reader should not try to grasp an author's intent) . . . Derrida thus abandons this position, just as others do, when he feels the need to replace a misstatement of his view with an adequate statement of it. (Ellis, pp. 13–14)

Once again there are so many confusions at work in this passage that one scarcely knows where to begin in sorting them out. Four main points must suffice for now. (1) If meaning turns out to be *strictly undecidable in certain*

---

* Jacques Derrida, *Limited Inc*, 2nd edn., incorporating 'Signature Event Context', with an Afterword, 'Toward an ethics of discussion', introd. and ed. Gerald Graff (Evanston Ill.: North-western University Press, 1989).

instances, this cannot be taken as synonymous with the claim that meaning is always and everywhere 'indeterminate', a claim (like the widespread misunderstanding of 'freeplay') which Derrida has often been at pains to disavow.[10] (2) There is simply no question of Derrida's 'rejecting' the idea of authorial intention, an idea that provides the 'indispensable guardrail' for any reading of a text, deconstructive or otherwise, even if – as he argues – the *de facto* evidence of unlooked-for textual complications counts against the prescriptive *de jure* appeal to 'intentions', pure and simple.[11] (3) Ellis cannot have it both ways, attacking what he sees (mistakenly) as Derrida's resort to a 'textualist' strategy of open-ended hermeneutic licence, then complaining when Derrida turns out to offer strong arguments and specific evidential grounds, as in the response to Searle. (4) Deconstruction is indeed susceptible to reasoned argument and counter-argument, a point that Derrida is far from wishing to deny, not only (as Ellis would have it) when presuming to correct misreadings of his work, but at every stage of his production to date. In short, the whole charge-sheet falls to shreds if one only takes the trouble to read what Derrida has written, instead of relying on a handful of simplified slogans ('all reading is misreading', 'there is nothing outside the text', 'meaning is always indeterminate' and so forth) which are no doubt well suited to the purpose of knock-about polemics, but which just do not begin to engage deconstruction at anything like an adequate level. Thus when Ellis deplores what he sees in Derrida – and 'French intellectuals' at large – as highbrow 'contempt for a stationary target of simplemindedness', his phrase not only misses the mark but comes back like a boomerang.

III

It would take too long to go right through Ellis's book picking out every instance of routine misunderstanding. Let me offer one further case in point, a case with particular relevance here since it has to do with Derrida's reading of Husserl, the one major portion of his work that philosophers in the 'other' (analytical) tradition have shown some sign of acknowledging at its true worth. This is not the place for a detailed exposition of the two early books (*Husserl's 'Origin of Geometry'* and *Speech and Phenomena*) where Derrida conducts a sustained close-reading and a rigorously-argued analytical critique of Husserl's grounding suppositions.[12] After all, the texts are there – along with a growing volume of informed commentary[13] – for anyone willing to suspend their preconceived notions of what Derrida has to say and to read those texts at their own (albeit demanding) level of philosophic argument.

Ellis, on the contrary, offers one brief passage on Husserl which at least has the merit of laying all his errors open to view in a usefully condensed form.

> Extraordinary verbal complexity is not excluded by this concern with primitive ideas; no one could deny that Derrida's texts are extraordinarily difficult and obscure. But though, for example, his making Husserl the starting point for a discussion of meaning in *La Voix et la phénomène* involves him immediately in highly convoluted and difficult writing, it is Husserl's simple and logically vulnerable assumptions about intentions, reference, and essences (i.e., that speech is the vehicle for conveying meaning and intention that is separate from itself) that draw him to begin there. Simple ideas are not incompatible with tortuous prose – on the contrary, it is when the clouds of tortuous prose are dispelled that primitive ideas are often found hiding from a light that they could not survive. (p. 142)

One can see (just about) how Ellis arrived at this contorted understanding of Derrida's text. Since deconstruction – on his view – can only maintain its appearance of high sophistication by picking out naïve or 'simple-minded' targets, *therefore* it must follow that Husserl's ideas fall into this category, displaying all the features that Derrida requires in order to practise his usual rhetorical games. But this does nothing to explain or excuse the sheer wrong-headedness of Ellis's account, offered as it is with the kind of breezy, commonsensical assurance that comes of a downright refusal to read what is there in the texts under discussion.

His argument misfires for the following reasons, all of which are rehearsed with demonstrable force and precision in Derrida's two early books on Husserl. First, there is no question of Derrida's having upstaged the whole project of Husserlian phenomenology – picked it out as a naïve, simple-minded or 'logically vulnerable' target – merely in order to display his own more subtle or sophisticated strategies of reading. On the contrary: Derrida insists over and again that Husserl's meditations are a paradigm case of philosophy at its finest, most rigorous and intensely self-critical stretch; that any effort to think 'beyond' such enquiries will have to go by way of a close and detailed engagement with Husserl's texts; and that deconstruction has nothing in common with those fashionable forms of postmodernist thought which reject the heritage of Western 'metaphysical' concepts and categories only to fall back unwittingly into various postures of naïve or pre-critical awareness. And this error is compounded by Ellis's simply taking it for granted – no doubt on the authority of Ryle, Searle and other thinkers in the Anglo-American tradition – that there is no need for such strenuous dealing with the project of transcendental phenomenology since Husserl's talk of 'intentions, reference and essences' is 'logically vulnerable' (for which read 'just a bad case of bother-headed Continental theory'), and therefore not worth the effort. Here again there is a curious structural irony about Ellis's argument which leads him to adopt exactly the stance of self-deluding superior knowledge that he claims to detect in Derrida's readings of Saussure, Husserl and others. For it should be apparent to anyone who has read these texts that deconstruction is *not* just a species of destructive or all-purpose nihilist rhetoric; that it resumes the pro-ject of Husserlian thought at a point where that project may indeed be ques-tioned as to its presupposed values, metaphysical commitments, hidden axiomatics, structuring oppositions and so forth, but only as the upshot of an immanent critique that respects Husserl's arguments even while refusing on principle to accept them as a matter of intuitive self-evidence or a priori truth. So it is quite simply wrong – a manifest case of very stubborn preconceptions at work – to treat Derrida's reading of Husserl as a piece of mere 'textualist' gamesmanship, or as setting out to score easy points against a 'stationary target' of typecast philosophical naïvety.

Of course I could not hope to convince Ellis by offering the judgement that *Speech and Phenomena* stands as one of the finest achievements of modern analytical philosophy, taking that description to extend well beyond its cur-rent, strangely narrowed professional scope. In order to debate the issue to any purpose one would have to take for granted at least a certain measure of shared intellectual ground, as for instance by assuming that Ellis had made some attempt to overcome his deep hostility to everything in the other ('Conti-nental') tradition, or any philosophical writing that did not fall square with his own ideas of a decent, perspicuous, commonsense style. But this dialogue would scarcely get off the ground since it is one of his chief complaints against deconstruction that it exploits what Ellis calls 'the equation of obscurity and profundity that has been available in European thought since Hegel and Kant', thus giving rise to the pernicious idea that 'an obscure text is difficult, and difficulty presents a *challenge* to readers' (p. 147). Again one is hard put to decide just how such passages ask to be read: whether every text that is 'difficult' should therefore be consigned to the category of wilful obscurantism, or whether Ellis sees any important differences between (e.g.) the kinds of intellectual 'challenge' that arise in the reading of Kant, Hegel, Nietzsche, Heidegger, Austin, or Derrida. What mostly comes across in his writing is a settled antipathy to any form of discourse that questions the orthodox (Anglo-American) thinking on such matters, that is, the notion of philosophic style as a transparent means of access to a priori concepts, argu-mentative grounds, clear and distinct ideas or whatever. And of course there is a sense – a well-publicised sense – in which deconstruction does indeed mount a challenge to any such self-assured policing of the bounds between philosophy and other, less rigorous or disciplined kinds of language. But if one then turns back to Derrida's texts on each of the above figures it will not be found – as Ellis would have us believe – that these are wayward, exhibitionist performances devoid of any genuine argumentative force. On the contrary, they are conducted at the highest level of sustained analytical grasp, with respect not only to the letter of the text (which may often give rise to a reading at odds with the orthodox, consensual wisdom), but also in the matter of authorial intentions, since there is – and on this point Derrida insists – no question of simply discounting or ignoring the intentionalist ground of appeal, even where such meanings appear caught up in signifying structures which it is beyond their power fully to determine or control. His statements to this effect are found at numerous points in *Of Grammatology* and elsewhere, although these passages are always passed over in silence by those – like Ellis – who choose to regard deconstruction as a species of all-licensing sophistical 'freeplay'.

On this question, as on so many others, the issue has been obscured by a failure to grasp Derrida's point when he identifies those problematic factors in language (catachreses, slippages between 'literal' and 'figural' sense, sublimated metaphors mistaken for determinate concepts) whose effect – as in Husserl – is to complicate the passage from what the text manifestly *means to say* to what it actually says when read with an eye to its latent or covert signifying structures. Thus 'freeplay' has nothing whatsoever to do with that notion of out-and-out hermeneutic licence which would finally come down to a series of slogans like 'all reading is misreading', 'all interpretation is misinterpretation', etc. If Derrida's texts have been read that way – most often by literary critics in quest of more adventurous hermeneutic models – this is just one sign of the widespread *deformation professionelle* that has attended the advent of deconstruction as a new arrival on the US academic scene. Of course there are passages in his work – notably the closing sentences of 'Structure, sign, and play' – which opponents like Ellis can cite out of context in support of this 'anything goes' interpretation. Thus Derrida: 'one could call *play* the absence of the transcendental signified as limitlessness of play, that is to say, as the destruction of onto-theology and the metaphysics of presence'. And again: 'the meaning of meaning (in the general sense of meaning and not in the sense of signalization) is infinite implication, the infinite referral of signifier to signifier'.[14] But one should at least recall – a point strategically ignored by Ellis – that these passages occur at the close of an essay (a deconstructive reading of Lévi-Strauss and the discourse of structural anthropology) which has argued its case up to this point through a rigorous critique of certain classic binary oppositions, notably the nature/culture antinomy, and which goes clean against the idea of 'freeplay' as a pretext for endless interpretative games without the least regard for standards of logic, consistency and truth. What the statements in question should be taken to signify is the fact that *at the limit* there is no compelling reason – no form of *de jure* or a priori principle – that could restrict the 'play' of oppositions in a text to the terms laid down by our received (logocentric) order of concepts and priorities.

It is the same basic point that Derrida makes when he interrogates the axiomatics of Austinian speech-act theory and denies that any appeal to intentions or to context could ever provide sufficient grounds in theory for distinguishing authentic from feigned (or 'felicitous' from 'infelicitous') examples of the kind. But he is no more denying that successful speech-acts *do* in fact occur, as a matter of everyday experience, than he is suggesting that interpretation is always faced with an infinitised 'freeplay' of textual meaning which can only be kept within tolerable bounds by some arbitrary act of will on the part of this or that self-authorised tribunal. His purpose is rather to direct our attention to those various forms of *de facto* interpretative grasp which operate everywhere in philosophy, criticism, everyday conversation, and especially – as Austin makes clear – in the ethical dimension of these and other activities. But it is also to insist, as against Searle's confidently orthodox reading of Austin, that such facts about the way we standardly 'do things with words' cannot be erected into a *de jure* theory (or generalised speech-act philosophy) that would henceforth determine what shall count as an instance of serious, authentic, good-faith, or 'felicitous' utterance. What is so difficult to grasp about Derrida's work – and what causes such confusion in critics like Ellis – is the fact that he arrives at these (seemingly) anti-philosophical theses through a highly disciplined process of argument, but does so in order to point up the limits of systematic thought when exposed to the kinds of displacement brought about by a deconstructive critique.

Hence the very different responses to that work manifested by the various schools of commentary that have already grown up around it. On the one hand there are those – Searle and Ellis among them – who just cannot see how any 'serious' philosopher could raise the sorts of question that Derrida raises, or write in such a 'playful', performative style that the questions are posed in and through the very act of writing. On the other one finds an assortment of largely sympathetic commentators (literary critics, neo-pragmatists like Richard Rorty, postmodernist thinkers of various persuasion) who praise Derrida for exactly the same reason. That is to say, they admire him for having knocked 'philosophy' off its pedestal by treating it as one more culture-specific 'kind of writing', a discourse whose truth-claims can henceforth be discounted since in the end they amount to nothing more than a choice among different 'final vocabularies', a self-interested preference for talking in terms of concepts, transcendental deductions, a priori knowledge, 'conditions of possibility', etc. On this view – argued most consistently by Rorty in his recent essays[15] – what is best about Derrida is his usefulness in debunking all those outworn epistemological pretensions which have left philosophy, or its mainstream exponents, lagging so far behind the times as signalled by the postmodern turn in recent cultural debate. From which it follows, conversely, that the *least* valuable parts of Derrida's work are those – like the early texts on Husserl – that still seem engaged with the tedious, old-fashioned business of offering arguments, criticising truth-claims, or coming up with new terms (*'différance'*, 'supplementarity', etc.) which then become just another technical jargon, despite their avowedly radical break with the discourse of Western metaphysics. One can see how nicely this approach dovetails with the reading of Derrida that enjoys wide currency among literary critics – and others of a broadly hermeneutical bent – who likewise have an interest in promoting the view that interpretation, so to speak, goes all the way down; that there is nothing distinctive about philosophical texts that would give philosophers an intellectual edge over people in departments of English or Comparative Literature. For them, as for Rorty, the texts of Derrida that exert most appeal are those (like *Glas* and *The Postcard: from Socrates to Freud*)[16] that seemingly enact this disciplinary stand-off with the maximum degree of stylistic brio and the smallest regard for what conventionally counts as 'serious' philosophical argument. To this extent one can see why critics like Ellis should regard deconstruction as indeed nothing more than old relativist doctrine writ large, or dressed up in extravagant Nietzschean rhetorical colours.

But this all has more to do with the reception-history of Derrida's work than with anything like an adequate assessment of that work in its proper intellectual context. For the latter, one must look to those qualified commentators – among them notably Rodolphe Gasché and John Llewelyn [17] – who possess both a detailed knowledge of the relevant philosophical background and a capacity for closely-worked textual exegesis which offers something more than a neat variation on the age-old 'literature-versus-philosophy' debate. What then becomes apparent is that Derrida is not merely collapsing the genre-distinction between those categories – a charge brought against him by Habermas[18] – but showing it to rest on a series of unstable oppositions (concept/metaphor, literal/figural, constative/performative, reason/rhetoric, etc.) whose structural economy is none the less prerequisite to any discourse, his own included, that attempts to think beyond their more traditional or typecast formulations. This argument is best represented by the essays brought together in *Margins of Philosophy*, a text which – symptomatically – tends to be ignored by Ellis, Habermas and other hostile commentators. For here Derrida argues very pointedly *against* what might be called the vulgar-deconstructionist position: the idea that philosophy is just a 'kind of writing', that all concepts come down to metaphors in the end, that the truth-values governing Western 'logocentrism' are merely the result of our having forgotten their contingent origin, the fact that they derive – as Benveniste had suggested – from certain features (like subject-predicate grammar) specific to ancient Greek language and thought.[19] In each case, he argues, one has to go further and ask what are the *conditions of possibility* that enable these issues to be raised in the first place, or to assume the kind of salience they have long possessed for thinkers in the Western philosophical tradition. And to pose this question is also to grasp that criticism cannot stop short at the point of simply inverting those deep-laid categorical distinctions; that (for intance) all our operative concepts of metaphor, literature, style, rhetoric, figural language and so forth have been produced and refined within a history of thought whose terms are inescapably marked or inflected by the discourse of philosophic reason.

So it is unthinkable – in the strictest sense of that word – that we should now follow the lead of postmodern-pragmatists like Rorty and learn to treat philosophy as just one more voice in the cultural 'conversation of mankind', on a level with literature, criticism and other such styles of 'edifying' discourse. For this is nothing more than a line of least resistance, a refusal to acknowledge the very real problems that arise as soon as one posits an alternative 'final vocabulary' – in Rorty's case, an idiom of strong misreading, creative renewal, poetic redescription, etc. – conceived as a preferable substitute for all those dead-end philosophical debates.[20] What such thinking cannot acknowledge is the fact that any suggested alternative will always involve a covert appeal to distinctions – like that between 'concept' and 'metaphor' – which are so far from breaking with the language and resources of Western philosophy that they reproduce its characteristic features at every turn.

IV

So it is simply a *mistake* – a determinate misreading of Derrida's work – to argue, like Ellis, that it all comes down to a species of rhetorical 'freeplay', or a Nietzschean desire to turn the tables on philosophy by subverting every last protocol of reason and truth. In fact one could take each chapter of *Margins*

and demonstrate not only that its arguments possess a rigorously consequential logic but also the regular pack-of-cards effect whereby it brings down a
whole body of received ideas about deconstruction. Let me take just one
example: 'White mythology: metaphor in the text of philosophy', an essay
which for sheer critical acumen and intellectual grasp – not to mention stylistic brilliance – far surpasses anything written on this topic by philosophers in
the Anglo-American tradition. Now it is certainly the case that Derrida here
continues the critique of philosophical concepts and truth-claims that
Nietzsche pursued through the analysis of language in its rhetorical (or
performative) aspects. Thus,

> there is no properly philosophical category to qualify a certain number of tropes
> that have conditioned the so-called 'fundamental', 'structuring', 'original'
> philosophical oppositions: they are so many 'metaphors' that would constitute
> the rubrics of such a tropology, the words 'turn' or 'trope' or 'metaphor' being
> no exception to this rule. (*Margins*, p. 229)

In which case it might seem that his critics are right when they treat deconstruction as merely the most recent – and rhetorically sophisticated –
version of a wholesale Nietzschean scepticism with regard to truth, logic and
the protocols of rational argument.

But this is to ignore some crucial points about Derrida's procedure in
'White mythology'. One is the quality of extreme analytical precision that
everywhere marks his discourse, even at the stage when that discourse
broaches the sheer *impossibility* of ever adequately thinking through this
relationship between 'concept' and 'metaphor'. What Derrida is striving to
articulate here is an order of insight into the workings of language that necessarily eludes the kind of clear-cut conceptualisation which 'mainstream'
philosophers – from Aristotle to Max Black or Donald Davidson – have
traditionally sought in their dealing with such topics. But this is not to say (as
Rorty would have it, or as Ellis takes Derrida to be arguing) that deconstruction can henceforth blithely disregard that whole legacy of analytic thought,
including the concept/metaphor distinction and its various correlative terms.
For it is still the case – unavoidably so – that 'the concept of metaphor, along
with all the predicates that permit its ordered extension and comprehension, is
a philosopheme' (p. 228). From which it follows necessarily that any proposition on the topic of metaphor – even one that adopts a Nietzschean stance of
extreme epistemological scepticism – will always take rise from a history of
thought whose structural economy is determined in advance by the discourse
of philosophic reason.

What this thesis amounts to in its weak, negative form is that no claim on behalf of metaphor (or literature) as against the rule of concepts (or philosophy) can possibly do more than rehearse the old quarrel while preserving the selfsame terms of debate. In its stronger version the argument holds (1) that all definitions of metaphor are *philosophical* definitions, elaborated by thinkers from Plato and Aristotle to the present; (2) that these thinkers have always been subject to a certain blindness with regard to the 'fundamental' figures or tropes that constitute their own discourse; but also (3) that any adequate or theoretically accountable treatment of the topic will have to go by way of a complex prehistory whose logic is inscribed – whether knowingly or not – in each new attempt to make sense of this tangled relationship. 'To permit oneself to overlook this *vigil* of philosophy', Derrida writes,

> one would have to posit that the sense aimed at is an essence rigorously independent of that which transports it, which is an already philosophical *thesis*, one might even say philosophy's *unique thesis*, the thesis which constitutes the concept of metaphor, the opposition of the proper and the nonproper, of essence and accident, of intuition and discourse, of thought and language, of the intelligible and the sensible. (p. 229)

In which case the philosopher who writes on metaphor will be subject to a twofold – and, it might seem, a contradictory – order of imperatives. First, there is the necessity of thinking these distinctions through with the maximum degree of analytical clarity and rigour. Second, there is the obligation to remark those points in the discourse of philosophic reason where metaphor turns out to elude or exceed the compass of any such self-assured project. But in fact what is involved is not so much a contradiction as a double gesture of fidelity, on the one hand to standards of argumentative consistency and truth, and on the other to the need for textual close-reading (or rhetorical analysis) as a form of critical symptomatology, an attempt to explain more clearly where philosophers have erred in taking those standards too much for granted, or in failing to perceive where they invoke certain metaphors (like the idiom of 'clear and distinct ideas') whose figural origin is forgotten in the drive for conceptual mastery and truth. At which point 'the appeal to criteria of clarity and obscurity would suffice to confirm . . . [that] this entire philosophical delimitation of metaphor already lends itself to being constructed and worked by "metaphors" ' (p. 252). But it is none the less true – necessarily so – that any such assertion will be couched in terms that presuppose the possibility of distinguishing literal from figural language, or conceptual definitions (the province of philosophic reason) from metaphors or tropes (the province of art, literature, rhetoric, sophistics, etc.). And once again, those terms are *philosophical* through and through, not merely as a local or contingent fact about Western intellectual history, but by virtue of their place among that handful of constitutive topics and concerns by which philosophy has been characterised as a discipline of thought from Plato to the present.

Hence Derrida's (no doubt rhetorical) question: 'can these defining tropes that are prior to all philosophical rhetoric and that produce philosophemes still be called metaphors?' (p. 210). His answer is not to be found in the form of any summary statement that would settle the question one way or the other. It can only be approached through the kind of meticulous analytical close-reading that 'White mythology' brings to bear on the texts of philosophical tradition. (Paul de Man's essay 'The epistemology of metaphor' is another work that achieves something like the same level of combined argumentative rigour and rhetorical self-awareness.)[21] This is what makes it so absurd for opponents like Ellis to claim that deconstruction is philosophically naïve, or that it trades on the age-old sophistical trick of targeting naïve assumptions in others (e.g. Husserl), while strategically ignoring any alternative (more sensible or logically compelling) viewpoint that would resolve the question once and for all, though of course without providing such welcome opportunities for ingenious self-display. It is tempting to respond – as Derrida does at one point in his latest rejoinder to Searle – that 'if things were that simple, word would have gotten around'. Where Ellis goes wrong is in his fixed belief that to 'deconstruct' a text is to take it apart merely for the pleasure of showing up its local inconsistencies, blind spots, non-sequiturs, moments of unwitting aporia and other such well-known Derridean motifs. And of course one can hardly deny that this strategy does play a prominent role at various stages in his writings on Plato, Kant, Husserl, Austin and others. But it is missing the point in quite spectacular fashion to conclude, like Ellis, that Derrida's 'tortuous prose' is merely a sign that he has hit on certain 'primitive ideas' in Husserl – intentionality, reference, essence, etc. – which would not stand up for a moment if subjected to a different, more orderly and logical approach. What Derrida brings out in his reading of Husserl (as likewise in 'White mythology) is the *absolute and principled necessity* of thinking both with and against these ideas, since on the one hand they provide the only possible starting-point for any philosophical reflection, while on the other they lead to a point where such thinking runs up against significant problems or obstacles, factors which considerably complicate Husserl's argument but which cannot be brushed aside in the name of straightforward commonsense logic. In short, Derrida's relation to Husserl bears absolutely no resemblance to Ellis's knock-down caricature, a reading that raises serious doubts as to the extent of his acquaintance with the work of either philosopher.

One main plank of Ellis's argument that collapses under the least pressure of detailed examination is his idea that deconstruction is just another variant of reader-response criticism. For both schools of thought, as he interprets them, '[c]ritics are given freedom to read texts without constraints, texts can mean an infinity of meanings, and readers use unrestrained creativity to discover meaning' (Ellis, p. 158). I can think of few advocates of reader-response theory – let alone deconstruction – to whom this statement could apply with any semblance of fair or accurate description.[22] Moreover, there is a massive confusion at work in the idea that 'textuality', as Derrida conceives it, amounts to nothing more than a licence for interpreters to make what they will of philosophical or literary works. Once again, this error results from the habit of reducing deconstruction to a handful of misconceived slogans ('all interpretation is misinterpretation', etc.) which enjoy wide currency only among those who evince small knowledge of the primary texts. (That there is no such thing as a 'primary text' since all texts – whether novels, poems, critical commentaries, works of philosophy, undergraduate-level 'theory' primers and so forth – partake of a generalised 'intertextuality' is another grossly reductive slogan presently doing the rounds.) In face of such manifest refusals to read what Derrida has written one can only turn Ellis's argument around and protest that it is he, not Derrida, who makes a habit of setting up imaginary simple-minded targets the more easily to shoot them down.

These tactics go along with what I have noted already: a tendency, on the part of Ellis and others, to restrict their understanding of Derrida's work to its role as one more novelty import on the US academic scene, a product of the rapid turnover in literary-critical fashions. Hence Ellis's myopic view of deconstruction as first and foremost a trend among literary theorists, with no philosophical credentials to speak of despite all the heavyweight allusions to Plato, Kant, Hegel or Husserl. Perhaps this movement had some point – he concedes – in its original French context, since here the tradition of positivist scholarship still reigned supreme, so that 'there really *was* a single authoritative opinion on literary texts, administered to all'. But it is a very different matter when deconstruction gains a following among American critics and theorists. For here the main problem is *not* the persistence of a rigidly orthodox line but, on the contrary, the dismal lack of any rational (truth-seeking) standards of debate that would serve to adjudicate the various competing creeds and ideologies. In short, 'there is something logically very odd about this mismatch between a critical theory that in its obsession with conformity could only have arisen in France and its acceptance in America, the pluralistically cheerful accepter of diversity' (p. 86). And if the metaphors here sound a cautionary note – a suggestion that maybe the country needs somewhat tighter immigration controls, at least where intellectual fashions and their bearers are concerned – it is a note that Ellis's next sentence does little or nothing to dispel. 'In one sense', he writes, 'this acceptance is very much in the spirit of America's acceptance of European refugees; in another sense, it might seem contrary to that spirit, since there is here no adequate soil to nourish deconstruction's basic thrust' (p. 86).

One could spend a lot of time unpacking the implications of this passage, not least the idea of intellectual value as rooted in the 'soil' of a native tradition that preserves itself only by maintaining a degree of healthy resistance to exotic imported ideas. There is a certain (presumably) unlooked-for irony in Ellis's remarks, since deconstructionists like Hartman and de Man were indeed European refugees, and they have both – de Man especially – had much to say on the topic of 'aesthetic ideology' and its resort to mystified organicist notions of national culture and temperament.[23] But my point is not so much to draw out sinister suggestions from this fairly harmless sentence as to remark just how inconsequent the argument looks if one treats it to the kind of logical critique that Ellis so insistently demands. If North American culture lacks 'adequate soil to nourish deconstruction's thrust', then surely it is wrong – a manifest non-sequitur – to conclude from this that deconstruction is nothing more than an exercise of shallow ingenuity, a product of that taste *pour épater les bourgeois* that Ellis thinks indigenous to French intellectual life. At this stage the national stereotypes come thick and fast, though the single most blatant instance is culled from Leo Bersani, as if to make the point while not entirely endorsing its cruder implications. Bersani writes of the 'arrogant frivolity' of the French, 'arrogant' – as Ellis obligingly explains – 'because the French intellectual defines himself [*sic*] through his feeling of superiority to the common herd in his more sophisticated values and perceptions', while 'frivolity' comes in on account of the fact that this same superior intellectual 'never tires of startling and chic new postures to shock and affront the bourgeois in his deadly serious commitment to his old routine' (p. 84). But again one has to ask what kind of logical force this passage could possibly claim, resting as it does on a well-tried mixture of folk-psychology, unargued imputations and manipulative rhetoric designed to head off any question as to what those 'French intellectuals' might actually have to say.

Ellis makes a bid for the moral high ground by opening his book with a call to serious, responsible debate on these matters, followed up by a complaint that deconstructors (unspecified) too often fall back on obscurantist arguments or an attitude of sovereign disdain toward their typecast naïve opponents.

> The test of whether they [the opponents] have sufficient intellectual sophistica-
> tion to discuss deconstruction will be that they are able to appreciate so sophist-
> icated a position. Those who question that evaluation ipso facto fail the test and
> deserve to be regarded with scorn. (p. ix)

There is – one has to admit – some truth in what he says, at least with regard to
those high-toned apostles of the deconstructionist cult who reject as mere
impertinence any attempt to criticise Derrida's work from a less than ideally
sympathetic standpoint. But the charge applies more aptly to Ellis's techniques of knock-down polemical assault and his habit of treating deconstruction as merely a short-lived fashionable craze among jaded literary theorists.
The three greatest virtues of Derrida's writing are also – and non-
coincidentally – the three qualities most strikingly absent from Ellis's treatment of the subject. That is to say, he combines a quite extraordinary range
and depth of philosophic thought with a keen analytical intelligence *and* (by
no means incompatible with these) a degree of stylistic virtuosity that allows
his writing to reflect at every point on its own performative aspect, or on
issues raised in and through the practice of an answerable 'literary' style.

Ellis is of course not the only commentator to have problems in seeing how
these attributes might go together, or how Derrida could be both a 'serious'
philosophical thinker and a writer of uncommon stylistic resource. Habermas
for one builds his entire case against deconstruction on the argument that these
functions have increasingly separated out in the 'philosophical discourse of
modernity' to the point where such an enterprise as Derrida's can only appear
a species of latter-day Nietzschean unreason, one that effectively abandons or
repudiates the 'unfinished project' of enlightenment.[24] That these readings are
mistaken – that they derive from a deep-laid logocentric prejudice which
Derrida has done much to expose and contest – is a case that I have argued at
length elsewhere, and which Ellis is perfectly entitled to dispute on the evidence of Derrida's texts.[25] But any convincing challenge will have to do more
than just rehearse what amounts to a litany of anti-deconstructionist *idées
reçues*. It will need to show precisely where Derrida's arguments go wrong;
where he misreads or misconstrues his philosophical source-texts; or where
the claims of deconstruction themselves fall prey to a better, more adequate,
historically informed, or cogent theoretical critique. One can readily endorse
Ellis's statement that

> 'theory of criticism' is surely best thought of, not as a set of dogmas but rather as
> an activity – the activity of analyzing, reflecting on, and thinking through the
> current practices of criticism to uncover its possible inconsistencies and

insufficiencies and to improve on those parts of it that cannot stand up to careful analysis. (p. 153)

But all the signs so far are that deconstruction has a much better claim to represent those values than the arguments routinely mustered against it by the partisans of a self-assured commonsense orthodoxy.

Notes

1. See especially Friedrich Nietzsche, 'Of truth and lie in an extra-moral sense', in Walter Kaufmann, trans. and ed., *The Portable Nietzsche* (New York: Viking, 1954), pp. 42–6.
2. Richard Rorty, 'Philosophy as a kind of writing', in *Consequences of Pragmatism* (Minneapolis: University of Minnesota Press, 1982), pp. 89–109. See also Christopher Norris, 'Philosophy as *not* just a "kind of writing"': Derrida and the claim of reason', in Reed Way Dasenbrock (ed.), *Redrawing the Lines: analytic philosophy, deconstruction, and literary theory* (University of Minnesota Press, 1989), pp. 189–203 and Rorty, 'Two meanings of "Logocentrism"': a reply to Norris', *ibid.*, pp. 204–216.
3. John M. Ellis, *The Theory of Literary Criticism: a logical analysis* (Berkeley and Los Angeles: University of California Press, 1974).
4. See especially the essays collected in Paul de Man, *The Resistance to Theory* (Minneapolis: University of Minnesota Press, 1986).
5. See Jacques Derrida, *Dissemination*, trans. Barbara Johnson (London: Athlone Press, 1981) and 'Living on: border-lines', in *Deconstruction and Criticism*, ed. Geoffrey Hartman, Harold Bloom *et al.* (London: Routledge & Kegan Paul, 1979), pp. 75–176.
6. See especially Derrida, *Margins of Philosophy*, trans. Alan Bass (Chicago: University of Chicago Press, 1982).
7. Derrida, 'Signature Event Context', *Glyph*, vol. 1 (Johns Hopkins University Press, 1977), pp. 172–97; John R. Searle, 'Reiterating the differences' (reply to Derrida), *Glyph*, vol. 1 (1977), pp. 198–208; Derrida, 'Limited Inc abc', *Glyph*, vol. 2 (1977), pp. 162–254. The new edition of *Limited Inc* (particulars on p. 147) contains both of Derrida's essays along with his 'Afterword: toward an ethics of discussion', responding to questions submitted by the editor, Gerald Graff. For discussion of the debate between Derrida and Searle, see Jonathan Culler, 'Meaning and convention: Derrida and Austin', *New Literary History*, vol. 8 (1981), pp. 15–30; Stanley Fish, 'With the compliments of the author: reflections on Austin and Derrida', *Critical Inquiry*, vol. 8 (1982), pp. 693–721; Christopher Norris, *Derrida* (London: Fontana, 1986), pp. 172–193; Gayatri Spivak, 'Revolutions that as yet have no model: Derrida's *Limited Inc*', *Diacritics*, vol. 10 (1980), pp. 29–49.
8. Searle, 'Reiterating the differences' (*op. cit.*), p. 201.
9. J.L. Austin, *How To Do Things With Words* (London: OUP, 1963).
10. See for instance Derrida, 'Afterword: toward an ethics of discussion' (*op. cit.*), pp. 111–54.

11. The point is already made with notable precision in Derrida, *Of Grammatology*, trans. Gayatri Spivak (Baltimore: Johns Hopkins University Press, 1976). See especially 'The exorbitant: question of method', pp. 157–64. Let me cite one passage from this early text – a passage that Ellis ignores, along with various others to similar effect – lest it be thought that Derrida has indeed changed tack in response to hostile or uncomprehending criticism.

> To produce this signifying structure [i.e. a deconstructive reading] obviously cannot consist of reproducing, by the effaced and respectful doubling of commentary, the conscious, voluntary, intentional relationship that the writer institutes in his exchanges with the history to which he belongs thanks to the element of language. This moment of doubling commentary should no doubt have its place in a critical reading. To recognize and respect all its classical exigencies is not easy and requires all the instruments of traditional criticism. Without this recognition and this respect, critical production would risk developing in any direction at all and authorize itself to say almost anything. But this indispensable guardrail has always only *protected*, it has never *opened*, a reading (p. 158).

One could work through this passage sentence by sentence and show how it specifically disowns the attitude of free-for-all hermeneutic licence – or the downright anti-intentionalist stance – that Ellis so persistently attributes to Derrida. And of course it must also create problems for those among the deconstructionist adepts who likewise take him to have broken altogether with values of truth and falsehood, right reading, intentionality, authorial 'presence' and so forth.

12. Derrida, *Edmund Husserl's 'Origin of Geometry': an introduction*, trans. John P. Leavey (Pittsburgh: Duquesne University Press, 1978); Derrida,'*Speech and Phenomena' and other essays on Husserl's theory of signs*, trans. David B. Allison (Evanston, Ill.: Northwestern University Press, 1973).

13. See especially Rodolphe Gasché, *The Tain Of The Mirror: Derrida and the philosophy of reflection* (Cambridge, Mass.: Harvard University Press, 1986).

14. See Derrida, 'Structure, sign, and play in the discourse of the human sciences', in *Writing and Difference*, trans. Alan Bass (London: Routledge & Kegan Paul, 1978), pp. 278–93.

15. See Rorty, 'Philosophy as a kind of writing' (*op. cit.*); also 'Deconstruction and circumvention', *Critical Inquiry*, vol. 11 (1984), pp. 1–23.

16. Derrida, *Glas*, trans. John P. Leavey and Richard Rand (Lincoln, Nebraska: Nebraska University Press, 1987); *The Postcard: from Socrates to Freud and beyond*, trans. Alan Bass (Chicago: University of Chicago Press, 1987).

17. Gasché, *The Tain of the Mirror* (*op. cit.*); John Llewelyn, *Derrida on the Threshold of Sense* (London: Macmillan, 1986).

18. Jürgen Habermas, *The Philosophical Discourse of Modernity: twelve lectures*, trans. Frederick Lawrence (Cambridge: Polity Press, 1987).

19. See Derrida, 'The supplement of copula', and 'White mythology: metaphor in the text of philosophy', in *Margins of Philosophy* (*op. cit.*), pp. 175–205 and 207–71. All further references to 'White mythology;' given by page-number in the text.

20. See Rorty, *Consequences of Pragmatism* (*op. cit.*) and *Irony, Contingency, and Solidarity* (New York and Cambridge: CUP, 1989).

21. Paul de Man, 'The epistemology of metaphor', *Critical Inquiry*, vol. 5, no. 1 (1978), pp. 13–30.

Limited think: how not to read Derrida

22. For a useful survey of the field, see Jane P. Tompkins (ed.), *Reader-Response Criticism: from formalism to post-structuralism* (Baltimore: Johns Hopkins University Press, 1980).
23. On this topic, see Norris, *Paul de Man: deconstruction and the critique of aesthetic ideology* (New York and London: Routledge, 1988).
24. Habermas, *The Philosophical Discourse of Modernity* (*op. cit.*).
25. See especially Chapter 1 of this volume and Norris, *Deconstruction and the Interests of Theory* (London: Pinter Publishers; Norman, Oklahoma: University of Oklahoma Press, 1988).

Chapter 4

Lost in the Funhouse: Baudrillard and the Politics of Postmodernism

I

'Forget Foucault' was Baudrillard's title for a nifty piece of polemics which, in the current French manner, staked his claim to be 'post-' just about everything, post-structuralism and Foucault included.* I think we would do well to forget Baudrillard, though not without treating his texts to more in the way of argued critique than Baudrillard sees fit to provide when dealing with his own precursors and rivals on the intellectual scene. An opportunity is now offered by the appearance of Baudrillard's *Selected Writings* in a volume edited by Mark Poster and presenting a useful overview of work published during the past two decades.[1] The book contains sizeable excerpts from nine of Baudrillard's texts, some of which have already been translated in full, while others are here published in English for the first time. There is enough to give the reader a lively sense of Baudrillard's rhetorical strategies, his frequent shifts of political ground, and his unwillingness to occupy any 'position' that might need defending in principle or theory. Baudrillard is undoubtedly the one who has gone furthest toward renouncing enlightenment reason and all its works, from the Kantian-liberal agenda to Marxism, Frankfurt Critical Theory, the structuralist 'sciences of man', and even – on his view – the residual theoreticist delusions of a thinker like Foucault. The nearest equivalents are Richard Rorty's brand of postmodern neo-pragmatist anti-philosophy and the strain of so-called 'weak thought' (not unaptly so called) that has lately been canvassed by Gianni Vattimo and other Heideggerian apostles of unreason.[2] But one suspects that Baudrillard would reject these comparisons, regarding

---

* *Jean Baudrillard: selected writings,* ed. Mark Poster (Cambridge: Polity Press, 1988). All further references to this volume given by page-number only in the text.

them as moves in a pointless game whose rule-book has been endlessly rewritten and should now be torn up for good and all.

Mark Poster's introduction is by no means given over to a wholesale celebration of these writings. It raises certain doubts as to Baudrillard's style ('hyperbolic and declarative, often lacking sustained, systematic analysis when appropriate'), his tendency to extrapolate far-reaching conclusions from limited evidence, and his habit of ignoring any hopeful signs that might complicate the otherwise dire prognosis for civilisation and its discontents. All the same Poster takes it as read that Baudrillard has important things to say and that his work engages the most salient features of our current 'postmodern' situation. More specifically, it offers new bearings in an age when 'the instant, worldwide availability of information has changed human society forever, probably for the good' (p. 8). No longer can we fall back on those old 'meta-narratives' or enlightenment myths of information, grounded as they were (or as they claimed to be) in a capacity to distinguish truth from falsehood, progress from reaction, knowledge from the various kinds of pseudo-knowledge (or mere 'ideology') that passed themselves off as the genuine thing. Of course other thinkers (among them Rorty and Lyotard) have argued to similar effect.[3] But none of them has maintained such an extreme oppositional stance toward every last truth-claim, every form or vestige of enlightened critical thought. In Lyotard's case there has been a marked shift of emphasis, from a work like *The Postmodern Condition* where enlightenment values are seen as the source of manifold errors and evils, to those recent texts where a certain (albeit heterodox) reading of Kant is applied to questions of history, politics and interpretation.[4] But with Baudrillard the movement is in an opposite direction, starting out from the critique of Marxism and other such 'foundationalist' or 'epistemological' paradigms, and then – as the very notion of critique becomes suspect – embracing a wholesale postmodernist creed where the ideas of truth, validity or right reason simply drop out of the picture.

This is where Poster locates the significance of Baudrillard's work: in the way that it 'shatters the existing foundations for critical social theory, showing how the privilege they give to labor and their rationalist epistemologies are inadequate for the analysis of the media and other new social activities' (p. 8). Thus, despite his detailed reservations, Poster accepts the basic claim that we have moved into a new (and as yet unthinkable) stage of postmodern evolution; that the old paradigms (whether Kantian, Marxist, structuralist or whatever) are of no use at all in grasping this emergent phase; and that therefore we had best help the process along by not putting up any kind of misguided theoretical resistance. Philosophers and political theorists since Plato have taken it as axiomatic that thought must at some point distinguish between truth and falsehood, reason and rhetoric, essence and appearance, science and ideology. One way of describing Baudrillard's project is to see it as a species of inverted Platonism, a discourse that systematically promotes the negative terms (rhetoric, appearance, ideology) above their positive counterparts. It is no longer possible to maintain the old economy of truth and representation in a world where 'reality' is entirely constructed through forms of mass-media feedback, where values are determined by consumer demand (itself brought about by the endless circulation of meanings, images and advertising codes), and where nothing could serve as a means of distinguishing true from merely true-seeming (or ideological) habits of belief. Such is the world we now inhabit, according to Baudrillard, and such are the governing conditions for any project of thought that hopes to make sense of the postmodern epoch.

Hence Baudrillard's quarrel with Marxism, developed most fully in *The Mirror of Production* (1973). Here he sets out to deconstruct the opposition between use-value and exchange-value, the one conceived in terms of 'genuine' needs and productive resources, the other identified with a late-capitalist or consumer economy which invades and distorts every aspect of human existence. But this is to get the matter backward, Baudrillard argues, since any definition of use-value will have to take account of the socialised desires, needs and expectations which constitute the sphere of values in general. Thus the positive terms of Marxist theory – labour-power, production, use-value, needs – are still caught up in a form of essentialist or metaphysical thinking which in effect reproduces the discourse of eighteenth-century political economy. That is to say, they are subject to an 'anthropological postulate', one that starts out from the Marxian premise that 'men begin to distinguish themselves from animals as soon as they begin to produce their means of subsistence' (p. 98). In a just social order such needs would be satisfied through a system based on use-values alone, or on the capacity of human individuals to create and enjoy the fruits of their own labour. It is only with the advent of exchange-value – of an artificial system created and sustained by capitalist market forces – that workers become 'alienated' from their real conditions of existence, thus falling victim to various forms of ideological false consciousness. It is this line of argument that Baudrillard rejects, since he sees it as just another version of the classical (Platonist) doctrine that holds out for truth against the snares of illusion and false seeming. More specifically, Marxism invests concepts like 'need', 'labour' and 'production' with an abstract generality or universal value which places them beyond further question. And to this extent it betrays its own critical imperative, the will to demystify naturalised, commonsense modes of perception (like those of classical free-market doctrine) by showing them to rest on stipulative values derived from some particular class interest or ideological world-view.

There are close parallels to be drawn between Baudrillard's *Mirror of Production* and Richard Rorty's *Philosophy and the Mirror of Nature* (published some seven years later).[5] Rorty rejects the idea of philosophy as a foundational or first-order discipline, one that explains how knowledge comes about by working to achieve an accurate match between real-world objects or states of affairs and concepts of pure understanding. Such was the decisive wrong turn that philosophy took when, with Descartes and Kant, it seized upon certain privileged metaphors – centrally those of the mind as a 'glassy essence' or 'mirror of nature' – and allowed these tropes to determine its entire future project. The result was a discourse that increasingly specialised in the discovery of unreal 'solutions' to unreal 'problems', a narrative whose chief episodes would include the entire history of post-Kantian debate on the powers and limits of knowledge, along with much of the modern analytical tradition (where, according to Rorty, these topics are merely recast in linguistic as opposed to epistemological terms). The exchange of one technical vocabulary for another brought nothing in the way of improved understanding or enhanced social relevance. What should now be apparent, after so much wasted ingenuity, is the fact that no solutions will ever be forthcoming, that epistemology was a pointless endeavour from the outset, and that therefore philosophers should give up this deluded quest and rejoin the cultural 'conversation of mankind' on equal terms with sociologists, literary critics and others who never entertained such high-flown ambitions. And this would mean dispensing with a whole set of pseudo-solutions ('clear and distinct ideas', a priori concepts, sense-data, transcendental arguments and so forth) which have hitherto managed to exert such a spellbinding power.

Rorty sees nothing to regret in this mood of postmodern disenchantment with enlightenment reason in its various forms. On the contrary, he hopes that it will bring philosophers around to the belated recognition that there is no ultimate truth to be had, no language that would 'cut nature at the joints' or achieve an ideal, one-to-one match between concepts and sensuous intuitions. 'True' can then be redefined for all practical purposes as 'good in the way of belief', a label of convenience attached to those ideas that currently enjoy widespread approval, or which make good sense in the context of this or that language-game, discipline or cultural 'form of life'. Of course we can carry on using those old conceptual idioms – Kantian, Hegelian, Marxist or whatever – in the hope that they might come up with some argument proof against time and change. But really they amount to nothing more than a range of alternative 'final vocabularies', styles of talk that serve well enough to keep the conversation going, but no longer possess much persuasive power in an age of neo-pragmatist (or 'postmodern bourgeois liberal') culture. In fact we should do better – so Rorty argues – to give up these outworn habits of thought and instead make every effort to multiply the language-games and thereby create as many conversational openings as possible. Philosophy to date has been hooked on a handful of metaphors masquerading as concepts, poetic ideas that were taken as absolute truths, thus losing whatever they once possessed of imaginative vigour and force. On the Nietzschean view that Rorty adopts, this process started out with the victory of Socratic rationalism and achieved its bad apotheosis with Descartes, Kant and their successors. Its last major episode was the rise of Anglo-American analytical philosophy, a movement that has now lost its way among various competing (and wholly undecidable) claims and counter-claims. So our best option is to drop the old metaphors – especially those that still trade on ideas of privileged epistemic access, or the mind as a mirror of nature – and try out whatever promising substitutes now come to hand.

Baudrillard is arguing a similar case with regard to the concepts and categories of Marxist theory. Like Rorty, he denounces such thinking as just another variant on the old, self-deluding enlightenment theme, the idea that one can criticise existing beliefs from some superior vantage-point of truth, reason or scientific method. Marxism compounds this error, according to Baudrillard, by basing its critique on a series of essentialist or anthropological concepts, among them the privilege accorded to economic use-value and the notion of 'man' as a creature defined by *needs* on the one hand and *productive capacity* on the other. It is in this sense that the Marxist 'mirror of production' takes its place among the governing metaphors of modern (post-Kantian) thought. When Marx set out to stand Hegelian dialectic back on its feet – to invert the terms of idealist philosophy by restoring the material forces of production to their rightful primacy over everything pertaining to the social and cultural spheres – he provided just one more delusive variation on the old metaphysical theme. And this applies all the more to those latter-day exponents who argue, like Althusser, for a reading of the Marxian text that would separate the elements of a dialectical-materialist 'science' from the residues of a humanist or 'ideological' project that persists into the early ('pre-Marxist') writings.[6] For it is a mark of their historical obsolescence that such arguments cling to the old enlightenment paradigm, the idea that we might yet come up with some *theory* – some infallible method or technique – for separating truth from the various currencies of true-seeming ideological belief.

What these thinkers fail to grasp – as Baudrillard sees it – is the fact that we have now moved on into an epoch where no such distinctions hold, where truth is entirely a product of consensus values, and where 'science' itself is just the name we attach to certain (currently prestigious) modes of explanation. Marxism especially invites this charge since it holds out the prospect of a liberating break with earlier paradigms (e.g. those of idealist metaphysics and eighteenth-century political economy) while in fact reproducing the selfsame structures of thought through its appeal to use-value, labour-power, forces of production, etc. For these categories still pay homage to a certain residual 'essence of man', one that is defined precisely in terms of *natural productive capacities* on the one hand and *elemental human needs* on the other. They are thus caught up in a specular relation or a pattern of unwitting dialectical reprise that ends up by confirming every last theorem of the 'false' sciences that Marx set out to controvert. And so it happens that, according to Baudrillard,

> the weapon Marx created turns against him and turns his theory into the dialectical apotheosis of political economy . . . The concept of critique emerged in the West at the same time as political economy and, as the quintessence of Enlightenment rationality, is perhaps only the subtle, long-term expression of the system's expanded reproduction . . . [P]erhaps, under the guise of producing its fatal internal contradiction, Marx only rendered a descriptive theory. The logic of representation – of the duplication of its object – haunts all rational discursiveness. Every critical theory is haunted by this surreptitious religion, this desire bound up with the construction of its object, this negativity subtly haunted by the very form that it negates. (p. 116)

And if critical theory is thus fated to undo itself – to fall straight back into the errors and delusions of some antecedent discourse which it aims to criticise – then we might as well give up on the whole attempt to get beyond existing consensus-values in the name of some better, more 'enlightened' or adequate understanding. This project would at best be a mere waste of time, and at worst a form of repressive instrumental reason that reduces all history to its own meta-narrative system of concepts and categories. For in Baudrillard's view such arguments must always be deluded, based as they are on an outworn (epistemological) paradigm which still thinks to distinguish *truth* or its various surrogates – 'science', 'the real', 'objectivity', 'use-value' 'need' or whatever – from the ideological representations which currently lay claim to that title.

It is for this reason that Marxism stands squarely within the line of mainstream Western intellectual descent, a line that begins with the Platonic distinction between *doxa* (mere opinion) and *episteme* (genuine knowledge), and which then comes down via Descartes and Kant to the present-day human sciences. Such is the fate of all critical concepts as soon as they claim any kind of explanatory power beyond the historical context that produced them or the circumstances that gave rise to their first elaboration. In short, theories can only be of use in so far as we apply them reflexively to the material or socio-political conditions under which they came into being. To suppose otherwise – to credit (say) the Kantian or Marxist critiques with any kind of ultimate validity – is to lapse into a form of 'metaphysical' thinking which persistently ignores this lesson.

So Marx may have managed to 'transform the concepts of production and mode of production at a given moment', and thus brought about a 'break in the social mystery of exchange-value' which helps to understand the conditions prevailing at that moment. But Marxism goes wrong when it attempts to universalise such insights, building them up into a full-scale critical theory or 'science' with claims to non-contingent, categorical truth. At this point, Baudrillard writes, such concepts

> become canonical and enter the general system's mode of representation . . . They set themselves up as expressing an 'objective reality'. They become signs: signifiers of a 'real' signified. And although at the best of times these concepts have been practised as concepts without taking themselves for reality, they have nonetheless subsequently fallen into the *imaginary of the sign*, or the *sphere of truth*. They are no longer in the sphere of interpretation but enter that of *repressive simulation*. (p. 114)

This passage is clearly much indebted to Nietzsche. It repeats his genealogical account of how 'truth' came about through a process of forgetting its own formative prehistory; how certain originary metaphors were subsequently mistaken for concepts, and philosophy was thereby launched on its quest for ideas and essences that never existed outside this jargon specialised for the purpose of systematic self-deception.[7] It is an argument – or a piece of enabling background narrative – that unites Baudrillard with other thinkers like Foucault, Lyotard and Rorty, all of them committed to a postmodern-pragmatist or anti-enlightenment viewpoint. But it is Baudrillard, more than anyone, who has pushed this kind of rhetoric as far as it will go and used it as a weapon against every last claim of truth, validity and critical reason. For if Baudrillard is right – setting aside the question of what 'rightness' could amount to, given this degree of epistemological scepticism – then it is hard to envisage any way forward other than a total abandonment of all such ideas and a willing embrace of the so-called 'postmodern condition'.

II

His case therefore rests on the following propositions: (1) that theory is a discredited enterprise, since 'truth' has turned out to be a fictive, rhetorical or imaginary construct; (2) that this prevents (or ought to prevent) our engaging in activities of 'rational' argument or *Ideologiekritik* and (3) that we must henceforth drop all talk of 'the real' as opposed to its mystified, distorted or 'ideological' representation, since such talk continues to trade on old assumptions that no longer possess any force or credibility.

Now one could hardly deny that Baudrillard's diagnosis does have a bearing on our present situation in the 'advanced' Western democracies. That is to say, it speaks directly to a widespread sense that we are living in a world of pervasive unreality, a world where perceptions are increasingly shaped by mass-media imagery, political rhetoric and techniques of wholesale disinformation that substitute for any kind of reasoned public debate. This process has undoubtedly intensified in recent years, as anyone will know who took more than a passing interest in the latest British and American election campaigns. In which case it might seem that Baudrillard's arguments are amply borne out by the evidence nearest to hand. Any notion that people are at liberty to think for themselves on the most important issues – that this is indeed what distinguishes the 'free world' from its 'totalitarian' counterpart – is surely belied by the extent to which their ideas, attitudes and voting behaviour are thus programmed in advance. Saturation coverage in the mass media has the effect, not of creating a better-informed electorate, but of reducing the whole business to a dead level of mindless slogans, trivialised issues and a near-total absence of genuine debate on substantive policy issues. Bush's victory in 1988, like Thatcher's the previous year, was a melancholy lesson in the way that elections can be stage-managed so as to distract attention from anything that might create problems for the party (or the cross-party nexus of interests) currently in power. 'Public opinion' is relentlessly monitored through a system of polls and so-called 'random sampling' which can always be adjusted – by suitably framing the questions or the method of statistical analysis – so as to produce the desired facts and figures. As a result it becomes neither necessary nor desirable for candidates to engage in serious discussion on matters of public concern. The antic performances of a Reagan or a Quayle may cause some occasional embarrassment – even a short-term dip in the polls – but are soon enough forgotten with the next round of mass-media polemics.

In short, it is hard to argue with Baudrillard's contention that ours is an age of postmodern 'hyperreality' where truth is merely what counts as such according to the latest media consensus, or as defined through the various loops and circuits of a highly evolved feedback mechanism. And from here it might seem a very short distance to the standpoint that renounces all competence to judge in questions of reality and illusion, truth and falsehood, reasoned argument and rhetorical or suasive effect. Baudrillard's systematic inversion of these concepts – his treatment of 'truth' as the mere by-product of a generalised fictive economy, or of use-value as determined through and through by the currencies of exchange-value – would then be nothing more than a fair extrapolation from the evidence of an epoch that has at last witnessed the definitive collapse of those old, self-deluding ontologies. If 'simulation' is the postmodern name of the game it is not some misfortune that has lately overtaken us but a condition that was always already in force despite the best efforts of truth-seeking theorists, from Plato on down, to pretend otherwise.

Baudrillard develops this case in his essay 'Simulacra and simulations', which again follows Nietzsche in its genealogical undoing of truth as an effect of multiplied errors and illusions.

> These would be the successive phases of the image: (1) It is the reflection of a basic reality. (2) It masks and perverts a basic reality. (3) It masks the *absence* of a basic reality. (4) It bears no relation to any reality whatever; it is its own pure simulacrum. (p.170)

Thus the story starts out, in Hegelian fashion, with primitive sense-certainty; goes on to a principled mistrust of appearances that unites idealists like Plato with critical thinkers like Kant, Hegel and Marx; arrives (item 3) at the Nietzschean stage of a thoroughgoing epistemological scepticism; and finally comes round to the postmodern viewpoint that everything is appearance, that 'truth' was always a species of self-promoting fiction, and that scepticism misses the point since it still makes a big dramatic scene of this belated discovery. For Baudrillard, it is not a question of our now having lost the old confidence in reason and truth as a result of fairly recent upheavals or mutations in the socio-political sphere. Nor is it the case that these changes could be treated as a form of widespread pathological affliction, a loss of the capacity to discriminate truth from falsehood, or the will to exercise reason in matters of political judgement. What we are experiencing now is an ultimate stage of disenchantment with the concepts and categories of enlightenment thought. And it is pointless to deplore or to criticise this process, since it represents not only an accurate diagnosis of our present conditon but, beyond that, a readiness to cope with the absence of all 'metaphysical' guarantees, all those old self-deluding appeals to reason, truth, reality and so forth.

In fact Baudrillard goes out of his way to block any reading of his work that would still find solace in traditional (enlightenment) notions of truth as arrived at by criticising false appearances. Like the Marxist distinction between use-value and exchange-value, these ideas betray not only a false nostalgia – false because premised on a purely imaginary difference – but also a desire to pass themselves off as the real thing, and thus to perpetuate what Baudrillard calls the regime of 'repressive simulation'. This effect comes about through a kind of perverse compensatory mechanism, a process whereby the perceived loss of truth (or the sheer unreality of present-day experience) goes along with an hysterical desire to prove otherwise. 'When the real is no longer what it used to be', Baudrillard writes,

> nostalgia assumes its full meaning. There is a proliferation of myths of origin and signs of reality; of second-hand truth, objectivity and authenticity. There is an escalation of the true, of lived experience . . . And there is a panic-stricken production of the real and the referential, above and parallel to the panic of material production. This is how simulation appears in the phase that concerns us: a strategy of the real, neo-real and hyperreal, whose universal double is a strategy of deterrence. (p. 171)

And it is clear from what he says elsewhere on this topic that Baudrillard 'believes in' nuclear deterrence.[8] It is something that has demonstrably worked, he thinks, at least to the extent that it has produced a continuing strategic stand-off, a situation where the exchange of 'simulated' threats and counter-threats is so hyperbolically unreal – so far beyond the grasp of any rational decision-making power – that we have managed to survive thus far through the waging of a purely rhetorical warfare. But this effect depends entirely on the refusal of each side to call the other's bluff, or on the way that deterrence is confined to a realm of simulation or 'hyperreality' where nobody (nobody in their right mind) would think to try conclusions in a practical way. 'In its orbital and ecstatic form warfare has become an impossible exchange, and this orbitalness protects us' (p. 191). So we had much better stick to the crazy 'logic' of deterrence, make believe that nuclear weapons have indeed 'kept the peace' these past forty years, and not get too worried when each new stage of rhetorical escalation creates a new threat, a new endgame scenario and – most often – a new weapons system to give it 'credible' force. For the only alternative, as Baudrillard sees it, is to think these questions through to a 'rational' or 'realistic' conclusion. And the upshot of this would be to undermine deterrence, substitute serious (war-fighting) plans for simulated (war-game) scenarios, and thus bring about the very catastrophe that we have so far managed to avoid. From which he draws the lesson that any critique of nuclear doublethink – any attempt to get at the truth behind appearances, or to lay bare the sophistries that maintain this illusion– is necessarily a mistaken and dangerous endeavour.[9]

Baudrillard offers various examples of the way that criticism is played off the field by this 'hyperreality' that supposedly extends to every aspect of postmodern life. One of them is Disneyland, often treated (as by de-mythologising commentators like Louis Marin)[11] as 'a digest of the American way of life, panegyric to American values, idealized transposition of a contradictory reality' (p. 172). But such analyses take for granted what Baudrillard is out to deny: namely, the possibility of drawing a line between real and fictive, or authentic and inauthentic modes of knowledge. Thus

> Disneyland is presented as imaginary in order to make us believe that the rest [i.e. the world outside Disneyland] is real, whereas in fact all of Los Angeles and the America surrounding it are no longer real, but of the order of the hyperreal and of simulation. (p. 172)

To think otherwise – like critics who locate the 'truth' of Disneyland in its power to legitimise a world elsewhere, a real world of pressing 'contradictions' which are here resolved in imaginary form – is to fall straight back into the old enlightenment trap. In short, 'it is no longer a question of a false representation of reality (ideology), but of concealing the fact that the real is no longer real, and thus of saving the reality principle' (p. 172). Thus the Marxists go wrong – in company with the Platonists, Kantians and culture-critics like Marin – when they claim to strip away the accretions of mythology (or commonsense belief) and expose the truth that has hitherto sheltered behind these saving appearances. The effect of such thinking would then be precisely to *endorse* the Disneyland myth, the idea that there exists an alternative world where the reality-principle reigns, where illusions come up against hard fact and theory will inevitably have the last word. For, according to Baudrillard, there is nothing to choose between this kind of self-deceiving attitude on the part of left-wing intellectuals and the other, more 'naïve' or spontaneous kind that simply enjoys Disneyland and never gives a thought to its 'ideological' function. In fact he strongly implies that the latter is preferable in so far as it avoids the theoreticist mistake of constructing just one more alibi for truth, and thus reinforcing the selfsame mythical message.

Another case in point (as Baudrillard reads it) is the Watergate affair and the way that this episode gave rise to a wholesale media campaign of 'public morality' versus the lies, intrigues and abuses of state power. Here again, the basic trick was to represent Nixon's behaviour as if it were a scandalous departure from the norm, a criminal folly that could then be brought to light by the courageous detective-work of two *Washington Post* journalists, inspired (as their book and the subsequent film made clear) by a dogged belief in truth, good reporting and the virtues of American democracy. Baudrillard sees this as a prime instance of the way that 'capitalism' can turn anything to advantage, even in the case of a political scandal that would seem to strike directly at its own vested interests. For such events help to confirm the idea that there is nothing wrong with the system itself; that abuses like Watergate are the exception, not the rule, and may in fact lead to a welcome renewal of the 'true' American spirit. Thus 'Watergate above all succeeded in imposing the idea that Watergate *was* a scandal – in this sense it was an extraordinary operation of intoxication: the reinjection of a large dose of political morality on a global scale' (p. 173). But one can grasp all this and still misinterpret the signs, as Baudrillard remarks of Pierre Bourdieu, who had analysed Watergate in terms of its ideological effect in dissimulating the *real* power-interests that lay behind the rhetoric of outrage, public morality, democratic values and so forth. Thus Bourdieu sets out to show how these 'relations of force' are both disguised and maintained by a periodic outbreak of moral panic which 'spontaneously furthers the order of capital'. But in adopting this position he unwittingly repeats the very gesture that his argument seeks to expose. For on Baudrillard's reading,

> this is still only the formula of ideology, and when Bourdieu enunciates it, he takes 'relation of force' to mean the *truth* of capitalist domination, and he *denounces* this relation of force as itself a *scandal*; he therefore occupies the same deterministic and moralistic position as the *Washington Post* journalists. (p. 173)

And if Baudrillard is right then the same must apply to all versions of *Ideologiekritik* and all attempts to distinguish falsehood from truth on a basis of reasoned argument.

III

I have offered this lengthy account of Baudrillard's work because I think there is an urgent need both to grasp the sources of its widespread appeal and to put up a resistance to it on principled theoretical grounds. The appeal is after all not so hard to understand, given the current political climate in Britain and the United States. The New York *Village Voice* made this connection in a number of articles on the Bush campaign and the 'hyperreality' of US electoral politics. Were Baudrillard's arguments not borne out by the absence of serious debate, the extent of mass-media manipulative influence and the ease with which the electorate was swung into believing such a mass of ungrounded allegations, half-truths and downright lies? How could one explain Bush's victory except by acknowledging the total obsolescence of ideas like truth, public accountability and the need to answer for past acts and decisions?

The *Voice* had done some good work in revealing not only the mendacity of Bush's campaign rhetoric but also the depth of his involvement with Irangate and other such shady (not to say criminal) episodes of the Reagan years. But of course this knowledge had currency only among a small readership, at least as compared with the mass-circulation papers and TV channels where the charges were treated, if at all, as mere distractions from the ongoing media charade. And any comfort in the fact that the Democrats fought a relatively 'clean' campaign was more than outweighed by their having given up on just about every major point of principle. In his televised 'debates' with Bush one had the impression that Dukakis was reading from a script drawn up by the Republican publicity team and designed to present him as an amiable half-wit who simply had not learnt the new rules of the game. By sedulously avoiding any use of the dread word 'liberal' – the Reaganspeak equivalent of 'communist' in McCarthy's era, or 'atheist' in Renaissance drama – Dukakis sacrificed his own best chance of staging an effective comeback. When he *did* start using it, in a last-minute change of strategy, his campaign showed signs of a limited revival. But of course the change came too late and the election was won on what amounted to a wholesale anti-liberal crusade, an Orwellian use of rhetorical tricks and whipped-up populist fervour to which the Democrats more or less surrendered from the outset.

So the *Voice* had some reason for turning to Baudrillard in hopes of understanding just what had gone wrong. One line of argument much canvassed in the run-up was that opinion polls were perhaps having a harmful influence on the democratic process since voters were unduly swayed by the wording of questions, the 'hidden agenda', or the feedback-effect which told them what to think before they had even started to make their minds up. But Baudrillard rejects such arguments as just another case of the old enlightenment dream, the craving for a 'truth' behind appearances, in this case truth that would win out in elections were it not for the polls and their mischievous influence. 'All this would be serious enough', he writes, 'if there were an objective truth of needs, an objective truth of public opinion' (p. 209). But there is no such thing – no *reality* of human needs, desires or interests – and hence no telling whether the polls have an effect on 'public opinion' for better or worse. Thus in Baudrillard's view we should agree neither with those who praise the beneficial use of the media, nor with those who scream about manipulation, for the simple reason that there is no relationship between a system of meaning and a system of simulation. Publicity and opinion polls would be incapable, even if they wished and claimed to do so, of alienating the will or the opinion of anyone at all, for the reason that they do not act in the time-space of will or of representation where judgment is formed. (p. 209)

He does go on to speak of this phenomenon as an 'obscenity', a kind of 'hyperchondriacal madness', persuading the electorate that 'it must at all times know what it wants, know what it thinks, be told about its least needs, its least quivers, *see* itself continually on the videoscreen of statistics' (p. 209). But he also makes it clear that these comments should be taken as a neutral diagnosis of the way things are, and not as an appeal to some saving principle of truth, reality or reason. And indeed Baudrillard is in no position to adopt such a critical stance, having argued repeatedly against the idea – the deluded 'enlightenment' idea – that we could ever think beyond this realm of false appearance to that which it supposedly dissimulates or masks.

But the question remains as to whether this persuasive *diagnosis* of postmodern politics necessarily entails a wholesale abandonment of truth-claims and the reality-principle. That is to say: does the fact that we currently inhabit an unreal world – a realm of mass-media distortion, nuclear deterrence, manipulative opinion polls and the rest – justify Baudrillard in his further assumption that there is no way out, since reality just *is* (to the best of our knowledge) the world which we thus inhabit? The *Village Voice* was understandably reluctant to draw this conclusion since it had made great efforts, during the run-up period, to uncover some of the facts about Bush's past record and the real power-interests at work behind the Republican campaign. All the same one can understand how the election result might have dented this confidence, suggesting as it did that the line between truth and falsehood had indeed been erased, that the politics of unreality had won out at last, and therefore that no amount of reasoned argument or factual reporting could turn back the tide of mass-media falsification. In fact – as more than one writer suggested – Bush's victory signalled a worse condition in the body politic than Reagan's two terms of office. At least with Reagan there was a sense that this business could not be for real; that the B-movie actor had somehow managed to impose his own crazy view of things, but that surely the episode would come to an end when people woke up to the true situation. There were no such comforting thoughts to be had with regard to George Bush and his very different brand of hard-headed cynical opportunism. It looked very much as if Baudrillard had been proved right – whatever that could mean – and the time of false appearances had now given way to a grim new reality-principle, one that no longer had need of Reagan's so-called 'charismatic' appeal.

I think there is good reason to reject this idea, along with the whole postmodernist line of last-ditch sceptical retreat. But it is not enough to say that such thinking has undesirable effects, that it leaves us bereft of argumentative grounds upon which to challenge the current, massively distorted consensus-view. To Baudrillard this would seem just one more instance of the old enlightenment nostalgia, the failure to perceive how those grounds were always (and are now more than ever) a species of wishful thinking. It would amount to nothing more than a pragmatist case for continuing to believe in truth and reason, since without such beliefs one could muster no defence against the lies and falsehoods put around by unscrupulous opponents. And if this were the bottom line of argument – one that took truth as what is currently 'good in the way of belief' – then Baudrillard would always have the last word in so far as he could point to the various signs that people (or the great majority of people) just do not have any use for such obsolete ideas. There is a parallel here with neo-pragmatists like Richard Rorty and Stanley Fish, those who hold that since all theories, truth-claims, ethical principles, etc. *must* be construed in terms of some given consensus or 'interpretive community', then we might as well give up such abstract talk and accept that the best we can ever hope to do is argue persuasively within that existing context of belief.[11] These thinkers would certainly reject the claim that their position has disabling political consequences, or that it leads to an attitude of passively accepting just any kind of current consensus-belief. For if Fish managed to convince us – that is to say, if we lost all faith in the idea that theory has 'consequences', that it is able to affect what we presently believe, one way or another – then it need not follow from this that we would be stuck for arguments and lose all interest in politics, philosophy, literary theory or whatever. In fact we would carry on debating these matters in pretty much the same old way, except that we would now be aware (at some level) that there were no ultimate truths to be had, no ground-rules or principles beyond those offered by the range of currently available beliefs.

So theory may have results in so far as it gets us to put things differently by shifting the terms of debate or persuades us to attach importance to some new set of problems and principles. But there is no question of theory having 'consequences' in the stronger sense of that term, that is, in the sense that one could come up with reasons – purely theoretical reasons – for rejecting what one does in fact believe.[12] There is simply no difference, on Fish's view, between saying 'I believe x to be the case' and claiming to *know* that x is the case on factual, theoretical or other such grounds. More precisely, the difference can only be a matter of rhetorical emphasis or the degree of psychological conviction involved. Knowing just *is* that particular state of mind in which we claim good reason for believing this or that to be the case. And it is wholly inconceivable that anyone could ever arrive at the position of rejecting *in theory* what they took to be true at the level of mere 'ideology' or 'commonsense' belief. For this would entail a contradiction in performative terms, as well as – psychologically speaking – a form of advanced schizophrenic disorder. From which Fish concludes (1) that truth-claims and beliefs are synonymous for all practical purposes, (2) that theory can never do more than appeal to some existing idea of what counts as a good theoretical argument, and (3) that we should therefore give up the notion that theorising makes any difference, aside from its usefulness in persuading us (and others) to think we have 'grounds' for believing what we do. As for the question whether his own line of argument had 'consequences', Fish can afford to take a relaxed view of the matter. Of course nothing follows in theory from establishing the point that theory is a strictly inconsequential activity. But if everyone were suddenly converted to Fish's persuasion then this would have the wholly desirable result, as he sees it, of putting an end to such misguided talk and getting us to argue things out on a basis of straightforwardly differing beliefs. Nothing would have changed except the realisation that nothing had changed, and that theory had therefore been pointless or redundant all along.

Now Fish would most certainly object to being classified with Baudrillard as a 'postmodern' thinker or exponent of the new irrationalism. In fact he makes a point of arguing – like Rorty – that his views just reflect what normally goes on in the way of civilised exchange among members of the various 'interpretive communities' (professional, academic and so forth) whose conversation sets the tone of a liberal-democratic culture. If they stopped talking theory it would scarcely affect this conversation, except to the extent that people found more time for discussing their genuine, substantive differences of view. So there would still be room for all manner of debate on issues of politics, ethics, philosophy, literary interpretation or whatever, just so long as the participants did not lay claim to any kind of theoretical warrant. If this position might itself seem politically loaded – if it serves (as with Rorty) to endorse the self-image of late twentieth-century North American liberal culture – then Fish can quite happily acknowledge this fact, believing as he does that there is no real option except to keep talking on the terms offered by one's own intellectual community. Like Baudrillard, he flatly rejects the idea that it could ever make sense to look *outside* that community – beyond its currently available range of meanings, values and assumptions –

whether in search of legitimising grounds or a basis for radical critique. But unlike Baudrillard he clearly thinks that North American culture is healthy enough – or sufficiently in touch with social realities – to warrant an attitude of sturdy pragmatist confidence, a belief that all is well with the current conversation, and therefore with society at large.

I want to suggest that Baudrillard is much nearer the mark in his characterisation of present-day society; that Fish could bring up no arguments against him, since he (Fish) has abandoned the grounds on which such an argument would need to be conducted; and – the main point at issue – that they are both mistaken in rejecting all appeals to anything beyond what is currently 'good in the way of belief'. For Baudrillard, this means that there is just no alternative to the realm of illusory appearances that constitute 'reality' as presently known and experienced. For Fish, less alarmingly, it means that we can carry on believing in the principles of democracy, justice, reason, 'truth at the end of enquiry' and so forth, provided we do not make the further claim of having a *theory* to back up those principles. Thus according to Fish it is an obvious fact that we believe what we believe, and that no amount of theorising can change our minds unless we are already – at some level of awareness – either half-way convinced or open to persuasion. His response to Baudrillard would no doubt be in keeping with what Fish has to say about Marxist, deconstructionist and other such challenges to consensual wisdom. That is to say, he would argue that postmodernism reduces to manifest nonsense in so far as it thinks to raise questions about truth, meaning, 'commonsense' belief, etc. which cannot be raised – at least, not *seriously* – if one wants to get a hearing and be rightly understood by members of one's own (or any other) 'interpretive community'. But it is far from obvious why Fish should exhibit such undiminished faith in the power of this community (roughly speaking: the North American academic, cultural and professional elite, with support from the mainstream of public opinion) to keep the conversation going and preserve the currency of liberal-democratic values. For there is plenty of evidence to the contrary, not only in Baudrillard's extravagant scenario but everywhere in the mass-media coverage of recent political events. It is hard to see what counter-arguments Fish might offer to anyone who claimed, like Baudrillard, that the conditions of a working consensus (or informed public sphere) had now broken down irretrievably, and that henceforth we had better adjust to living in a world of pervasive hyperreality.

But if Baudrillard is right to this extent – right in diagnosing what is manifestly wrong with the postmodern body politic – we are not, for that reason, necessarily obliged to accept the whole package of irrationalist ideas that he mounts on this gloomy prognosis. That is to say, there is something highly suspect in his habit of constantly jumping from one language-game to another, from descriptive accounts of the way we live now to generalised pronouncements on the postmodern condition, the obsolescence of truth, the non-availability of critical grounds, of rational criteria, and so forth. In fact it proves impossible for Baudrillard to present his case without falling back into a language that betrays the opposite compulsion at work. Thus he often communicates a sense of sickened loathing for the media, the opinion polls, the whole apparatus of 'dissimulation', even while insisting that there is just no point in deploring its effects since they constitute 'the real' in so far as we can possibly know it.

This ambivalence comes across most clearly in those passages from his recent text *The Masses* where Baudrillard suggests that stupidity or apathy – the sheer indifference to truth – may be the most effective weapon against forms of ideological indoctrination. 'About the media', he writes,

> you can sustain two opposing hypotheses: they are the strategy of power, which finds in them the means of mystifying the masses and of imposing its own truth. Or they are the strategic territory of the ruse of the masses, who exercise in them their concrete power of the refusal of truth, of the denial of reality. (p. 217)

The first is yet another form of that old Platonist delusion that would treat the intellectual as a figure apart, a knower of truths ideally exempt from the errors and follies of 'commonsense' belief. The second (absurdly) is Baudrillard's one remaining counsel of hope, his idea that 'the masses' might finally arrive at a stage of such total, unresisting imbecility that they would simply not respond to techniques of mass-persuasion, media hype or whatever. It is only the intellectuals, the heirs of Enlightenment – politicians, television pundits, cultural theorists and their ilk – who deplore the idiocy of everyday life and hold out for the saving power of critical reason. In which case, 'if only for a change, it would be interesting to conceive the mass, the object-mass, as the repository of a finally delusive, illusive, and allusive strategy, the correlative of an ironic, joyful, and seductive unconscious' (p. 217).

This is – to say the least – a pretty desperate line of argument, and one that sits oddly with Baudrillard's attack on 'enlightened' thinkers for their patronising attitude to 'the masses'. But it is also worth noting how his language at this point reproduces the old truth/falsehood distinction in the very act of denouncing its complicity with modern techniques of surveillance and control. Thus

> the media are nothing else than a marvellous instrument for destabilizing the real and the true, all historical or political truth . . . And the addiction that we have

for the media . . . is not a result of a desire for culture, communication, and information but of this perversion of truth and falsehood, of this destruction of meaning in the operation of the medium. (p. 217)

So it would seem that there is (or maybe once was) a 'reality', a 'truth' to be destabilised or perverted, a meaning that was somehow subject to 'destruction', a 'medium' that furthered this process by confusing truth and falsehood to the point of an ultimate undecidability . . . Baudrillard in effect contrives to have it both ways by playing on these distinctions – without which he could not even begin to articulate his case – while rhetorically denying that they possess any kind of operative force. So long as we do not read too carefully he can thus carry off the performative trick of conjuring away with one hand those same criteria (truth, reality, history, etc.) which he then summons up with the other for purposes of contrastive definition. This trick is fairly common (maybe universal) among celebrants of the 'postmodern'. For the term has no meaning except in relation to those various, supposedly obsolete notions that make up the discourse of modernity.

But this is not just to score the odd point off Baudrillard by remarking his occasional lapses into a pre-postmodern way of thinking. On the contrary: his work is of value only in so far as it accepts – albeit against the grain of his express belief – that there *is* still a difference between truth and falsehood, reason and unreason, the way things are and the way they are commonly represented as being. Baudrillard is a first-rate diagnostician of the postmodern scene but thoroughly inconsequent and muddled when it comes to philosophising on the basis of his own observations. For it just does not follow from the fact that we are living through an age of widespread illusion and disinformation that *therefore* all questions of truth drop out of the picture and we cannot any longer talk in such terms without harking back to some version of Platonist metaphysics. Baudrillard's mistake is to move straight on from a descriptive account of certain prevalent conditions in the late twentieth-century lifeworld to a wholesale anti-realist stance which takes those conditions as a pretext for dismantling every last claim to validity or truth. What this amounts to is, again, a kind of systematically inverted Platonism: a fixed determination to conceive no ideas of what life might be like outside the cave.

IV

As I have said, it is not enough simply to urge on pragmatist grounds that this makes for bad politics, or leads to a position where no amount of reasoned argument would count against the current 'realities' of public opinion, media influence, manufactured consensus-values and the like. Certainly there is every sign of its having this effect, as witnessed by the scramble of left-wing thinkers (among them contributors to journals like *Marxism Today*) to take on board not only Baudrillard and other postmodernist gurus but a good deal of Thatcherite ideological baggage besides. What begins as a softening-up of the position on various 'liabilities' in the old Marxist line – critique, ideology, class conflict, forces of production, the labour-theory of value – ends in a more or less total conversion to the postmoderist viewpoint. Thus one finds Dick Hebdige, in a recent article, expounding Baudrillard's ideas with some enthusiasm and advising his readers (or the old-guard socialists among them) that they had better catch up with these latest rules of the game. 'It is no longer possible', he writes,

> for us to see through the appearance of, for instance, a 'free market' to the structuring 'real relations' beneath (e.g. class conflict and the expropriation by capital of surplus value). Instead, signs begin increasingly to take on a life of their own referring not to a real world outside themselves but to their own 'reality' – the system that produces the signs.[13]

Hebdige goes on to admit a few doubts as to just what this program might mean in political terms, given its attitude of virtual acquiescence in the 'banal seductions' and 'mindless fascination' of current mass-media psychology. But in general the message is clear enough: that if such arguments do not make sense according to the 'orthodox left analysis', then the fault lies more with thinkers on the left – or their old-fashioned Marxist concepts and categories – than with anything intrinsic to the postmodern condition. And this attitude often goes along with a suggestion that Thatcherite consensus-values have now managed to capture the high ground of public opinion, so that any workable strategy for change will have to make terms with this new situation.

> If the generalized scepticism towards mainstream media reportage moves beyond issues of 'fact' and interpretation – what happened when, where and why and what does it mean? – to question the line between truth and lies itself, then the whole 'economy of truth' collapses.[14]

And it is clear – despite the scattering of queasy quotation marks – that Hebdige thinks of this as a fair statement of the problems confronting socialist thinkers in an age of post-enlightenment politics.

One's response to such arguments could take a variety of forms. It could begin by pointing out that Baudrillard's strategy of persuasion itself presupposes the truth/falsehood distinction when he offers what purports to be an accurate account – or an informed diagnosis – of the way things stand with us now. In fact he ends up in something very like the classic relativist predicament. That is to say, if he succeeds in undermining all appeals to truth, validity, or rational warrant, then there can be no grounds for counting him right on this or any other question. And if he does not thus succeed – or if his work turns out to be the one exception to its own rule – then we are equally entitled to reject his case. Philosophers since Plato have often used this as a knock-down argument against relativism, scepticism and other such apparently self-refuting doctrines. But those doctrines have proved remarkably resilient, reviving periodically in various updated or modified forms, only to meet with some new counter-argument that reiterates the same basic line.[15] Thus Baudrillard might say – in fashionable speech-act parlance – that his claims should be construed as performatives, not constatives; that they are simply not engaged in the language-game of giving reasons, theoretical grounds, etc., and therefore cannot be caught off-guard by the old anti-relativist argument. And the same would apply (as we have seen) to any pragmatist objection that started out from the supposed existence of a liberal-democratic consensus, and used this as a pretext for rejecting Baudrillard's extremist views. For he could then muster all kinds of evidence that in fact this consensus has more or less collapsed, and along with it the very possibility of appealing to 'truth' as a matter of agreed-upon language-games or shared cultural values.

So any adequate response to Baudrillard will need to do more than denounce postmodernism for its defeatist implications or its role in promoting what Fredric Jameson calls the 'cultural logic of late capitalism'.[16] It will have to come up with strong counter-arguments of precisely the kind that Baudrillard rejects as belonging to an outworn enlightenment regime of rationality and truth. I have addressed these issues at length elsewhere, and now have room for only a brief indication of the shape such an argument might take.[17] The most important task would be to point out the various cogent alternatives to Baudrillard's assumption that truth is nothing more than a localised product of consensus-belief, in which case it can no longer make sense to invoke truth-conditions or engage in any form of *Ideologiekritik*. One could then push back to the origins of postmodernism in that widespread structuralist 'revolution' across various disciplines – linguistics, anthropology, political science, literary theory –which took a lead from Saussure in treating language as the paradigm of all signifying systems, and moreover in excluding (or bracketing) any consideration of language in its referential aspect. For Saussure, this exclusion was strictly a matter of methodological convenience, a heuristic device adopted for the purpose of describing the structural economy of language, that is, the network of relationships and differences that exist at the level of the signifier and the signified.[18] For his followers, conversely, it became a high point of principle, a belief – as derived from the writing of theorists like Althusser, Barthes and Lacan – that 'the real' was a construct of intra-linguistic processes and structures that allowed no access to a world outside the prison-house of discourse.

In Althusser's case this belief went along with an attempt to reconstitute Marxist thought by sharpening the distinction between 'science' and 'ideology', identifying the latter with lived experience in its various mystified forms, and reserving the term 'science' for that strictly theoretical discourse whose truth was guaranteed by its own structural logic or system of articulated concepts and categories.[19] It was therefore vital (as Althusser argued) to locate the precise point in Marx's own work where there occurred an 'epistemological break', a transition from the residual humanism of his earlier writings to the truly 'scientific' Marxism that resulted from this labour of conceptual critique. Only then would it be possible to specify exactly what distinguished Marxist 'theoretical practice' from those various misreadings, distortions or perversions that had so far prevented such a science from emerging. And if a model was required – a paradigm instance of this new-found analytic rigour – then it lay in Saussure's demonstration of the need to separate the study of language in its structural aspect (*la langue*) from the sheer multiplicity of individual speech-acts comprised under the term *parole*. In Lacan also, the 'return to Freud' was simultaneously a return to Saussure and Jakobson.[20] It involved not only a studious attention to the detail – the 'letter' – of the Freudian text, but also a reading that took full advantage of these discoveries in the realm of structural linguistics. And indeed, as Althusser noted in his essay on Lacan, this held out the prospect of a certain convergence between Marxism and psychoanalysis, since the Lacanian 'Imaginary' could now be construed in terms of its ideological function, its role in producing effects of specular 'misrecognition', while the 'Symbolic order' could likewise be treated as an analogue of the pre-given social structures which constitute the field of meaning and desire.[21] In short, the appeal to structural linguistics seemed to promise a degree of theoretical rigour that would utterly transform these and other disciplines.

As this prospect receded – as Marxism went out of fashion among French intellectuals and the structuralist paradigm came under attack from various quarters – so postmodernism emerged as the upshot of a generalised incredulity with regard to all theories, truth-claims or 'scientific' notions of system and method. Thus Foucault offered the lesson that truth was nothing more than a product of the will-to-power within discourse, a value attached to certain privileged ideas thrown up from time to time within the shifting orders of language and representation. Post-structuralists (notably the later Barthes) renounced all versions of the quest for method, invariant narrative structures, the 'grammar' of rhetorical codes, etc., and henceforth embraced the idea of an 'intertextuality' that exceeded the grasp of any possible structuralist approach. Lacan was taken up – mainly by literary theorists – with the object of showing how illusory was the notion of psychoanalysis as a 'method' applied to literary texts; how the relation between work and commentary – like that between patient and analyst – was subject to manifold symptoms of transference and counter-transference, such that no line could possibly be drawn between literature and criticism (or language and meta-language). It then remained for thinkers like Lyotard to declare the whole modernist epoch at an end in so far as we could no longer place any trust in Kantian, Marxist or other such claims for the emancipating power of enlightened critical reason. Baudrillard's position can thus be understood as the furthest stage yet reached in this widespread disenchantment (widespread at least among French intellectuals) with 'theory' in just about every shape and form.

So the case against postmodernism could best make a start by examining the basic assumptions of structuralist method, those same assumptions that later proved vulnerable to various forms of sceptical critique. One direction for this enquiry is to ask whether Saussure's foundational project – more specifically, his treatment of the sign as a two-term relation between signifier and signified, renouncing all concern with its referential aspect – might not itself have been responsible for a good deal of subsequent confusion. For there exists an alternative to this way of thinking in the work of analytical philosophers in the post-Fregean line of descent, a tradition that has been more or less ignored by exponents of recent French ideas. From Frege one can take the argument that 'sense determines reference' *only up to a point*; that although what words refer to is partly established by their role in various sentences, language-games or signifying systems, nevertheless it is the referential aspect of language that fixes truth-conditions and thus serves as a paradigm-case for all linguistic understanding.[22] This position finds support in the work of present-day philosophers like Hilary Putnam and Donald Davidson. What they provide – very briefly – is an argument against the relativist doctrine that every language encodes its own distinctive set of referential or semantic criteria; that truth-values can only be assigned in terms of some particular language (or 'conceptual scheme'); and thus that any act of translation between different languages, discourses or schemes will always be underdetermined with respect to the various possible ways of construing their semantic or conceptual fit. Davidson comes up with some powerful objections to this line of reasoning, a line that brings together such otherwise diverse thinkers as W.V. Quine (on ontological relativity), B.L. Whorf (on ethno-linguistics) and Thomas Kuhn (on the radically 'incommensurable' character of different scientific paradigms).[23] In each case, Davidson argues, they have created unnecessary problems by supposing that issues of truth only arise in the context of this or that particular language. In fact it makes more sense to start out from the opposite premise; namely, that the *precondition* for our knowing any language – for our ability to produce, recognise or interpret sentences in our own or any other tongue – is the ascription to it of certain basic properties (truth-values, predicative structures, referring expressions, etc.) in the absence of which understanding just could not make a start. And this argument would also apply to those forms of post-structuralist or postmodernist thinking that likewise fall into error (as Davidson sees it) by relativising truth and reference to the supposed multiplicity of languages, cultures or 'conceptual schemes'. Their mistake is in simply not perceiving that truth is a kind of logical primitive, a starting-point for any genuine attempt to comprehend what is involved in acts of translation, successful or otherwise.

This is just one example of the way that developments in analytical philosophy might challenge some of Baudrillard's rhetorical claims with regard to the obsolescence of truth, the non-availability of rational grounds and the need to break with all forms of 'enlightened' conceptual critique. One could also point to work in the areas of epistemology, philosophy of science, historiography, the analysis of knowledge (or veridical truth-claims) and other such disciplines where a strong case exists for *not* simply adopting the pragmatist stance and equating 'truth' *tout court* with what is currently 'good in the way of belief'. The arguments against this position are too many and complex for any adequate summary here. But they would include (for example) some intensive recent work on the question of what constitutes knowledge, as opposed to justified true belief;[24] various instances from the history of science that presuppose some form of epistemic access (as distinct from making sense only on the terms of an existing consensus or research program);[25] and arguments in the analytical philosophy of mind and language that stress – like Kant, though with less in the way of 'metaphysical' baggage – that such issues are posed by every act of self-conscious critical reflection on the powers and limits of rational understanding.[26] In short, the postmodernist 'turn' in recent French thinking begins to look less credible – or more closely tied to its own rather narrow intellectual prehistory – if one takes some account of these alternative views.

The same applies to Baudrillard's more specific critique of Marxist concepts and categories. Here again, it is the Saussurian paradigm – or a form of structural-linguistic a priori – that stands behind Baudrillard's wholesale reduction of economic, political and social issues to questions of symbolic exchange and the 'dissimulating' agency of the sign. Thus 'the crucial thing', he writes,

> is to see that the separation of the sign and the world is a fiction, and leads to a science fiction . . . This 'world' that the sign 'evokes' (the better to distance itself from it) is nothing but the effect of the sign, the shadow that it carries about, its 'pantographic' extension . . . Now the homology between the logic of signification and the logic of political economy begins to emerge. For the latter exploits its reference to needs and the actualization of use value as an anthropological horizon while precluding their real intervention in its actual functioning and operative structure . . . In fact, it is now clear that the system of needs and of use value is thoroughly implicated in the form of political economy as its completion. And likewise for the referent, this 'substance of reality', in that it is entirely bound up with the logic of the sign. Thus, in each field, the dominant form . . . provides itself with a referential rationale, a content, an alibi and, significantly, in each this articulation is made *under the same metaphysical 'sign'*, i.e. need or motivation. (pp. 84–5)

I have quoted this passage at length because it brings out very clearly the extent to which Baudrillard transforms Saussure's descriptive-analytical project into a form of wholesale anti-realist doctrine. That is to say, he assumes that 'reality' is structured through and through by the order of signs or symbolic equivalences; that our knowledge of the world can amount to nothing more than our mode of insertion into this all-encompassing economy of signs; and thus that any attempt to distinguish 'real' needs or use-values from their order of 'imaginary' representation is necessarily a vain effort and chimerical delusion.

The response to all this could take various forms, among them the flat rejoinder that there are real and present facts of experience – inequality, deprivation, urban squalor, unemployment, massive and increasing differentials of wealth and power – which make nonsense of Baudrillard's sophistical case that nothing exists outside the endless circulation of ungrounded arbitrary signs. At a more philosophical level, one could cite the work of thinkers such as G.A. Cohen and Jon Elster who analyse cardinal concepts in the Marxian text – concepts like base/superstructure and 'forces and relations of production' – but who do so (and herein lies their difference from Althusser) on the assumption that those concepts will or should make logical sense quite apart from any mode of discursive production peculiar to Marxist 'theoretical practice'.[27] This difference is crucial for the reason I suggested above: that the restriction of truth (even 'scientific' truth) to its role within this or that specific order of discourse will always leave room for sceptics like Baudrillard to push yet further and conclude that truth is nothing more than a species of rhetorical imposition. In short, the disenchantment with Marxism among present-day French intellectuals has perhaps as much to do with problems intrinsic to the Althusserian-structuralist paradigm as with anything in the broader context of socio-political events.

It may be said – and pragmatists like Rorty or Fish would certainly take this line – that positions 'in theory' are always adopted on the basis of prior commitments or principles, and that far from providing 'grounds' for such beliefs they merely act as a source of heightened conviction or suasive appeal. Any argument would then come down to the choice of some favoured rhetoric – or what Rorty calls a 'final vocabulary' – in which to pursue the conversation. Thus liberal thinkers would opt for a language of rights, first principles, equal opportunity, constitutional guarantees, etc., while Marxists would invoke a whole range of alternative notions like alienation, class conflict, ideology, late-capitalist modes of production and so forth. But there could be no deciding the issue between them on other than rhetorical grounds, since their languages would be wholly incommensurable, and any such decision-procedure could only work by appealing to some alternative rhetoric, some 'final vocabulary' that still carried weight in terms of current consensus-values. If this were the case then Baudrillard would surely have the last word. For it is impossible to deny much of what he says about the 'hyperreality' of present-day politics, the disappearance of truth as an operative standard and the failure of critical reason – whether liberal, Marxist or whatever – to effect any visible change in this condition. And if validity-claims only have force when understood against a background of agreed-upon values and assumptions, then it would indeed appear that truth is a thing of the past and criticism powerless to make itself heard above the media babble, the opinion-poll feedback and the endless stream of state-sponsored disinformation.

But this case will appear convincing only to those who are swept along by Baudrillard's relentless hyperboles and his otherwise distinctly familiar 'end-of-ideology' rhetoric. Against it one needs to reassert the basic claim that issues of truth and right reason are *inescapably* raised by any discourse that presents itself for serious appraisal in the mode of diagnostic commentary. Nor are such arguments confined to the tradition of Anglo-American analytical philosophy. Equally relevant would be Habermas's case for a form of 'transcendental pragmatics', one that adopts a normative standpoint – what he calls the 'ideal speech situation' – from which to criticise existing social arrangements and consensus-beliefs.[28] Thus, according to Habermas, there is a critical dimension built into every act of communicative grasp, each attempt to understand what others are saying or to make our own meaning clear despite the various obstacles of ignorance, prejudice or misinformation that stand in our way. Progress comes about through the shared human interest in overcoming such obstacles by achieving a better, more enlightened consensus or a willingness to engage in reasoned debate with viewpoints other than our own. One can thus conserve what is vital to the Kantian tradition – its commitment to values\of rationality, truth and the critique of repressive social institutions – without the appeal to foundationalist arguments which would then be vulnerable to Rorty's line of attack. For Habermas it is crucial to maintain this distinction between a pragmatist outlook which simply equates 'true' with 'true for all present purposes' (or 'good in the way of belief'), and on the other hand a transcendental pragmatics which allows for critique of existing consensus-values. His argument takes in a vast range of evidence from speech-act theory, philosophical hermeneutics, the history of science, the sociology of knowledge and issues in present-day (especially West German) political debate. At every point his aim is to mobilise the resources of critical reason against a levelling consensus-view of meaning and truth, a view that would render criticism powerless to diagnose the signs of a false (i.e. a partial or massively distorted) consensus.

Baudrillard's alternative is stated clearly enough: 'a hyperreal henceforth sheltered from the imaginary, and from any distinction between the real and the imaginary, leaving room only for the orbital recurrence of models and the simulated generation of difference' (p. 167). It is a vision which should bring great comfort to government advisers, PR experts, campaign managers, opinion-pollsters, media watch-dogs, Pentagon spokesmen and others with an interest in maintaining this state of affairs. Baudrillard's imagery of 'orbital recurrence' and the 'simulated generation of difference' should commend itself to advocates of a Star Wars program whose only conceivable purpose is to escalate East–West tensions and divert more funds to the military-industrial complex. There is no denying the extent to which this and similar strategies of disinformation have set the agenda for 'public debate' across a range of crucial policy issues. But the fact remains (and this phrase carries more than just a suasive or rhetorical force) that there is a *difference* between what we are given to believe and what emerges from the process of subjecting such beliefs to an informed critique of their content and modes of propagation.

This process may amount to a straightforward demand that politicians tell the truth and be held to account for their failing to do so. Of course there are cases – like the Irangate–Contra affair or Thatcher's role in events leading up to the Falklands war – where a correspondence-theory might seem to break down since the facts are buried away in Cabinet papers, the evidence concealed by some piece of high-level chicanery ('Official Secrets', security interests, reasons of state, etc.), or the documents conveniently shredded in time to forestall investigation of their content. But there is no reason to think – as with Baudrillard's decidedly Orwellian prognosis – that this puts the truth forever beyond reach, thus heralding an age of out-and-out 'hyperreality'. For one can still apply other criteria of truth and falsehood, among them a fairly basic coherence-theory that would point out the various lapses, inconsistencies, non-sequiturs, downright contradictions and so forth which suffice to undermine the official version of events. (Margaret Thatcher's various statements on the Malvinas conflict – especially the sinking of the *General Belgrano* – would provide a good example here.)[29] It may be argued that the truth-conditions will vary from one specific context to another; that such episodes involve very different criteria according to the kinds of evidence available; and therefore that it is no use expecting any form of generalised *theory* to establish the facts of this or that case. But this ignores the extent to which theories (and truth-claims) inform our every act of rational appraisal, from 'commonsense' decisions of a day-to-day, practical kind to the most advanced levels of speculative thought. And it also ignores the main lesson to be learnt from Baudrillard's texts: that any politics which goes along with the current postmodernist drift will end up by effectively endorsing and promoting the work of ideological mystification.

Notes

1. Jean Baudrillard, *Oublier Foucault* (Paris: Editions Galilée, 1977). Trans. Nicole Dufresne, 'Forgetting Foucault', *Humanities in Society* No. 3 (Winter 1980), pp. 87–111.

2. See for instance Gianni Vattimo, *The End of Modernity*, trans. Jon R. Snyder (Cambridge: Polity Press, 1988).

3. See the essays collected in Richard Rorty, *Consequences of Pragmatism* (Minneapolis: University of Minnesota Press, 1982).

4. Jean-François Lyotard, *The Post-Modern Condition: a report on knowledge*, trans. Geoff Bennington and Brian Massumi (Minneapolis: University of Minnesota Press, 1983).

5. Richard Rorty, *Philosophy and the Mirror of Nature* (Princeton, NJ: Princeton University Press, 1980).

6. See for instance Louis Althusser, *For Marx*, trans. Ben Brewster (London: New Left Books, 1977).

7. See especially Friedrich Nietzsche, 'On truth and lie in an extra-moral sense', in Walter Kaufmann (trans. and ed.), *The Portable Nietzsche* (New York: Viking, 1954), pp. 42–7.
8. See Baudrillard, *Les Stratégies Fatales* (Paris: Bernard Grasset, 1983). Also Poster (*op. cit.*), pp. 185–206, for a partial translation of this text.
9. There is a rapidly growing body of work on this question of 'nuclear criticism' and on the possible uses of textual theory (semiotics, post-structuralism, deconstruction etc.) in analysing forms of nuclear-strategic doublethink. Baudrillard's stance of extreme referential agnosticism is just one of the positions adopted by parties to this debate. Others have argued that we can, indeed must, maintain some version of critical realism – some means of addressing a 'nuclear referent' or real-world state of affairs – while acknowledging the extent to which perceptions of the arms race are constructed in and through the various rhetorics that compete for public acceptance. By far the most ambitious attempt in this vein is J. Fisher Solomon's *Discourse and Reference in the Nuclear Age* (Norman, Okl.: Oklahoma University Press, 1988). Solomon puts the case for a 'potentialist' metaphysics, one that would recognise the strictly unthinkable (aporetic) nature of the nuclear 'real', but not go on to argue – like Baudrillard – against any form of rational critique or resistance on principled grounds. The alternative, as he sees it, is to adopt something more like Aristotle's view of the different criteria applicable to those objects, processes or events that exhibit a certain latent reality, a *tendenzraum* or capacity for change that is none the less amenable to analysis.
    On this topic see also the Cardiff Text Analysis Group, 'Disarming voices (a nucclear exchange)', *Textual Practice*, vol. 2, no. 3 (Winter, 1988), pp. 381–93; Jacques Derrida, 'No apocalypse, not now: full speed ahead, seven missiles, seven missives', *Diacritics*, vol. 14, no. 2 (Summer, 1984), pp. 20–31; Michael Allen Fox and Leo Groarke (eds.), *Nuclear War* (New York: Peter Lang, 1985); Robert Mielke, 'Imaging nuclear weaponry: an ethical taxonomy of nuclear representation', *Northwest Review*, vol. 22, no. 1 (1982), pp. 164–80; Christopher Norris, 'Against postmodernism: Derrida, Kant and nuclear politics', *Paragraph*, vol. 9 (March, 1987), pp. 1–30; Christopher Norris and Ian Whitehouse, 'The rhetoric of deterrence', in Nikolas Coupland (ed.), *Styles of Discourse* (London: Croom Helm, 1988), pp. 293–322; Daniel L. Zins, 'Teaching English in a nuclear age', *College English*, vol. 47, no. 4 (1985), pp. 387–406.
10. See Louis Marin, *Utopiques: jeux d'espace* (Paris: Minuit, 1973).
11. See for instance Richard Rorty, *Consequences of Pragmatism* (*op. cit.*) and Stanley Fish, *Is There a Text in this Class? the authority of interpretive communities* (Cambridge, Mass.: Harvard University Press, 1980).
12. See the essays by Fish and others collected in W.J.T. Mitchell (ed.), *Against Theory: literary theory and the new pragmatism* (Chicago: University of Chicago Press, 1985).
13. Dick Hebdige,'After the masses', *Marxism Today*, January 1989, pp. 48–53; p. 51.
14. *ibid.*, p. 51.
15. For a useful recent account, see Barry Stroud, *The Significance of Philosophical Scepticism* (London: Oxford University Press, 1984).
16. Fredric Jameson, 'Postmodernism, or, the cultural logic of late capitalism', *New Left Review*, no. 146 (July/August 1984), pp. 53–92.

17. See the essays collected in Christopher Norris, *Deconstruction and the Interests of Theory* (London: Francis Pinter & Norman; Okl.: University of Oklahoma Press, 1988).
18. Ferdinand de Saussure, *Course in General Linguistics*, trans. Wade Baskin (London: Fontana, 1974).
19. See especially Louis Althusser, *For Marx* (*op. cit.*) and Louis Althusser and Etienne Balibar, *Reading Capital*, trans. Ben Brewster (London: New Left Books, 1970).
20. See Jacques Lacan, *Écrits: a selection*, trans. Alan Sheridan-Smith (London: Tavistock, 1977).
21. See Louis Althusser, 'Freud and Lacan', in *'Lenin and Philosophy' and other essays*, trans. Ben Brewster (London: New Left Books, 1971), pp. 177–202.
22. See Gottlob Frege, 'On sense and reference', in Max Black and P.T. Geach (eds.), *Translations from the Philosophical Writings of Gottlob Frege* (Oxford: Basil Blackwell, 1952), pp. 56–78. On this topic see also Solomon (*op. cit.*) and Christopher Norris, 'Sense, reference and logic: a critique of post-structuralist theory', in *The Contest of Faculties* (London: Methuen, 1985), pp. 47–69.
23. See especially Donald Davidson, 'On the very idea of a conceptual scheme', in *Inquiries into Truth and Interpretation* (London: OUP, 1984), pp. 183–98. Also Norris, 'Reading Donald Davidson: truth, meaning and right interpretation', in *Deconstruction and the Interests of Theory* (*op. cit.*), pp. 59–83.
24. Much of this work has to do with cases (so-called 'Gettier problems') where veridical knowledge involves something more than (1) believing x to be the case, and (2) having good grounds or evidential warrant for holding that belief. See Edmund Gettier, 'Is justified true belief knowledge?', *Analysis*, vol. 23 (1963), pp. 121–3. For a useful survey of the subsequent debate, see Robert K. Shope, *The Analysis of Knowing: a decade of research* (Princeton, NJ: Princeton University Press, 1983).
25. See for instance Karl-Otto Apel, *Towards a Transformation of Philosophy* (London: Routledge & Kegan Paul, 1980).
26. For examples from two rather different traditions of thought, see P.F. Strawson, *The Bounds of Sense* (London: Methuen, 1958) and Hilary Putnam, *Realism and Reason* (Cambridge: CUP, 1983).
27. See especially G.A. Cohen, *Karl Marx's Theory of History* (Oxford: Clarendon Press, 1978) and Jon Elster, *Making sense of Marx* (Cambridge; CUP, 1982). See also Alex Callinicos, *Marxism and Philosophy* (London: OUP, 1985); Robert Paul Wolff, *Understanding Marx: a reconstruction and critique of Capital* (Princeton, NJ: Princeton University Press, 1984).
28. See for instance Jürgen Habermas, *Communication and the Evolution of Society*, trans. Thomas McCarthy (London: Heinemann, 1979).
29. See Arthur Gavshon and Desmond Rice, *The Sinking of the Belgrano* (London: Secker & Warburg, 1984), especially Appendix 7, 'A catalogue of inconsistencies', where they establish beyond doubt – on the principle of non-contradiction – that the British government put out more than one item of false propaganda. See also Tam Dalyell, *Misrule* (London: Grafton Books, 1988) for further examples of this Thatcherite 'economy of truth' as applied to the management of awkward facts.

Chapter 5

Derrida and Kant

Irene Harvey makes it plain from the outset that *Derrida and the Economy of Différance** is a philosopher's book, designed in large part to rescue Derrida from the false characterisation of his work put about by literary critics. Her reading will proceed by way of textual explication, but not – most certainly – the kind of exuberant verbal 'freeplay' espoused by his admirers in departments of literature. Rather, its approach will be to place Derrida's writings in a post-Kantian tradition where issues of epistemological critique are still very much on the agenda. Deconstruction may seem to have shelved such questions in its will to break with the prevailing discourse of Western 'logocentric' reason. Certainly this has been the reading canvassed by those who want to argue that philosophy is just another kind of writing, with no privileged truth-claims that would set it apart from poetry, criticism or the human sciences at large. Some (like Geoffrey Hartman) have seized upon those elements in Derrida's work that seem to subvert such merely institutional boundary-lines, and to open up a space of liberated intertextuality where languages endlessly merge or migrate.[1] Then there are philosophers – among them Richard Rorty – who applaud Derrida for much the same reason; for having borne out their own neo-pragmatist claim that 'truth' is what presently counts as such in the ongoing plural discourse of civilised exchange.[2] If philosophy is indeed just a diverse collection of *texts* with no monopoly on wisdom or truth, then one way of making that point is by showing (with Derrida) that its concepts come down to metaphors in the end, or that its arguments are everywhere subject to a play of rhetorical undecidability. And so it has come about that deconstruction is perceived –

---

* Irene Harvey, *Derrida and the Economy of Différance* (Bloomington: Indiana University Press, 1986).

especially by philosophers in the 'mainstream' analytical tradition – as a mere 'literary' bag of tricks with no serious claims on their attention. Harvey has nothing expressly to say about this current line of easygoing pragmatist *rapprochement*. She wants a more strenuous reading of Derrida, a more 'philosophical' reading, in precisely the sense of that word that Rorty thinks Derrida has played off the field. The following brief excursion into the history of ideas may help to establish a context for her arguments. Deconstruction takes up the main problems bequeathed to modern thought by the Kantian project of enlightened rational critique. That is to say, it has to do with strictly *transcendental* modes of reasoning, those which raise first-order questions about the limits and conditions of knowledge in general. According to Kant, philosophers had got things wrong by failing to distinguish clearly between ontological and epistemological issues. In short, they had assumed that the proper business of philosophy was somehow to prove that reality conformed to our ideas or representations of it, thereby establishing an exact correspondence between real-world objects and objects of knowledge. When this program did not work out – when Hume, for example, was forced to admit the lack of any ultimate logical grounds for our commonplace assumptions and beliefs – then these thinkers either despaired of the attempt (falling back into various kinds of epistemological scepticism) or elected to save appearances by denying that these problems had any real bearing on everyday, practical experience. Thus Hume famously divided his day between the reassuring pleasures of social intercourse and the lonely, at times almost maddening pursuit of (perhaps non-existent) philosophical grounds. Time, causality, the existence of other minds, natural laws and regularities of sense perception – these all became subject to a corrosive sceptical doubt as soon as one asked, like Hume, what *logically* compelling reasons there were for accepting their absolute and unconditional necessity. And this because Hume took it largely for granted, in the standard empiricist fashion, that any argument addressing these questions had to do so on the basis of direct acquaintance with a world of indubitable sense-perceptions which alone could guarantee its claims to truth. But clearly this led to a form of circular reasoning, since the possibility of attaining such knowledge was itself both the premise and the wished-for conclusion of all these arguments. Thus Hume had to recognise the limits placed upon thought by the fact that all its ideas and representations might *not* correspond to anything objectively 'there' in external reality. Cause and effect – to take the best-known instance – could always be construed as just a useful fiction, a means of imposing regularity and shape on the otherwise chaotic data of sensory experience. And the same applied to all those other deep-grained habits of thought whose logical validity Hume was unable to establish, despite their persisting (in his own more sanguine moments) as the plainly indispensable basis of commonsense reason.

Kant's 'Copernican revolution' in philosophy consisted of his turning these problems round to ask a whole different set of questions. What must be the nature of our cognitive capacities, given the various intelligible aspects under which experience presents itself to us? How far can philosophy go in providing a foundationalist account of the powers that enable us, as rational subjects, at once to interpret that experience and to occupy a shared world of human understanding? Where exactly had traditional thinking gone wrong in its desire to make reality conform at every point to the projections of speculative reason? By asking these questions Kant thought it possible to break the closed circle of empiricist reasoning and hence provide an answer to last-ditch sceptics like Hume. If ontological issues were indeed beyond reach of a priori adjudication – if the very act of raising them created all kinds of insuperable problems and paradox – then philosophy still had its work cut out in beating the bounds of conceptual analysis and showing exactly how our forms of understanding constitute a world of shared objects and experiences. It would now be a matter of examining those various cognitive modes (intuition, understanding, pure and practical reason, aesthetic judgement and so forth) whose powers and limits could be assigned by means of transcendental deduction, or by asking the distinctively Kantian question: what must be the case with our cognitive faculties – our knowledge-constitutive categories – for the world to make sense for us in the way it does?

Kant's three *Critiques* were devoted to expounding this program in all its intricate ramifications. The tripartite division served, broadly speaking, as a means of respecting the boundaries between understanding (epistemology), practical reason (ethics) and judgement (aesthetic understanding). But these faculties were *not* to be conceived as so many separate or self-enclosed realms of knowledge. Rather, they existed in a state of complex reciprocal determination, so that – for instance – the link between sensory intuition and concepts of pure understanding could only be grasped by way of an appeal to aesthetics, which thus came to play a crucial mediating role far beyond its usual confinement to matters of artistic sensibility and taste. Practical reason was likewise linked to both pure reason and aesthetic judgement through a network of articulated contrasts and dependences which precluded the reduction of Kant's thinking to a species of typecast faculty-psychology. To follow the *Critiques* in all their detailed process of argument was also to grasp the central doctrine of Kantian enlightenment: that philosophy can only arrive at mature self-knowledge through the exercise of a reason whose nature is revealed in the act of independent critical reflection. And this doctrine applies equally to the realms of religious and political belief, where it is – Kant argues – the rightful prerogative of each individual to criticise existing value-systems and to grant or withhold rational assent according to the dictates of conscience. If this condition fails to obtain – if the subject passively consents to laws which brook no kind of reasoned critique – then state and individual alike have forfeited their claim to membership of a genuine participant democracy. Hence the strong ties between Kantian philosophy on its 'technical' side and the politics of enlightened or liberal-progressive thought.

These themes are prominent in Derrida's recent essays, especially his writings on the role of philosophy in relation to the state and teaching institutions.[3] Here he addresses the Kantian 'principle of reason' from a deconstructive standpoint which questions its juridical truth-claims, and which shows up the various rhetorical strategies that work to maintain the appearance of pure, 'disinterested' reason. Yet Derrida also declares more than once that there is simply no escaping the demands laid down by this 'lucid vigil' of enlightened critique. Any project which aims to break altogether with the Kantian heritage – as with certain forms of current postmodern or pragmatist thinking – effectively loses all critical force and reduces to a species of passive conformist ideology. Such (for instance) would be Rorty's attempt to enlist deconstruction in the pragmatist cause of demonstrating once and for all that philosophy is just another 'kind of writing' with no special claim to authority or truth. However problematical Kant's appeal to the tribunal of disinterested reason, still there is a need to think those problems through with a sense of their rigorous necessity and lasting pertinence.

Now Harvey is not concerned – explicitly at least – with these political dimensions of Derrida's work. Nor is she out to vindicate the Kantian enlightenment tradition as against its latter-day pragmatist detractors. Her interest focuses squarely on the ways in which deconstruction relates to Kant's epistemological concerns and (more specifically) his use of a priori or transcendental-deductive forms of argument. Here she finds a number of detailed correspondences which justify the claim that Derrida belongs within this Kantian tradition, despite his having pressed its arguments to the point where they open on to strictly unthinkable problems in the nature of their own undertaking. Derrida begins, in a sense, where Kant leaves off: with the question of what grounds can finally be offered for the principle of reason itself. In several notoriously obscure passages Kant declined to address this question or referred it back to the supposed self-evidence of a knowledge beyond reach of further explanation. It was here precisely – at the crucial stage of joining up 'sensuous intuitions' with 'concepts of pure understanding' – that aesthetics came to occupy its mediating role. But there seems no way that

Kant can possibly prove the existence of a preordained or necessary fit between these two orders of cognition. Quite simply,

> the answer must be: It (the totality of rules that we call nature) is only possible by means of the *constitution* of our understanding, according to which all the above representations of the sensibility are *necessarily* referred to a consciousness and by the particular way in which we think, namely by rules. (cited by Harvey, p. 19)

In short, the correspondence has to be assumed – effectively taken on trust – for experience to make any kind of intelligible sense. So Kant is obliged to posit this grounding principle as a matter of a priori truth, something known without question at a level of awareness that requires no further justification. Hence his recourse to a grounding 'constitution' and to 'rules' which must be the precondition of all knowledge whatsoever. 'Although *what* they are and precisely *how many* there are can be precisely determined, *why* they are just these and not others and from whence they come cannot be known' (Kant, cited by Harvey, p. 18).

It is at this stage that Derrida's critique draws out the un-self-acknowledged problems and antinomies of Kantian reason. It does so, not by abandoning the forms of rational argument, but rather by pressing beyond their sticking-point in Kant to ask what might be their ultimate justification. For Derrida, as Harvey reads him, this quest for first principles must always lead on to a moment of aporia, or insurmountable paradox, where thought comes up against the non-availability of any such legitimising grounds. But their absence cannot be taken for a sign (as Rorty would have it) that philosophy took a wrong turning with Kant when it became obsessed with all those pointless epistemological puzzles.[4] What is required is a more rigorous attention to precisely the passages where Kant had to stipulate that no further questions were in order. The upshot may indeed be to shake the foundations of Kantian thinking, since these passages are so many cornerstones – defective cornerstones, as it seems – in the edifice of the three *Critiques*. But to deconstruct a set of philosophical assumptions is *not* to discredit or simply reject the whole enterprise of which they form a constitutive part. Rather it is to ask (in distinctly Kantian vein) what might be the basic presuppositions that make such an enterprise possible, but whose presence is necessarily concealed or obscured by the desire that its logic should appear self-evident.

Harvey spells out this relationship between Derrida and Kant in a sentence which – as with much of her writing – one has to read at least twice over before the sense comes clear.

That which leads Kant to rely on the notion of *constitution* as such, which cannot be known further, since in the process we would always necessarily rely on that same 'object of investigation', is that which Derrida aims to reveal the *conditions of possibility of* and in turn, necessarily, the conditions of the – more rigorously speaking – impossibility of. (p. 19)

Despite its lamentable awkwardness of style this passage articulates the central points of Harvey's argument. Derrida provides the most rigorous, indeed the most authentically *Kantian* reading of Kant precisely through his willingness to problematise the grounds of reason, truth and knowledge. Deconstruction refuses to rest content with the notion of an end-point to critical enquiry, a stage at which thinking simply has to accept the self-evidence of its own rational laws. Kant's appeal to 'a priori forms of intuition' thus appears a kind of stopgap measure and one, furthermore, that avoids the more radical implications of his own thinking. It is in the nature of transcendental arguments to push back the process of enquiry from stage to stage and ask at every point what grounds exist for our claim to know truly what we think we know. And it is the virtue of Derrida's reading to raise this question to the highest point of visibility, to demand a reason for reason itself, without resorting to premature forms of intuitive self-evidence or circular argument.

This is not to say – far from it – that Derrida succeeds in breaking altogether with 'Western metaphysics' or the Kantian desire for some terminal point to the giving of reasons for reason. In fact deconstruction is always, inescapably, bound up with that same ubiquitous system of concepts and categories which it claims to reveal in the texts of 'logocentric' thinkers from Plato to Saussure. Thus Harvey observes that Derrida's arguments depend at every point on the conceptual resources of an age-old philosophical tradition which effectively determines the form and possibility of reasoned argument in general. They presuppose (among other things) the 'if . . . then' structure of deductive or syllogistic reasoning; the existence of *criteria* for judging the validity of (more or less rigorous) deconstructive readings; and the use of terms like 'origin', 'proper', 'legitimate', 'necessary' and so forth, terms which – on a simplified view of deconstruction – should have no place in Derrida's vocabulary. But this is to misunderstand the very nature of his critical engagement with the concepts that organise philosophic discourse. What Derrida seeks to bring out is the deep and unavoidable complicity between Western metaphysics and the various efforts – Kant's and his own included – to think the limits of that same tradition. As Harvey writes, 'any attempt to understand Derrida's work is a movement toward its reappropriation by metaphysics, and thereby a movement, paradoxically, toward the former's recognition and thus destruction' (p. 124). 'Destruction' *not* in the sense that metaphysics would henceforth be relegated to the history of outworn or ruined ideas, its truth-claims shown up once and for all as so many metaphors or fictions masquerading as genuine concepts. What is destroyed is the assurance that those concepts *must* be the end-point of rational enquiry; that any thinking so rash as to question their ultimate validity will lose itself (as Kant believed) in a realm of unanchored speculative reason where paradoxes loom at every turn. For Derrida, these problems cannot be outfaced by laying down laws for the proper, self-regulating exercise of reason. Hence his very different way of posing the transcendental question: namely, by asking what conditions of *im*possibility mark out the limits of Kantian conceptual critique.

Writing, supplement, trace, *différance* – these are some of the terms that Derrida uses in order to unsettle the presumed deep foundations of philosophic discourse. But he does so always in the knowledge that there is no getting 'beyond' metaphysics, no language that would not be in some sense complicit with the language it seeks to deconstruct. And by the same token Derrida can argue that deconstruction is *always already* at work in those cardinal texts of the Western tradition that invest most heavily in a logocentric scheme of values. On the one hand these thinkers establish a series of loaded binary distinctions between speech and writing, presence and absence, authentic living memory and mere mechanical recollection. But on the other – if one reads more attentively, with an eye to certain symptomatic blind spots and evasions – their arguments turn out to depend at crucial points on the supposedly derivative or secondary term. In each case there operates a perverse double logic which constrains these writers not to mean what they say or effectively and consistently say what they mean.

Thus Plato in the *Phaedrus* has Socrates argue that writing is a 'poison', a bad substitute for the inward, authentic knowledge that can only be gained through the living communion of souls made possible by spoken language. But the Greek word for 'poison' (*pharmakon*) can also signify 'remedy', 'medicine' or 'cure', an ambivalence which – according to Derrida – marks the very logic or structural economy of Plato's dialogue.[5] In Rousseau likewise, the opposition between speech and writing goes along with that between nature and culture, the second term in each case held to represent a falling-away from original innocence and grace into a state of unnatural dependence on various kinds of civilised artifice. Yet here also the 'dangerous supplement' of writing comes to occupy a pivotal role in Rousseau's reflections on the origin of language, on social evolution, ethics, politics and other related themes. Indeed Rousseau is more than once forced to admit that his own life-history is more real to him when he subsequently writes or narrates it – in texts like the *Confessions* – than it had been at the time when his experiences were actually taking place. He puts this down to the combined bad influence of solitary day-dreams, of auto-erotic fantasy and the writer's habit of living in a world remote from present (natural) forms of spontaneous human intercourse. But what these apologies conceal – according to Derrida – is that curious 'logic of supplementarity' which operates everywhere in Rousseau's text and effectively subverts the metaphysics of presence vested in the notion of authentic, living speech.[6] However strong his desire to prove otherwise, Rousseau inadvertently sets this logic in train through a whole series of covert metaphors and narrative ploys.

With Husserl and Saussure we reach the two modern thinkers most germane to the project of deconstruction. Husserlian phenomenology renews the attempt – the perennial attempt, since Descartes and Kant – to provide indubitable grounds or foundations for the exercise of philosophic reason. It does so by means of a 'transcendental reduction', a Cartesian mode of disciplined, abstemious enquiry which suspends all reliance on the 'natural' or common-sense attitude in order to isolate the primordial structures of thought and perception. The two aspects of this program which chiefly interest Derrida have to do with Husserl's theory of language and his phenomenology of time-consciousness.[7] In each case Husserl seeks to distinguish a moment of authentic self-presence – the *Jetztzeit* of punctual perception and plenary sense – from those other modalities of knowledge which involve memory, anticipation or traces of an absent experience. Thus time and language alike bear witness to the primacy of that which reveals itself directly to a consciousness intent upon 'eidetic inspection', or the bringing-to-light of structures implicit in the act of subjective understanding. The logic of temporality can only be grasped by reference to a 'now' where the subject is presently, knowingly located and from which point the receding horizons of past and future are experienced as so many forms of strictly derivative representation. And in the case of language, according to Husserl, one has to keep a similar distinction in mind, namely that between 'expressive' and 'indicative' signs. These terms signify on the one hand a language authentically possessed of self-present meaning and intent, on the other a merely token or conventional usage that deprives words of their expressive force and reduces them to so many lifeless, arbitrary marks. Husserl is concerned with language only in so far as it reveals the *intentional* character – the signs of animating purpose and sense – manifest in linguistic forms. So he has to lay down a firm distinction between 'expressive' and 'indicative' signs, the latter being counted merely parasitical upon language in its natural, authentic state.

But on closer examination it appears that Husserl is unable to maintain this clear-cut separation of realms. For it is a necessary fact about language – a 'condition of possibility' in the Kantian sense – that it can only be perceived *as* language in so far as it belongs to a system of articulate terms and relationships which must always precede the individual act of utterance. Such of course is the basis of modern structural linguistics, as theorised by Saussure: the principle that meaning consists in the differences, the distributive economy of sound and sense, rather than depending on a one-to-one relation between signifier and signified.[8] But this creates problems for the Husserlian project, since language in its structural or differential aspect necessarily exceeds the conscious grasp of even the best-trained phenomenological observer. Speech-acts are always already caught up in a network of pre-existent codes and conventions which enables them to signify – to work for all practical purposes – regardless of the speaker's avowed intentions. And the same kind of problem arises with Husserl's attempt to account for the modalities of time-consciousness from the standpoint of a transcendental ego which can only exist in the momentary grasp of a pure, self-present understanding. For there is simply no conceiving of time present except in terms of a layered, differential temporality where what is happening *now* is defined by contrast with what has just happened and what is about to take place. Husserl distinguishes the long-term aspects of memory and anticipation from those other, more immediate 'retentions' and 'protentions' which exist at every point in the stream of consciousness and compose (so to speak) a moving pocket of authentic temporal awareness. But this is to imply – against the whole drift of his manifest intentions – that presence is a purely *differential* concept, unthinkable outside the structural economy of a time that can nowhere be found to coincide with the punctual self-presence of a transcendental ego.

So Derrida mounts his critique of Husserl very largely on the basis of Saussurian structural linguistics. But when he directs his attention to Saussure (in *Of Grammatology*), that program turns out to have logocentric blind spots of its own, passages where the argument self-deconstructs into chains of contradictory assertion. Thus Saussure recommends that linguistics should concern itself as far as possible with spoken language; that writing should be treated as a merely derivative or supplementary system of signs, and one moreover that often works mischief with the primary medium of speech, since it introduces all manner of corrupting influence through its use of arbitrary spelling conventions, anomalies which can then feed back into speech by a kind of unnatural contagion. In this respect Saussure is simply repeating the standard, prejudicial view of writing which Derrida finds everywhere at work in the Western philosophical tradition. But with Saussure that prejudice is all the more visible for the fact that he conceives of language as a differential system of relationships, marks and traces; a system whose most obvious analogue is precisely that of writing. Like Rousseau and Husserl, he often has recourse to graphematic models and metaphors at those crucial points where his argument comes up against its own explanatory limits. How *can* language be conceived or represented as a structural economy 'without positive terms', a network of signifying elements whose meaning is constituted wholly in the play of differences among and between them? Only by resisting the temptation to reify the idea of 'difference' itself, which would merely be to replace one kind of positivity with another. But this means that writing, not speech, must be the privileged model for a general linguistics, since writing most perfectly exemplifies the notion of a system of differential marks and traces irreducible to self-present sense. What Saussure quite explicitly *means to say* is at odds with what his argument *compels him to mean*: namely, that a certain idea of writing engenders the very possibility of systematic thought about the nature and workings of language.

Now Derrida is not denying the validity, on their own terms, of Husserl's or Saussure's particular projects. A passage from *Of Grammatology* (cited by Harvey) makes the point clearly enough. 'I think Saussure's reasons are good', Derrida writes.

> I do not question, on the level on which he says it, the truth of what Saussure says . . . I would rather announce the limits and the presuppositions of what seems here to be self-evident and what seems to me to retain the character and validity of evidence.[9]

And even more strikingly, with regard to Husserl: 'this [Derrida's reading in *Speech and Phenomena*] does not place in question the apodicticity of the phenomenological-transcendental description, and does not disrupt the founding value of presence.'[10] What Derrida sets out to reveal is the deep-laid structure of assumptions that cannot *expressly* be acknowledged as such by Husserl or Saussure if their arguments are to claim unconditional validity. But these are not 'false premises' in the sense that thinking could ultimately do without them or find some alternative basis for the conduct of rational critique. If they are (as Derrida says at various points) 'unfounded', 'illegitimate' or strictly *de jure* – as opposed to the *de facto* evidence of what these thinkers actually wrote – it is not owing to some corrigible weakness in Husserl's or Saussure's reasoning. Rather it is the case that they serve *necessarily* as grounding presuppositions, but still lead on to paradoxical results when one asks (like Derrida) what reasons exist for accepting their ultimate truth. As Harvey says:

> At the same instant that Derrida reveals the contradiction between the 'declared' and the 'described' aspects of both Husserl's and Saussure's projects respectively, he insists that these contradictions are irreducible and therefore a necessity . . . indeed, it is toward the condition of this necessity that he turns with his deconstructive project. (p. 78)

This is why Harvey sees Derrida (rightly) as having not so much broken with the Kantian tradition of epistemological critique as drawn out its furthest, most unsettling implications. Again, her reading is thoroughly remote from the Rortyan-pragmatist or postmodern view that would count such interests merely a sign of lingering attachment to outworn ways of thinking.

In fact Harvey goes yet further with this project of seeking out instructive parallels between Derrida and Kant. She focuses again on those passages in the first *Critique* where Kant draws limits to the exercise of pure reason and describes some of the bad results that follow when thought runs free in speculative regions of its own airy devising. This is why concepts must always be matched up with sensuous intuitions, or reason held in check by a due regard for the certitudes of commonsense experience. Otherwise thinking will be tempted to abandon the firm ground of its inherent 'constitution' and then to indulge in all kinds of delusive metaphysical quest. Such are the 'antinomies of pure reason' – the paradoxes beyond reach of any arbitrating judgement – that Kant puts forward as cautionary instances of what must happen when reason gets out of hand. But there is also a sense of insecurity betrayed by the strength of this desire to save philosophy from the toils of metaphysical abstraction. It comes out clearly in Kant's descriptions of the discipline required to preserve and enforce this self-denying ordinance of method. As Harvey notes:

> the 'transgressions' Reason is given to can only be explained as 'aberrations', 'illusions', fictive flights of fantasy, the 'pure beings of the Understanding' which necessarily 'arise' – unfounded in experience – which cannot therefore be proven to be either true or false . . . they are the 'troublesome' aspects which we must 'struggle against by scientific instruction yet with much difficulty'. (p. 19)

This is why, as Kant argues, metaphysics is 'the favourite child of reason', providing all manner of tempting opportunity for thought to take wing in the heaven of pure concepts. Only by an effort of strenuous self-discipline – by obeying the maxim 'no concepts without intuitions' – can philosophy be sure to avoid these perils.

Deconstruction should be seen (Harvey suggests) as the project which follows from suspending that maxim, but suspending it only in order to grasp its absolute *necessity* for the purposes of Kantian critique. Nor can deconstruction itself escape that necessity, even at the point of raising questions which appear to go beyond the ground-rules established by Kant. It is here – in his attempt to think the limits of philosophy – that Derrida introduces the term *différance* as a means of resisting the drive toward premature system and method. It first comes to light in his reading of Husserl, where Derrida is concerned with the paradoxes engendered by any such attempt to reduce language or representation to a self-present order of intelligible sense. *Différance* is not so much a 'concept' as a name for whatever eludes and baffles the project of Husserlian enquiry. It is a neologism, untranslatable into English, whose meaning is allowed to oscillate (as it were) between the two French words signifying 'difference' and 'deferral'. It thus brings together the Saussurian claim (that language is a structure of differences, irreducible to any straightforward logic of identity) with the radical implications of Husserl on the nature of time-consciousness (that the 'present' is a moment endlessly deferred through the non-self-identical nature of temporal experience). And of course the anomalous spelling of 'différance' registers only in its *written* form, since French pronunciation is unable to distinguish an 'a' from an 'e' in the word's last syllable. So Derrida's purpose in adopting this strange portmanteau form is to reinforce the link between writing (or graphic representation) and everything that works to complicate the notion of speech as ideal self-presence.

'The economy of *différance*' is therefore in some sense an untranscendable horizon for any thinking that would press further along the path of enquiry opened by Kant and Husserl. It is a 'general' as opposed to a 'restricted' economy,[11] one that renounces the assurances of concept and system, and thereby willingly exposes itself to the dislocating forces which Kant so feared. It can only be thought of in structural terms, in the same way that Saussure conceived the economy of language-as-difference. Yet it also creates real problems for the structuralist paradigm, since (as Derrida writes) 'differences are the effects of transformations and from this point of view the theme of *différance* is incompatible with the static, synchronic, ahistoric motif of the concept of structure'. Saussurian linguistics and its various latter-day offshoots – the so-called structuralist 'sciences of man' – are *at a certain level* called to account by this deconstructive critique. But there is no question here of moving decisively beyond that level in order to expose its limited grasp and hence facilitate the passage to a better, more adequate theory. Even if, as Harvey says, 'the notion of structure as such does not exist for Derrida', still he is unable to attach any sense to the term *différance* without calling upon structural metaphors or analogues. In short, '*différance* produces what it forbids, makes possible the very thing that it makes impossible' (p. 202). And in this respect it brings out exactly the pattern of mutual interrogative exchange that Harvey finds everywhere at work in the relationship between Derrida and Kant. Deconstruction no more claims to supersede structuralism than it thinks to invalidate the project of Kantian critique. What it does in each case is establish precisely the limits (or conditions of intelligibility) that mark out a given conceptual terrain. And this means acknowledging the extent to which its own operative terms and strategies necessarily partake of a 're-stricted economy', a given set of enabling philosophical assumptions.

Harvey's book is welcome for several connected reasons. It marks a definite stage of progress beyond the 'literary' reception of Derrida's work, a reception that has consistently ignored or misconstrued its philosophical implications. Among literary critics the term *différance* is mostly taken as a licence for deconstructive 'freeplay', a convenient shorthand for the notion that meaning is always, irreducibly indeterminate, and that texts can therefore be subjected to any number of novel interpretations. Harvey's reading of Derrida alongside Kant should help to turn back this damaging misapprehension. It is also (as I have argued) a timely corrective to the fashionable pragmatist view which sees nothing but multiplied error and delusion in the quest for philosophical reasons and grounds. At last the signs are that Derrida is receiving the kind of sustained analytical attention that his work absolutely demands. Of other recent studies, two stand out in this regard: Rodolphe Gasché's *The Tain of the Mirror* (mainly on Derrida's relation to Kant and Hegel)[12] and John Llewelyn's *Derrida on the Threshold of Sense* (placing him within the broad context of modern Continental philosophy).[13] It is a pity that Harvey's prose so often manifests an indifference not only to the niceties of English style but to straightforward requirements of grammatical sense. Still her book is a notable achievement and deserves careful reading, most of all by those philosophers as yet unprepared to take serious account of Derrida's work.

Notes

1. See especially Geoffrey Hartman, *Saving the Text: literature/Derrida/philosophy* (Baltimore: Johns Hopkins University Press, 1981).
2. See Richard Rorty,'Philosophy as a kind of writing', in *Consequences of Pragmatism* (Princeton, NJ: Princeton University Press, 1980), pp. 89–109.
3. See for instance Jacques Derrida, 'The principle of reason: the university in the eyes of its pupils', *Diacritics*, vol. 13 (Autumn, 1983), pp. 3–20; also 'The age of Hegel', *Glyph*, vol. 1, new series (Minneapolis: University of Minnesota Press, 1986), pp. 3–35.

4. This line of argument is developed most fully in Rorty, *Philosophy and the Mirror of Nature* (Princeton, NJ: Princeton University Press, 1980).
5. See Derrida, 'Plato's pharmacy', in *Dissemination*, trans. Barbara Johnson (Chicago: University of Chicago Press, 1980), pp. 61–171.
6. Derrida, *Of Grammatology*, trans. Gayatri Chakravorty Spivak (Baltimore: Johns Hopkins University Press, 1976).
7. See especially Derrida, *'Speech and Phenomena' and Other Essays on Husserl's Theory of Signs*, trans. David B. Allison (Evanston, Ill.: Northwestern University Press, 1973).
8. Ferdinand de Saussure, *Course in General Linguistics*, trans. Wade Baskin (London: Fontana, 1974).
9. Derrida, *Of Grammatology* (*op. cit.*), p. 39.
10. Derrida, *Speech and Phenomena* (*op. cit.*), p. 8.
11. Concerning this distinction, see Derrida's essay on Hegel, 'From restricted to general economy', in *Writing And Difference*, trans. Alan Bass (London: Routledge & Kegan Paul, 1978), pp. 251–77.
12. Rodolphe Gasché, *The Tain of the Mirror: Derrida and the philosophy of reflection* (Cambridge, Mass.: Harvard University Press, 1986).
13. John Llewelyn, *Derrida on the Threshold of Sense* (London: Macmillan, 1986).

Chapter 6

Music, Language and the Sublime

I

Kevin Barry's book *Language, Music and the Sign** pursues two lines of argument, the one having to do with a chapter of late eighteenth-century intellectual history, the other with certain ideas about language and music which he thinks of great interest and value on their own account. It is a well-researched and often fascinating piece of work which genuinely breaks new ground in the area of music theory and comparative aesthetics. We are wrong, Barry argues, to take it on trust (or on the word of influential scholars like Jean Hagstrum) that poetry and painting were the 'sister arts' whose natural kinship was acknowledged by just about every major thinker in this period.[1] For in fact there were problems with the classical doctrine – 'ut pictura poesis' – and these problems gave rise to an alternative way of thinking in which music figures as the model, paradigm or test-case for other kinds of language.

We are familiar enough with the role that music played in the discourse of nineteenth-century philosophers, poets and critics, those who thought of it (like Mallarmé) as a language ideally removed from the crass contingencies of everyday usage or referential meaning, a language *sui generis* existing in the space of its own self-authenticating truth. This tradition goes back to Pythagoras and the belief that music, like mathematics, embodies certain ultimate laws of reason, proportion or formal harmony which cannot be grasped by way of mere sense-perception. Then again, for Schopenhauer and Nietzsche, music gave access to a realm of primordial intuitive knowledge unattainable by the other arts, since these could only *represent* such feelings in

* Kevin Barry, *Language, Music and the Sign: a study of aesthetics, poetics and poetic practice from Collins to Coleridge* (Cambridge: CUP, 1987).

written, graphic or material form. That all aesthetic experience should therefore 'aspire to the condition of music' was a theme that unified these otherwise quite disparate movements of thought. But the idea took hold – so Barry argues – a good bit earlier than is often supposed, and in a form that raises certain crucial questions about art, language and the history of ideas. The analogy between language and visual perception gave way to various metaphors of a musical provenance, figures of thought which expressly challenged the predominance of sight over hearing.

Barry finds several likely reasons for this shift of aesthetic priorities. One was a growing sense of unease with that Lockeian empiricist philosophy which sought to explain all concepts or ideas – no matter how abstract – on the basis of immediate sense-perception. This theory worked well enough so long as one assumed that language was a strictly *representational* medium, a sign-system where individual words matched up with their real-world referents through a one-to-one relation of mimetic truth. Such was the doctrine expounded by writers like Sir Joshua Reynolds, according to whom (in Barry's words) 'painting stands as the type of the ''full'' sign, and holds first place in any theory of representation' (pp. 1–2). But this doctrine came under increasing strain as critics and philosophers attempted to work out its full implications. Firstly there was the problem of metaphor and other such 'deviant' tropes, a problem that Locke had attempted to resolve by insisting that these were at best a mere ornament, and at worst a hindrance to the conduct of proper, well-regulated thought.[2] But metaphor remained a vexatious topic, as can be seen from those numerous passages – in Locke himself and in critics like Dr Johnson – which commend the virtues of a plain-speaking, honest, literal style, but do so very often in a language shot through with metaphorical hints and suggestions. And this gave rise to another difficulty: namely, the fact that Lockeian empiricism reduced language to a stimulus-response model, one that apparently left no room for imagination or artistic creativity. Thus one finds various writers beginning to speculate on language as a system of 'empty' signs, words that convey no immediate, positive or self-present meaning, but whose sense we can grasp only through a form of inward, sympathetic recreation.

It is here that music seemed to provide a more promising source of analogies:

> Given that a piece of instrumental music must appear, according to Lockeian principles, to be empty of signification, its enjoyment is evidence of the necessity for an aesthetic complex enough to include the pleasures of uncertainty in interpretation and of some free subjectivity in response. (p. 3)

As a new kind of music came into fashion – chamber works and symphonies that lacked any definite programme, any 'content' of pre-given verbal or dramatic ideas – so the need arose for a new aesthetic that would somehow account for this mysterious autonomy of musical language. Barry provides some very useful documentation of the debates that went on among composers, critics and musicians of the period, mainly in the two great performing centres, London and Edinburgh, where audiences were most receptive to these musical innovations. In particular he shows how the late Haydn symphonies – imported with great success by the impresario Salomon – obliged the critics and the musical public to adopt new ideas about meaning, content and form. And it is no coincidence, Barry suggests, that this was the period, and these the most active centres, of a new philosophy which set out to challenge the dominant Lockeian paradigm. In short:

> At the moment when eighteenth-century epistemology noticed that the signs of music evade the categories of distinctness and clarity of ideas, it became possible (1) to locate the significance of music in its composition, in its structure or source; and (2) to locate the significance of music in its emptiness, in its absence of meaning, and therefore in the act of listening, in the energy of mind which its emptiness provokes. (p. 65)

Thus he cites – among others – Adam Smith's 1795 essay distinguishing music from the 'imitative arts', and a treatise by Smith's compatriot, James Beattie, whose title *An Essay on Poetry and Music as they Affect the Mind* is evidence enough of the new way of thinking. This was, after all, the most active period in that Scottish enlightenment tradition which had set about revaluing the dominant forms of philosophy, political economy and other disciplines from a standpoint deeply schooled in rhetoric and the arts of linguistic analysis. So we can see why these thinkers were quick to respond to a music whose style and formal innovations offered such a challenge to existing canons of taste.

But the same reaction is visible elsewhere, as part of that widespread upheaval in the arts and the history of ideas loosely but conveniently termed 'pre-Romanticism'. It is a main theme of Edmund Burke's *Philosophical Enquiry into the Origin of our Ideas of the Sublime and the Beautiful* (1757), where Burke argues strongly – as against Locke – that the 'common effect of words' is *not* their 'raising of ideas of Things' in the mind, but rather their power to summon up feelings or affects beyond the grasp of any such reductive, phenomenalist account. And of course it was in these terms that the sublime came to figure for Kant, Coleridge and others as the highest reach of creative imagination, that point where the mind, having failed to objectify its sense of wonder in the face of some overwhelming experience, falls back upon its own inward resources and thus gains access – albeit momentarily – to the realm of 'supersensible' ideas. Hence the increasing tendency of thinkers after Burke to privilege the sublime over the beautiful, as a mode of experience surpassing all forms of sensuous cognition, and opening (as Kant was to argue) on to the realm of ethics or practical reason. What Barry demonstrates to striking effect is the extent to which these or cognate ideas had already, by the mid-eighteenth century, managed to shift the analogical bias away from painting toward music as the art which most aptly prefigured such concerns.

Thus he cites Oliver Goldsmith, in a review of Burke's *Enquiry*, declaring that 'so far is clearness of imagery from being absolutely necessary to influence the passions, that they may be considerably operated upon, as in music, without presenting any image at all' (p. 28). Then again there was James 'Hermes' Harris, a philosopher-grammarian whose three-volume study of music, painting and poetry followed Burke on this question of expressive autonomy and made a point of devaluing 'imitative' music, in particular those settings of religious or secular texts where content was allowed to dictate in matters of musical form and style. Harris's language indeed anticipates Kant when he describes music as possessing 'a power . . . which consists not in Imitations, and the raising *Ideas*; but in the raising *Affections*, to which Ideas may correspond' (p. 30).

So by this time it was almost a commonplace to treat music as a language of 'empty' signs, a language that somehow subsisted (to adopt the Saussurian formula) 'without positive terms', or in the absence of any determinate semantic content. And this shift of phenomenological values – from *sight* to *hearing* as the privileged instance – went along with a growing taste for purely instrumental or orchestral music, as opposed to those older forms (like Handelian oratorio) which were now felt to rely too heavily on scriptural, dramatic or literary sources. One of Barry's most interesting points is the way that this undoubted revolution in taste was carried forward simultaneously on various fronts: by composers, philosophers, critics and of course those members of the concert-going public whose opinions registered not least through their habits of attendance. At one point he suggests, without pressing the argument, that 'in the early years of the eighteenth century the invention, within the state's finances, of the national debt placed at the centre of social life a determining and ultimate "empty sign" ' (p.183). But this idea is floated as a 'pleasing conjecture' with no real evidence to support the claim. Otherwise Barry is content to leave it an open question just which way the influence worked, or whether it suggests (no doubt 'in the last instance') some form of socio-economic determinism.

II

Of course one could turn this question around and ask what kinds of present-day interest might have gone toward the shaping of Barry's critical project. In fact he has a good deal to say on this topic, since the 'empty sign' has played a prominent role in recent literary theory, especially the writings of Derrida and Paul de Man. Here it figures as a source of demystifying insights and arguments, a concept opposed to those forms of 'logocentric' thinking (Derrida) or 'aesthetic ideology' (de Man) which involve a premature sinking of the differences between language and phenomenal cognition. Thus Barry cites the well-known passage from de Man's essay 'The rhetoric of temporality' where he sets up two, antithetical models for the reading of literary texts, and suggests quite plainly that the choice comes down to a good-faith ('allegorical') mode of understanding as opposed to a bad-faith ('symbolist') mode.

> Whereas the symbol postulates the possibility of an identity or identification, allegory designates primarily a distance in relation to its own origin, and renouncing the nostalgia and the desire to coincide, it establishes its language in the void of this temporal difference. In so doing it prevents the self from an illusory identification with the non-self which is now fully, though painfully, recognised as a non-self. It is this painful knowledge that we perceive at the moments when early romantic literature finds its true voice.[3]

De Man offers two main grounds for this argument that readings conducted under the sign of allegory are more truthful, rigorous or un-self-deluding than those which subscribe to a symbolist aesthestic. One has to do with the *temporal* aspect of all understanding, the absence of any possible guarantee that what a text means now – for some historically situated reader – will also turn out to be its ultimate meaning *sub specie aeternitatis*. For de Man, as for Derrida, this hope is bound up with the belief in a 'transcendental signified', a source of authoritative meaning and truth that would finally put an end to the conflict of interpretations. And the symbolist aesthetic compounds this error by egregiously collapsing ontological distinctions. That is to say, it clings to the illusory faith that language in its highest, most creative forms can effectively transcend this condition and achieve what amounts to a hypostatic union of signifier and signified, subject and object, mind and nature. Allegory, by contrast, holds out against any such premature conflation of realms. It brings home the fact that signs are always 'empty' in so far as their meaning necessarily eludes any last instance of assured, self-present hermeneutic grasp.

Elsewhere, in his 1971 review-essay on Derrida's *Of Grammatology*, de

Man makes Rousseau his main point of reference for this 'early-romantic' attitude, as well as placing music – and Rousseau's writings on music – at the centre of his own argument. Thus 'the priority of music over painting . . . [is asserted by Rousseau] in terms of a value-system which is structural rather than substantial: music is called superior to painting despite and even because of its lack of substance'.[4] In fact de Man takes issue with Derrida on the question of whether or not Rousseau really managed to articulate a theory of the 'empty' sign as the basis of musical as of other kinds of language. For Derrida – at least as de Man reads him – Rousseau was still very much in the grip of a logocentric ethos, a prevailing 'metaphysics of presence', such that his texts must be read against the grain in order to reveal how that ethos is undone by a 'supplementary' logic that questions all its overt truth-claims and values.[5] Thus writing turns out to be the *condition of possibility* for speech, culture for nature, absence for presence, harmony for melody, and so on through the various structural oppositions that organise Rousseau's discourse. For de Man, on the contrary, it is almost an article of faith that Rousseau's text should itself rehearse this deconstructive reading at every point, and thus take full credit for rhetorically undermining its own (on occasion) less circumspect claims.

There is something rather odd about de Man's argument here, since in fact Derrida goes out of his way to insist that deconstruction is *not* just an exercise of perverse ingenuity on the critic's part, and that Rousseau's text shrewdly anticipates everything that he (Derrida) will have to say.[6] But on the main point he agrees with de Man: that is, in treating music as a crucial instance of the passage from a doctrine of language founded on ideas of mimesis, self-presence and adequate representation to one that acknowledges the 'empty' or non-self-identical nature of the sign. And this same transition is to be found in various eighteenth-century writers on music, philosophy and the fine arts. James Usher, for one, thinks of poets and musicians as 'hav[ing] a confused idea, without ability to arrive at it . . . But although they know it not they are sensible when they approach the unknown object, that seems at the same time to appear and hide from the imagination' (Barry, p. 62). This passage remarkably anticipates Kant on the moment of sublime imagining: that moment when the mind, at a loss to comprehend its experience by finding concepts adequate to phenomenal intuitions, is thereby driven back to seek within itself a power transcending all other modes of knowledge. What emerges very clearly from Barry's documentation is the fact that, for many of its earliest proponents, this awareness took shape in and through the experience of music as a uniquely privileged art-form.

Thomas Twining develops similar ideas in the two essays (on poetry and music) appended to his 1789 critical edition of Aristotle's *Poetics*. Twining is one of Barry's most intriguing discoveries: a keen amateur musician, friend and correspondent of (among others) Thomas Gray and Charles Burney, admirer of Haydn and the newly-emergent classical style, and a scholar whose response to David Hume's sceptical essay 'On miracles' was to look toward music as a realm of experience irreducible to sensuous or phenomenal cognition. It seems that Twining found support for these ideas in the difference between harpsichord and pianoforte, both of which he continued to play, but with a growing preference for the new instrument. 'There are times', Twining writes,

> when one's ears call only for harmony, and a pleasant jingle, when one is disposed to merely sensual music, that tickles the auditory nerves . . . But as soon as ever my spirit wakes, as soon as my heart-strings catch the gentlest vibrations, I swivel me round incontinently to the pianoforte. (p. 98)

What evokes this response is not – or not only – the piano's far greater range of tonal and dynamic expressiveness. Rather, it is the absence of that clear-cut sonority, that precise articulation of note with note which the harpsichord possesses to a high degree and which leaves relatively little (so Twining argues) to the listener's creative imagination. One measure of this difference is in the matter of tuning, where the harpsichord approximates to a pitch-system based on perfect (mathematical) proportions, while the piano has to be tuned more in keeping with its power to call forth a rich, complex and inherently more subjective range of musical responses. And so it comes about – in Barry's words – that ' "imperfection" is the opportunity for "strong" listening . . . The quality of sound on a piano, because of its imprecision, offers the larger access to subjectivity. The relatively "perfect" harpsichord offers less' (p. 100).

In fact he might have looked to some of de Man's later essays (like 'The resistance to theory') for a further development of this anti-phenomenalist case.[7] It involves a denial that language – *any* kind of language, even that of music – can ever be reduced, so to speak, without remainder to the realm of naturalised or sensuous cognition. What de Man perceives in all such attempts is a form of that potent 'aesthetic ideology' which works by effacing ontological distinctions and identifying language with nature, or with ideas of 'organic' development borrowed, by illicit metaphorical transfer, from the world of natural forms. And one result of such thinking is the widespread tendency, especially among German post-romantic philosophers, to equate *one particular* language or national tradition with the voice of authentic destiny or revealed poetic truth. Hence de Man's relentless deconstruction of aesthetic ideology in its various forms: on the one hand his insistence that we think back to Kant for a rigorous treatment of issues glossed over by subsequent thinkers, and on the other his proposal that a form of rhetorical critique – an 'epistemology of tropes' – is the best means of revealing the confusions engendered by this seductive habit of thought.[8] For otherwise there is always the danger that thinking will relinquish its critical powers and lend itself more or less knowingly to the purposes of an ersatz jargon of authenticity.

Nor is de Man alone among present-day theorists in his belief that the Kantian sublime marks a crucial point of intersection between language, politics and the discourse of representation. For Lyotard also, the sublime figures as a strictly unthinkable category, one that can never be present to thought in some form of existing reality or phenomenal cognition, but which none the less exists (like Kant's 'ideas of pure reason') in a realm of as-yet unrealised future potential.[9] It is precisely by virtue of this tentative, open-ended character that democracy functions – in Lyotard's view – as a discursive space where various narratives, language-games or ruses of legitimising reason are able to coexist without any one truth-claim assuming ultimate power. Whereas it is the case with other (e.g. fascist or totalitarian) orders that there is always some form of meta-narrative constraint, some limit placed upon the sheer multiplicity of language-games, often – as in Nazi Germany – through the appeal to a manifest destiny conceived in mythic nationalist terms. Such appeals can only work in so far as they efface the Kantian distinction between concepts of understanding (which take for their object a real-world experience given to intuition) and ideas of reason (which lack such empirical self-evidence and whose validity is strictly confined to the realm of speculative thought). Thus, according to Lyotard,

> [t]he importance of the philosophy of the beautiful and the sublime . . . lies both in the derealisation of the object of aesthetic feelings, and in the absence of a real aesthetic faculty of knowing. The same thing holds, perhaps even more radically, for the historico-political object, which as such has no reality, and for any political faculty of knowing, which must remain inexistent . . . With this *Begebenheit* [i.e. presentation of ideas with no phenomenal or real-world content] we must get as close as possible to the abyss to be crossed between mechanism on the one hand and liberty or finality on the other, between the domain of the sensory world and the field of the supersensible – and we should be able to leap across it without suppressing it, by fixing the status of the historico-political – a status which may be inconsistent and indeterminate, but which can be spoken, and which is, even, irrefutable.[10]

I have quoted this passage at length because it helps to explain just what is at stake when present-day theorists (like Lyotard and de Man) invoke the Kantian sublime as a check to misplaced or delusive aesthetic ideologies. Their aim is primarily to deconstruct that mystifying tendency of thought whereby ideas of reason are falsely conflated with some given (empirical) reality, and discourses of all kinds reduced to the order of phenomenal or naturalised cognition. For the effects of such confusion are by no means confined to philosophy, aesthetics or literary theory. Their repercussions may be felt in the political sphere, and never more so than at moments – like the period of German High Romanticism and its nationalist aftermath – when critique gives way to the notion of truth as residing in some single, uniquely privileged language or culture. This is why, in de Man's words,

> [t]hose who reproach literary theory for being oblivious to social and historical (that is to say ideological) reality are merely stating their fear at having their own ideological mystifications exposed by the tool they are trying to discredit. They are, in short, very poor readers of Marx's *German Ideology*.[11]

III

It is no part of Barry's argument to follow out these further implications of the Kantian sublime in its socio-political aspect. All the same his book provides plentiful evidence of the close relationship that existed in this period between aesthetic theory and questions in the realm of moral and political debate. Here again, the most suggestive analogies have to do with music as an 'empty' sign, a language whose very lack of determinate meaning gives it this peculiar power to awaken the listener's faculties, and thus to stimulate a level of productive involvement that exceeds all merely sensuous or passive understanding. Of course this story is familiar enough from the mainstream historians of Romanticism, those (like M.H. Abrams in *The Mirror and the Lamp*) who trace the passage from an old, eighteenth-century, empiricist paradigm to a new way of thinking, much influenced by Kant, where imagination is conceived as an active, form-giving faculty, a power that is to some degree involved in our most elementary acts of cognition, but is witnessed more impressively by those moments of sublime overreaching achieved by poets like Wordsworth, Coleridge and Shelley.[12] Up to a point this is pretty much the tale that Barry has to tell, with the difference that he places music alongside poetry as an index of the change in aesthetic sensibility. But he also – like de Man – takes issue with Abrams on the question of whether art can actually *achieve* that state of 'unmediated expressiveness' that often features in high-romantic claims for the superiority of symbol over allegory, or for metaphor as a trope that transcends the limitations of other, more prosaic devices like metonymy. Such thinking is itself a version of aesthetic ideology in so far as it ignores the ontological difference between word and world, the sheer *impossibility* that language might annul this difference and thus overcome all the classic antinomies of mind and nature, subject and object, ideas and sensuous perceptions.

For Barry, as indeed for de Man, this delusion is one that overtakes the discourse of Romanticism when it forgets those un-self-deceiving lessons handed down by strong precursors like Rousseau. We should, he says,

> note the continuity between Rousseau's definition of the musician, as one who is 'affected more by absent things as if they were present', and Wordsworth's definition of the poet, as one who has 'an ability of conjuring up in himself passions, which are indeed far from being the same as those produced by real events'. (p. 179)

One way of unpacking this sentence would be to read it in terms of the changes wrought upon romantic ideology by the powerful conservative backlash that followed in the wake of the French Revolution. (Again, it is not an argument that Barry takes up in any detail, but his book does provide a good deal of supporting documentary evidence). One could then see the architects of later romantic tradition – Wordsworth and Coleridge among them – as offering a kind of rearguard defence, a mystified doctrine of aesthetic value that precisely negates or collapses those hopes once vested in French political events. For Kant, after all, the Revolution stood as a test of those ultimate ideals – republican justice, universal peace, the progress of mankind toward a state of enlightened world government – which as yet had no demonstrable grounding (since the outcome was utterly uncertain), but which none the less demanded an absolute commitment *for or against* in the minds of all qualified observers.[13] What is figured in the upheaval of 1789 is thus – according to Lyotard – a virtual transposition of the Kantian sublime into the realm of history and politics. The very chaos or formlessness of current events is an index of their power (like that of the sublime in nature) to call forth responses far surpassing the limits of commonplace knowledge or perception.

Kant himself was of course no friend to revolutions, at least in so far as they involved the overthrow of existing monarchical or state structures. Hence no doubt his desire to maintain that crucial separation of realms whereby freedom, progress and justice are held to be ideas of pure reason, and therefore not concepts that could ever be translated into the here-and-now of revolutionary action. Thus, in Lyotard's words:

> What best determines the sublime is the indeterminate, the *Formlösigkeit* . . .
> The same must be the case for the Revolution, and for all great historical
> upheavals – they are the formless and the figureless in historical human nature.
> Ethically there is nothing valid about them: on the contrary they come in for
> critical judgement . . . they are the result of a confusion (which is the political
> illusion itself) between the direct presentation of the *gemeine Wesen* [communal
> existence] and the analogical presentation of the Idea of a Republican contract.[14]

And there is – as I have argued elsewhere – a similar ambivalence in de Man's
writings, a treatment of political motives and ideals as somehow belonging to a
realm apart from all hope of secular or this-worldly fulfilment.[15] It comes out
especially in those middle-period essays (like 'Wordsworth and Hölderlin')
where the poets supply an ironic gloss on the claims of revolutionary justice, a
chastened self-knowledge that eventually perceives how deluded was the notion
of translating such ideals into any kind of activist programme.[16] Lyotard himself – as a theorist of the 'postmodern condition' – rejects all forms of that
enlightenment belief (whether Kantian, Hegelian, Marxist or whatever) that
would seek out a providential meaning in history, a master-plot imposed in the
name of progress, freedom or universal truth. But this message is qualified by
his constantly returning to those passages of argument in Kant which attempt to
keep open a space for the critique of existing political structures, despite all the
dangers – as Kant and Lyotard see it – of confusing such ideas with any real-
world change in the state of political affairs.

What is now required, according to Lyotard, is a step beyond the author-
itarian discourse of enlightenment reason, and a willingness to accept the
diverse language-games that make up a postmodern socio-political 'dissen-
sus'. This step would be evidenced, he writes,

> in the fact that it is not only the Idea of a *single* purpose which would be pointed
> to in our feelings, but already the Idea that this purpose consists in the formation
> and free exploration of Ideas *in the plural*, the Idea that this end is the beginning
> of the *infinity of heterogeneous finalities*.[17]

There remain – to say the least – certain problems in assessing just how this
attitude might work out in political terms. In fact it seems to me that Lyotard's
mistrust of premature 'totalising' creeds is pushed to the point where thinking
very nearly renounces its power to criticise existing realities. But he does
make it clear that these Kantian issues go deep into the philosophic discourse
of modernity, and need to be addressed by any critical theory that warrants the
name. Furthermore, it is in the region of the Kantian sublime – of the difference (to repeat) between concepts of understanding and ideas of pure

reason – that this debate takes on its most crucial aspect. For Kant, as Lyotard reads him, '[t]he progress of a common being for the better is not to be judged on the basis of empirical intuition, but on the basis of signs.' That is to say, events like the French Revolution have a capacity to signify those ultimate values of progress, democracy and freedom despite what must appear as a sequence of disheartening set-backs and failures in the practical realm. To interpret them as *signs* in this specific sense – as what Kant calls 'hypo-typoses', or ideas that possess a meaning quite apart from all present or empirical self-evidence – is to place the sublime at the very heart of socio-political thinking. 'This sign [i.e. the French Revolution for Kant] *is* progress in its present state, as far as can be, although civil societies are not, far from it, close to the Republican regime, nor States close to worldwide federation.'[18] What preserves the necessary margin of hope is precisely this refusal to misread the signs, or to treat history as merely the sum of its determinate manifestations to date.

These questions are all within reach of what Barry has to say about music as an 'empty sign' and its relation to eighteenth-century ideas of aesthetic rep-resentation. In particular they help to explain why music should have figured increasingly as the focus of a certain dissatisfaction with analogies drawn from the visual or plastic arts. 'The meaning of music depends upon the enigmatic character of its signs which, instead of replacing a source which they would imitate or express, turn the listener's attention to his own inventive subjectivity' (p. 104). Barry is here using the word 'sign' with something much akin to its force in Lyotard's argument: that is, as an index of music's power to summon up ideas beyond the grasp of determinate concepts on the one hand, or phenomenal intuitions on the other. And he also makes it clear that the 'inventive subjectivity' in question is *not* just a matter of impres-sionistic whims attaching to this or that mood of listener-response, but should rather be seen as a decisive shift of epistemological categories. In short,

[t]he difference between seeing and hearing, whereby one does and the other does not designate a coordinating perspective and objectivity, affects the status of the subject. For the perceiving subject who *sees* is situated and placed within a set of clarities and distinctions, but the perceiving subject who *hears* is dis-placed within a set of obscurities. (p. 50)

Thus music becomes something more than a source of aesthetically appealing images and metaphors. It assumes the central role in a new way of thinking about language, art and representation whose effects reach far beyond the discourse of art criticism.

Barry finds a similar process at work in the poetry of this period, one that begins with the pastoral figure of the poet-as-musician evoked in Collins's 'Ode to Evening', and achieves its fullest, most articulate form in the writings of Wordsworth and Coleridge. Here again there is a marked shift of priorities in the later eighteenth century, as notions of language based upon visual or painterly metaphors give way to an aesthetics of the Kantian sublime and a stress on those 'obscure', 'enigmatical' meanings that elude such phenomenal characterisation. His chapter on Coleridge makes excellent use of the numerous passages, scattered through the prose writings, which lend support to Barry's argument for the ascendance of a music-alised poetics. My one reservation about this chapter is that it tends to underestimate the conflict between Coleridge's symbolist-organicist creed – as developed in his later, more conservative texts – and that idea of music and poetry as 'empty' signs which would surely present a radical challenge to any such aesthetic ontology. At this point the argument seems oddly out of touch with its own more searching implications. But there is every reason to welcome Barry's book as a valuable piece of scholarly research and one that opens up some intriguing prospects for further work in the field.

Notes

1. See especially Jean H. Hagstrum, *The Sister Arts: the tradition of literary pictorialism and English poetry from Dryden to Gray* (Chicago: University of Chicago Press, 1958).
2. On the topic of figural language in Locke and other philosophers, see Paul de Man, 'The epistemology of metaphor', *Critical Inquiry*, vol. 5, no. 1 (Autumn, 1978), pp. 13–30.
3. Paul de Man, 'The rhetoric of temporality', in *Blindness and Insight: essays in the rhetoric of contemporary criticism* (London: Methuen, 1983), pp. 187–228; p. 207.
4. De Man, 'The rhetoric of blindness: Jacques Derrida's reading of Rousseau', in *Blindness and Insight* (*op. cit.*), pp. 102–41; p. 128.
5. See Jacques Derrida, *Of Grammatology*, trans. Gayatri C. Spivak (Baltimore: Johns Hopkins University Press, 1976), especially pp. 280–95.
6. This question is taken up again by Derrida in *Mémoires: for Paul de Man* (New York: Columbia University Press, 1986).
7. See for instance de Man, 'The resistance to theory' and 'The return to philology', in *The Resistance to Theory* (Minneapolis: University of Minnesota Press, 1986), pp. 3–20 and 21–6.
8. See especially de Man, 'Phenomenality and materiality in Kant', in Gary Shapiro and Alan Sica (eds.), *Hermeneutics: questions and prospects* (Amherst:

University of Massachusetts Press, 1984), pp. 112–44 and 'Hegel on the sublime', in Mark Krupnik (ed.), *Displacement: Derrida and after* (Bloomington: Indiana University Press, 1983), pp. 139–53.

9. See Jean-François Lyotard, *The Postmodern Condition: a report on knowledge*, trans. Geoff Bennington and Brian Massumi (Minneapolis: University of Minnesota Press, 1984).
10. Lyotard, 'The idea of history', in Derek Attridge, Geoff Bennington and Robert Young (eds.), *Post-Structuralism and the Question of History* (Cambridge: CUP, 1987), pp. 162–80.
11. De Man, 'The resistance to theory' (*op. cit.*), p. 11.
12. M.H. Abrams, *The Mirror and the Lamp: romantic theory and the critical tradition* (London: OUP, 1953).
13. See Kant, *Political Writings*, ed. H. Reiss (Cambridge: CUP, 1973) and *On History*, ed. L.W. Beck (New York: Bobbs-Merrill, 1963).
14. Lyotard, 'The idea of history' (*op. cit.*), pp. 173–4.
15. See Norris, *Paul de Man: deconstruction and the critique of aesthetic ideology* (New York and London: Routledge, 1988).
16. De Man, 'Wordsworth and Hölderlin', in *The Rhetoric of Romanticism* (New York: Columbia University Press, 1984), pp. 47–65. See also his essays 'The Image of Rousseau in the poetry of Hölderlin', in *The Rhetoric of Romanticism* (*op. cit.*), pp. 19–45 and 'Heidegger's exegeses of Hölderlin', in *Blindness and Insight* (*op. cit.*), pp. 246–66.
17. Lyotard, 'The idea of history' (*op. cit.*), p. 179.
18. *ibid.*, p. 177.

Chapter 7

Settling Accounts:
Heidegger, de Man and
the ends of philosophy

I

The facts of the case are sufficiently well known by now, and Lacoue-Labarthe has little to add by way of documentary evidence.* Nor is he concerned to find grounds for excusing or downplaying Heidegger's involvement with Nazi cultural politics in the period of his Rectorship at Freiburg University after 1933. This book starts out from the clear-eyed, sober recognition that Heidegger not only espoused the Nazi cause – espoused it in the most unequivocal and public terms – but also found in it a singular confirmation of everything that had occupied his own teaching and writing up to that time. It makes no attempt to minimise the impact of these latest 'discoveries' about Heidegger's pre-war career, or to argue that they manifest a brief 'flirtation' with Nazi ideology in a thinker whose work was otherwise devoted to higher philosophical ends. Nor (to his credit) does Lacoue-Labarthe go in for the kind of last-ditch saving strategy adopted by Richard Rorty in a recent article on Heidegger's life and work.[1] For Rorty, it is just a sentimental error – a species of category-mistake – to suppose that great thinkers ought to be good human beings, or that intellectual eminence should somehow guarantee a high standard of ethical behaviour. One had much better face up to the unfortunate truth (in Heidegger's case, that he was 'a nasty piece of work – a coward and a liar, pretty much from first to last . . . an egomaniacal, anti-Semitic redneck'), since this does not entail any consequent revision to our sense of his intellectual worth (that Heidegger was, quite simply, 'as original a philosopher as we have had in this century').

---

* Philippe Lacoue-Labarthe, *Heidegger, Art and Politics*, trans. Chris Turner (Oxford: Basil Blackwell, 1990). All references to this work are given by page-number in the text.

Such a line of defence might perhaps seem attractive when dealing with the kind of crude *ad hominem* abuse heaped upon thinkers of various (mostly left-wing) persuasions by Paul Johnson in his lamentable volume *Intellectuals.*[2] But this attitude just will not do as a matter of serious, responsible debate, and one is thankful to find Lacoue-Labarthe adopting a more principled and ethically rigorous stance. For what we are dealing with here is not, he insists, some momentary 'error' or lapse of judgement on Heidegger's part, some strange aberration that led him – however briefly – to identify Nazism as the authentic voice of German cultural renewal. On the contrary: this was 'not an error, but a consequence . . . And if that consequence had as its consequence, even if only for a period of ten months, *consenting to* Nazism – to something of that order – then we must speak, not of committing an error, but of *doing wrong*' (p. 22).

At the same time Lacoue-Labarthe has small patience with what he sees as the current bout of sensation-mongering sparked off by the appearance, in 1987, of Victor Farias's book *Heidegger et le Nazisme.*[3] Most of this material (the book included) he considers mere journalistic chatter, or at best a kind of 'factical' enquiry that evades the real issues – the philosophical issues – posed by the so-called 'Heidegger affair'. To this extent Lacoue-Labarthe seems committed to a line of argument that takes its main bearings from Heidegger's pronouncements on the hermeneutic circle of tacit foreknowledge, the idea that interpretation goes all the way down, and the need to approach thinkers from within the horizon of 'pre-understanding' that alone makes it possible to comprehend their work. 'To evade that question [i.e. the issue of Heidegger's political commitment] by adopting the rather simple stance of an "external critique", and arguing that one has to "call a spade a spade", is not necessarily to set things back in their right place' (p. 131). More specifically, it ignores the crucial distinction – crucial for Heidegger at least – between matters of an 'ontic' or straightforwardly evidential character and matters of a deeper, 'ontological' significance that cannot be settled by any such appeal to the manifest facts of the case. In so far as he respects the need for this distinction – along with others of a kindred nature like 'historical' and 'historial' – Lacoue-Labarthe is clearly committed to the view that any *authentic* discussion of Heidegger must take the form of an immanent critique, or a reading conducted on terms laid down by that same Heideggerian project.

In short, there is no choice but to accept those terms if we wish to understand how it ever came about that philosophy could identify its own deepest interests with what Heidegger called the 'inner truth and greatness of this [i.e. the Nazi] movement'. For it is taken pretty much for

truths of existence. Again, Lacoue-Labarthe rejects any notion that Heidegger can somehow be excused on these grounds, or his pronouncements treated as somehow beyond reach of ethical judgement. Indeed, he makes a point of citing those few passages in the later texts where Heidegger does acknowledge his own 'greatest stupidity', that of having once identified such truth with the emergence of a merely historical movement (or a surrogate entity, the German *Volk*) whose meaning was thereby – disastrously – obscured from view. Nor does he attempt to make excuses for Heidegger's notorious evasiveness on this issue and his failure to address it in anything other than a cryptic and roundabout fashion. But there is still a real sense, according to Lacoue-Labarthe, in which Heidegger's thought has pre-empted the terms of any serious debate and provided the only possible means of understanding the 'essence' of Nazi politics.

Take the following passage, where he offers what amounts to a characterisation of Heidegger's fault in language that Heidegger would surely have endorsed as faithful to his own deepest thoughts and intentions. The involvement with Nazism was arrived at, he suggests,

> on the basis, essentially, of a kind of 'transcendental illusion' bearing on the people and restoring a subject (of history) at a point where the thinking of ekstatic *Dasein* and finitude . . . should have prevented any confusion of *Mitsein* with a notion of community as substance or even, quite simply, with an entity (the people, whether Greek or German, which is to say, their language). (p. 78)

This passage reads like an unwitting parody of everything that hostile (especially Anglo-American) commentators have seized upon as typical of Heidegger's jargon-ridden, obfuscatory style. One can see – just about – what the argument comes down to: that Heidegger espoused the Nazi cause through a fateful dereliction of his own thinking as regards the 'ontological difference' between matters of fact and issues of a deeper (authentic or truly 'historial') import. What Lacoue-Labarthe never quite gets round to asking – for all his subtlety of argument and ethical concern – is the question whether this whole line of talk does not reproduce exactly the kind of 'transcendental illusion' that allowed Heidegger to raise the Nazi movement into a principle of manifest truth. That is to say, it implies that Heidegger after all understood these dangers better than anyone else; that we can only grasp the 'essence' of Nazi politics through a rigorous reading of Heidegger's post-1933 texts; and that no amount of mere historical chatter (or 'factical' research) can provide any glimmer of enlightenment as regards the truth of these matters.

For it is Lacoue-Labarthe's chief contention throughout this book that Nazism took rise from a history of thought which encompassed the entirety of 'Western metaphysics', from Plato to Hegel, Nietzsche and Husserl, and whose meaning Heidegger alone has pursued to the point of revealing its ultimate (nihilist) conclusion. His thinking would thus provide 'a privileged access – and perhaps the only possible access – to the essence of the political that is simultaneously veiled and unveiled by National Socialism' (p. 7). And furthermore, any critic who sought to expose that thinking as somehow complicit with Nazi ideology – as an ersatz 'jargon of authenticity', in Adorno's phrase, inherently prone to such uses – would thereby manifest a failure to grasp what is *essentially* at stake in this affair.[4] From which it follows, again, that there is no coming to terms with the 'fact' of Heidegger's Nazi involvement except by way of an authentic (i.e. Heideggerian) approach that in principle refuses to treat of such questions from a standpoint of 'external' critique. Lacoue-Labarthe does acknowledge at one point that perhaps a degree of scepticism might be in order; that 'it can be very useful – even healthy – to take certain Heideggerian statements literally, to be on one's guard for euphemisms and observe the greatest caution towards a rhetoric (Heidegger's) that is governed by a refusal of the ontically obvious' (p. 130). But in general he maintains – as against thoroughgoing sceptics like Adorno – that this refusal is both justified and necessary in so far as it enables us to grasp more fully what Heidegger could have meant by that notorious reference to the 'inner truth and greatness' of the Nazi movement. For his reading is staked on the premise that such utterances *must* be capable of a deeper, more 'authentic' mode of explication, one that has learned – after Heidegger's example – not to rest content with merely 'ontic' or socio-historical terms of understanding.

II

So Lacoue-Labarthe has set himself a different (some might say impossible) task. He must explain how it is that Heidegger's thought could *on the one hand* provide our most authoritative source of insight into the Nazi evil, and *on the other* give rise to a massive aberration of political judgement which led him – at whatever 'philosophical' remove – to endorse that same evil in the name of authentic Being and truth. This still necessitates our asking the question: 'Why is historial *Dasein* determined as the *Dasein* of a people?', or again, 'in more everyday political terms . . . [w]hy was Heidegger committed to the idea of a national revolution, and why did he never repudiate this commitment?' (p. 112). But any answer to this question will fall far short of Heidegger's own (albeit deeply compromised) project of thought if it persists in treating Nazism as an aberrant phenomenon, a socio-historical 'fact' that needs explaining, or Heidegger himself as a thinker betrayed by some 'choice' that could be judged according to the standards of enlightened ethical critique. At this point discussion must be opened, as Lacoue-Labarthe writes,

> not on the evaluation of Nazism, but on *thinking* Nazism (after all, the phenomenon was not born out of nothing, but came from us, 'good Euro-peans that we are') and thinking through its stunning success, its power of seduction, its project and its victories etc., and above all in thinking what it might have represented for intellectuals of the period, not all of whom – far from it – were imbeciles or opportunists. (p. 127)

This passage goes to the heart of his argument and therefore merits the closest attention. By 'thinking' we are clearly given to understand what Heidegger means by the word, that is, a contemplative questing-back for the 'essence' of that which has concealed itself within or beyond the inherited categories of Western 'metaphysical' thought.[5] Only thus can philosophy be set upon the path of authentic truth, a path that involves nothing less than the undoing (or the deconstructive passing-in-review) of that entire tradition and its various forms of deep-laid forgetfulness with regard to the primordial 'question of Being'. And this applies just as much to the 'essence' of Nazism, a movement that Heidegger once acclaimed as the looked-for awakening of the German *Volk* to its emergent national destiny, but which he then came to view – in chastened retrospect – as the last, most degraded and bankrupt form of that same metaphysical tradition.

In short, 'we could not speak of "archi-fascism" [i.e. the true meaning of the Nazi phenomenon] if Heidegger himself had not taught us to think philosophically what fascism, plain and simple, is about' (p. 110). For Lacoue-Labarthe firmly rejects the idea that Heidegger's 'error' was contingent upon his *choice* of a certain philosophical outlook; that he might somehow have avoided his fateful misjudgment of the Nazi phenomenon had he not gone in for that particular style of pseudo-historical archaising thought joined to an irrationalist 'jargon of authenticity' which promptly fell in with the purposes of Nazi propaganda. Any such argument will ignore the most crucial point: namely, that 'metaphysics, at least in the form of that ineradicable *Trieb* recognised by Kant and Nietzsche, is at the most secret heart of thought itself' (p. 19). And again: '. . . "thought", if there is such a thing, can never proclaim itself "disengaged" from metaphysics . . . [since]

this is what always leaves it *engagé* in this world, however great its prudence or its disillusionment' (p. 19).

This is why Lacoue-Labarthe has no time for commentators – like Adorno – who argue that there exists a close relation between Heidegger's mystified ontology of Being and his temporary 'lapse' into a strain of 'vulgar' pro-Nazi rhetoric. On the contrary: what made Nazism possible was that long prehistory of Western metaphysical thought whose limits (or 'closure') Heidegger was the first to think through in a rigorous and consequent manner. Thus Adorno gets it wrong on three main counts, according to Lacoue-Labarthe. First, he mistakes Heidegger's language of Being, *Dasein*, 'fundamental ontology', etc. for a mere line of talk, a rhetoric adopted (whether wittingly or not) in the service of a potent irrationalist mystique with dire political consequences. Second, he assumes that the question of Heidegger's 'politics' is raised most acutely by those scandalous pronouncements that belong to the so-called Nazi phase, the period of his Rectorate at Freiburg when Heidegger explicitly aligned his thinking with the National Socialist cause. For Lacoue-Labarthe, conversely, this reveals a hopelessly inadequate grasp, and above all a failure to recognise the fact that *Heidegger's entire life's work* – before, during and after the Nazi 'interlude' – was devoted to a questioning of that which constituted the 'essence' of National Socialism. Thus:

> it is not in the discourse of 1933 that 'Heidegger's politics' is to be found (that discourse, including his *Rectoral Address*, is far too compromised in advance), but in the discourse which follows the 'break' or the 'withdrawal' and which presents itself in any case as a settling of accounts with National Socialism, *in the name of its truth*. (p. 53)

Hence Adorno's third great error, as Lacoue-Labarthe sees it: his belief that Heidegger's Nazi involvement was a short-lived but symptomatic episode, that it compromised his thinking as a whole ('right down to its innermost components', in Adorno's phrase), but did so precisely on account of his refusal to acknowledge that complicity or face up to its deeper implications.

Lacoue-Labarthe takes the contrary view on each of these counts. So far from ignoring or evading the issue, Heidegger's writings after 1933 continued to address the Nazi phenomenon, but at a level which opponents like Adorno could scarcely be expected to grasp, committed as they were to a standpoint of 'external' critique, an attitude that rendered them incapable of thinking the 'essence' of Nazi ideology. That 'essence' was Heidegger's constant theme in the works that followed his rapid disillusionment with the

National Socialist cause. What he came to understand – belatedly, no doubt, but all the more forcefully for that – was the intimate link between Nazi mythology and that entire prehistory of Western metaphysics whose latest expression was the will-to-power bound up with technological or scientistic reason. It is not surprising, then, that Adorno should signally have failed to grasp this deep-laid connection, given his attachment to a mode of enlightened demystifying thought ('negative dialectics') whose antecedents included Kant, Hegel, Marx and all the other main figures in that same prehistory that Heidegger set out to deconstruct.[6] For it is precisely the distinction – the 'essential' value – of Heidegger's later writings to have laid bare the complicity that exists between Nazism and those various forms of enlightenment critique which conceal that dialectical will-to-power behind a rhetoric of disinterested reason and truth.

Lacoue-Labarthe puts the case as follows in a passage that again requires detailed scrutiny. Did Adorno, he asks, 'possess a concept of fascism which was fascism's truth and which, in particular, made it possible to detect it in places where it was not self-evidently present: in the thinking of Being, for example?' (pp. 106–7). This question must receive a negative answer, he thinks, since

> Adorno's 'critique' of fascism never freed itself from its Marxist or para-Marxist presuppositions and therefore revealed itself incapable of reaching the place where, a long way this side of their reciprocal hostility (which was in fact irreducible), and therefore a long way this side of 'ideological' or 'political' divergences or oppositions, the ontological-historial co-belonging of Marxism and fascism . . . can be established. Perhaps Adorno, who was as eager as could be to speak about it, said less about fascism than did Heidegger in the very parsimony of his declarations . . . (p.107)

At this level of thought – so the argument runs – the difference between Marxism and fascism becomes just a matter of localised dispute, a falling-out among the parties to a common 'metaphysical' heritage of thought. In which case Adorno's critique of Heidegger would amount to nothing more than the programmed replay of a superficial quarrel whose terms cannot fail to reproduce all the inbuilt values and assumptions of Western enlightenment reason. The 'co-belonging' that Lacoue-Labarthe speaks of is something that can only be revealed if one adopts the Heideggerian stance of suspending all reference to merely 'ideological' or 'political' differences, and asking instead what unites Marxism and fascism despite their appearance of 'reciprocal hostility' (and even while allowing that such hostility is 'in fact irreducible'). In this perspective it is the merest of

illusions to suppose that one could criticise Heidegger on ethical or political grounds that had not already been brought into question by Heidegger's thinking on the 'essence' and the destiny of Western metaphysics. In
short, 'all denunciations of the Heideggerian idiom . . . never manage to
avoid the trap of counter-ideology. To espouse Marxism against Heidegger is to miss the essentials of his thought – including his political thought'
(p. 15).

The trouble with this whole line of argument is that it simply takes over
the jargon of authenticity – all the talk of 'essences', historial *Dasein*,
ontological difference and so forth – and uses it as a stick to beat any critic
who rejects such mystifying verbiage. Indeed, Lacoue-Labarthe goes out
of his way to cast Adorno in the role of an intellectual dupe, a thinker
whose extreme dialectical contortions did nothing to prevent his falling
prey to bad faith and political misjudgement. Thus he digs up the fact (first
publicised by a Frankfurt student newspaper in 1963) that Adorno had
once written favourably about a song-cycle to words by Baldur von
Schirach, a poet much acclaimed in National Socialist circles. In fact it was
by way of responding to this attack that Adorno used the phrase about
Heidegger so resented by Lacoue-Labarthe ('it ought to be impossible for
anyone who inspects my work in its continuity to compare me with
Heidegger, whose philosophy is fascist right down to its innermost components').[7] It seems to me that Adorno more than earned the right to this
riposte, and that Lacoue-Labarthe is here applying what amounts to a
shifty double standard, since elsewhere – defending Heidegger – he sees fit
to remind us of Valéry's dictum: 'qui ne peut attaquer le raisonnement,
attaque le raisonneur' (p. 14). But one can well understand why Adorno
should figure as the thinker whose arguments need demolishing (by whatever means) if Heidegger is to emerge in a light undimmed by the charge
of Nazi complicity. For Adorno's critique cannot easily be dismissed (like
the Farias book and other such largely documentary sources) as just a piece
of trifling 'factical' research, unconcerned with the 'essence' of Heidegger's thinking or the 'essence' of National Socialism. What Adorno brings
out with admirable force is the close relation – so to speak, the elective
affinity – between Heidegger's mystified ontology of Being and his
espousal (however short-lived) of a Nazi rhetoric that likewise traded on
notions of authentic national spirit and other such 'profound' pseudo-
truths.

Lacoue-Labarthe has great contempt for such arguments, regarding
them as just another symptom of the superficiality – the failure to 'think' in
the strong (Heideggerian) sense of that word – which has so far

characterised this whole debate. 'For Adorno's accusation to hit its mark', he writes,

> at least two conditions have to be fulfilled: (1) we must know what fascism is in its essence; (2) we must show what *effective* relation there is between the accused (or suspect) 'philosophy' – also in its essence – and a fascism rigorously delimited in this way. (p. 106)

And of course this entails the foregone conclusion that Adorno will have nothing of importance to say on the matter, or nothing that could possibly advance discussion to a point where it began to catch up with Heidegger's thinking. For Adorno's whole case must be seen to rest on a principled resistance to such vacuous (but all-too-beguiling) talk of essences, primordial truths, concealments of Being, historial *Dasein* and other such quasi-mystical absolutes dressed up in an oracular jargon that claims some privileged access to truths beyond reach of argued critique. 'Quite naturally Adorno wanted to have nothing of that. And after all, that is something one can *also* understand' (p. 106). That is to say, Adorno's stance on the question of 'Heidegger's politics' needs to be viewed in a diagnostic light, as the upshot of a bankrupt 'metaphysical' tradition which could only turn aside from the knowledge of its own historial obsolescence, taking refuge in a mode of 'external critique' which – for all its negative-dialectical rigour – was predestined to rejoin that same outworn tradition. And of course this leaves little room for thinkers of a different (non-Heideggerian) persuasion. Heads I win, tails you lose: if you don't go along with Heidegger's claim to have thought more deeply, more *authentically* on the 'essence' of Nazism than those (like Adorno) who never heard the call of its 'inner greatness and truth', then you show yourself simply unfit to pronounce on such matters.

This is not to say that Lacoue-Labarthe has nothing more specific to offer when it comes to explaining just what it was that Heidegger perceived (belatedly) as the truth or essence in question. On the contrary: his book has a thesis, a distinctive line of argument on the topic of 'Heidegger's politics', for all that he rejects the very notion of judging or taking up a position for or against. What Heidegger at last came to realise, he argues, was that Nazism amounted 'in essence' to a form of *national aestheticism*, a thinking that conflated the realms of politics and art to a point where society itself became a kind of total spectacle, a *Gesamtkunstwerk* in which the artist's vision (or the Führer's will) could no longer be distinguished from the thoughts and desires of the people whose privileged destiny it was to act out this magnificent drama. Such thinking identified the highest political good with the image of an ideal organic community, a *Ge-meinschaft* united by intimate ties of national and cultural character. And one major impulse behind this development was the heritage of German post-Kantian idealist thought, as witnessed (for instance) by Schiller's great theme of 'aesthetic education' as a means of overcoming those various hateful antinomies – mind and nature, subject and object, freedom and necessity – which Kant had effectively left in place, or failed to transcend through the exercise of critical reason.[8] Thus it was that philosophy entered upon the path of a 'national aestheticism' which progressively blurred the distinction between art and politics, and whose most extreme statement was Nietzsche's belief that existence could only be 'justified' as an aesthetic phenomenon. What Nazism achieved – according to Lacoue-Labarthe – was the deployment of such notions on a massive, unprecedented scale; the carrying-over of Nietzsche's doctrine (along with its various Romantic ante-cedents) into a fully-fledged 'society of the spectacle' where every last national resource was enlisted in the Nazi pageant of power.

So this is the tradition of thought that Heidegger inherits, one which

> originates in the Jena of Schiller (and not Goethe), the Schlegels, Hölderlin, Schelling and, in part, the 'young Hegel' – and which, through Wagner and Nietzsche, ultimately wins out and certainly at least dominates, in very varying forms, the Germany that did not resist the 'movement' of the 1930s. (p. 57)

And moreover, there is no question of his having espoused this aesthetic ideology only during that brief period (1933–4) when Nazism appeared to represent the 'inner truth and greatness' of German national destiny. For it is Lacoue-Labarthe's chief contention here that Heidegger never swerved from this essential insight, that is, his understanding of the Nazi phenom-enon as deeply bound up with the entire prehistory of Western metaphy-sical thought, a history whose underlying impulse was precisely the will to 'aestheticise politics', or to treat historical events as fit material for the artist's shaping vision. Indeed, he goes so far as to claim that

> it was not until ten years after the collapse of the Third Reich that Heidegger had the definitive revelation that National Socialism (national-aestheticism) was the truth of the inversion of Platonism or of the restoration of what Plato had fought against – though not without yielding to tyranny himself – in other words, the thinking of the technical or the political as *fiction*: the last attempt at 'mythizing' the West. Though not, probably, the last aestheticization of the political. (p. 86)

In support of this claim he can point to the following main pieces of evidence. (1) Heidegger continued to believe in the deep (historial) affinity that existed between ancient Greek and latter-day German culture, a belief which found expression in his well-known thesis that thinking – authentic philosophical thinking – was impossible in any other language. (2) The only hope of 'settling accounts' with Nazism was to grasp that affinity as it bore upon the 'essence' of national-aestheticist thought, namely, the heritage of a 'Western metaphysics' whose deepest, most persistent drive was to substitute aesthetic for political terms of judgement. (3) The best way to achieve such insight was to ponder deeply on the work of those poets – Hölderlin pre-eminent among them – whose language somehow managed to recall 'the grandeur of the Greek beginning, in so far as that grandeur . . . is still in reserve in the future, that is to say, is still to come' (p. 56). From all of which it followed (4) that thinking had still to go by way of that grievous 'revelation' which came to Heidegger in the years after 1933, and which could not be side-stepped by treating Nazism as a mere 'pathological' episode, a fateful swerve from the authentic path opened up by that privileged relation to the Greeks. For it was – and remained – Heidegger's conviction that nothing could account for that episode except the kind of thinking that 'resolutely' acknowledged this kinship between the highest and the worst, most degraded aspects of German cultural tradition.

Thus in Lacoue-Labarthe's words, summarising Heidegger:

> Germany will accede to itself and to History when it is capable of giving resonance to the unsaid and the unthought that is proffered, though still locked away, in the words of the Greeks. For then it will have found its own language. (p. 56)

Hence the importance of Hölderlin's poetry – his 'interpretation/translation of the Greeks' – for Heidegger's subsequent coming-to-terms with the inner truth and meaning of the Nazi phenomenon. By reading that poetry in light of what had occurred – not only of recent political events but of everything in the history of Western thought, from Plato to Kant, Hegel and Nietzsche, which had somehow (obscurely) prepared for those events – it might yet be possible to reach an understanding beyond the merely 'factical' or social-diagnostic. More plainly: 'there will be no salvation for the Germans as a people entering (Western/World) history and fulfilling their spiritual-historical destiny, unless they listen to Hölderlin' (p. 55).

233

As so often in this book, it is difficult to know whether Lacoue-Labarthe is simply paraphrasing Heidegger, endorsing his claims, or offering them up to critical assessment as a massive warning instance of what goes wrong when thinking falls prey to such potent forms of 'national-aestheticist' delusion. At any rate he takes them seriously enough to make a point of distinguishing between Heidegger's version of that creed and the versions put about by Nazi ideologues of a less reputable character. For on the face of it one might be tempted to suppose that this difference did not amount to much, since they – like Heidegger – extolled the virtues of organic community, national tradition, the *Führerprinzip* as source of all values, and the nation-state as living embodiment of the leader's will made manifest in concrete socio-political form. Lacoue-Labarthe suggests as much when he writes that

> it is a Romanticism of this kind that structures, both in its caricatural forms (for mass consumption) or its more elaborate (but still degraded) ones, the official – though not always very homogeneous – ideology of the Reich: this is the language of Goebbels and also of Rosenberg, Bäumler or Krieck. (p. 57)

But he none the less maintains that there is a crucial difference between Nazi ideology in these (more or less 'degraded') variants and Heidegger's involvement with 'national aestheticism' even at the time when he overtly embraced the major tenets of Nazi cultural politics. For in Heidegger's case the involvement was that of a thinker who in some sense *could not have escaped* such complicity, and whose subsequent 'settling of accounts' with the Nazi phenomenon *for that very reason* affords the best hope of understanding its deepest import.

But of course this argument will carry little weight – or be seen as just another piece of mystified special pleading – unless Lacoue-Labarthe can say more precisely what it was that elevated Heidegger's thought above the run of Nazi cultural propaganda. After all, his book offers some striking instances (from Rosenberg, Goebbels, Jünger and others) of the way that this 'vulgar' aestheticising drive was able to exploit certain themes taken over from the German Romantic tradition, themes which also played a crucial role in Heidegger's thought both during and after the period of Nazi hegemony. (Thus Goebbels in a letter to the conductor, Wilhelm Furtwängler: 'Politics, too, is perhaps an art, if not the highest and most all-embracing there is . . . only an art that draws on the *Volkstum* as a whole may ultimately be regarded as good . . .' [cited pp. 61–2]). And it is at this point that Lacoue-Labarthe puts forward his own most distinctive and far-reaching claim as regards the 'essence' of Heidegger's thinking, or the trait that decisively marked it off from such forms of crude propaganda. For with Heidegger – so he argues – the matter of this relationship between art and politics is thought in terms of an aesthetic ideology that goes far back beyond the Nazi instance to its origin in that 'inversion of Platonism' which opened the way to all later variants on the same metaphysical theme.

III

This argument is developed in much greater detail in Lacoue-Labarthe's essays on the theme of *mimesis* and its complex role *vis-à-vis* the categories of Western theoretical and speculative thought.[9] One would need to take full account of those texts – to read them more closely than is possible here – in order to grasp what is involved in his claim that the destiny of European thought is in some sense prefigured, played out in advance, through Plato's 'quarrel' with the poets and the ambivalence that marks his dealing with the question of authentic, revealed truth (*aletheia*) as opposed to its bad, derivative substitute (*mimesis*, or artistic representation). For it is here that we perceive the first signs of that deep disturbance – that failure to distinguish the two kinds of discourse, to separate knowledge from mimetic desire, or truth from the various second-order forms of simulacrum, fiction, impersonated wisdom, etc. – whose after-effects have comprised the whole history of Western thinking on these topics. The 'inversion of Platonism' that Lacoue-Labarthe speaks of would then come to figure as the source and model of all aesthetic ideology, the aboriginal swerve or 'trope' of thought through which philosophy ('metaphysics') compulsively re-enacted its own failed attempt to establish truth on a basis of clear and distinct ideas unbeholden to *mimesis* and its bad, dissimulating ways. For it would then emerge that the question of 'art and politics' was inseparable from the question of how – since Plato – thinking had attempted this 'settling of accounts' with a highly dubious legacy, one whose character was such as to deny (or to render intensely problematic) any confident beating of the bounds between truth and aesthetic ideology.

To summarise such work – writing of the highest exegetical force and subtlety – is of course to risk all manner of distortion and convenient shorthand paraphrase. Nevertheless one may venture the following ten propositions as bearing most directly on the Heidegger 'affair' and the related topic of national-aestheticist thought. (1) Any attempt (any serious attempt) to address these questions will have to go by way of their inaugural instance in the Platonist metaphysics of mind and knowledge. (2) It will also need to take account of that conflict between the truth-claims of art and philosophy – or *mimesis* and speculative reason – which Plato was himself unable to resolve, since (3) it is evident from Plato's writings that philosophy relies upon a range of essentially mimetic devices (impersonation, imaginary dialogue, the dramatic *mise-en-scène*, allegorical or fictive modes of utterance, etc.) which cannot be reduced to the self-present voice of authentic first-person wisdom. (4) It is precisely on account of this compromised beginning that philosophy has had such problems in maintaining its distance from the snares and illusions of aesthetic ideology. (5) It was Heidegger's deepest insight that this whole problematics of art, knowledge and truth took rise within a certain history of thought – albeit a history more or less coterminous with the Western post-Socratic tradition at large – which had followed Plato's ambivalent lead in suppressing or forgetting the primordial 'question of Being', and had thus come to think of truth in terms of an adequate *correspondence* or matching-up between ideas and things, subjects and objects, truthful propositions and real-world states of affairs. From which it followed (6) that such thinking must be destined to an endless repetition of the same root dilemma, that which had confronted Plato's attempt to delimit the sphere of authentic truth and prevent *mimesis* from working its sophistical effects. For the only result of this endeavour (7) was to show up the limits of metaphysical (i.e. representationist) thought when exposed to the continuing seductive force of an aesthetic ideology which had always inhabited such thinking even at its moments of greatest critical vigilance. Hence (item 8) the crucial respect in which Heidegger's thinking differed from those other, more crudely doctrinaire versions of 'national aestheticism'. Where Heidegger specifically opposed such ideas – whether advanced by downright propagandists like Goebbels or party-line ideologists like Jünger – was in coming to see (9) how this renewed German spirit of national self-assertion involved a kind of *agon* or 'mimetic rivalry' with the Greeks. This amounted to the most extreme form of 'inverted' Platonism in the sense that it aspired to emulate the achievements of Greek thought and culture through a species of direct imitation, a tap-root (so to speak) straight back to the sources of that ancient wisdom, and thus fell into the basic gesture that Plato identified with mimetic illusion at its most seductive and dangerous. And so it becomes possible for Lacoue-Labarthe to argue (10) that Heidegger maintained a critical distance from the purveyors of Nazi ideology precisely in so far as he saw in that doctrine a vulgar and unwitting repetition of issues that had vexed Western philosophy from its earliest times, and which here re-emerged in the form of a full-blown national-aestheticist creed.

Such, in broad outline, is the case presented in this book and the essays that need to be read alongside it in order to grasp the more detailed implications of Lacoue-Labarthe's argument. It is stated most explicitly in the following passage from *Heidegger, Art and Politics*, a passage that I shall cite at some length since it addresses so many of the above issues.

> Since the Renaissance, Europe as a whole has been prey to the Ancient and it is *imitatio* which governs the construction of the modern. What distinguishes Germany, however, is the fact that, from the [French] Revolution onwards, or rather from its imperialistic accomplishment, which coincides with the appearance of speculative idealism . . . Germany rejected the neo-classical – and Latin – style of that *imitatio* (which also implies the rejection of the political form in which neo-classicism ultimately clothed itself, i.e. the Republican form) and sought, not without difficulty, to find a style of its own . . . A mimetic *agon* with France was thus added to that with Greece . . . What the German *imitatio* is seeking in Greece is the model – and therefore the possibility – of a pure emergence, of a pure originality: a model of self-formation. And this also explains the implacable contradiction that inhabits the *imitatio* when radicalized to this point . . . Germany, in its attempt to accede to historical existence and to be, as people or nation, 'distinguishable in the world's history', quite simply aspired to genius. But genius is by definition inimitable. And it is therefore in the impossibility of this imitation of genius that Germany literally exhausted itself, succumbing to a sort of psychosis or historico-spiritual schizophrenia, of which certain of its most highly regarded geniuses, from Hölderlin to Nietzsche, were the heralds (and premonitory victims). And besides, only a schizophrenic logic was capable of allowing that unthinkable event, the Extermination; and the present division of Germany is virtually a symbolic outcome of that process. Germany still does not exist. Except in the distress of not existing. (pp. 78–9)

There are two chief points that need to be made about this passage, aside from its sheer speculative sweep and confidence in matters of large-scale historical generalisation (not to mention the way that recent events in Eastern Europe have rendered the last few sentences strikingly obsolete). One is the fact – as I have remarked already – that Lacoue-Labarthe is himself heavily committed to the Heideggerian project of fundamental ontology, a project that informs every detail of his argument here, even where he seeks to account for Heidegger's period of seeming complicity with Nazi doctrine. That is to say, he assumes that any *serious*, philosophically accountable treatment of the question will need to acknowledge Heidegger's pre-eminent status as the one great thinker who addressed the 'essence' of Nazism, as opposed to merely offering (like Adorno and others) an 'external critique' on grounds unrelated to anything in Heidegger's thought. And the second point follows directly from this, since it concerns the basic Heideggerian principle – shared in large measure by Lacoue-Labarthe – that philosophy can only give voice to its own innermost meaning and truth by respecting this authentic ('historial') vocation, despite all the evidence of its deep-laid kinship with themes and motifs characteristic of Nazi ideology. For it is clear from the above passage that Lacoue-Labarthe sees *no other way* that Heidegger's thinking could possibly have gone, given the essentially predestined character of German national tradition, its 'mimetic rivalry' with the ancient Greek model (as well as with 'Republican' France), and its working-out of the tensions installed within European culture as a result of Plato's ambivalent legacy. In short, there is a rigorous necessity inscribed within that whole prehistory of Western thought which begins with the 'inversion' of Platonist metaphysics, and whose latest (though by no means assuredly final) stage is National aestheticism in its degraded Nazi form.

Hence Lacoue-Labarthe's contemptuous treatment of commentators on the 'Heidegger affair' who adopt one or another handy escape-route, *either* by adducing the documentary record (Farias), *or* by treating it as a matter for socio-political analysis, *or again* – and here he is equally dismissive – by holding Heidegger personally to account for his utterances in 1933–4.

> I have no wish to put Heidegger on trial. By what right could I do so? I want to confine myself to a question – a question for thought. This is why it seems pointless to me to go back again over the facts. (p. 32)

Thus the relevant 'question for thought' is one that should take us beyond any dealing with matters of a merely 'factical' import, like the argument (favoured by a number of Marxist or left-wing critics) that Heidegger's project took rise within a certain, distinctively German context of reactionary social attitudes. This is why, as Lacoue-Labarthe sees it,

> all denunciations of the Heideggerian idiom . . . though they may be politically apposite and confirm his affinities with some particular lexicon within the National Socialist movement, such as Swabian agrarianism for example, never manage to avoid the trap of counter-ideology. To espouse Marxism against Heidegger has always been to miss the essentials of his thought – including his political thought. (p. 15)

Of course they cannot fail to miss the point of such thinking since that point is so closely identified by Lacoue-Labarthe with the essential truth of what Heidegger himself had to say on the topic of Marxism as just another variant of the old 'metaphysical' paradigm. Quite simply, Heidegger taught us to think 'that fascism – like Marxism and "Americanism" – resulted from a misapprehension, which in this case was fundamental, regarding the essence of *techne*' (p. 110). So anyone who presumes to criticise Heidegger's thinking from a Marxist or (more broadly) a socio-political standpoint will merely demonstrate their own deep failure to grasp the essence of that thinking. And the same applies to those critics who adopt an ethical or overtly moralising stance, as if unaware of all that Heidegger had written on the present-day crisis of ethical discourse, its complicity with 'Western metaphysics' at large, and the bad faith involved in any such attempt to turn that discourse back upon Heidegger himself.

This is why, as Lacoue-Labarthe claims, 'it would be no overstatement to describe the sight of the philosophical pose loftily reasserting itself today as "derisory" ' (p. 4). And again: this recourse to a language of choice, accountability and humanistic values 'is and can only be a mere tinkering around in inessential and subordinate matters (ethics, the rights of man etc.), journalistic socratism or anthropological approximations. It is nothing that has to do with the work of thought' (p. 4). In which case it seems that the 'work of thought' – that is to say, of *authentic* philosophical thinking – can only be advanced in so far as it renounces all concern with questions of an ethical or political character. For the very desire to pose such questions, at least in the way that they have been posed up to now, is evidence enough – for Heidegger as for Lacoue-Labarthe – that thought has failed in its essential task of overcoming the inherited weight of 'metaphysical' concepts and categories. Those who reproach Heidegger as if it were a matter of his having somehow *chosen* to offer those pronouncements about the 'essence' of Nazi ideology are thereby not only 'missing the essentials of his thought' but failing to grasp how their own ethical stance falls under the same judgement that Heidegger brought against all such 'enlightened' standards of moral accountability. They are, in short, very poor readers of Heidegger, or readers whose understanding is still captive to those forms of deep-laid metaphysical illusion whose consequences he more than anyone sought to expose. For, according to Lacoue-Labarthe,

> ethics . . . also suffers from the general exhaustion of philosophical possibilities and manifestly cannot claim to stand outside that exhaustion except

at the cost of a certain blindness towards it and its origin: how and from where could one *philosophically* get back beyond Heidegger's delimitation of ethics and humanism? (p. 31)

And this verdict applies even to thinkers (like Levinas) who acknowledge the crisis – the terminal 'exhaustion' – of Western ethical philosophy, but whose work none the less continues that project in ways that necessarily fail to take account of our present, impoverished condition.[10]

Of course this does not mean that we can henceforth abandon those inherited 'norms and prescriptions', those values that still provide a work-ing basis for the conduct of everyday life. Nor should it be read – and Lacoue-Labarthe is very anxious to make this point – as a means of excus-ing or exonerating Heidegger on grounds of his having merely *uttered the truth* of this post-humanist, post-'ethical' predicament. On the contrary: Lacoue-Labarthe insists not only that Heidegger must be held account-able for those pro-Nazi statements but also that he *did wrong* to his colleagues, students and humanity at large by allowing his thought to be thus seduced by the discourse of a degraded 'national aestheticist' ideo-logy. In fact he is diligent in seeking out passages – mainly from post-war interviews and recorded conversations – where Heidegger himself ac-knowledged as much, especially with regard to the matter of his Freiburg Rectorship and the 'human failing' which he latterly perceived in his deal-ing with erstwhile colleagues or mentors like Husserl. But this phrase 'doing wrong' comes equipped with such a mass of qualifications, caveats and escape clauses that in the end it seems devoid of any remnant of ethical or judgemental force. Thus:

> We are, of course, forced to live and act according to the norms and pre-scriptions of ethics . . ., but no one can any longer be in any doubt, unless they wish simply to indulge in re-legitimizing the obsolete, that we are in this regard entirely without resources. It is no doubt still possible to answer the question 'how are we to judge'? It is certainly no longer possible to answer the questions, 'From what position can we judge?' 'In the name of what or of whom?' For what we are lacking, now and for the foreseeable future, are names, and most immediately 'sacred names', which in their various ways governed, and alone governed, the space (public or other) in which ethical life unfolded. (p. 32)

And of course it is in Heidegger's resolute attempt to think this condition through to the limit – to the 'closure' of Western metaphysics, along with all its epistemological, ethical and political categories – that thinking now discovers the only 'resources' for continuing to address such questions. In which case nobody who had read Heidegger *as he asks to be read* could possibly set up to judge or to criticise that thinking on grounds that Heidegger will always turn out to have deconstructed in advance.

But of course these arguments will only hold good if one acknowledges, like Lacoue-Labarthe, the epochal significance of Heidegger's thinking and the need to suspend all commonplace standards of judgement as regards the 'essence' of that thinking. For otherwise it will appear that the whole case amounts to a form of purely circular special pleading where the Heideggerian 'jargon of authenticity' is used to head off any questions that would call its own motivating interests and values into doubt. What Lacoue-Labarthe cannot for a moment entertain is the idea that Heidegger's philosophical concerns might not, after all, have come down to him as a legacy of 'Western metaphysics' from Plato to Nietzsche, but that they might – on the contrary – be products of his own, deeply mystified and reactionary habits of mind. 'To object, as some have done, that the question of Being . . . is somehow an "invention" of Heidegger's and in some way arises from a "choice" that is his alone, or simply from his philosophical "position", cannot be regarded seriously' (p. 10). And this on the grounds that we *know* – from whom better than from Heidegger himself? – that the question had been posed *inescapably* throughout the entire preceding history of Western thought; that it is 'from philosophy, via Brentano and Husserl that he receives the question of Being'; and that finally this path leads back all the way (through Nietzsche, Hegel, Kant, etc.) to 'the anxiety felt by Plato barely minutes after the first beginnings' (p. 10). All of which is taken by Lacoue-Labarthe as sufficient proof of the non-seriousness – the misunderstanding or mere bad faith – involved in any discussion of Heidegger's work that resorts to a language of 'choices' or philosophical 'positions'. For this is to ignore what that work should communicate to anyone capable of heeding its message: namely, that Heidegger is not offering philosophical 'theses' of a kind that might be subject to counter-argument or principled objection on ethical grounds. Thus, in Lacoue-Labarthe's words,

> [t]o be or call oneself 'Heideggerian' has no meaning, no more than to be or call oneself 'anti-Heideggerian'. Or rather, both mean the same thing, that one has missed the essential point in Heidegger's thinking, and one is condemned to remain deaf to the question which the age poses through Heidegger. (p. 11)

So once again, those who think to criticise his 'position' on non-

Heideggerian (ethical or political) grounds must thereby reveal a hopeless incapacity to grasp what is 'essentially' at stake in Heidegger's work. Still less can they claim to have seen through his thinking to its origins in this or that socio-cultural context or specific ideological formation. For at this point Heidegger – or his apologist – will always come back with the familiar response: that such claims are inherently self-deluding since they presuppose the continued availability of 'resources' which belonged to that old (metaphysical) order of thought.

IV

It seems to me that the real puzzle here is not why so many critics have failed to heed the message of Heidegger's work, but much rather why certain intellectuals – among them thinkers of great acuity and power like Lacoue-Labarthe – should have gone to such lengths of ingenious argumentation by way of protecting that work from any form of reasoned assessment or critique. For it is indeed a striking fact that these defences have often come from thinkers (notably Derrida)[11] whose writing far surpasses Heidegger's own in point of argumentative subtlety and rigour. Of course there is a vigorous counter-tradition of philosophers in the 'other', analytical camp who protested that this was all nonsense, pure and simple; that Heidegger's talk of 'Being' – along with all his other portentous abstractions – was just a kind of primitive word-magic, deriving from an elementary muddle about the logical grammar of such words; and therefore that the whole of Heidegger's thinking should be treated as one of those massive aberrations to which philosophy is prone when it gets out of touch with the sense-making standards of logical discourse (or, alternatively, 'ordinary language'). No doubt some of them arrived at this position without actually reading Heidegger, or at least on the basis of minimal acquaintance with his work. Others – including Gilbert Ryle – started out from a position of qualified respect for the arguments in *Being and Time*, but ended up by rejecting Heidegger's approach as just a species of misplaced psychologism, a philosophical dead-end which had best be abandoned in favour of conceptual and linguistic analysis.[12]

At any rate there soon emerged a broad consensus: that he (like most 'continental' thinkers) had taken a wrong turn among the paths opened up in the wake of Kant's critical philosophy. That is to say, Heidegger was the latest – and worst – representative of a tradition that continued to pose 'metaphysical' issues (i.e. questions as to the meaning of 'Being', the essence of things, their 'historial' conditions of possibility, etc.), rather than following the alternative Kantian lead toward a scaled-down descriptive enterprise whose terms translated readily enough into the idiom of modern analytical thought. And this error was compounded – so the argument goes – by Heidegger's penchant for dressing up his dubious truth-claims in a yet more dubious rhetorical show of arcane etymologies, portentous word-play, or suspect appeals to the wisdom of the ages enshrined in some piece of mystified pseudo-philological verbiage. One result of all this was his habit of hypostatising abstract notions (like 'Being', as distinct from mere 'beings'), and then erecting a wholesale metaphysics on that basis, i.e. on the supposed 'ontological difference' revealed by this verbal sleight of hand. Thus Heidegger ignores the criticism brought against arguments of this kind by philosophers from Kant to Russell: namely, that 'existence is not a predicate', since the question whether or not objects exist is not at all the same as the (nonsensical) idea of their having some attribute ('existence') which shows forth their deepest, most essential mode of Being.

Paul Edwards puts this case in a recent (markedly hostile) essay which more or less repeats the standard line on Heidegger adopted by Carnap, the logical positivists and most Anglo-American philosophers since. 'To begin with,' he writes,

> Heidegger totally fails to distinguish between the 'is' of predication ('the sky is blue'), the 'is' of identity ('a triangle is a plane figure bounded by three straight lines') and the 'is' of existence ('there is a God'). Thus he mistakenly believes that 'the lecture hall is illuminated' is an existential statement of the same form as 'the lecture hall is, that is, exists' . . . The assumption that existence is the most basic characteristic of existing things . . . may at first seem plausible because of the grammatical form of existence-statements. However, a little reflection shows it to be false . . . because it is not a characteristic at all; and it is not an ingredient or ground or source of things either.[13]

It seems to me that this criticism hits the mark and cannot be deflected or made to look hopelessly naïve by any ritual invocation of the standard Heideggerian line. The confusion analysed by Edwards in this passage is closely akin to the confusion that takes *etymology* – or the mere fact of words having once meant this or that – as a royal road to truth or the essence of Being. This latter is of course a very widespread and tenacious idea, responsible for all kinds of folk-wisdom and high-toned moralising down through the ages. It is especially marked in religious thinkers like

Archbishop Trench, one of the founding fathers of the Oxford English Dictionary, to whom it was a matter of self-evident truth that (for instance) the word 'pain' signified both *torment* and *punishment*, since the Latin *poena* carried both of these meanings, and their conjunction had an obvious moral import when linked to the Christian doctrine of original sin.[14] The very notion of proof by etymology is one that lends itself to mischievous uses, or at any rate to uses that jump clean over any standards of rational accountability. And in Heidegger's thinking – as Adorno saw clearly - it works to promote a mystified language of Being, essences, primordial truths, predestined national greatness, etc. which fitted in readily with the purposes of Nazi cultural propaganda.

Of course Lacoue-Labarthe would regard all this as a gross misreading of Heidegger's work and a failure to respect the 'ontological difference', i.e. the distinction between matters of contingent, historical fact and matters of a deeper ('historial') concern. Moreover, he would have little time for the argument that Heidegger's philosophy only pays attention to the privileged ('continental') line of descent running from Kant to Hegel, Nietzsche and Husserl, and thus fails to reckon with the powerful objections voiced by thinkers in the latter-day analytical school. Indeed, it is a major contention of his book that Heidegger has effectively rehearsed or pre-empted *everything* that philosophy now has to say, whether overtly 'for' or 'against' his pronouncements on finitude, Being-unto-death, fundamental ontology, existential hermeneutics and other such themes. For it is Lacoue-Labarthe's fixed idea – impervious to any kind of counter-argument – that Heidegger not only 'receives' these concerns, but receives them from 'the whole of philosophy since its origins', or at least from those thinkers (notably Plato, Aristotle, Kant, Hegel, Nietzsche and Husserl) who figure in Heidegger's elective prehistory as having thought the 'question of Being' at a level of profundity commensurate with his own. And this leaves little room for opposing voices or thinkers outside that privileged tradition. Thus, as Lacoue-Labarthe placidly observes,

> if one were to go on to say then that all this is simply a matter of 'point of view' and that Heidegger does not in the least take account, for example, of ancient materialism, the Sophists, British empiricism or analytic philosophy, what has one added which Heidegger, starting out from the question of *philosophy*, that is from an unshakable allegiance to the initial definition of philosophy, has not already precisely delimited as a regional and subordinate point of view? (p. 11)

In short, such an argument would simply go to show that the questioner had mistaken Heidegger's thinking for just another set of philosophical 'theses', or one more available 'position' on a range of accredited topics for debate. And to this extent their own position would emerge as a strictly 'delimited' or 'regional' area of concern, quite possibly one that possessed a certain interest (e.g. on analytic or logico-linguistic grounds), but still very much a 'subordinate' affair when set against Heidegger's unswerving address to issues at the heart of Western cultural tradition. Least of all could one take the analytical philosophers seriously when they claim – like Russell, Ayer or Ryle – that the whole misbegotten project of 'fundamental ontology' can be seen to rest on a deep confusion as regards the logical grammar of predicative statements. For it is an article of faith to committed Heideggerians – Lacoue-Labarthe among them – that philosophy can only *think the essence* of its own historial vocation in so far as it hearkens to the message implicit in those languages (pre-eminently the Greek and German) which have managed to conserve at least something of the authentic, primordial relation to Being and truth. In which case the modern analytic tradition would appear as simply the latest variant of that deep-laid oblivion with respect to such questions that overtook the history of 'metaphysical' thinking from Socrates to the present.

Needless to say, this rejoinder will carry little weight with philosophers trained up in that other ('subordinate') tradition where the worth of any new contribution to thought is assessed in terms of argumentative probity, analytic rigour, and regard for the protocols of reasoned debate. On each of these counts – they would argue – Heidegger falls far short of the requisite norm. And the same must apply to any treatment of Heidegger's work that seeks exemption from commonplace standards of validity and truth on the ground that those standards are relevant only to some 'regional' sub-branch of philosophic thought, and can gain no purchase on an enterprise (like Heidegger's) aimed toward the 'essence' of philosophy as such. For clearly this argument could be used to justify any amount of confused reasoning or uncritical, self-promoting verbiage just so long as the thinker in question had a firm enough conviction of his own 'essential' rightness and a total disregard for criticism based on altogether different (logical or ethical) grounds. Lacoue-Labarthe is prepared to grant Heidegger this kind of privileged status because he thinks, quite simply, that *no such options exist*; that any real facing-up to our present situation has to live with the knowledge that we are utterly 'without resources', since we lack any criteria that would make it possible to criticise Heidegger's thinking from an alternative, more enlightened or ethically accountable standpoint.

His reasons for so thinking are familiar enough from the currency of

French postmodernist debate. That is to say, they derive from an odd mixture of intra-philosophical argument (the 'exhaustion' of Western metaphysics, the collapse of ethical values, 'enlightened' meta-narratives, etc.) and 'factical' or socio-historical grounds (the sheer impossibility of continuing to honour humanist or liberal-enlightenment ideals in the wake of such appalling events as were witnessed in the period of Nazi – or indeed of Stalinist – rule). Like Lyotard, Lacoue-Labarthe sees this as principally a question of 'sacred names', or of the loss of such names that inevitably comes about when thinking is forced up against the manifest failure of history to bear out its hopes for the advancement of progressive social and ethical values. Just as Lyotard recites a gloomy catalogue of place-names and dates ('Berlin 1953', 'Hungary 1956', 'Prague 1968', 'Poland 1980') by way of 'refuting' all notions of enlightened critique,[15] so Lacoue-Labarthe takes it pretty much for granted that any hopeful – especially socialist – philosophy of emancipatory values will always run aground on the massive counter-evidence of things as they have been or things as they are. And along with this drive to discredit such illusory sources of historical hope goes a deep hostility to everything in the (broadly Kantian) enlightenment tradition that would criticise the appeal to 'sacred names' as just a form of self-legitimating word-magic, a mystification of language closely allied to a mystification of history and politics. For it is Heidegger's habit of solemn-sophistical word-play – his investing of language with a power of 'primordial' recollection beyond the capacities of mere human reason – that leads him (along with thinkers like Lyotard and Lacoue-Labarthe) to conclude that we have now lived on into a 'postmodern' epoch when the sacred names have lost all their resonance and philosophy lacks the most basic 'resources' for thinking this condition through in ethical or political terms. And this follows directly from his notion of language – especially poetic language – as the sole means of access to truths long forgotten down through the history of Western 'metaphysical' thought. That is to say, the whole Heideggerian thematics of Being, *aletheia* (truth-as-unconcealment), historial *Dasein*, language as the dwelling-place or man as the 'shepherd' of Being and so forth is premised on the notion that thinking has no choice but to live with this terminal 'exhaustion' of philosophy and the consequent lack of any alternative (ethical) 'viewpoint' from which to criticise those – like Heidegger – who spoke the 'truth' of this condition.

Hence the extreme contortions of argument that Lacoue-Labarthe gets into when he strives to explain how Heidegger indeed 'did wrong' in making those pro-Nazi statements, but also how wrongdoing *at this level of thought* cannot be treated according to commonplace (ethical or enlightened) standards of judgement. This is why – in a passage I have cited already – we find him contemptuously dismissing such talk as 'mere tinkering around in inessential and subordinate matters (ethics, the rights of man, etc.) . . .' (p. 4). The implications of this attitude are spelled out more fully in the following two passages which between them illustrate the painful dilemma that Lacoue-Labarthe faces:

1. It might be thought then that we have before us here, hastily sketched out, all the elements required for a 'critique' of Heidegger. But this is not the case at all. From where might one 'criticize' Heidegger? From what 'point of view'? This much, however, is true: recognition of the importance of his thought – or indeed unreserved admiration for it – in no way excludes infinite mistrust. Not of the thinker himself . . . but of what his thought entails or carries with it, what it sanctions and justifies. This comes back to saying that the situation with Heidegger is just as impossible and hardly more 'tenable' than it is with philosophy. (p. 14)
2. Contrary to what has been said in a number of places, Heidegger's commitment is entirely consistent with his thought. And the 'political' and the 'philosophical' were so interwoven that practically all his teaching from the so-called 'turn' (*Kehre*) up until 1944 was devoted to a 'settling of accounts' with National Socialism, which in reality reveals *a contrario* the truth that Heidegger had perceived in it . . . That such a belief should have given rise to a properly philosophical act . . . is not the product of some accident that has happened to 'thought' but reveals what constantly threatens the said 'thought' – its danger. Which is less, as Heidegger will write in 1947, 'the bad and thus muddled danger' of 'philosophizing' than the danger 'which is the evil and thus keenest danger', i.e. thinking itself. (p. 19)

Whatever is one to make of all this? More specifically: how is one to square Lacoue-Labarthe's professed 'mistrust' of Heidegger's thinking with his belief that this thinking not only expressed the inner 'truth' of Nazi ideology, but expressed it in a form that responded 'essentially' to questions at the heart of Western philosophy, indeed at the heart of 'thinking itself'? In which case – since such 'thinking' is here identified implicitly with Heidegger's usage of the word – it would seem (contrary to Lacoue-Labarthe's major thesis in this book) that there is no real difference between Nazi ideology and Heidegger's more circumspect pronouncements. At any rate it seems that some caution is in order when dealing with passages like the two cited above.

To the extent that it is capable of rational reconstruction the argument goes roughly as follows. Axiom I: Heidegger was undeniably a great thinker. Axiom II: his greatness consisted in his having pondered the 'question of Being' more profoundly than anyone else in our time. Axiom III: Nazism was a great evil, perhaps the greatest in world history, and certainly one that must be taken into account by any future discourse on ethics, politics or philosophy's responsibility in these matters. Proposition 1: Heidegger was compromised by his expressions of support – however qualified in detail – for the Nazi regime and its social, political and cultural aims. Proposition 2: that involvement went beyond any short-term pragmatic or accommodating 'line', and in fact took the form of a sustained meditation on the 'essence' and (in some sense) the inward 'truth' of the Nazi phenomenon. Axiom IV: such questions are inherently beyond the reach of any criticism that would treat 'the facts' of Heidegger's 'case' as material for ethical or social-diagnostic judgement. Proposition 3: thinking of this order – i.e. at the level attained by Heidegger's (no matter how deeply compromised) reflections on Nazism and its relation to 'national aestheticist' ideology – cannot be regarded as an 'accident', an 'error', or itself a mere product of ideological conditioning. Proposition 4: Heidegger received the 'question of Being' from a long line of philosophers (and poets) for whom – as for him – it constituted the single most imperative task of thinking. Proposition 5: Nazism was also a response to that question, albeit a 'degraded' response, one that only Heidegger – who had felt its seductive power – was able to comprehend in its innermost essence. Conclusion I: there was nothing contingent or accidental about Heidegger's (to say the least) ambivalent dealings with Nazi cultural politics. Conclusion II: it is therefore wrong – a naïve misunderstanding – to separate his 'politics' from his 'philosophy' by 'imput[ing] the commitment of 1933 to a failing or a sudden loss of vigilance . . . or to the pressure of a thinking as yet insufficiently disengaged from metaphysics' (p. 19). Rather we should acknowledge (Conclusion III) that *thinking itself* – the 'essential' task of thought – is fraught with those dangers that appear all too clearly in Heidegger's (however short-lived) espousal of the National Socialist cause.

Thus any thought of judging Heidegger on ethical grounds, or of explaining his 'error' through some form of enlightened *Ideologiekritik*, will not only misconstrue that thinking but manifest its own utter lack of 'resources' in regard to such ultimate questions. And again: we shall understand nothing of Heidegger's significance – of the 'greatness' or 'essence' of his thought – if we fail to see how closely 'interwoven' were the questions of philosophy and politics. For that thinking could scarcely have developed as it did – achieved, that is to say, such a radical break with the discourse of 'Western metaphysics' – had Heidegger not experienced the encounter with Nazism and come to see in it the latest, most degraded form of 'national aestheticist' ideology. This is no doubt why Lacoue-Labarthe rejects the term 'error' as applied to Heidegger's utterances of 1933–4 and declares, on the contrary, that they reveal the very *truth* of the Nazi phenomenon, albeit a truth whose decadent nature Heidegger at the time seemed unable or unwilling to recognise. Thus:

> there would have been an error if Nazism, whatever its 'reality' in other respects, had not borne within it the possibility Heidegger saw there. Now manifestly it bore that possibility, at least in certain of its features, with respect to the destiny of Germany and that of the West. The distress (*Not*) which underlies the National Socialist insurrection, as it underlies Heidegger's protest in the *Rectoral Address*, is not simply the economic vortex into which Germany is sinking and the collapse of the Weimar Republic that followed defeat and the Treaty of Versailles . . . nor is it simply the disarray of a Germany that has known for over a century that it has received the spiritual heritage of the whole of the West and which knows equally well that it cannot for all that arrive at existence as such, condemned as it is either to remain painfully in abeyance or to find itself crushed in the 'vice' formed by Russia and America . . . it is also, and perhaps even principally, the anxiety and even the dread arising from the acknowledged exhaustion of the modern project in which the catastrophic Being of that project stands revealed. (p. 20)

This passage – along with the two cited directly above – may help to explain what is so utterly wrong with Lacoue-Labarthe's whole line of argument. (Also why my attempted 'rational reconstruction' lacks the least semblance of adequate reasoning.) Indeed, it offers a useful starting-point for anyone wishing to understand the nature of Heidegger's peculiar hold over minds that would otherwise seem well-equipped to resist such forms of coercive mystification.

To begin with, there is the attitude of lofty disdain for socio-historical, economic or other such documentary details ('Versailles and all that'), consigned as they must be to the realm of merely 'factical' data, neither here nor there for the purposes of truly comprehending what is at stake in Heidegger's thought. Then again there is the constant shifting in and out of *oratio obliqua* or 'free indirect' style, a device that enables Lacoue-Labarthe to maintain a certain (undefined) distance from full-blown Heideggerspeak while still half-crediting his oracular talk of 'the spiritual heritage of the whole of the West', 'the acknowledged exhaustion of the modern project', 'the catastrophic Being of the modern project' and suchlike portentous phrases. Finally this passage brings out with particular force the *politics* implicit in Lacoue-Labarthe's refusal to distinguish between various episodes in the so-called 'metaphysical' history of thought which Heidegger treats as pretty much an indivisible and monolithic whole. Thus he (Lacoue-Labarthe) takes the whole Heideggerian doctrine on board, including the idea that Marxism ('Russia') and capitalism ('America') are just different names for the same root phenomenon, that which Heidegger accurately diagnosed under the cover-term of *techne* – or technocratic reason – and which 'Germany' suffered as a massive affront to its frustrated quest for 'existence as such', or the 'spiritual heritage' that German thinkers (Heidegger pre-eminent among them) were properly destined to receive. And from this point it is no great distance to the idea of National Socialism as the 'degraded' *but in some sense truthful* expression of a national destiny baulked of its fulfilment by these misfortunes of historical time and place.

One could instance many passages in Lacoue-Labarthe's book where he adopts this same Heideggerian line of discounting real (social and political) differences, or holding them to apply only at the level of vulgarised 'factical' enquiry. What follows is a fairly representative sample. 'Who in this century', he asks,

> in the face of unprecedented world historical transformations that have taken place, in face of the apparent radicalism, whether of 'right' or 'left' of the various revolutionary projects, has not been duped? . . . But what of those who were great figures in their respective ways? I cite at random Hamsum, Benn, Pound, Blanchot, Drieu and Brassilach . . . Or in the other camp, Benjamin, Brecht, Bataille, Malraux (I do not except Sartre, whose moral authenticity is quite beyond question). What did the old world have to offer them with which they could have resisted the irruption of the so-called 'new world'? From this point of view, all things considered, the merit of Heidegger will have been to have succumbed for only ten months to this Janus-headed illusion of 'New Times. (pp. 21–2)

It is worth looking closely at the rhetoric of this passage, in particular its way of lumping together right-wing and left-wing thinkers – figures like Pound and Brecht – as if the difference between them amounted to nothing more than a choice of 'revolutionary' idioms or styles from the range currently on offer. For this is how it must indeed appear if one takes the standard Heideggerian line, i.e. that which treats all forms of overt political commitment, along with any theories, principles or arguments adduced in their support, as belonging to the realm of mere anecdotal evidence, beneath the attention of serious thought. Such 'apparent radical-ism' is inherently self-deluding whether it issues from *soi-disant* 'left' intel-lectuals or right-wing (even proto-fascist) ideologues like Hamsum, Pound and Brassilach. And any difference *within* those opposed 'camps' – such as recent intellectual historians have been at some pains to point out[16] – would count for nothing at this elevated level of thought, a stand-point from which such arguments would look very like the quarrel be-tween Tweedledum and Tweedledee.

Moreover, this message is shrewdly reinforced – rather than qualified – by Lacoue-Labarthe's parenthetical remark about Sartre, namely that, in this case at least, a left-wing thinker's 'moral authenticity is quite beyond question'. For the effect of this comment, taken in context, is to drive a wedge between 'moral authenticity' and any arguments that Sartre may have fetched up in support of his political views. After all, it was partly on account of those views – allied as they were to a radically different under-standing of praxis, engagement, ethical accountability, etc. – that Sartre progressively distanced his thinking from that of Heidegger. What Lacoue-Labarthe thus contrives to suggest in the above passage is that political options simply *do not count* when it comes to taking stock of a thinker's 'moral authenticity', or the extent to which thought measures up to the demands placed upon it by historial *Dasein*. From this point of view (which is no 'point of view' at all, according to Lacoue-Labarthe, but a simply inescapable predicament, one that we can ignore only through strategies of self-willed 'voluntarist' illusion) – from this (let us then say) *authentic* standpoint – it will appear that the signal 'merit' of Heidegger's thought was that which enabled him to figure among the genuinely 'great' thinkers of his time (Hamsum, Pound, Brassilach and the others), to have known the 'inner truth and greatness' of the Nazi phenomenon, and yet to have 'succumbed' to its cruder (socio-political) manifestation only for that ten-month period when he overtly espoused the Nazi cause. In other words, it was precisely Heidegger's openness to the primordial 'question of Being' that also left him open – for however short a time – to the seductions of National Socialist ideology.

So we shall mistake the essential nature of Heidegger's 'wrongdoing' if we think to comprehend it on terms that derive from the outworn stock of humanist ethical resources, or again, on terms that merely reproduce the unthinking 'left'/'right' dichotomy. Such talk has trivialised the conduct of debate – as Lacoue-Labarthe sees it – by substituting various 'revolu-tionary projects' or styles of 'apparent radicalism' for the deeper concerns that have always preoccupied genuine thinkers like Heidegger. Thus

'[Heidegger] knew, as early as the "break" (and doubtless also before, which is where he committed a wrong) that fascism – like Marxism and "Americanism" – resulted from a misapprehension, which in this case was fundamental, regarding the essence of *techne*' (p. 110). From which it follows that those 'great figures' on the intellectual left – Brecht, Benjamin, Malraux, Sartre – would enjoy such status not at all on account of their overt political engagement, and still less by virtue of having opposed Nazism on grounds of principle and theory. Their greatness would consist, like Heidegger's, in their facing up to questions that inherently elude such superficial treatment, and whose essence was revealed (albeit in 'degraded' form) by the Nazi appropriation of national-aestheticist doctrines and values. In which case – for such is the curious logic of Lacoue-Labarthe's argument – we must stand all the more indebted to Heidegger for his not having taken refuge in any kind of shallow left-political critique or analysis, but allowed his thinking to continue resolutely on its appointed path, even where that path exposed him to the worst, most dangerous temptations.

V

I think we are now in a position to see why an intelligent commentator like Lacoue-Labarthe can be reduced to such desperate twists of argument in defence of Heidegger's position. Let me cite one further passage from his book since it brings out these problems with particular clarity and force. Again, his remarks are directed against Adorno, in particular the latter's uncompromising charge that Heideggerian philosophy is 'fascist right down to its most intimate components'. But, according to Lacoue-Labarthe, this can only be a charge

> produced by superficiality and ill will if fascism is defined, in its German form, as National Socialism. That philosophy is, admittedly, opposed to any form of internationalism, rationalism (but *also* irrationalism), humanism, progressism etc.; it rails against the *Aufklärung* (though it does so in terms of the Kantian theme of finitude); but it also manages to wrest itself free, though with some difficulty, from the subjectivistic-voluntaristic ontology of the latest metaphysics (which also happens to be Nietzsche's). If one has to provide a political definition it can be said to be a heroico-tragic *and* revolutionary philosophy 'of the Right'. It could therefore, in the effectively revolutionary circumstances of 1933, allow scope, *volens nolens* (or rather at the cost of a certain number of serious – philosophically serious – compromises) for a political commitment, by which I mean something more than mere support. But everything about it – or almost everything – ran

counter to that commitment being a lasting one (I would not say quite so much for the support), once the (immodest and naive) illusion had passed that the movement might be open in some way to possible 'entryism'. And in fact, so far as the essentials of Nazism's *metaphysical* positions were concerned, the break was inevitable. (p. 109)

This passage reproduces all the grounding assumptions that characterise both Heidegger's thinking and Lacoue-Labarthe's tortuous attempts to redeem it from the charge of straightforward ideological complicity. That is to say, it supposes that 'political definitions' (like the 'right' versus 'left' dichotomy) are a matter of superficial interest only; that the real question – the question for thought – has to be engaged at an altogether deeper, more 'philosophical' level; that Heidegger's 'support' for the Nazi cause (i.e. his overt and public stance) was something quite distinct from his 'commitment' to it, the latter a far more complex and ambivalent affair; that 'rationalism' and 'irrationalism' (or enlightenment and counter-enlightenment) are mere flipsides of the same exhausted 'metaphysical' currency, like the typecast 'right'/'left' distinction as applied to 'effectively revolutionary circumstances' such as those of 1933; that Heidegger's 'compromises' with Nazi ideology, although very real (indeed 'philosophically serious'), were none the less in some sense the portals of discovery, since they enabled him to perceive all this more clearly than anyone else, then or since; that his 'commitment' to National Socialism and his 'settling of accounts' with that movement were part of the same, immensely difficult process, one that continued through all his later work; that this work therefore focused in large part on Nietzsche, the 'last metaphysician' (and hence the most immediate precursor of German 'national aestheticism', so that 'Heidegger devotes more than four years of his teaching between 1936 and 1941 to "delimiting" Nietzsche's metaphysics');[17] that Heidegger 'received' these questions (*volens nolens*), along with their scope for political 'wrongdoing', as the one philosopher at that time capable of thinking them through; and – finally – that his 'break' with Nazi ideology was *also and simultaneously* a break with everything in the Western 'metaphysical' tradition (culminating in Nietzsche) that had made Nazism possible.

In which case Adorno would inevitably figure as one more thinker in that same exhausted tradition, vainly attempting (through his 'negative dialectics') to turn the resources of enlightenment reason back against itself in the interest of a better, more self-critical or genuine enlightenment, but failing on account of his ultimate commitment to a politics of rational critique. For we *know* from Heidegger (or ought to know, according to Lacoue-Labarthe) that 'rationalism' and 'irrationalism' are just two variants of the same metaphysical illusion, namely, the idea that the prospects for humanity are somehow bound up with the fate of that faculty (reason or enlightenment) whose truth-claims are at stake right down through the tradition of Western thinking from Plato to Nietzsche. But if we can only let go of that tradition – only learn to treat it, in Heidegger's fashion, as a symptomatic interlude in the history of thought – then we will perhaps come out on the far side of all such deluded (metaphysical and political) ideas. And at the same time we will have learned to see that Heidegger is our last, best teacher in such matters, the one philosopher to have thought the 'essence' of Western metaphysics (along with its national-aestheticist outcome) in a way that both conserves its undeniable 'truth' and points beyond it to whatever strange wisdom may survive this encounter with the limits of enlightened reason. After all,

> we are not talking about any old person being politically compromised, about some teacher or other or party member so and so. If this were the case, we would not even spend five minutes on the subject. We are talking about the greatest thinker of our age. It is in his thought therefore that the question of political responsibility is posed. (p. 135)

Take that as self-evident – as Lacoue-Labarthe does – and you will find yourself wondering whether maybe Adorno, Farias and the other dissenters have not really missed the point of Heidegger's thinking in some very basic and crucial regard.

If one rejects that premise, on the other hand, then the whole case assumes a very different aspect and becomes more a topic for treatment from the socio-pathological or diagnostic standpoint. That is to say, the possibility arises that Heidegger's thinking is compromised *through and through* by its recourse to a mystified 'jargon of authenticity' which supposedly sets us on the path back through language to authentic Being and truth, but which in fact – as Adorno convincingly argues – serves to smuggle in all manner of irrational prejudice. And Adorno's critique finds striking confirmation, albeit from a somewhat different angle of approach, in some essays by Paul de Man – notably 'Heidegger's exegeses of Hölderlin' – which likewise focus on the symptomatic blind spots produced by this will to identify language (especially the German language) with the voice of authentic revelation.[18] Thus for Heidegger, as de Man reads him,

Hölderlin is the greatest of poets ('the poet of poets') because he states the essence (*Wesen*) of poetry. The essence of poetry consists in stating the parousia, the absolute presence of Being. In this Hölderlin differs from the metaphysicians Heidegger dismisses; all, at least in some degree, are in error; Hölderlin is the only one whom Heidegger cites as a believer cites Holy Writ. (*BI*, p. 250)

But de Man is able to show, through a detailed close-reading of the passages in question, that Heidegger has in fact misconstrued those passages, sometimes to the point of making them say *exactly the reverse* of what Hölderlin expressly states.[19] He does so by ignoring certain crucial (most often grammatical) details, among them Hölderlin's pointedly subjunctive verb-forms, modal inflections that make all the difference between a poetry that *claims access* to revealed truth and a poetry that *voices the desire* for such truth but also – inevitably – the failure to attain it. Thus

as soon as the word is uttered, it destroys the immediate and discovers that instead of stating Being, it can only state mediation . . . For man the presence of Being is always in becoming, and Being necessarily appears under a non-simple form. (*BI*, p. 259)

Not that Heidegger's readings of Hölderlin are thereby deprived of all value, or judged simply inadequate by orthodox (scholarly or literary-critical) standards. On the contrary: de Man makes a cardinal point of distinguishing 'mistakes' (which come about through mere carelessness, incompetence, or inattentive reading) from 'errors' (which occur in consequence of some deep-laid bias or prejudgment on the reader's part, and which therefore possess a much greater diagnostic interest). Thus 'at this level of thought it is difficult to distinguish between a proposition and that which constitutes its opposite' (*BI*, p. 255). In which case Heidegger's exegeses would at least possess the signal virtue of having brought out the 'central concern' of Hölderlin's poetry, a respect in which (as de Man thinks) they 'surpass all other studies'. But the fact remains that they mistake the meaning of that poetry, and do so moreover through a predisposition to read it in accordance with Heidegger's motivating interests.

The comparison with de Man takes on an added relevance in light of what is now known about his journalistic writings in Belgium under the German occupation. These writings have been the focus of much recent controversy – along with Heidegger's pre-war Nazi involvement, as amply documented in the Farias book – and I do not propose to discuss them in any detail here.[20] Sufficient to say that de Man's journalism reproduced many of the same ideological motifs, including the predestined hegemony of German language and culture, the emergence of a new (post-war) European order under German spiritual guidance, the privileged suprahistorical *rapport* between modern German and ancient Greek thought, and the evolution of national spirit through deep-laid 'organic' laws of development whose nature eluded all the concepts and categories of mere 'enlightened' reason, just as it transcended those typecast political distinctions ('left' versus 'right', etc.) whose currency derived from that same outworn heritage. For the most part these articles – some two hundred in all – are ephemeral stuff, written to a regular deadline and ranging between crude cultural propaganda and portentous world-historical pronouncements on a basis of hastily worked-up comparatist scholarship. Nobody who has read them would think of comparing de Man's juvenilia (for this is really what they amount to) with anything that Heidegger published either before or after his period of Nazi involvement. But my point is not so much to establish common philosophical ground between them as to show how decisively de Man reacted – in the essays of his middle and late periods – against any form of that 'aesthetic ideology' that had once exerted a powerful hold upon the thinking of many intellectuals during the pre-war period.

In *Blindness and Insight* this reaction is clearly evident in the way that de Man distances his critical approach from any version of the ontological imperative that reads poetry as a uniquely privileged means of access to the realm of primordial Being or truth. It is an argument pursued not only in the essay on Heidegger but also through a series of intense meditations on Blanchot, Poulet, Lukács, the American New Criticism, and mainstream Romantic scholarship as exemplified in the work of M.H. Abrams and others. Already there is a strong indication that 'aesthetic ideology' is more widespread and deep-rooted than might be supposed if one attended only to its more extreme (e.g. Heideggerian) forms of expression. What it amounts to is a permanent temptation of thought, a desire – especially marked in the discourse of post-Kantian idealist aesthetics – to conflate the two realms of phenomenal experience and conceptual understanding (or linguistic representation). *Blindness and Insight* is perhaps best read as a full-scale critical symptomatology of this desire and its diverse manifestations, from Lukács's early (pre-Marxist) nostalgic broodings on the origins of the novel to Poulet's phenomenological 'criticism of consciousness', Abrams's attempt (via Wordsworth and others) to recapture the 'one life within us and abroad' of high Romantic argument, or the New Critics' use of organicist images and metaphors by way of presenting the poem as a 'verbal icon', a self-possessed unity of meaning and form beyond all the vexing antinomies of plain-prose reason. In each case – and despite their manifest differences of view – these interpreters have recourse to a mystified ontology of language that cannot be sustained if one examines their texts with an eye to the various problematic details, the 'blind spots' of rhetorical implication or discrepancies between meaning and intent, that emerge through a rigorous deconstructive reading.

Hence de Man's chief contention in this book: that such moments of 'blindness' in the discourse of philosophy or literary criticism can in turn become a source of demystifying 'insight' for the reader alert to their presence. And moreover – as the essay on Heidegger shows – there is a great deal at stake in what might easily appear just a game of ultra-specialised critical one-upmanship. For the blind spots in question are also (and inseparably) moments of *ideological* prejudice, moments when reading falls prey to some form of unquestioned doctrinal adherence or over-riding interpretative aim. In Heidegger's case, according to de Man, one has to take account of certain 'secondary reasons', motives of a 'senti-mental and national' character that led him, firstly, to elevate Hölderlin to the highest rank among German poets, and secondly to misread Höld-erlin's texts in keeping with his own preconceptions. Thus 'Heidegger's commentaries were thought out just before and during World War II, and are directly linked to an anguished meditation upon the historical destiny of Germany' (*BI*, p. 254). But at this point – perhaps understandably – de Man elects not to press any further with questions of a socio-political nature, describing them as merely a 'side issue that would take us away from our topic'. One could also surmise that such questions must have borne too directly on de Man's own experience, writing as he was – in the early 1950s – with a melancholy knowledge of just how far thought could be corrupted by such forms of national-aestheticist doctrine in the guise of 'fundamental ontology'. This knowledge echoes like a subdued but obses-sive refrain through the essays collected in *Blindness and Insight*, especially those on Heidegger, Blanchot and – more improbably – Husserl. In each case, it is a question of locating what might be called the unthought axiomatics – the governing prejudice or *parti pris* – which is both the *condition of possibility* for their project and the blind spot that prevents its realisation in anything like the intended form.

Thus Husserl, as an enlightened European intellectual, addressed what he saw as a 'crisis' in the natural and human sciences, a crisis brought about by the growth of irrationalist doctrines and the failure of philosophy to reflect adequately on its own grounding interests and truth-claims.[21] He conceived of transcendental phenomenology as primarily, in de Man's words, 'a self-interpretation by means of which we eliminate what he calls *Selbstverhülltheit,* the tendency of the self to hide from the light it can cast on itself' (*BI*, p.15). But in treating that crisis as a strictly *European* affair – a disaster threatening the inherited cultural, intellectual and scientific resources of the West – Husserl contravenes the most basic principle of his own 'enlightened' project. Such are those passages where Husserl 'speaks repeatedly of non-European cultures as primitive, prescientific and pre-philosophical, myth-dominated and congenitally incapable of the disinterested distance without which there can be no philosophical meditation' (*BI*, p. 15). And this despite the fact that, *by his own definition*, philosophy acknowledges no such limits to the spread of enlightened critical reason, and indeed finds its principal justification in the idea of a 'supranational' community of thought transcending all merely ethnic or cultural boundaries. In short,

> the crucial, determining examination on which depends Husserl's right to call himself, by his own terms, a philosopher, is never in fact undertaken . . . As a European, it seems that Husserl escapes from the necessary self-criticism that is prior to all philosophical truth about the self. (*BI*, p. 16)

Again, it is worth recalling de Man's insistence that Husserl was 'a man of superior good will', one against whom – and this would seem to be the point – nobody could honestly bring the charge of ethical bad faith, knowing duplicity, or collusion with racist ideology. But then, what of Heidegger, the facts of whose Nazi involvement were not so widely known at the time de Man wrote his essay, but who certainly could not be classed with Husserl as an 'enlightened' thinker unwittingly betrayed into statements at odds with his own deepest values and beliefs? And again, what shall we make of de Man's role in all this, his skirting the question of Heidegger's politics and also the curious mixture of motives – simultaneously counsel for the prosecution and the defence – that marks his ambivalent dealing with Husserl? For de Man is quite capable of noting the massive historical irony of Husserl's attitude, namely 'the pathos of such a claim at a time when Europe was about to destroy itself as center in the name of its unwarranted claim to be the center' (*BI*, p. 16). What seems to be happening here is a certain displacement of guilt away from Heidegger (and implicitly away from de Man) by discovering in Husserl a version – however unwitting or 'goodwilled' – of the same basic error of thought. At any rate it is clear that these essays of his middle period find de Man addressing the issues of collaboration, war-guilt, bad faith and ideological complicity in a manner which, however oblique and (maybe) self-deceiving, still raises those issues *inescapably* for anyone who reads de Man with his own critical imperatives in mind. That is to say, the dialectic of 'blindness and insight' must apply self-reflexively to de Man's own writings, at least if one is to give those writings credit for uncovering – as they claim – a pattern of alternating self-knowledge and self-ignorance which criticism can only point out by way of salutary warning and not lay to rest once and for all in its own 'enlightened' discourse. For any such presumption would of course invite the same kind of symptomatic reading that de Man applies to Husserl's quasi-universalist rhetoric of transcendental critique.

Opinions differ – to say the least – on the question of de Man's ethical good faith in addressing these issues at such a rarified level of interpretative theory or literary-critical debate. In his later writings the distance increases to a point where questions of guilt and moral accountability are treated as instances of a 'linguistic predicament', one that exemplifies the endlessly problematical relationship between 'grammar' and 'rhetoric', 'constative' and 'performative' speech-acts, or statements that refer to some real-life (past or present) situation and statements that have meaning purely by virtue of their own self-engendering rhetorical force.[22] Critics of de Man have mostly seen such arguments as a species of sophistical self-exculpation, an attempt to convince others (and maybe himself) that there is no present responsibility for past actions and choices; that 'confessions' are a pointless and redundant exercise (as de Man appears to say in his reading of Rousseau); that history is in any case a product of narrative contrivance (Nietzsche); and therefore that any act of personal 'atonement' can just as well proceed through the rhetorical deconstruction of other, more naïve or self-deluded confessional texts. And certainly there is a sense in which de Man's readings complicate the issue of ethical (or political) accountability to a point where it is difficult – maybe impossible – to treat of such matters without taking stock of their linguistic or narrative dimension. But this is not to say that de Man's whole enterprise comes down to an elaborate escape-mechanism, a means of retroactively disclaiming guilt for actions or utterances (and an utterance is indeed an action for de Man) which after all can only be conjured up by an act of narrative deconstruction, and which therefore exert no ethical claims upon the conscience of their present-day narrator.

That this is a gross misreading of de Man's work – more likely, a determined non-reading – should be clear enough to anyone who has approached that work with a reasonably open, unprejudiced mind. Having written about these questions at much greater length elsewhere[23] I can perhaps risk a simplified summary at this point by way of remarking the contrast with Heidegger's high-handed attitude on matters of ethical judgement. For de Man, the language of ethics is essentially a language of *resistance*, a force-field (so to speak) of tensions, aporias and conflicts – as between the 'rhetorical' and 'grammatical' or the 'constative' and 'performative' aspects of utterance – that cannot be held straightforwardly accountable to standards of plain, self-evident, veridical statement. Thus the act of confession – as de Man remarks about Rousseau – can always be read in the mode of excuse, or as a form of covertly self-exculpating discourse which invents all manner of fictive scenarios for the public display of a writer's guilty conscience. Hence de Man's reading of the well-known episode where Rousseau 'confesses' to having implicated a servant-girl (Marion) in the theft of a ribbon which in fact he had stolen himself, a deception which led to her dismissal (and probable ruin), and which Rousseau counts among the worst acts of his life by reason of its sheerly random, unmotivated character. 'What Rousseau *really* wanted', according to de Man,

> is neither the ribbon nor Marion, but the public scene of exposure which he actually gets . . . This desire is truly shameful, for it suggests that Marion was destroyed, not for the sake of [his] saving face . . . but merely in order to provide him with a stage on which to parade his disgrace, or, what amounts to the same thing, to provide him with a good ending for Book II of his *Confessions*.[24]

Hostile commentators have seen this passage – and others like it – as pointing not only to de Man's stance of extreme cognitive scepticism (i.e. his belief that 'real-life' events are always a product of narrative contrivance or textual representation), but also to a highly dubious strategy of self-willed ethical evasion, a desire to discount all questions of blame or moral accountability by showing how language 'dissociates the cognition from the act', or makes it simply impossible to judge in such matters. And from here it is a short step to the argument – much canvassed by recent critics – that de Man's whole production in the post-war period amounted to nothing more than a series of increasingly elaborate gambits or pretexts for disavowing guilt over those early articles.

Indeed, one can find any number of passages that lend themselves to just such a reading so long as one ignores the context of argument and treats them as fragments of a thinly-veiled autobiographical narrative. In his middle-period essays – preceding the 'turn' toward an austerely rhetorical or linguistic mode of analysis– de Man most often strikes this note in connection with the topic of romantic irony, a topic that can likewise be seen as an 'excuse' for strategies of self-evasion masquerading as rigorous philosophical argument. Thus 'ironic language', as de Man interprets it,

> splits the subject into an empirical self that exists in a state of inauthenticity and a self that exists only in the form of a language that asserts the knowledge of this inauthenticity. This does not, however, make it into an authentic language, for to know inauthenticity is not the same as to be authentic.[25]

It is clear enough how this passage must strike any reader who starts out convinced of de Man's moral delinquency, and who then looks sharp for corroborating evidence wherever the eye hits print. For it seems to discount the very possibility of 'authentic' self-knowledge or ethical good faith, regarding such notions as necessarily *in*authentic in so far as they postulate a unified, autonomous subject of experience, a self that reflects on (and accepts responsibility for) its own past thoughts and actions, while also – paradoxically – reviewing the past from a standpoint that cannot for a moment coincide with the self whose activities are now (belatedly) under review. In short, one is faced with the unenviable choice between a notion of 'authentic' selfhood that inherently falls into naïvety or sheer bad faith, and an awareness of that same predicament that allows of no escape from the unhappy consciousness bound up with all reflection on the nature and modalities of human self-knowledge. Such would appear to be the only alternatives if de Man's argument holds and there is no way beyond the aporetic structure – in the end, as he insists, a linguistic predicament – that emerges most clearly in the reading of 'confessional' texts. The best that one can hope for, it seems, is the kind of rigorously undeceiving knowledge – the remorseless dialectic of 'blindness' and 'insight' – that eschews all appeals to authentic selfhood and thus, at very most, achieves the kind of negative 'authenticity' which comes of not falling prey to such naïve illusions.

So it is not hard to see why de Man's opponents have had such a field-day hunting out passages to suit their reading of his work. By selective quotation and shrewdly-angled commentary one can make it appear that de Man is not only excusing himself for having written those wartime articles but also rejecting every last principle of ethical judgement or accountability. Moreover, there is a similar case to be made – albeit (as I shall argue) an erroneous case – with regard to some of de Man's more cryptic pronouncements on the nature of historical understanding and the politics of interpretation. Thus for instance, in his reading of Rousseau's *Social Contract*, '[i]t turns out . . . that the "law of the text" is too devious to allow for such a simple relationship between model and example, and the theory of politics inevitably turns into the history, the allegory of its inability to achieve the status of a science'.[26] And again: it is here, 'in the description of a political society, [that] the "definition" of a text as a contradictory interference of the grammatical with the figural field emerges in its most systematic form'.[27] These, and other sentences like them, have been held up as irrefutable evidence that de Man subscribed to a thoroughgoing 'textualist' creed, one that effectively debarred any access to a world outside the all-encompassing domain of textual or narrative representations. From this point his opponents can quickly go on to remark the fairly obvious advantages, for someone in de Man's situation, of treating history as just one version of a generalised linguistic (or textual) predicament, the 'meaning' of which has nothing to do with any putative *facts* that might be discovered by empirical research in – for instance – a Belgian newspaper archive. And when it comes to the matter of political commitment – a matter supposedly way off bounds for sophisticated theorists like de Man – then it is clear (on this reading) that deconstruction provides any number of convenient bolt-holes. For if history is indeed, as de Man conceives it, a figment of narrative or textual contrivance, then of course there is no appeal to any ground of judgement – any good reason for acting this way or that – which might once have made it seem both *ethically and politically wrong* to write articles in support of Nazi cultural propaganda. Thus when de Man comments (in a typically provocative statement) that 'textual allegories on this level of complexity generate history', his remark can be read as just one more damning instance of a drive to dissociate questions of textual meaning from questions (more simply) of *who said what*, in what precise historical circumstances, and with how great a knowledge of what might follow from their having uttered such things.

VI

This reading of de Man is wrong on several counts, not least in its failure (or refusal) to consider the many passages in his later work which engage quite explicitly with questions of an ethical or socio-political import. As Geoffrey Harpham has noted, these passsages have to do with the topic of *resistance*, of that which holds out against simplified or premature habits of reader-response, whether conceived - as most often with de Man – in terms of the 'linguistic interference' between disparate (e.g. rhetorical and grammatical) codes, or expressed more directly as the conflict between desire and moral law which has characterised the discourse of ethical philosophy at least since Kant. Indeed Harpham goes so far as to claim that deconstruction 'might be seen most profitably, not as a product of ethical reading, but as a hyperarticulated instance of ethical discourse'.[28] And this despite the fact that de Man seemingly goes out of his way to complicate issues of ethical choice, responsibility and commitment by subjecting them to a form of rhetorical analysis that would seem to leave little if any room for judgements of right and wrong. For it is none the less the case, with de Man as with Kant, that 'the subject itself has a self-interfering, self-resisting, self-overcoming ethical "thickness", and that the moral law or the inhumanity of the text is no more external to the subject than are its desires'.[29] What de Man brings out with peculiar force, according to Harpham, is the way in which deconstruction takes up and elaborates this language of ethical self-resistance, a language still present in those passages of hard-pressed rhetorical exegesis where de Man speaks of reading as an 'argument', one moreover that 'has to go against the grain of what one would want to happen in the name of what has to happen'.[30] At such points we can see how the 'law of the text' becomes for de Man a kind of Kantian ethical imperative, a demand that holds out against the easier satisfactions to be had by treating language in aesthetic (or phenomenalist) terms, that is to say, as if it could be understood by analogy with objects and processes in the natural world. Such 'resistance' thus becomes identi-fied, in de Man's late essays, with the project of a rigorous *ethics of reading* squarely opposed to all forms of ideological mystification.[31]

What chiefly distinguished de Man from Heidegger – at any rate in the post-war years – was his determination henceforth to resist the effects of that same 'aesthetic ideology' that had once so grievously confused his thinking. This involved, among other things, a detailed account of the way that aesthetic philosophy after Kant had taken a decisive (and fateful) wrong turn, a development made possible by the widespread misreading of specific passages in the *Third Critique*. A central concern of de Man's late essays – especially those collected in *The Resistance to Theory* (1986) – is to show how this aberrant tradition took hold, how its influence reached out beyond the specialised domain of aesthetics and art-criticism into the realms of ethical and socio-political thought, and also (most importantly) how close-reading in the deconstructive mode could work to undo this pernicious legacy of mystified concepts and values.[32] Thus 'whenever the aesthetic is invoked as an appeal to clarity and control, wherever, in other words, a symptom is made into a remedy for the disorder that it signals, a great deal of caution is in order' (*RT*, p. 64). And all the more so when the category of aesthetic judgement becomes a model, metaphor or analogue for some imaginary form (or utopian ideal) of socio-political life where conflicting interests would at last be perfectly reconciled, to the point of transcending all mere contingencies of time and place. Such notions derived much of their persuasive force from the 'organic' work of art as envisaged by thinkers like Goethe, Hegel and Coleridge, a work where each and every detail co-operates toward achieving the overall effect, and where 'unity in multiplicity' is the touchstone of aesthetic worth. For it then becomes possible to conceive of society – or more specifically, the emergent nation state – as embodying the authentic spirit of the age and also the generalised will of the people, expressed not so much through their particular interests, political choices, desires, etc. as through their role in a process of world-historical evolution whose highest stage is reached at the point where such conflicts (e.g. between state and civil society) would no longer have any relevance. And it is here that the discourse of 'aesthetic ideology' feeds back most directly – and with the most insidious effect – into that whole way of thinking about art, language, culture and politics which has played such a prominent role in the modern (post-romantic) tradition.

The results are most evident – so de Man argues – in the line of idealist or speculative thought that begins with Schiller's all-embracing notion of 'aesthetic education', and which descends through Hegel to such diverse schools as the American New Criticism, reader-response theory, phenomenological poetics, Hans-Robert Jauss's *Rezeptionsaesthetik* and – perhaps most strikingly – the present-day mainstream interpreters of English romanticism. These latter would include critics like M.H. Abrams who take it virtually as an article of faith that poetry can indeed – in Coleridgean terms – transcend all those vexing philosophical antinomies between time and eternity, subject and object, mind and nature, or the phenomenal and noumenal realms.[33] What enables them to assert such (strictly unthinkable) claims is a failure to register the force of Kant's critical arguments concerning the constitutive powers and limits of aesthetic understanding. One point that Kant stresses (and the commentators often miss) is the fact that this faculty belongs on the side of *reflective judgement*, i.e. to our subjective representations of the beautiful or the sublime, as distinct from yielding any direct knowledge of (or phenomenal acquaintance with) those various objects – whether natural forms or artefacts – that occasion the aesthetic response. The failure to observe this crucial distinction gives rise to all manner of delusive aesthetic ontologies, among them Hegel's talk of the work of art as the 'sensuous embodiment of the Idea',[34] the New Critics' (likewise Hegelian) theory of the poem as a 'concrete universal' or 'verbal icon',[35] the formalist – and also Leavisite – notion of poetry as a kind of 'sensuous enactment', revitalising language through its powers of vivid, quasi-visual or even tactile evocation, and the idea among reception-theorists like Jauss that textual understanding comes about through a cognitive process much akin to the perception of salient details against a background 'horizon' of intelligibility conceived (once again) on the phenomenalist model of direct sensory acquaintance.[36] In short, de Man is claiming that *every major school* of present-day critical thought – with the possible (but by no means guaranteed) exception of rhetorical exegesis in the deconstructive mode – can be traced back to that misreading of Kant by philosophers like Schiller and Hegel.

Thus for Jauss, 'the condensation of literary history and structural analysis occurs by way of the category of the aesthetic and depends for its possibility on the stability of this category' (*RT*, p. 64). In which case Hegel would stand behind both the great opposing schools of present-day critical thought, the two lines of approach that Jauss strives to reconcile through his theory of historical *Rezeptionsaesthetik*. For it is in Hegel that a mystified (phenomenalist) conception of language and form goes along with a full-scale synthesising drive to explain every aspect of human cultural development in terms of the world-historical process that alone makes such understanding possible. 'Nowhere else,' de Man writes, 'does the structure, the history, and the judgement of art seem to come as close to being systematically carried out, and nowhere else does this systematic synthesis rest so exclusively on one definite category . . . called the aesthetic'.[37] And this Hegelian legacy is everywhere present in the discourse of modern (post-romantic) critical thought, even where interpreters reject the very notion of 'literary history' in favour of some strictly formalist, synchronic, immanent or text-based mode of analysis. For in this case – as de Man brings out most adroitly in his essays on Jauss and Riffaterre – they will once again be opting for a hermeneutic model that always relies at some point on the notion of meaning as *perceived* in the encounter of reader with text, an encounter that can only take place through the 'fusion' of interpretative horizons, in other words, through a certain *phenomenology* of reader-response whose dialectical 'model to end all models' is the grand Hegelian synthesis which these critics so strenuously seek to avoid. As de Man writes, 'these categories are susceptible to infinite refinement, and their interplay can undergo numberless combinations, transformations, negations, and expansions'.[39]

But this is not to say – far from it – that we are thereby condemned to enter all unwittingly into the 'hermeneutic circle' that has induced so many critics and philosophers to misread (or ignore) those cardinal passages in Kant, and hence to conflate the disjunct orders of phenomenal experience and linguistic meaning.[40] What makes it so important to resist this move is the fact that it leads to further such confusions in the complex system of inter-articulated values and truth-claims that make up Kant's critical doctrine of the faculties. More specifically, it allows the faculty of aesthetic judgement to overstep the strictly mediating role that Kant assigns it, a role both crucial to the entire argumentative structure of the three *Critiques* and capable of drastically distorting that structure if its workings are thus misconstrued. In the more technical sense of the term it serves – notably in that section of the First *Critique* entitled the 'Transcendental Aesthetic' – as a bridge, so to speak, between sensuous intuitions and concepts of understanding.[41] For it is only by postulating the existence of this faculty that Kant can explain how we achieve knowledge of phenomenal objects, processes or events, i.e. how we 'bring intuitions under concepts' and thereby secure the basic claims of cognitive enquiry in general. Otherwise there would simply be no point of contact between sensuous experience – or the 'manifold' of perceptual data as given prior to any act of understanding – and those forms of a priori conceptual grasp that alone make it possible to interpret such experience. So the 'aesthetic' here has a sense far wider (and more deeply involved with epistemological issues) than the meaning it has assumed in latter-day art-critical parlance. And on the other hand it also figures for Kant as a means of conveying what is distinctive about *ethical* questions, those that pertain to 'practical reason', or the realm of suprasensible ideas where there can be no appeal to phenomenal self-evidence or matters of empirical fact. For aesthetic judgements in the narrower sense (i.e. judgements of taste as applied to natural phenomena or artefacts) have this much in common with the dictates of practical reason: that they implicitly claim *universal* validity, or the character of holding good for all subjects fitted to pronounce on such matters, while at the same time manifestly lacking any title to *objective* or demonstrable truth.[42]

This is why Kant makes such a cardinal point of arguing that differences of judgement in the realm of aesthetics cannot be settled – or conveniently shelved – by having recourse to the old relativist line, 'de gustibus non est disputandum.' No doubt this applies to matters of mere subjective preference, disagreements where nothing is at stake save a personal taste for this or that mode of sensuous gratification. But when it comes to aesthetic judgements we cannot (or should not) be willing to accept such a handy compromise formula. For it is at this point, according to Kant, that

> taste would discover a transition of our judging faculty from sense enjoyment to moral feeling; and so not only would we be the better guided in employing taste purposively, but there would be thus presented a link in the chain of the human faculties *a priori*, on which all legislation must depend.[43]

Thus aesthetic judgement – in this Kantian sense – is analogous to that realm of 'suprasensible' ideas whence derive the maxims of practical reason, and which imposes ethical dictates and values quite apart from any appeal to subjective self-interest on the one hand, or determinate objective knowledge on the other. And it is able to perform this privileged role on two main conditions: firstly, that judgements of taste lay claim to subjective universality, and secondly – following from this – that they *not* be determined (like cognitive judgements) according to the model of an adequate 'fit' between concept and sensuous intuition, but should rather derive from the 'free play' of the faculties when raised to their highest power of self-knowledge or reflective critical awareness. In Kant's words:

> the unsought, undesigned subjective purposiveness in the free accordance of the Imagination with the legality of the Understanding presupposes such a proportion and disposition of these faculties as no following of rules . . . can bring about, but which only the nature of the subject can produce.[44]

In which case – and here we return to de Man on the topic of 'aesthetic ideology' – it is an error to suppose that such judgements have anything in common with the process of phenomenal cognition, or with qualities manifested by the work itself as an object of aesthetic understanding.

Hence de Man's relentless – as it might seem, obsessive – concern to deconstruct those numerous variants of the basic phenomenalist error, from Hegel's notion of symbolic art as the 'sensuous embodiment of the Idea' to W.K. Wimsatt's Hegelian talk of the poem as 'concrete universal' or 'verbal icon' and, beyond that, the assumption – common to formalists like Jakobson and Shklovski, reader-response theorists like Iser and students of reception-history like Jauss – that literary meaning is somehow *perceptible* through a process of aesthetic 'concretisation' analogous to the way in which objects present themselves in the field of phenomenal perception. For de Man, on the contrary, it is eminently open to question 'whether aesthetic values can be compatible with the linguistic structures that make up the entities from which these values are derived' (*RT*, p. 16). And again: 'the resistance to theory [in literary studies] . . . is a resistance to language itself, or to the possibility that language contains factors or functions that cannot be reduced to intuition' (*RT*, pp. 12–13). For it is de Man's chief point in these late essays – and also the ground of his earlier difference with Heidegger over the interpretation of Hölderlin's poetry – that this move to aestheticise language by collapsing ontological distinctions is an error that all too readily falls in with a mystified conception of Being, nature and truth as revealed through certain privileged *national* languages (i.e. the Greek and German) that enable us to 'dwell' poetically in the presence of a wisdom long forgotten down through the history of Western 'metaphysical' thought. In de Man's words:

> The ineffable demands the direct adherence and the blind and violent passion with which Heidegger treats his texts. Mediation, on the other hand, implies a reflection that tends towards a critical language as systematic and rigorous as possible, but not overly eager to make claims of certainty that it can substantiate only in the long run. (*BI*, p.263)

This passage already (*circa* 1950) suggests a good deal about the course of de Man's post-war critical thinking, especially his sense that the issues confronting literary theory were also matters of great political moment, requiring the kind of 'systematic and rigorous' reflection that Heidegger had failed to exhibit in his readings of Hölderlin. But it is only with the essays produced during his last decade that de Man arrives at an adequate understanding of 'aesthetic ideology', its historical sources and the reasons for its continued, multiform presence in the discourse of present-day criticism. For the aesthetic is, as de Man describes it, 'a seductive notion that appeals to the pleasure principle, a eudaimonic judgment that can displace and conceal values of truth and falsehood likely to be more resilient to desire than values of pleasure and pain' (*RT*, p. 64). That is to say, it enables criticism to satisfy its desire for an immediate, self-present access to truth through a mode of delusory inwardness with the text whose condition is precisely that of the 'hermeneutic circle', the perfect reciprocity of textual meaning and readerly 'pre-understanding' which Heidegger raised into a high point and principle of interpretation in general.

This is no doubt what de Man has in mind when he asserts that 'the ultimate aim of a hermeneutically successful reading is to do away with reading altogether' (*RT*, p. 56). And by 'reading' de Man clearly means something other – and more – than the circular process of interpreting texts with a tacit foreknowledge of their meaning as somehow yet to be revealed against this or that background of informing assumptions or in-place 'horizon' of intelligibility. For it is only if we think of language in phenomenalist terms, that is to say, by anology with objects in the field of sensuous perception, that we will be led to subscribe to some version of the hermeneutic circle, or the idea that meaning is *always and inevitably* a product of foregone interpretative assumptions. This is what happens when Jauss offers his theory of reception-history as a dialogue of reiterated questions and answers, yet one whose 'horizon' is always marked out in advance by the enabling conditions (which are also the limits) of a situated reader-response.

> As the answer metamorphoses into a question, it becomes like an individual, tree, or portrait, set within a stylised landscape and it reveals, by the same token, a live background behind its background, in the form of a question from which it can now itself *stand out*. (*RT*, p. 59)

So the phenomenalist reduction of linguistic meaning goes along with a failure to conceive how language could ever put up any kind of resistance to the effects of aesthetic ideology. And this failure is linked in turn to the fact that such criticism misreads (or ignores) the twofold Kantian injunction, i.e. that judgements of aesthetic taste are *not* to be confused with phenomenal cognitions, and that in so far as they bear upon questions of ethics, politics or 'practical reason' that bearing has a strictly *analogical* significance, and cannot (or should not) be treated as a matter of direct or immediate correspondence. For one result of this confusion – as in Heidegger's exegeses of Hölderlin – is to elevate language (more specifically: the German language, as brought to its highest powers of expressiveness by poets in the Graeco-German line of descent) to a truth-telling status supposedly exempt from all the normative standards of enlightened critique or ethico-political judgement.

On de Man's account of it, the history of this error goes back at least to Schiller and his idea of 'aesthetic education' as a means of transcending the Kantian disjunction between knowledge (or cognitive truth-claims) on the one hand and imagination (or the power of inward, sympathetic under-standing) on the other.[45] Such would be the end-point of Schiller's re-demptive project: 'a wisdom that lies somehow beyond cognition and self-knowledge, yet can only be reached by ways of the process it is said to overcome'.[46] Aesthetics would thus become the natural home ground for a different, altogether 'higher' mode of awareness that disowned the antinomies of Kantian critical reason and claimed to effect a reconciliation of the various faculties whose separate domains Kant had attempted to delimit. But the result of this enterprise, as de Man sees it, is a species of 'aesthetic formalisation' which collapses the difference between ethics (practical reason) and phenomenal cognition, and thus makes reason entirely subject to the laws or dictates of natural necessity. 'The "state" that is here being advocated [in Schiller's *Letters on Aesthetic Education*] is not just a state of mind or of soul, but a principle of political value and authority that has its own claims on the shape and the limits of our freedom.'[47] And these claims are by no means a mere 'aberration' or an isolated instance of aesthetic philosophy overstepping its legitimate domain. On the contrary, as de Man writes: 'aesthetic education by no means fails; it succeeds too well, to the point of hiding the violence that makes it possible.'[48] And if we wish to understand the sources and nature of that 'violence', then the best we can do is reread de Man on 'Heidegger's exegeses of Hölderlin', since it is here that he begins – albeit obliquely – to confront the issues thrown up by this convergence between aesthetic ideology and totalitarian politics. In fact one could go beyond de Man's analysis and suggest that it is specifically in Heidegger's reading of Kant – a reading that elevates the 'productive imagination' to a status far beyond anything envisaged by Kant himself – that this error takes hold and opens the way to all manner of aestheticist confusion.[49]

VII

Lacoue-Labarthe puts the case for Heidegger's later writings as representing by far the most profound, sustained and rigorous attempt to 'think the essence' of Nazi ideology in its wider philosophical and cultural context. But this argument fails on one major count: that nothing in Heidegger's post-1933 production – or in Lacoue-Labarthe's treatment of it – gives any indication that Heidegger attained the kind of critical distance from that earlier involvement that would justify such claims for his preeminent status as the intellectual conscience of his age. Thus Heidegger *continued to believe* that the innermost essence of the Nazi phenomenon could only be revealed by a thinking that concerned itself with the question of Being as vouchsafed to philosophy (German philosophy) by the Greeks. Moreover, he *persisted in maintaining* that any authentic, 'serious' contribution to this debate would have to be posed in terms quite other than those of received (post-Kantian) ethical discourse, since ethics was itself part and parcel of that Western 'metaphysical' tradition of thought whose resources were inadequate to the task in hand. And lastly, Heidegger held firm in his conviction that the language of poetry – especially Hölderlin's poetry – gave voice to primordial truths beyond reach of that debased 'metaphysical' currency. And so the question for thought bequeathed to us by Heidegger is also the question that came down to Heidegger from Plato, Kant, Hegel, Nietzsche and Husserl: namely, how to interpret that strain of 'mimetic rivalry' which had marked every stage of the agonistic struggle between Europe and its Greek antecedents, and which Nazism was able to exploit in the form of a full-blown national-aestheticist creed. For it is, we recall, from 'the whole of philosophy since its origins' that Heidegger receives the question of Being, and not from any 'choice' on his part (as if that question were just one of many that he might have taken up), and still less on account of some 'position' adopted from the range of philosophical alternatives currently on offer.

In which case critics like Adorno would clearly be mistaken in thinking to hold Heidegger *ethically accountable* for those confusions brought about by his adherence to a mystified 'jargon of authenticity', one that involved this delusory appeal to a language of primordial Being and truth. And the same would presumably apply to de Man's argument in 'Heidegger's exegeses of Hölderlin', that is to say, his carefully documented case that Heidegger not only *misread* Hölderlin but did so as a consequence of deep-laid ideological values and convictions. For as Lacoue-Labarthe sees it this would be just another instance of 'external critique', or the kind of commentary that ignores what is essential to Heidegger's thought and contents itself with criticisms of a wholly extraneous character. Least of all could he accept de Man's central argument that the entire Heideggerian project derives from a basic misconception about language, a failure to perceive the sheer *impossibility* that language could ever 'state' Being in the mode of immediate, self-present truth. For it is Heidegger's claim – faithfully echoed by Lacoue-Labarthe – that such truth was once manifest in the sayings of the pre-Socratics, that it has since been overlaid by the accretions of 'Western metaphysics', but that it may yet be glimpsed in the work of those poets whose language conserves something of that ancient wisdom. Thus, for Lacoue-Labarthe,

[a]t the beginning of philosophy or, in other words, in the initial indication that being and thinking are the same and that that 'same' is the site of truth, there was a store of possibilities: the determinations of thinking, which is to say, in each case, an interpretation of Being, or, if one prefers, an experience of what is (das Seiende). Successively adopted in an order which owed nothing to chance but a great deal to the stage-by-stage emancipation of the sciences and to the domination of a 'critical' concept of truth, these possibilities which we have to imagine from the beginning as finite in number, have been exhausted – and this has occurred ever more rapidly and precipitately since the West has entered what it has itself called its modern age. (p. 3)

Hence his disdain for 'ethical' (or political) criticisms of Heidegger that still think to draw on that supposedly exhausted stock of conceptual resources. And from this point it follows (as night follows night) that Heidegger's most valuable insights into the 'essence' of Nazism were arrived at through persisting more deeply, more authentically in the same kind of thinking that had once given rise to his professions of National Socialist allegiance.

Such, after all, is the central hypothesis of Lacoue-Labarthe's book; that

it is not in the discourse of 1933 that 'Heidegger's politics' is to be found (that discourse . . . is far too compromised in advance), but in the discourse which follows the 'break' or the 'withdrawal' and which presents itself in any case as a settling of accounts with National Socialism, *in the name of its truth*. (p. 32)

In which case the only valid criticism of Heidegger would be one that accepted all his major theses, including the argument (duly repeated by Lacoue-Labarthe) that it makes no sense to talk of 'theses', premises, philosophical 'positions', etc. with respect to a thinker whose work went so far beyond anything describable in those terms. And by the same token one would have to concede that Heidegger's pro-Nazi statements (those belonging to the 'discourse of 1933') can only be read, understood or criticised from the standpoint achieved *by Heidegger himself* in the 'discourse' that followed his putative break with national-aestheticist ideology in its cruder (National Socialist) guise. In other words, this whole argument rests on an appeal to the 'hermeneutic circle', the horizon of tacit 'pre-understanding' which – according to Heidegger – delimits or circumscribes each and every act of interpretative grasp. But it is (to say the least) a very dubious application of this argument that would have us treat Heidegger's own post-1933 pronouncements as the only 'discourse' sufficiently in touch with the truth of the Nazi phenomenon – more specifically, its 'inner truth and greatness' – to avoid the vulgar error of reproaching Heidegger from a standpoint of 'external' critique. And the argument takes on a yet more vicious circularity if one adds to it the fact – fully recognised by Lacoue-Labarthe – that Heidegger's 'break' was so far from complete that the entire subsequent course of his thinking can be seen as a sustained meditation on themes continuous with those of the Rectoral Address. Heidegger's 'blindness' (i.e. his falling prey to the seduction of National Socialist ideology) would then have to be seen as the *essential precondition* for his own unique 'insight' into the sources and workings of that same ideology.

But there is no question of these terms applying in anything like the sense that de Man gives to them in the essays of his middle period. For there it is a case of insights that derive from a process of sustained and rigorous critique, an undeceiving discourse that exposes the errors bound up with national-aestheticist thought. And there is no such process to be observed in the writings that Heidegger produced after 1933, including those texts where Lacoue-Labarthe finds evidence of his 'settling accounts' with the Nazi phenomenon. For these writings do not so much condemn, repudiate or criticise the national-aestheticist doctrine as make of it something in the nature of a passing distraction, a vulgar misconstrual of truths that are otherwise *authentically* bound up with Germany's dawning self-awareness of its role as predestined inheritor of the question of Being handed down from the ancient Greeks. Thus: '. . . beneath Adorno's insult, the real question still remains: did fundamental ontology and the analytics of *Dasein* harbour within them the possibility of a commitment to fascism?' (p. 108). To which Lacoue-Labarthe returns the confident response: that this error (even 'wrongdoing') on Heidegger's part was the product of a short-lived compromise or lapse in his thinking, one that amounted to a 'certain overdetermination of historial *Dasein,* co-extensive with its relegation to a secondary place, by the concept (itself also unquestioned) of "people" (*Volk*)' (p.108). From which one is evidently meant to conclude, *first* that Heidegger's political compromise did not involve the deepest, most essential aspects of his thinking, and *second* that the only way of 'settling accounts' with that compromise – or indeed with the Nazi phenomenon as a whole – is to follow Heidegger in his subsequent reflections on the name and nature of 'historial *Dasein*' as revealed through a 'fundamental ontology' of language, Being, and truth. For otherwise we will just produce some further variant of 'Adorno's insult', that is to say, the argument that *all* such talk amounts to a species of mystified aestheticist jargon; that Heidegger's commitment of 1933 is *wholly of a piece* with his other, more 'authentic' or (seemingly) less 'compromised' discourse; that Heidegger was indeed ethically accountable for those pronouncements in the name of 'historial *Dasein*', 'fundamental ontology', etc.; and that Lacoue-Labarthe in the end does nothing more than beg all the relevant (philosophical, ethical and political) questions by merely restating Heidegger's case in the same Heideggerian terms. That Adorno got it right on all the main counts is an idea that Lacoue-Labarthe – understandably – cannot bring himself to entertain.

Nevertheless Adorno *did* get it right, along with those other critics of Heidegger (de Man among them) who have recognised the deep-laid elective affinity between a rhetoric of primordial, self-authenticating truth and a politics premised on national-aestheticist doctrine. In de Man's case this recognition led to an ever more determined and rigorous attempt, both to locate the sources of that widespread 'aesthetic ideology' and to explain how criticism could resist its influence through the close-reading of texts (philosophical or literary) where such values came into play. Thus:

> [m]ere reading, it turns out, prior to any theory, is able to transform critical discourse in a manner that would appear deeply subversive to those who think of the teaching of literature as a substitute for the teaching of theology, ethics, psychology, or intellectual history. Close reading accomplishes this in spite of itself because it cannot fail to respond to structures of language which it is the more or less secret aim of literary teaching to keep hidden. (*RT*, p. 24)

Those 'structures of language' show up in various forms, always with the effect of resisting or inhibiting that aestheticist drive within the discourse of (mainly post-Kantian) critical thought. They include – for instance – the obtrusive metonymical figures that complicate Proust's high claims for the transcendent, visionary powers of metaphorical language;[50] the discrepancies between meaning and intent that emerge when various critics (from Coleridge to Abrams) attempt to articulate an organicist union of mind, nature and language;[51] the signifying surplus of language that cannot be reduced to any form of quasi-phenomenal or sensuous apprehension; and those problematic passages in Kant's third *Critique* that are commonly misread (or passed over in silence) by commentators in the high Romantic tradition, from Schiller on down. Elsewhere – in the essays of his last period – de Man makes the point more often in terms of the 'structural interference' between disjunct orders of meaning, as for instance between logic, grammar and rhetoric, the constative and performative dimensions of utterance, or language in its referential and figural aspects.

What these various terms of distinction all have in common is a capacity to question or subvert that appeal from language to the realm of phenomenal experience which marks, for de Man, the likely presence of 'aesthetic ideology' in one or another guise. Thus, '[w]hat we call ideology is precisely the confusion of linguistic with natural reality, of reference with phenomenalism' (*RT*, p. 11). From which it follows, again, that 'more than any other mode of enquiry . . . the linguistics of literariness is a powerful and indispensable tool in the unmasking of ideological aberrations, as well as a determining factor in accounting for their occurrence' (*RT*, p.11). For it is precisely by way of that persistent confusion between *meaning* (or linguistic structures) on the one hand and *phenomenal cognition* on the other that critics have so often sought access to a truth beyond all the Kantian antinomies of thought. But this desire gives rise to some far-reaching errors, not least as regards the role of aesthetic judgement *vis-à-vis* the truth-claims of epistemology on the one hand and ethics (or practical reason) on the other. Such is indeed de Man's major point about the angled misreading of Kant's third *Critique* which took hold with Schiller's all-embracing philosophy of 'aesthetic education', and the effects of which are everywhere to be seen in the discourse of present-day Romantic scholarship, reception-theory, reader-response criticism and so forth. This misreading came about – so de Man argues – through a failure to respect Kant's vital distinction between truths of experience (as given in the form of phenomenal intuitions that are then 'brought under' adequate concepts) and those other kinds of judgement (ethical and aesthetic) where reason 'gives the law' *not* as determined by the powers and limits of phenomenal cognition, but in accordance with the 'supra-sensible' dictates of morality, taste, and other such normative principles. It is on this account that de Man attaches such significance to the character and workings of 'aesthetic ideology'. For the confusion between these modalities of judgement is liable to lead - as in Heidegger's case – to a thinking that subordinates ethical judgements to a mystified, pseudo-organicist notion of 'authentic' historial destiny, such that (for instance) any criticism of Heidegger's politics *on other than his own elective terms* would have to be seen as mere 'journalistic chatter', intellectual dishonesty, or 'tinkering around in inessential and subordinate matters (ethics, the rights of man etc.)'.

Hence de Man's stress on the errors that result when critics or philosophers take it as read that Kant somehow managed to *reconcile* the various orders of knowledge and experience, as by treating aesthetics as that privileged realm where the faculties attain an ideal state of harmonious balance between sensuous cognition and reflective judgement. Thus:

> [t]he link between literature (as art), epistemology, and ethics is the burden of aesthetic theory at least since Kant. It is because we teach literature as an aesthetic function that we can move so easily from literature to its apparent prolongations in the spheres of self-knowledge, of religion, and of politics . . . [But] neither has aesthetic theory succeeded in its admirable ambition to unite cognition, desire and morality in one single synthetic judgement . . . Whether a reading of *The Critique of Judgment*, as distinct from its simplified versions in Schiller and his offspring, would confirm this assertion certainly stands in need of careful examination. Contemporary literary theory has started this long overdue process. (*RT*, p. 25)

What de Man came to realise – having himself fallen prey to that delusion in his wartime articles – was that thinking can indeed resist such forms of seductive aesthetic ideology, but only in so far as it maintains the kind of *critical* vigilance that comes of a refusal to identify language (more specifically: some privileged *national* language) with the voice of authentic Being and truth. Of course this desire has a long prehistory, going back to the rise of the European vernaculars and the efforts then made to discover some deep, etymological (but also spiritual) kinship between those languages and their Greek or Latin sources.[52] As with Heidegger, this enterprise most often took the form of a 'jargon of authenticity' that exploited the findings of linguistic research – whether genuine or fake – in the interests of national self-assertion or the will to pan-European cultural hegemony.

In the early nineteenth century it took a more distinctly philosophical turn, especially among thinkers in the German universities, anxious to establish the world-historical significance of their work, and thus much given to claiming a unique affinity between ancient Greek and latter-day German thought. This case has been argued to controversial effect by Martin Bernal in his recent book *Black Athena: the Afroasiatic roots of classical civilization*.[53] According to Bernal we are still in the grip of this distorted historical picture, one that locates the main source of Athenian culture in those 'civilising' currents that supposedly came down from the North, and which thus underrates (or consistently ignores) the Egyptian, Phoenician and other such influences nearer home. But one need only look to Nieztsche's *The Birth of Tragedy* to see how even the strongest of revisionist interpreters in the German line could yet take it as a manifest truth that Germany was somehow predestined to revive the cultural hegemony of ancient Greek language and thought.[54] No doubt one should remember, as Lacoue-Labarthe points out, that 'Heidegger devote[d] more than four years of his teaching between 1936 and 1941 to "delimiting" Nietzsche's metaphysics and openly contesting its "diversion" into biologism and the use that is made of it by the official racist ideology' (p. 134).[55] But it is also the case that he continued to believe – as does Lacoue-Labarthe – in the crucial significance of that Graeco-German line of cultural descent, not only for assessing the Nazi 'phenomenon' in its deepest ('essential') character, but for any thinking that sought to go beyond the vulgarities of mere sociological analysis or 'external critique'.

Of course there is no question of simply conflating their two argumentative positions, as if Lacoue-Labarthe were offering nothing more than a straightforward assenting gloss on Heidegger's work. On the contrary, as he writes:

> One should not attribute to me the positions I am analysing. My 'Heideggerianism' in no way prevents me from thinking, amongst other things, that there are at least other scansions in the History of Being than those indicated by Heidegger and other trajectories in the constitution of the philosophical than those which Heidegger re-marks after Hegel. (p. 101)

But again, this disclaimer can apply only up to a point, since Lacoue-Labarthe's entire treatment of Heidegger proceeds on the assumption that his thinking not only *makes sense* – i.e., warrants such detailed and scrupulous commentary – but also that Heidegger is the one and only thinker of recent times who has addressed these questions at anything like an adequate depth of understanding. To hold a contrary opinion on either of these counts is to find onself dismissed by Lacoue-Labarthe to the company of those who, for whatever reason, simply have not grasped the 'essence' of Heidegger's thought. And this attitude appears most strikingly in the difference between his and de Man's way of reading those late texts on the poetry of Hölderlin. For Lacoue-Labarthe, they constitute a deeply problematic but none the less truthful and revealing commentary on the 'question of Being' as posed *inescapably* by the great poets and philosophers down through the history of Western thought. Thus '[t]he historial mission of a poet is to bestow his language upon a people . . . this was Homer's mission among the Greeks. It could also, for the Germans, be Hölderlin's mission, if they consented to listen to him' (p. 56).

Of course it would be wrong – and the more so in light of Lacoue-Labarthe's express disavowals – to read such passages as straightforwardly endorsing the doctrines they summarise. There is always (as here) the possibility of *oratio obliqua*, self-distancing paraphrase, implied reservations and so forth. But it is equally the case that Lacoue-Labarthe's whole line of argument takes for granted the essential *significance* of such claims, their capacity to illumine aspects of existence that lie beyond the grasp of mere 'external critique'. For de Man, on the other hand, Heidegger is quite simply *wrong* about Hölderlin – prone to certain highly specific and determinate forms of rhetorical misreading – and his errors cannot be set aside in the interests of a deeper, more 'authentic' access to Being and truth. To this way of thinking, 'a commentary on Heidegger's poetry must essentially be critical, if it wishes to be faithful to its author's definition of poetry, just as this poetry is critical of its own certitudes, their illusory character unveiled' (*BI*, p. 263). There can thus be no question of conserving what is 'essential' in Heidegger's (or Hölderlin's) work while failing to respect the critical imperatives of textual close-reading and analytic rigour. Hence the following passage, taken once again from his essay 'Heidegger's exegeses of Hölderlin', and offering perhaps the clearest indication of de Man's future work on aesthetic ideology and its various linguistic modes of propagation. 'As a control discipline', he writes,

> equally scornful of arbitrariness and pseudo-science, philology represents a
> store of established knowledge; to seek to supersede it, and it is far from
> obvious that this is possible, is without merit. When it is negated by equally
> excessive mysticism or scientism, it gains in increased self-awareness and
> provokes the development of methodological movements within the dis-
> cipline itself, which ultimately reinforce it. (*BI*, pp. 263–4)

The alternative is to treat Heidegger's texts as possessing an authority that may indeed be 'compromised' (in Lacoue-Labarthe's phrase) by their association with Nazi doctrine, but whose inner truth is none the less proof against criticism at an ethical, political, or merely philological level. And it is precisely the burden of de Man's late essays to demonstrate how the 'return to philology' – or the attention to those elements in language that resist any simplified (phenomenalist) account – may itself be the source of valuable insight into the workings of aesthetic ideology.[56]

To this extent at least one is justified in asserting that Lacoue-Labarthe is indeed a 'Heideggerian', and that moreover he subscribes – in all 'essential' respects – to certain *theses* that characterise Heidegger's thinking, early and late. These include his assurance that the 'question of Being' is one that can properly and intelligibly be raised as Heidegger raises it; that this question takes absolute priority over all other philosophical concerns, thus reducing them to side-issues or matters of a strictly limited ('metaphysical') import; that thinkers who reject or ignore this claim are thereby betraying their own incapacity for thought at such an elevated level; and finally, that Heidegger's post-1933 writings offer a sustained and uniquely authoritative statement on the Nazi phenomenon and his own brief period of involvement with it. What is clearly unthinkable to Lacoue-Labarthe is the contrary argument: that Heidegger's *entire philosophical production* – and not just that momentary lapse during the pre-war years – might best be accounted for in terms of aesthetic ideology, or the confusions engendered by a mystified appeal to language (one particular *national* language) as a source of revealed truth. It is this lesson that we are given to read in de Man's late essays, but which figures only as a massive and symptomatic silence in the texts that Heidegger supposedly produced by way of 'settling accounts' with National Socialism.

Notes

Note: For a useful selection of Heidegger's texts in English translation see David Krell (ed.), *Heidegger: Basic Writings* (New York: Harper & Row, 1977). Readers may also wish to consult the following sources: *The Question Concerning Technology: Heidegger's Critique of the Modern Age*, trans. William Lovitt (New York: Harper & Row, 1977); *Early Greek Thinking*, trans. David Krell and Frank Capuzzi (New York: Harper & Row, 1975); *The Question of Being*, trans. W. Kluback and J.T. Wilde (New York: Twayne, 1958). Separate references are given (below) for all works specifically cited in the text.

1. Richard Rorty, review of Victor Farias, *Heidegger et le Nazisme, London Review of Books*, 3 September 1967.
2. Paul Johnson, *Intellectuals* (New York: Harper & Row, 1988).
3. Victor Farias *Heidegger et le Nazisme* (Paris: Verdier, 1987).
4. T.W. Adorno, *The Jargon of Authenticity*, trans. T. Tarnowski and F. Will (London: Routledge & Kegan Paul, 1973).
5. See especially Heidegger, 'What is called thinking?', trans. F.D. Wieck and J.G. Gray (New York: Harper & Row, 1968); also *Discourse on Thinking*, trans. J.M. Anderson and E.H. Freund (New York: Harper & Row, 1969) and 'The end of philosophy and the task of thinking', in *On Time and Being*, trans. Joan Stambaugh (New York: Harper & Row, 1972), pp. 55–73.
6. See T.W. Adorno, *Negative Dialectics*, trans. E.B. Ashton (London: Routledge & Kegan Paul, 1973); also Adorno, *Aesthetic Theory*, trans. C. Lenhardt (London: Routledge, 1984).

7. The accusation – and Adorno's response to it – may be found in the January, 1963 number of the Frankfurt student newspaper *Diskus*. One should, I suppose, acknowledge Lacoue-Labarthe's diligence in bringing this unfortunate episode to light, although his reasons for so doing – and his obvious casting around for any stick with which to beat Adorno – strike me as less than admirable.

8. See Friedrich Schiller, *On the Aesthetic Education of Mankind, in a series of letters*, trans. E.M. Wilkinson and L.A. Willoughby (Oxford: Clarendon Press, 1967).

9. See especially the essays collected in Lacoue-Labarthe, *Typography: mimesis, philosophy, politics*, ed. Christopher Fynsk (Cambridge, Mass.: Harvard University Press, 1989). The following passage puts his case most concisely, and may therefore be helpful to readers unfamiliar with Lacoue-Labarthe's wider (and immensely intriguing) philosophical project.

> Plato is the first to betray, in the very text wherein he establishes them (the *Republic* is in fact a mixed narrative), the norms that he has himself prescribed and that govern, in his eyes, good fiction *as* a discourse of truth. But in fact the set-up is much more complex. Not only because Plato does not respect the law that he decrees, not only because an other, Socrates (who speaks in *his* name, in the first person) represents him and speaks in 'his' name, not even simply because this entire pedagogical program, in which the question of mimesis and of fiction is debated, is itself presented as myth, but because in reality Plato – and this is the height of the paradox – does not speak one word of the *philosophical discourse itself.* Unless this be *indirectly* – by what play of mirrors? – and in so far as we may consider the redressing and verification of fictive discourse to be regulated by the model of true discourse, in the form of the discourse of philosophy. But in the text it is Socrates, 'his' *mimos*, the mimetic part of 'himself', who speaks philosophically. The philosopher is here a figure. As for Plato . . . he *fictions*, content, perhaps, with playfully re-marking his 'own' name or the at least double sense that an (assumed) proper name can always take on. (*Typography*, pp. 134–5)

These essays contain some of the finest commentary anywhere to be found on the vexed relationship between philosophy, aesthetics and politics as inaugurated in Plato's dialogues, and thence transmitted – under various guises – down through the history of Western thought. They will surely become a major point of reference for anyone seeking to interpret that history in terms of its ambivalent origins and complex genealogy. My purpose here is not to contest the indubitable value of this work, but to point out the blind spots, the distortions of argument that overtake *even* so subtle and well-qualified a theorist as Lacoue-Labarthe when he tries to square the facts of Heidegger's political record with the fixed idea that Heidegger remains the most truthful, authentic, *indispensable* thinker of our time. That this conviction is shared by so many likewise intelligent and critically astute commentators is one good reason for asking just why Heidegger's thinking has continued to exert such a potent spell.

10. On Levinas and his relationship to Heidegger, see for instance the essays collected in *The Levinas Reader*, ed. Sean Hand (Oxford: Basil Blackwell, 1989).
11. See especially Jacques Derrida, *De l'esprit: Heidegger et la question* (Paris: Galilée, 1987).
12. See Gilbert Ryle, review of Heidegger's *Sein und Zeit*, in Ryle, *Collected Papers*, Vol. I (London: Hutchinson, 1971), pp. 197–214.
13. Paul Edwards, 'Heidegger's quest for Being', *Philosophy*, vol. LXIV, no. 250 (October, 1989), pp. 43–70.
14. For further examples, see Tony Crowley, *Standard English and the Politics of Language* (Illinois: University of Illinois Press, 1989); also, for a critique of Trench's special brand of theological humbug along logico-semantic lines, see William Empson's neglected masterpiece, *The Structure of Complex Words* (London: Chatto & Windus, 1951).
15. See Jean-François Lyotard, *The Differend: phrases in dispute*, trans. Georges van den Abbeele (Manchester: Manchester University Press, 1988), p. 179.
16. See for instance Gilles and Jean-Robert Ragache, *La vie quotidienne des écrivains et des artistes sous l'occupation, 1940–1944* (Paris: Hachette, 1988); also some of the essays collected in Hamacher, Hertz and Keenan (eds.), *Responses: on Paul de Man's wartime journalism* (Lincoln: Nebr.: University of Nebraska Press, 1988).
17. See especially Heidegger, *Nietzsche*, Vol. I: *The Will to Power as Art*, trans. David Farrell Krell (New York: Harper & Row, 1979).
18. Paul de Man, 'Heidegger's exegeses of Hölderlin', in *Blindness and Insight: essays in the rhetoric of contemporary criticism* (London: Methuen, 1983), pp. 246–66. All further references to this volume given by *BI* and page-number in the text.
19. For these readings of Hölderlin, see Heidegger, *Poetry, Language, Thought*, trans. Albert Hofstadter (New York: Harper & Row, 1971).
20. See Hamacher, Hertz and Keenan (eds.), *Paul de Man: wartime journalism* (Lincoln, Nebr.: University of Nebraska Press, 1988); also *Responses: on Paul de Man's wartime journalism* (*op. cit.*); Christopher Norris, *Paul de Man: deconstruction and the critique of aesthetic ideology* (New York & London: Routledge, 1988); and Herman, Humbeeck and Lernout (eds.), *(Dis)continuities: essays on Paul de Man* (Amsterdam: Rodopi, 1989).
21. Paul de Man, 'Criticism and crisis', in *Blindness and Insight* (*op. cit.*), pp. 3–19. See Edmund Husserl, *The Crisis of the European Sciences and Transcendental Phenomenology*, trans. D. Carr (Evanston: Northwestern University Press, 1970).
22. See especially de Man, *Allegories of Reading: figural language in Rousseau, Nietzsche, Rilke, and Proust* (New Haven: Yale University Press, 1979).
23. Norris, *Paul de Man* (*op. cit.*).
24. De Man, *Allegories Of Reading* (*op. cit.*), p. 285.
25. De Man, 'The rhetoric of temporality', in *Blindness and Insight* (*op. cit.*), pp. 187–228; p. 214.
26. De Man, 'Promises (*Social Contract*)', in *Allegories of Reading* (*op. cit.*), pp. 246–77; p. 271.
27. *ibid.*, p. 270.

28. Geoffrey Galt Harpham, 'Language, history, and ethics', *Raritan*, vol. VII, no. 2 (1987), pp. 128–46; p. 140. See also Harpham's remarks on de Man, deconstruction and the 'ethics of reading' in his excellent book *The Ascetic Imperative in Culture and Criticism* (Chicago: University of Chicago Press, 1987), pp. 239–69.
29. Harpham, 'Language, history, and ethics' (*op. cit.*), p. 141.
30. De Man, Foreword to Carol Jacobs, *The Dissimulating Harmony* (Baltimore: Johns Hopkins University Press, 1978), pp. vii–xiii; p. xi.
31. These arguments are taken up from de Man in J. Hillis Miller, *The Ethics of Reading* (New York: Columbia University Press, 1987); also by the present author in Norris, 'De Man unfair to Kierkegaard? an allegory of (non)-reading', *Deconstruction and the Interests of Theory* (London: Pinter, 1988), pp. 156–86.
32. De Man, *The Resistance to Theory* (Minneapolis: University of Minnesota Press, 1986). All further references to this volume given by *RT* and page-number in the text.
33. See especially M.H.Abrams, *Natural Supernaturalism: tradition and revolution in Romantic literature* (New York: Norton, 1971).
34. See de Man, 'Sign and symbol in Hegel's *Aesthetics*', *Critical Inquiry*, vol. VIII, no. 4 (1982), pp. 761–75; also de Man, 'Hegel on the sublime', in Mark Krupnick (ed.), *Displacement: Derrida and after* (Bloomington: Indiana University Press, 1983), pp. 139–53.
35. See especially W.K. Wimsatt, *The Verbal Icon: studies in the meaning of poetry* (Lexington: Ky.: University of Kentucky Press, 1954).
36. See Hans-Robert Jauss, *Toward an Aesthetics of Reception*, trans. Timothy Bahti (Minneapolis: University of Minnesota Press, 1982). De Man's essay on Jauss, 'Reading and history', first appeared as the Forword to this volume, pp. vii–xxv. It is reprinted in *The Resistance to Theory*, pp. 54–72.
37. De Man, 'Sign and symbol in Hegel's *Aesthetics*' (*op. cit.*), p. 762.
38. De Man, 'Hypogram and inscription', in *The Resistance to Theory* (*op. cit.*), pp. 27–53.
39. De Man, 'Sign and symbol' (*op. cit.*), p. 771.
40. On this topic see de Man, 'Phenomenality and materiality in Kant', in Gary Shapiro and Alan Sica (eds.), *Hermeneutics: questions and prospects* (Amherst: University of Massachusetts Press, 1984), pp. 121–44.
41. Immanuel Kant, *Critique of Pure Reason*, trans. N. Kemp Smith (London: Macmillan, 1933).
42. Kant, *The Critique of Judgement*, trans. J.C. Meredith (London: OUP, repr. 1978).
43. Kant, *Selections*, ed. Theodore M. Greene (New York: Scribners, 1957), pp. 381–2.
44. *ibid.*, p. 430.
45. Schiller, *On the Aesthetic Education of Man* (*op. cit.*).
46. De Man, 'Aesthetic formalization: Kleist's *Über das Marionnettentheater*, in *The Rhetoric of Romanticism* (New York: Columbia University Press, 1984), pp. 263–90; p. 265.
47. *ibid.*, p. 264.
48. *ibid.*, p. 289.

49. See Heidegger, *Kant and the Problem of Metaphysics*, trans. James Churchill (Bloomington: Indiana University Press, 1962).
50. De Man, 'Reading (Proust)', in *Allegories Of Reading* (*op. cit.*), pp. 57–78.
51. See especially de Man, 'The rhetoric of temporality' (*op. cit.*).
52. See Tony Crowley, *Standard English and the Politics of Language* (*op. cit.*).
53. Martin Bernal, *Black Athena; the Afroasiatic roots of classical civilization*, Vol. I: *The Fabrication of Ancient Greece* (New Jersey: Rutgers University Press, 1987).
54. Friedrich Nietzsche, *The Birth of Tragedy* and *The Case of Wagner*, trans. Walter Kaufmann (New York: Vintage Books, 1967).
55. See Heidegger, *Nietzsche* (*op. cit.*).
56. See de Man, 'The return to philology', in *The Resistance to Theory* (*op. cit.*), pp. 21–6.

Index

Index